THE SEXUAL ECONOMY OF WAR

A VOLUME IN THE SERIES

Battlegrounds: Cornell Studies in Military History

General Editor: David J. Silbey

Editorial Board: Petra Goedde, Wayne E. Lee, Brian McAllister Linn, and Lien-Hang Nguyen

A list of titles in this series is available at cornellpress.cornell.edu.

THE SEXUAL ECONOMY OF WAR: DISCIPLINE AND DESIRE IN THE U.S. ARMY

ANDREW BYERS

CORNELL UNIVERSITY PRESS
Ithaca and London

First published 2019 by Cornell University Press

Library of Congress Cataloging-in-Publication Data

Names: Byers, Andrew, author.
Title: The sexual economy of war : discipline and desire in the U.S. Army / Andrew Byers.
Description: Ithaca : Cornell University Press, 2019. | Series: Battlegrounds : Cornell studies in military history | Includes bibliographical references and index.
Identifiers: LCCN 2018040385 (print) | LCCN 2018040974 (ebook) | ISBN 9781501736452 (pdf) | ISBN 9781501736469 (epub/mobi) | ISBN 9781501736445 | ISBN 9781501736445 (cloth)
Subjects: LCSH: Soldiers—Sexual behavior—United States—History—20th century. | Military discipline—United States—History—20th century. | United States. Army—History—20th century. | War and society—United States—History—20th century.
Classification: LCC UH630 (ebook) | LCC UH630 .B94 2019 (print) | DDC 355.1/334—dc23
LC record available at https://lccn.loc.gov/2018040385

To Elizabeth

CONTENTS

Acknowledgments

This book would not have been possible without the guidance and help of many people who contributed valuable insights, assistance, time, and support over the course of many years.

First, I must heartily thank two scholars at Duke University, Alex Roland and Dirk Bönker, both excellent military historians who helped to guide me as a historian and shepherd this project through its various stages. I am profoundly grateful for the faith and confidence in me that you have each demonstrated over the years. Two of my closest academic colleagues—Patricia Stapleton and Francesco Crocco—with whom I have had the privilege of coauthoring and coediting other books have also been instrumental to my development as a scholar. I thank you all from the bottom of my heart.

My gratitude also extends to other scholars and colleagues, including Claudia Koonz, Anna Krylova, Jocelyn Olcott, Peter Sigal, and John Herd Thompson at Duke University; Joseph Glatthaar, Karen Hagemann, and Richard Kohn of the University of North Carolina at Chapel Hill; and scholars at other institutions outside the Triangle, including Fahad Bishara, Elizabeth Brake, George Chauncey, Gregory Daddis, Tamara Extian-Babiuk, Marie-Amelie George, Michael Grossberg, Marie Hicks, Walter Ladwig, Joanne Meyerowitz, Sean Parrish, James Perry, Richard Thornton, Willeke Sandler, and, especially, James Stutler. I am honored by the help and guidance you have offered over the years. I would also like to thank two staff members of Duke's History Department, Robin Ennis and Cynthia Hoglen, who were especially generous with their time and assistance. Three close friends from outside academia who kindly offered me their friendship, encouragement, and a place to stay in the Washington, DC, area while I was conducting research are Shawn Carman, Scott Kane, and Megan Sinesiou. You have all been friends in the truest sense.

At Cornell University Press, I would like to thank Emily Andrew for her confidence in the book; Bethany Wasik for her able assistance; the anonymous reviewers who helped improve the book immeasurably; and David J. Silbey, editor of Battlegrounds: Cornell Studies in Military History, for including my book as one of the inaugural titles in his series.

My research benefited from generous financial support provided by Duke University; an endowment from Anne Firor Scott, which made possible an early research grant; and a generous endowment from the late Dr. and Mrs. Arthur B. Ferguson, which made possible my first research foray into the archives.

In the course of my research, I have benefited from the help of many knowledgeable archivists and librarians who have graciously shared their time and expertise. Those most helpful include the staff of the U.S. Army Military History Institute, particularly Richard Sommers and David Keough; and the staff of the National Archives and Records Administration in Washington, DC, and College Park, Maryland. Joanne P. Tetreault Eldridge, Deputy Clerk of Court, and the staff of the U.S. Army Court of Criminal Appeals were also extremely helpful. At Duke University, I would especially like to thank Carson Holloway for his continuing help and kindness, as well as the rest of the staff of Duke University's Lilly and Perkins-Bostock Libraries.

I would be remiss if I did not acknowledge the support and guidance of a number of teachers who have guided me along life's journey. These have included the Sisters, Servants of the Immaculate Heart of Mary (IHM) who taught at Star of the Sea School, especially Sister Patricia Micklos, IHM, and the late Sister Edward Marie Dougherty, IHM. Several of my professors at Virginia Tech helped set me on the path that led to my own career as an academic and teacher. These include William Ochsenwald, K. Edward Spiezio, and Joseph Wieczynski. I would also like to thank my mentors, from whom I have learned so much over the years: Norman Edwards, Michael Lancaster, and Charles Miller, as well as the late Robert Bozzelli.

I must thank several members of my family who have been tremendously supportive as I pursued my education, from my first days in college to the present, especially Peggy Byers, Lorraine Byers, and the late George Denney.

The person who deserves the lion's share of the credit for helping me complete this project is my wife, Elizabeth. Mere words cannot express my gratitude for her time, patience, encouragement, and, above all, research assistance in the archives. She gave many weeks of her life to this book, taking countless digital photographs of documents at my side, and for that I am especially grateful. More importantly, without her, I never would have started, or finished, this book. It is dedicated to her, with tremendous love and gratitude.

THE SEXUAL ECONOMY OF WAR

Introduction
Society, Sexuality, and the U.S. Army in the Early Twentieth Century

> General Pershing is filled with anxiety about the sexual morale of troops.
>
> —Future Supreme Court Justice Felix Frankfurter to Secretary of War Newton D. Baker, August 15, 1917, on the condition of American troops in France during World War I

In June 1900, William B. Johnson published a sensational exposé, entitled "The Administration's Brothels in the Philippines," that alleged the U.S. Army had established a network of brothels in the Philippines for the exclusive use of American soldiers. The American League of Philadelphia, a group that opposed U.S. overseas expansion, soon republished Johnson's piece as a pamphlet entitled *The Crowning Infamy of Imperialism*, which garnered national attention, blasting the army for its immorality and urging the McKinley administration to withdraw its forces from the islands.[1] Three months later, American newspapers and moral reform organizations began publishing the "Custer Henderson Letter," a letter allegedly written by a young American soldier to his parents that detailed widespread sexual promiscuity and other vices among soldiers in the Philippines, seemingly offering corroboration for Johnson's allegations of official corruption and the pervasive moral hazards faced by American soldiers as they ventured abroad.[2]

In response, outraged citizens began sending letters and telegrams to William McKinley and the War Department urging withdrawal from the Philippines and an end to the army's regulation of prostitution. Letter writers used the issue to discuss their views on anti-imperialism, antimilitarism, miscegenation, temperance, morality, and venereal disease. As one U.S. anti-imperialist physician described it, the army had established "a system of nasty weekly medical inspections of hundreds of women by our army surgeons" so that "our officers and soldiers and sailors, and men and boys generally, might safely commit fornication and adultery, saving their bodies but destroying their souls."[3] Other doctors, such as U.S. Army Major Charles Lynch, advocated continuing the regulation regime, for without it, Lynch suggested, "venereal disease [would be] carried to innocent women and children in the United States, evil consequences which would follow unregulated prostitution here," presumably after American soldiers who contracted venereal diseases in the islands returned home and resumed sexual relations with their wives.[4] Lynch's view reflected the army's prevailing notion that men had irrepressible sex drives that made it impossible for them to remain sexually abstinent. It also highlighted the army's desire to mitigate the effects of venereal infections contracted by soldiers by intervening in the health of their civilian sexual partners.

What the American press and public failed to realize was that the U.S. Army had been regulating—and implicitly endorsing—prostitution in the Philippines since November 1898, when American troops first arrived in the islands and assumed control from the Spanish. Local prostitutes were required to regularly report to army physicians, who inspected the women for venereal infections and either issued them a certificate indicating a clean bill of health or ordered the women to be confined until their symptoms subsided. Army officials had understood that their actions would face a backlash if the American public learned of them, so they attempted to regulate prostitution with as little publicity as possible.

The public debates over prostitution and moral degeneracy in the Philippines triggered a congressional investigation. Governor-General of the Philippines (and future president) William Howard Taft was called to testify. He stated that while medical inspections had begun under military auspices and continued under colonial government authority, they had been discontinued by the time of his testimony in February 1902.[5] Taft failed to note that the formal inspection program had ended the day before his testimony, when the Secretary of War ordered the army to stop charging prostitutes inspection fees and issuing health certificates. Though army doctors were no longer allowed to charge prostitutes for their inspections or keep records on the women, the U.S. Army quietly continued to inspect the bodies of prostitutes in the Philippines until 1917, when a new federal law pushed through by moral reformers finally mandated that the army no longer permit prostitution near U.S. military bases. Despite the host of problems that the army's interventions in public sexual health caused, army officials believed that they needed to continue to be involved in the sex lives of soldiers and their partners, not just in the Philippines but everywhere the army deployed in the early twentieth century.

As with many other militaries, the U.S. Army believed that soldiers' sexual activities had the potential to cause a variety of problems. Most obviously, and perhaps most important from an institutional perspective, soldiers' sexual activities could lead to combat ineffectiveness because they might contract venereal diseases that rendered them unable to perform their military duties. Venereally infected soldiers would also consume sometimes scarce medical resources during treatment, and it might take days or weeks before the diseases' symptoms abated or—after the introduction of penicillin—were cured. Second, soldiers' sexual activities could get out of hand and generate considerable ill will and even active resistance in communities surrounding military bases.[6] Rapes by servicemen of local women in friendly or occupied areas could cause significant resentment by local civilian populations, as could unacknowledged or unwanted pregnancies, making placid civil-military relations extremely difficult. Vulgar displays by soldiers, especially when such behaviors were publicly exhibited by officers, could prove embarrassing to militaries. Last, soldiers' sexual partners could serve as sources of intelligence for enemies, especially during wartime.

The U.S. Army sought to address each of these perceived problems as it was called on to expand its reach across the Caribbean and into the Pacific and Europe in the early twentieth century. One of the army's key operational and logistical concerns—and one that hitherto has not been investigated comprehensively—was the effect of soldiers' sexuality on the establishment and maintenance of long-term military outposts and bases as part of the expanding overseas American military presence. Military planners, army leaders, War Department officials, and civilian observers of the military were intensely concerned about issues related to sexuality because they tended to believe that soldiers had irrepressible sexual needs that, when inevitably indulged, could cause harm to the army. They also believed that by instituting a series of legal regulations and medical interventions, the army could mitigate the damages to the institution arising from sex, while also shaping soldiers' sexuality in ways the army and interested civilian parties might find more acceptable.

This book explores how the U.S. Army of the early twentieth century, on institutional and individual levels, perceived and intervened in a host of issues related to sexuality: marriage and family life, prostitution and venereal disease, rape and sexual violence, same-sex sexuality, and masculinity, among others. It examines how the army sought to regulate and shape the sexual behaviors of soldiers and the civilians with whom they came into sexual contact. The sexual cultures, practices, and behaviors of soldiers and their partners, along with the U.S. Army's efforts to regulate their sexuality, constitute what I will describe as the "sexual economy of war."

Temporally, this study begins with 1898, as the Spanish-American War ushered in a new role on the world stage for the United States and the U.S. Army. Previously, the United States had steadily expanded its continental borders at the expense of its neighbors, but the war in 1898 represented a sharp break from what had gone before, catapulting the United States into its Caribbean backyard, as well as halfway around the world in Asia. With this expansion into global politics came imperialist foreign and military policies, as well as increasing efforts to manage and shape sexuality in far-flung locales. The narrative will trace the changing conditions brought about by these new military commitments and, later, involvement in World War I, when the American experience in Europe and the massive wartime conscription effort brought new challenges to preexisting notions of sexuality and increased concern with surveilling and regulating soldiers' sexuality. Following the war, the army's and, more broadly, American conceptions and categorizations of sexuality became more rigidly codified. The book ends on the cusp of American involvement in World War II and the tremendous changes triggered by the war.

Geographically, the book covers the complete breadth of the army's deployments throughout the period: within the United States itself, both at well-established bases and in new domestic training camps created for World War I; throughout the Pacific; and, beginning with World War I, in Europe. While American overseas deployments in the Caribbean and across the Pacific were particularly important formative experiences for the army as an institution, in the early twentieth century, the United States became a world power with a modernized, professional army. As such, the army's experiences both at home and in different overseas contexts—in the outposts of empire and in Europe—are vitally important to understanding the sexual economy of war.

One of the key objectives of this research is to situate the United States' military policies from the early twentieth century within a larger framework of gender, racial, class, national, and sexual politics, as well as Progressive Era medical and social-purity discourses. The book investigates the competing ideas of empire and masculinity of U.S. social purity activists[7] and anti-imperialists on the one hand, and U.S. civilian and military leaders who pursued imperial policies on the other. The soldiers charged with carrying out U.S. foreign and military policies and the people with whom they had sexual relations further complicated the debates between policymakers and critics because they highlighted competing conceptions of acceptable sexual behavior and demonstrated the difficulties in implementing and enforcing sexual regulations. These debates reveal conflicting conceptions of American masculinity and provide insights into the conceptions of race, class, and nation that were expressed and contested in the early twentieth century.

Transformation of the U.S. Army

Beginning in 1898 with the Spanish-American War and subsequent Philippine-American War, the United States began to look beyond its continental boundaries and acquire a new, far-flung empire, with territorial acquisitions in Hawaii, Samoa, Guam, the Philippines, Puerto Rico, and Cuba.[8] It staffed each of these new acquisitions with permanent military garrisons, necessitating the construction of a network of military bases throughout the Pacific and Caribbean. The nation's growing empire required the deployment of tens of thousands of U.S. soldiers at a time through the years leading up to World War II. The United States also engaged in other military interventions in Asia and Latin America, including China, Panama, Mexico, the Dominican Republic, Nicaragua, and Haiti, not to mention the massive mobilization required by American intervention in World War I and the subsequent occupation of Germany. Along with significant new overseas commitments, the U.S. Army underwent several major changes in the first four decades of the twentieth century, including massive growth in the army's forces, changes in the demographics of soldiers and an associated attempt to "Americanize" the army, and increased professionalization and internal reform as the army sought to improve its performance and increase its standing in the nation.[9] These changes all played significant roles in how the army came to perceive and regulate sexuality.

When it became clear that the United States would go to war with Spain in 1898, the McKinley administration rapidly realized that the small standing army would be inadequate to defeat the Spanish forces lodged in Cuba, so it raised a large body of temporary volunteers to bolster its forces; by war's end, the volunteer force numbered 216,000 and the Regular Army 59,000. Over the next four decades, the U.S. Army's strength continued to grow.[10] In 1890, there had been fewer than 28,000 soldiers in the army; by 1900, there were nearly 102,000. The National Defense Act of 1916 increased this number further, calling for an army of 175,000 men. The drafts of 1917–1918 brought unprecedented numbers of new soldiers into the army: over 4.7 million men served during World War I. Ultimately, the experiences of the war proved transformative for both the army as an institution and the men who served in it, particularly for the men deployed as part of the American Expeditionary Force to Europe.[11] The army rapidly demobilized after the war; the total number of men in the army fell to fewer than 140,000 in the 1920s and 1930s. Only in 1940, with fears of a new war involving the United States, did the army's strength begin to increase again.

It was not only the numbers of men in the U.S. Army that changed over time; the demographics of American soldiers likewise reflected the changes of the American population in the early twentieth century. A considerable number of immigrants—many nonnative English speakers—entered the army during this period. The War Department, often in close cooperation with civilian reformers, attempted to employ principles of social engineering to inculcate a sense of American national identity and pride in these men in an effort to Americanize the army, just as it would use the opportunity provided by wartime indoctrination of draftees to instill middle-class morality and sexual mores.[12] Racial differences also began to emerge as African Americans were admitted into the army in greater numbers.[13]

With the increase in sheer numbers of soldiers came an emphasis on internal reform, institution building, and enhanced professionalism. Following the army's poor performance in the Spanish-American War,[14] Secretary of War Elihu Root initiated a series of reforms amid calls for increased professionalization, interservice coordination, and new international responsibilities. Root's reforms included the Army Reorganization Act, which provided for an enlarged standing army and attempted to limit the power of army bureaus, as well as the General Staff Act, which marked the beginning of the modern command structure for the army. While Root's vision for the army was not completely achieved by the start of World War I, the army's expanded staff and planning capabilities significantly aided in the American war effort. Throughout this era, the army sought to remake itself into a highly professionalized force that would perform better militarily and have an improved standing in the nation as a whole. The army's efforts at professionalization were part of a broader trend in late nineteenth and early twentieth-century America involving the creation of increasingly specialized technical experts, such as doctors and lawyers; the army's officer corps was little different in its desire to become respected, professional, and technically expert.[15]

The U.S. Army and Sexuality

The U.S. Army exhibited concerns about soldiers' sexual behavior everywhere it went, though it sought to deal with the host of issues surrounding sex very differently in each setting. Outward-facing U.S. foreign policy, the growth in both the size of the army and the scope of its operations across the globe, and the nation's renewed investment and interest in the soldiers who served in the U.S. Army as a result of the national mobilization of World War I all resulted in increased public scrutiny of and interest in life inside the army. Domestic reformers attempted to reshape the army's policies on sexuality in order to reform an increasingly important American social and cultural institution. The army was thus not an institution autonomously choosing the proper way to consider and regulate soldier sexuality; instead, it was buffeted by domestic influences and constituencies that would significantly shape how the army would handle sexual matters.

The U.S. Army sought to create a series of policies to address the problems it perceived as stemming from soldiers' sexual relationships. Rates of venereal infection varied tremendously among U.S. Army units in the early twentieth century, but they became a particularly acute problem in the Philippines before World War I, where venereal infection rates climbed to 20–35 percent in some units.[16] Though no massive venereal epidemics appeared in American troops during World War I, fears that venereal infection rates would increase dramatically once American soldiers landed in France inspired major army sexual education and venereal treatment efforts. To combat this threat, the army chose to adopt a series of policies that in some ways mimicked those of other militaries.[17] These policies established regimes of medical surveillance and regulation of prostitutes to limit the transmission of venereal diseases to soldiers who frequently came into contact with these women. The U.S. Army instituted medical inspection and segregation regimes of prostitutes first in the Philippines and then later along the Mexican border, and it cooperated with civilian officials who maintained similar policies in Hawaii, France, and Germany. In contrast with more permissive regimes abroad—at least until negative publicity forced changes in places like the Philippines—in the continental United States the army cooperated with domestic moral reformers who sought to eliminate all traces of prostitution and other "vices" surrounding military bases within the continental United States. The U.S. Army never allowed its soldiers to rape indiscriminately, and there are certainly no indications that it ever pursued rape as a military strategy. Alleged rapes and sexual violence perpetrated by American soldiers in the Philippines, Hawaii, France, and Germany before World War II did, however, significantly complicate the army's relationships with local civilians. Furthermore, the army encouraged homosocial bonds between soldiers as a means of fostering unit cohesion, but it never endorsed homosexual activities between soldiers, increasingly condemning these kinds of behaviors after World War I.[18]

The U.S. Army attempted to control—via official policy, legal enforcement, indoctrination, and military culture—particular sexual behaviors that it found problematic for the institution as a whole and its overall military effectiveness. Allowing soldiers the opportunity to indulge some sexual desires but not others, while guarding against the problems that sex could cause for unit readiness and morale, became one of the key balancing acts that U.S. Army planners had to perform throughout the early decades of the twentieth century. The sexual behaviors the army found particularly troublesome included sexual encounters that resulted in venereal infections, marriage, or pregnancy, as well as those that created public embarrassment for the army as a whole or difficulties in relations between the army and local civilians. Over time, the army increasingly came to view sexual relationships between soldiers as undesirable because of changes in the way that most Americans, led by medical and psychoanalytic experts, viewed such same-sex relationships. In regulating these sexual behaviors, the army also indirectly (and unintentionally, in some cases) influenced particular views of sexual morality and sexual identities among soldiers. For example, in emphasizing sexual abstinence as a policy during World War I, the army publicly intervened in wider debates about sexual morality, helping to promote a particular brand of traditional, middle-class sexual morality favored by many influential moral reformers. It also implicitly endorsed the perceived linkage—especially from the early 1920s onward—between same-sex sexual activities and pathologized homosexuality, which came to be equated with both effeminacy and psychological degeneracy.

The U.S. Army seems to have embraced what scholars of masculinity have described as a changing conception of American manhood that emerged in the late nineteenth century as a result of larger cultural responses by white men to the disappearance of the American "frontier"; the increasing urbanization, bureaucratization, and industrialization of American society; and the slow but steady rise in the social and political rights of women, minorities, and other groups most white American men had previously dominated.[19] White men's increasing interest in martial virtues, physicality, strength, a robust male body, athleticism, competition, "primitive" warriors, and virility created what might be called militant masculinity. Hand in hand with this new kind of masculinity went a respect for fighting and an eagerness to engage in personal combat to test and assert one's manhood.[20] Theodore Roosevelt, colonel of the Rough Riders during the Spanish-American War and later president, embodied this new sense of manhood most explicitly in his "doctrine of the strenuous life," a regimen of physical training to enhance strength, vigor, and toughness that promoted struggle as a virtue.[21] Advocates of this conception of masculinity were profoundly concerned that modern civilization, with all its comforts, was making white American men decadent and effeminate by forcibly suppressing their "natural" masculine drive for independence, courage, and mastery.

American soldiers, who routinely engaged in intense physical labor and held a virtual monopoly on the legal use of violence, were able to embrace this new conception of masculinity to a greater degree than most civilian men. These constructed images of gender became central to soldiers' identities and highly charged with meaning, shaping the way that soldiers conceived of themselves as men and as soldiers. The army adopted and enlarged the concept of militant masculinity, using it to shape soldiers' sexual identities—particularly enlisted soldiers, some of whom were considered sexually problematic by army officials—by socializing them to generate that specific kind of masculinity in their public and private lives, behaving in particular "masculine" ways. Army officers, considered "gentlemen" in military culture and law, were required to exhibit different traits of masculinity and different standards of sexual behavior from the enlisted soldiers who served under them. The models of masculinity promoted by the U.S. Army during this period were examples of what psychologists have since described as "hypermasculinity," which can include callous sexual attitudes toward women, a conception of violence as a manly activity, and a view of danger as exciting.[22] The army required increasingly heteronormative sexual expression of soldiers, as the institution and American society became more aware of same-sex attraction. Soldiers were expected to conform to these specific gender and sexual norms and public performances, while also being forbidden from engaging in sexual practices and behaviors deemed effeminate. The resulting set of acceptable hypermasculinized sexual behaviors constituted part of a new sexual identity for soldiers, one that army leaders believed was the most effective for promoting aggressive, militant, and therefore *martial* behaviors in the new century.

The U.S. Army intervened in another important way in the personal lives of its members: it forbade most enlisted men—sergeants excepted, because of their age and seniority—and junior officers from marrying.[23] As the old saying about life in the U.S. Army goes, "If the army had wanted you to have a wife, it would have issued you one." Though some enlisted soldiers did marry while in military service, with or without their commanding officer's permission, they were forbidden from reenlisting once married and would be court-martialed if they attempted to conceal the fact that they were married at enlistment or reenlistment. The army ostensibly created this policy because large numbers of civilian dependents would have created a burden on the army to provide housing and support for the wives and children of soldiers. Maintaining large numbers of army families would have been especially difficult in the army's austere basing conditions in early twentieth-century Hawaii and the Philippines. Most middle-class Americans perceived enlisted military service as socially undesirable, and enlisted soldiers were also generally paid less than civilian blue-collar workers; these factors would have made supporting a family financially and socially problematic, even had the army permitted marriage. The army's antimarriage policy thus created a military culture in which most soldiers who desired romantic or sexual partnerships were forced to choose between consorting with prostitutes, thus risking venereal infection; violating army regulations by having illicit sexual relationships or marrying in secret, thus risking being court-martialed when the marriage or relationship came to the official attention of the army; and marrying and then being forced to leave military service when the current term of service had ended.

The United States in the Progressive Era

The U.S. Army was not alone in undergoing transition in the early twentieth century: unprecedented, sweeping changes were taking place across American society and culture at the same time. These changes included tremendous growth in immigration, especially from southern and eastern Europe, which began transforming the once-dominant Anglo-Saxon demographic makeup of the United States; urbanization and industrialization, especially in the Northeast; and the rise of more outward-looking foreign policies requiring new overseas military commitments. By the dawn of the twentieth century, many Americans, mostly members of the middle class, felt the need to increase the role of government in American society in order to address what they perceived as a host of growing social problems. Like the populists of the late nineteenth century who came before them, these middle-class reformers—most of whom have been described as progressives—believed that unregulated capitalism, the urban boom and its attendant problems, and the growing immigrant population, among other perceived social and cultural ills, required sweeping reforms that only stronger government supervision and intervention could bring. As the historian William Leuchtenburg describes it, "The Progressives believed in the Hamiltonian concept of positive government, of a national government directing the destinies of the nation at home and abroad. They had little but contempt for the strict construction of the Constitution by conservative judges, who would restrict the power of the national government to act against social evils and to extend the blessings of democracy to less favored lands. The real enemy was particularism, state rights, limited government."[24]

The Progressive movement was not a unitary movement, and the groups that can be reasonably described as "progressive" were extremely diverse, though they shared a commitment to reforming American government and society. Progressives tended to have great faith in the power and ability of a reformed American state to impose sweeping changes across all aspects of American society, reflecting beliefs that public and private life could not be disentangled and that the state should do more to ensure the moral and social welfare of its citizens. These reformers came from across the traditional American political spectrum—with leaders as disparate as Republicans Theodore Roosevelt, Robert M. La Follette Sr., Charles Evans Hughes, and Herbert Hoover, and Democrats William Jennings Bryan, Woodrow Wilson, and Al Smith—making progressivism one of the most widespread and influential American political movements of the twentieth century.

By the onset of American intervention in World War I, the Progressive movement had reached its height of influence in the United States. As the United States formally entered the war and began a massive military mobilization, some progressives began to express their anxieties regarding the threats American soldiers would, they believed, inevitably encounter, not on the battlefield but in the training camps and red-light districts of American cities before they even deployed to Europe. Fears about the social and moral dangers of prostitution and venereal disease that newly conscripted American servicemen would face were also intertwined with anxieties about urbanization and immigration, as well as the rise of a new commercial leisure culture that featured increasingly visible working-class women in public spaces. Many of these women were first- or second-generation immigrants who behaved in ways that ran counter to traditional middle-class values, which reserved sexuality for monogamous marriage; forbade other kinds of sexual expressions, including same-sex sexuality and masturbation; emphasized sexual purity in thought as well as behavior, especially in public and in male-female interactions; and stereotyped moral women as relatively asexual beings. These conceptions of sexuality would define and prescribe the kinds of sexual expression that many moral reformers advocated, as well as shape the ways in which they sought to legally mandate and regularize American sexuality in the decades before World War II.[25]

Though Prohibition was the reformers' most visible antivice success in social engineering, it was but one among many similar efforts to reshape

American society and morality through legal efforts to prohibit "immoral" activities. In 1910, in response to the "white slave panic" that swept the nation and instilled a fear of widespread enslavement of white women into prostitution, the U.S. Congress passed the Mann Act, which prohibited the transportation of women across state lines "for immoral purposes."[26] The Mann Act prevented very little coercive human trafficking, but for decades it was used to prosecute thousands of cases of consensual, noncommercial travel by unmarried adults. The Harrison Narcotic Drug Act of 1914's regulation and taxation of opiates represented the first federal involvement in what came to be the century-long War on Drugs.[27] In 1915 and again in 1918, the Comstock Act, which made it illegal to send any "obscene, lewd, and/or lascivious" materials through the mail, was also used to restrict the ability of sex educators and birth control advocates, like Margaret and William Sanger, to send information on contraceptive devices through the U.S. mail. A new federal agency, the Commission on Training Camp Activities (CTCA), was formed soon after the United States entered World War I to regulate soldiers' sexual morality. The CTCA succeeded in shutting down dozens of red-light districts throughout the United States and imprisoning thousands of women in work camps because they were alleged to be either prostitutes or promiscuous women who might lead soldiers astray. Previously, the use or abuse of alcohol and narcotics, along with sex between unmarried persons, had been perceived as social *conditions*, which, while objectionable, were present throughout society. During the Progressive Era, reformers considered these issues to be social *problems*, which could be identified by experts and solved through increased activism by reformers and legal action by the newly empowered federal government.

While social and moral reformers of all sorts enjoyed tremendous success in affecting sexual mores and the laws governing sexual and other personal activities in United States in the first decades of the twentieth century, their influence crested during World War I and the years immediately following. During the Roaring Twenties, America's sexual landscape began to change, and new sexual freedoms emerged.[28] Birth rates declined and divorce rates increased, as did the rate of premarital sex.[29] Popular images from the era, including those of flappers, speakeasies, F. Scott Fitzgerald's *The Great Gatsby*, petting parties, and the emergence of Hollywood sex symbols, only served to reinforce perceptions of increased sexual license. By the 1930s, reliable artificial birth control measures became increasingly available and socially (and legally) acceptable, further encouraging extra- and premarital sexual expressions. Sexual imagery, too, became more prevalent in many films and advertisements saturating American society. These factors all steadily eroded support for moral reformers' efforts to impose or maintain middle-class ideas about sexual morality and practices.

This era also witnessed the rise of psychoanalysis and the influence of Sigmund Freud's work in the United States, which ushered in new perspectives on human sexuality, including homosexuality, beginning in the 1920s.[30] As the American medical and psychoanalytical communities became professionalized in the early twentieth century, their monopoly over expertise in matters psychological and sexual grew. World War I only served to give them a new sense of mission in treating an increasingly pathologized populace and expand their role in society. By war's end, psychological and medical professionals, many of whom deemed themselves "sexologists"—experts in diagnosing and treating sexual dysfunctions—were regularly consulted in matters of public health and sexuality.

By the 1920s there was growing awareness of same-sex sexual attraction, which elicited considerable interest among psychoanalysts and sexologists, who increasingly viewed such behavior as pathological. Homosexuality came to be considered as more than just a set of behaviors, gestures, or demeanors and was instead perceived as a central feature of the identity of those who engaged in same-sex sexual activity. Michel Foucault later noted that "homosexuality appeared as one of the forms of sexuality when it was transposed from the practice of sodomy onto a kind of interior androgyny, a hermaphroditism of the soul. The sodomite had been a temporary aberration; the homosexual was now a species."[31] Freud called into question the idea that homosexuality was inborn and inherited, as previous sexologists like Magnus Hirschfeld and Richard von Krafft-Ebing, among many others, had believed. Freud instead asserted that it was the result of early childhood experiences and ultimately concluded that homosexuality, like other sexual conditions he regarded as perverse, was generally the result of interrupted sexual development.[32] To Freud, heterosexuality was the normal state of mature, adult psychosexual development: "One of the tasks implicit in object choice is that it should find its way to the opposite sex."[33] Later psychoanalytic clinicians in the United States and elsewhere—including many employed by the U.S. Army—came to perceive homosexuality as a profound, psychopathic disturbance.

The stigmatization of homosexuality as a pathological, even psychotic, condition, as well as its conceptual linkage with effeminacy, strongly influenced the ways in which the U.S. Army dealt with homosexuality within the ranks. Before World War I, the army occasionally prosecuted soldiers for committing acts of sodomy, though sodomy had never been included as an explicit offense under the Articles of War. The 1917 revision to the army's *Manual for*

Courts-Martial—which first introduced sodomy as an explicit offense—ushered in a series of new sodomy-related charges. The 1917 Ninety-Third Article of War defined sodomy as anal penetration of a man or woman by a man. In these regulations, penetration of the mouth did not initially constitute sodomy. In the regulations that accompanied the revision of the Articles of War in 1920, however, *The Manual for Courts-Martial* redefined sodomy as anal or oral copulation between men or between a man and a woman.[34] After World War I, the U.S. Army, reflecting changing common understandings and perceptions of same-sex sexual activity among men, began to perceive acts of sodomy as indicating a homosexual sexual identity, which the psychoanalytic profession had condemned as a form of psychopathy.

The U.S. Army and the Sexual Economy of War

War Department and army officials frequently described their concerns about soldiers' sexualities using the language of "military necessity."[35] They frequently argued that army interventions in sexuality were based on pragmatic, utilitarian concerns, with the army allegedly striving to balance health and morale, as well as managing the effects that matters of sexuality could have on military missions and broader U.S. geopolitical and diplomatic affairs. However, individual army officials also frequently shared the moral concerns of civilian commentators and reformers, and the army's policies were significantly affected by domestic discourses about public health and morality. These policies were not created in an ideological vacuum; while the army's military necessity approach sometimes involved different priorities and ends from those advocated by many moral reformers, it also represented an ideological approach to solving the army's problems related to sexuality.

Because of its concerns about the effects of sex on soldiers and the army as an institution, the army therefore strove to regulate sexuality in such a way that the inevitable meeting of soldiers' sexual needs would have the least deleterious effect on army operations. It is these collective attempts (and their effects) to regulate almost all aspects of soldiers' sexual lives, along with the regulated aspects of sexuality themselves, that I describe as a "sexual economy of war" in order to capture the complexity of the interactions between and among individuals, institutions, and legal, medical, and moral frameworks surrounding issues of sexuality. Just as conducting military operations and deployments required a political economy, the United States' projection of military force abroad as part of its expanded overseas mission incorporated a sexual economy of war, with exchanges taking place both inside and outside the sphere of military conflict, encompassing all aspects of soldiers' intimate lives: prostitution, venereal disease, same-sex attraction and later homosexuality, sexual violence and rape, sexual morality, military families, and ideas about masculinity, among others. The nature of the sexual economy and how it operated within the context of the nascent American state both at home and abroad are the central focus of the book. As conceived here, the sexual economy includes both those aspects of human sexuality that the army attempted to control and its means for doing so. Without considering and intervening in these aspects of the sexual economy, the army did not believe that it could sustain the military deployments brought about by the United States' new role on the world stage.

The sexual economy of war was a highly negotiated and contested exercise of power. The army's hegemonic discourses and institutional control competed directly with the agency, experiences, willful action, resistance strategies, and sexual and gender performances of the individuals affected. It involved a multitude of actors, both military—senior leaders, officers, and enlisted men—and civilian, including governmental officials and policymakers, moralists, sexual and medical "experts," and the local populations surrounding army bases and garrisons, whose members sometimes became the sexual partners of soldiers.

The sexual economy of war depended heavily on the asymmetries of power present throughout society, which ranged from the individual to the institutional. Individual soldiers, as men and male sexual partners, often had greater power than their female sexual partners because of inherent physical differences, the social privileges that men enjoyed over women, and, in the case of patronage of prostitutes, the socioeconomic and legal advantages that customers had over sex workers. Significant asymmetries of power existed among commissioned officers, noncommissioned officers, and enlisted men because of the hierarchical nature of the military institution to which they belonged. Different classes of military men experienced life in the army very differently because of separate military cultures and legal and disciplinary structures within the army, as well as differences in ages (young conscripts versus older veterans of military service, for example) and other personal characteristics. These differences resulted in tremendous disparities in how, for example, officers' and soldiers' sex lives were surveilled and regulated by the army and how they experienced military justice for sexual transgressions, and they sometimes allowed men of higher rank to use their military status to sexually exploit men of lower rank. There were also clear asymmetries of power in evidence regarding the treatment and status of nonwhite civilian sexual partners of soldiers due to prevailing ideas and theories about race and racial hierarchies.[36] Last, the U.S. Army as an institution clearly used its power over individual soldiers and their sexual partners to attempt to impose surveillance and regulatory regimes on their sex lives.

The sexual economy of war encompassed not a single national discourse but rather a series of discourses taking place in particular locations and at particular times. It took radically different forms depending on its geographic and temporal contexts, with sexuality being policed in very different ways in domestic settings from how it was treated abroad. Different overseas contexts mattered too: prostitutes were perceived and regulated very differently in the Philippines, for example, from how they were treated in wartime France or in postwar Germany. This has a great deal to do with the racial discourses surrounding the inhabitants of each of those locales, as well as American conceptions of whiteness.[37] Temporality is also important, as 1917–1918 represented a particular break from the periods that preceded and followed it. The American experience in World War I involved unprecedented levels of mass mobilization and conscription that brought with them massive civilian interest in army life and new ideas about the "citizen-soldier," all of which had profound implications for how the army, and American society more broadly, thought about and acted on the sexuality of soldiers. Many civilian moral reformers imagined the newly conscripted doughboys as a source of manpower that would help reinvigorate the nation's morality after the war. Thus, the military could be put to civilian purposes: the war represented an opportunity to reach out to millions of American men and inculcate in them new virtues, sexual and otherwise. This new mass army, once demobilized, could then become a tool for socially and morally reshaping the nation after the war.

Ultimately, the U.S. Army had a variety of goals for its many legal and medical interventions that played out in varying ways across time and space; these interventions, along with continuities and change in different settings and at different times, are highlighted across the case studies that are examined in this book. One of the army's major goals was to prevent the spread of venereal disease from making significant numbers of soldiers ineffective for duty and thereby causing a serious manpower problem. Because the army tended to perceive soldiers' sexual desires as irrepressible and female prostitutes as the most common sexual outlet for soldiers, where and when it could, the army sought to venereally inspect and regulate prostitutes as a means of meeting this goal. The army also consistently sought to maintain good order, morale, and military discipline inside the institution; it perceived a wide variety of sexual behaviors as being disruptive to military discipline, and it sought to prevent sexual expressions—especially public ones—from causing disciplinary problems. Once the United States decided to intervene in World War I, and consequently draft more than four million Americans into the army, both the army and civilian moral reformers attempted to enhance the public image of the United States and the U.S. Army by making soldiers models of virtue and sexual abstention, which required even more extensive interventions in the sexuality of soldiers and their partners. This effort also sought to instill particular ideas about morality that were intended to craft a generation of young men who would morally rejuvenate the nation when they returned to civilian life at war's end. After World War I, as the psychoanalytic community and American society at large became increasingly concerned about the perceived dangers of homosexuality, the U.S. Army sought to root out same-sex sexual activities within the army, which Army leaders linked with "deviant" homosexual identities, effeminacy, and psychologically maladjusted personalities, creating a "straight" army.[38]

Research Methodology

This project examines two main areas: the regulation of sexuality by the U.S. Army, often through the army's medicolegal interventions in sexuality; and the experiences of those whose sexuality was regulated by the army, including both soldiers and those civilians with whom they interacted sexually. Accordingly, this study has required extensive archival research in primary documents, both institutional and personal. The project has been undertaken along two lines of research. The first, and primary, avenue required delving into the official records of the U.S. government, including the U.S. Army, the War Department, and other federal agencies, such as the World War I–era CTCA. By taking this approach, I have sought to uncover how military and civilian officials and the institution of the army conceived of and discussed sexuality, what these individuals and organizations were attempting to accomplish by regulating and manipulating sexuality, and how they went about doing so. Through my second research avenue, I have attempted to uncover how individuals inside the institution or otherwise affected by it (that is, soldiers and their sexual partners) perceived, received, and sometimes resisted the army's efforts to control and use sexuality. I have done this by investigating personal documents that describe these individuals' firsthand experiences of the army's legal apparatus for prosecuting alleged sexual transgressions. Neither approach would have provided a comprehensive picture in isolation, but by integrating the two, I can shed light on research questions that have not yet been explored by either military historians or historians of gender and sexuality, and provide answers that will offer broad insights to scholars in both fields.

A key set of sources for this research were the disciplinary records (primarily courts-martial) for the period, because these help reveal how the army maintained sexual discipline and punished soldiers who violated army regulations. Because court-martial cases form such an important body of sources for my research, it is important to consider how they might best be used and what we might expect to learn from them, as well as their limitations.[39] First, it is important, if obvious, to note that courts-martial do not tell us whether someone actually committed a particular act, nor can they tell us the prevalence of certain kinds of activities. We also do not know what kind of informal policing went on within army units (below the level of court-martial through nonjudicial punishments) and what it took for an act to become sufficiently scandalous that a court-martial would be necessitated. However, close reading of these court transcripts is crucial to help reveal the exact language and categorization that the various historical actors—army prosecutors, witnesses, medical "experts," and the accused themselves—used to discuss transgressions and activities.[40] The historian William M. Reddy has described the concept of "emotives," which he defines as expressions of feelings through the use of language, specifically through verbal constructions that explicitly describe emotional states or attitudes.[41] By thinking of courts-martial as sources of language and categorization and seeking these emotives in court-martial transcripts as a means of uncovering attitudes toward sexuality, and by reading these transcripts and other legal documents "against the grain"—that is, considering what is *not* said, as well as what is; consciously considering the author or institution's perspective and how that affected what was recorded, or silenced, and how acts are discussed; and seeking alternative interpretations and explanations—we may be able to use them as sources for a kind of cultural history rather than a simple social or legal history.[42] We must be somewhat cautious in reading and extrapolating from these judicial records because of their relatively small number and idiosyncratic nature. It is certainly possible to generalize as to the ways in which the army thought about certain kinds of sexual behavior by examining how they were discussed in these courts-martial, but we must acknowledge that some degree of speculation is required in order to draw broader conclusions.

It is also important to note that the army did not always function as a unitary institution, and the disagreements within the army among various army leaders, policymakers, medical experts, and others remind us that we need to "unpack" the army in any study of the institution. The U.S. Army of the early twentieth century was divided by rank, race, class, investment in medical and psychoanalytic "expertise," and varying levels of interest in the army's role as an agent of moral reform and related concerns. Institutional regulators were not all of one mind and did not always function as though they were. The sexual regulations the army created and enforced were likewise not all applied or experienced in the same way by all those touched by the army as an institution.

Organization of the Book

The rest of this book aims to examine the U.S. Army's regulation of sexuality and responses to these regulations by soldiers and civilians alike. Chapter 1 covers the army's regulation of sexuality at Fort Riley in Kansas from the end of the nineteenth century, as the United States sought to find a place on the world stage as a great power, through the end of the 1930s. The domestic setting of a large, permanent garrison that existed throughout the period provides an opportunity to discuss the U.S. Army's military justice system and set of policies on sexuality as a whole throughout the first four decades of the twentieth century. Chapter 2 examines the experiences of the army in the Philippines, beginning with the U.S. occupation of the Philippines following the Spanish-American War through World War I. The racial mixture of the soldiers sent to the Philippines and the Filipinos with whom they interacted sexually created an environment that complicated the army's efforts to manage soldiers' sexuality, particularly once U.S. domestic reformers learned of the U.S. Army's sexual regulation overseas. Chapter 3 looks at the U.S. Army at Camp Beauregard, a training camp built in Louisiana during World War I, as it sought to regulate sexuality in civilian communities near the camp, including both Alexandria and New Orleans, Louisiana. Social reformers promoted and encouraged the army's goal of creating the "world's cleanest army" during the war because they viewed the war as a tremendous opportunity to train millions of American men along moral lines. This effort was greatly complicated by the "vice conditions" the army and federal officials encountered in the American South, as well as resistance to antivice efforts by local civilians. Chapter 4 explores the army's attempts to regulate sexuality in both France and Germany during and immediately after World War I. Along with the American war effort came massive numbers of conscripted soldiers from all walks of life and renewed public interest in the conditions of military service and life inside the army. Foreign and diplomatic relations between the United States, its ally France, and its defeated foe Germany also significantly complicated the army's efforts to regulate sexuality overseas. Here, racial politics once again played an important role in the inevitable encounters between white and black Americans and their European hosts. Chapter 5 tells the story of the army's regulation of sexuality from 1909 to 1940 in Hawaii, the cusp of U.S. involvement in World War II as the army struggled to manage its new responsibilities in the Pacific, as well as the effects of the post–World War I changes to army policies on sexuality.

CHAPTER 1

"Conduct of a Nature to Bring Discredit upon the Military Service"

Fort Riley, Kansas, 1898–1940

> Any officer or cadet who is convicted of conduct unbecoming an officer and a gentleman shall be dismissed from the service.
>
> —Ninety-Fifth Article of War, effective February 4, 1921

> All disorders and neglects to the prejudice of good order and military discipline, all conduct of a nature to bring discredit upon the military service, and all crimes or offenses not capital, of which persons subject to military law may be guilty, shall be . . . punished at the discretion of such court.
>
> —Ninety-Sixth Article of War, effective February 4, 1921

The U.S. Army experienced tremendous change in the early decades of the twentieth century.[1] We see all of those changes playing out at Fort Riley in Kansas in this era: growth and transformation in the size, scope, and demographics of the army and the men who served in it; professionalization and institutional transformation in response to the massive changes wrought by World War I ; and heated domestic debates surrounding morality and health, and how the army would revolutionize its legal system to accommodate these conceptual changes. Because Fort Riley was an old, established U.S. Army post in the Midwest by the late nineteenth century, it serves as a useful venue for exploring how the U.S. Army thought about issues related to sexuality—family life and marriage, sexual propriety, venereal disease, homosexuality, and sexual violence—in domestic settings. Fort Riley also housed both white and black soldiers, which offers a further opportunity to examine to what extent the race of individual soldiers mattered in how the army considered these issues. While most of those serving at Fort Riley were members of the Regular Army—that is, active-duty, professional soldiers who were considered by many civilians to be outside the mainstream of American society, especially before World War I—World War I also brought an influx of new men into the army who intended only to perform their military duty for the duration of the war. With these men, many of them draftees, came increased attention and interest by civilian reformers in army life. After the war, the army's justice system was significantly revised for the first time in more than a century. Examining how the army treated what it considered criminal violations of a sexual nature in its court-martial process provides insight into what behaviors the army considered transgressive, how it publicly discussed such transgressions, and how it dealt with offenders.

At Fort Riley we see how entangled the army's notions of marriage, the family, and sexual propriety were with social class and gender relations in its methods of policing contact between enlisted men and civilian women of various social classes. In many ways the army sought to maintain and reinforce the existing class, racial, and gender relations present in broader American society; as a profoundly hierarchical institution, it could do so starkly in ways that might be more obscured in a nominally egalitarian civilian society. We can also observe the perceived linkages between homosexuality and moral perversion present in how the army dealt with alleged cases of sexual contact between men, which only grew over time, as well as the discomfort that some middle-class observers had with the sometimes sexually charged banter and roughhousing of working-class men.

Fort Riley was initially established in Northeast Kansas in 1853 to protect the flow of settlers and goods over the Oregon, California, and Santa Fe Trails.[2] During the Civil War, it housed a prisoner-of-war camp, and after the war it served to protect key rail lines against Indian attacks. From the fort, the U.S. Army launched several campaigns against Native American tribes in western Kansas and eastern Colorado during the Indian Wars, though with the lessening of hostilities by the 1880s, Fort Riley faced closure, along with many of the army's other frontier outposts. In his annual report to Congress in 1884, Lieutenant General Philip Sheridan, commanding general of the U.S. Army, recommended that Fort Riley be retained as the army's primary cavalry post and site of the army's cavalry school. Sheridan's recommendation was accepted and the cavalry school was established at Fort Riley in 1887. Fort Riley later hosted many major training exercises in the early twentieth century (1902–1904, 1906–1908, and 1911), which lent added importance to the fort as a major training center for the army.

Fort Riley was also home to a variety of army units, including the famed Ninth and Tenth Cavalry Regiments, two units of the so-called buffalo soldiers, though official army histories of Fort Riley rarely even mention that black soldiers once served at the fort.[3] Staffed by black cavalry troopers serving under white officers, these regiments rose to prominence and national attention during the Indian Wars. By the turn of the century, they were considered elite units and were sources of racial pride for many African Americans. Nevertheless, African Americans continued to be forced to serve in segregated units, and except for a handful of black chaplains and Lieutenant Charles Young (one of the few African American graduates of West Point), black soldiers were commanded by white commissioned officers. Black units were also stationed exclusively at garrisons west of the Mississippi.[4]

World War I brought enormous changes to Fort Riley, which was expanded by thirty-two thousand acres to accommodate cavalry training of new army units before their deployment to Europe. As part of this effort, Camp Funston was created as one of the thirty-two new training camps for World War I doughboys on the extensive grounds of Fort Riley. Originally intended as a temporary training cantonment, Camp Funston is still in use in the twenty-first century. Construction of Camp Funston began in the summer of 1917; by September, when the camp opened, it housed just over ten thousand soldiers. Funston grew rapidly to accommodate over fifty thousand men by October 1918.[5] It was commanded by Major General Leonard Wood, of Spanish-American War and Rough Rider fame, and produced three divisions of soldiers deployed to France for the war. Camp Funston also has the distinction of being the site of the first diagnosed victims of the misnamed Spanish Flu, which likely originated in Haskell County, Kansas, before becoming a global pandemic that infected five hundred million people and killed fifty million to one hundred million.[6]

Fort Riley and Camp Funston are located between two small towns. The nearest, Junction City, is four miles away. Its turn-of-the-century population of about five thousand had increased to over eight thousand by the outbreak of World War II. The only other nearby town, Manhattan, Kansas, eight miles from Riley and Funston, began the century with just over three thousand civilians but had increased to nearly twelve thousand by World War II. The army population at Fort Riley varied tremendously in the early twentieth century as units were deployed from Fort Riley to the Philippines, the Mexican border, and elsewhere. The fort's population rarely fell below one thousand men, since the army's cavalry school was always manned, generally ranging around two thousand men, though it swelled to more than four thousand during and immediately following World War I.[7]

While Camp Funston trained two divisions of white soldiers during the war—the Tenth and Eighty-Ninth Divisions—it also trained elements of a black division, the Ninety-Second. As soon as the presence of twelve thousand African American soldiers at Camp Funston was announced in fall 1917, local civilians began to complain. Their resistance to the presence of additional black soldiers at Camp Funston was somewhat unusual because while the local black civilian population was very small (there were only 110 black families in Manhattan, Kansas, in 1920, for example), there had been black Regular Army soldiers periodically stationed at Fort Riley (which was called, after all, "home of the buffalo soldiers") for decades with no known negative reactions to their presence by local whites. The War Department dispatched a representative of the federal Commission on Training Camp Activities (CTCA), tasked with overseeing the training and recreation of wartime recruits, to Camp Funston to investigate the matter. The CTCA official, F. B. Barnes, wrote to Raymond B. Fosdick, chairman of the CTCA, to urge Fosdick to employ his "influence and strongest efforts to have the order" to send the additional black soldiers to Funston rescinded. Ostensibly, the rationale was that, while local civilian entertainment facilities were not segregated as they were in the South, the small number of local blacks meant that black soldiers would have few other blacks with whom to associate, creating what Barnes called "moral and recreational problems exceedingly difficult to solve."[8] Local white civilians echoed these concerns, stating that the "influx of large number of colored troops into parks, streets, and places of amusement . . . near Camp Funston would inevitably result in race conflicts which the local civilian authorities would be unable to control."[9] There is no indication that Fosdick ever attempted to use his influence to prevent blacks from being trained at Funston, and in January 1918, the first group of 2,700 black soldiers arrived at Funston. The CTCA set aside one camp theater for their exclusive use.[10] When a black sergeant was refused entry to a civilian theater in March 1918, the white commander of the Ninety-Second Division, Major General Charles C. Ballou, issued what became his infamous Bulletin No. 35. This order cautioned the black soldiers under his command against going where they were not wanted, urging them to give up their legal rights if pursuance of those rights would "provoke race animosity."[11] After this incident, there are no other recorded racially motivated disagreements between Funston's black soldiers and local whites, nor were there any disciplinary infractions by blacks accused of sexual crimes in Kansas during World War I. All told, Fort Riley represents a domestic army community that enjoyed relatively placid relations with the local civilian community throughout the first four decades of the twentieth century, though it did experience demographic and legal changes during this period that affected how local army officials would attempt to regulate sexuality.

Military Justice at Fort Riley

The American court-martial system used at Fort Riley (and elsewhere) drew on centuries of British military justice tradition that was gradually modified for use by the U.S. Army.[12] In 1775, the Provisional Congress of Massachusetts Bay adopted a virtually unchanged version of the 1774 British Articles of War as the Massachusetts Articles of War, which contained detailed guidance for conducting courts-martial and maintaining military discipline. Two years later, the Massachusetts Articles of War were revised slightly and adopted for use throughout the United States. The Articles of War thus represent a kind of legal framework older than the U.S. Constitution, predating all civilian courts authorized or instituted by the Constitution. Military courts-martial also differed in significant ways from civilian courts, including the use of a single judge advocate who acted as both prosecutor and defense counsel. The Articles of War were amended again in 1789 but otherwise remained in effect until 1806, when they were substantially revised for the first time by the U.S. Congress. These revisions prohibited double jeopardy, established a two-year statute of limitations, and granted the accused the right to challenge members of the court. The Articles of War were amended again in 1874, largely to reflect a growing consensus within civilian legal circles on due process considerations.

In 1890, Congress established the summary court-martial, which was designed to replace the regimental and garrison courts-martial for enlisted men charged with minor offenses during peacetime.[13] In a summary court-martial, the accused was to be brought before a single-officer court within twenty-four hours of arrest. This officer was the sole determiner of the accused's guilt or innocence and meted out any punishments. The accused was offered the choice of a summary court-martial or a higher-level court-martial; these higher-level courts-martial offered increased protection of due process but were more elaborate and involved many commissioned officers in court proceedings. It was only in 1895 that an executive order established a set of maximum punishments for each punitive Article of War or individual offense; this executive order also provided guidance on how courts-martial were to consider the accused's prior convictions and other factors in determining punishments.

For the first time in more than a century, Congress undertook a major revision of the Articles of War in 1916. The new legal guidelines established the three types of courts-martial that would exist within the U.S. military throughout the rest of the twentieth century: the general court-martial, the special court-martial (which replaced the regimental and garrison courts-martial), and the summary court-martial.[14] This 1916 revision included a number of important features, such as the requirement that a judge advocate be appointed to general and special courts-martial; the accused's right to receive legal representation at general and special courts-martial; a prohibition on the requirement of the accused to incriminate himself; and the requirement that the accused be tried within ten days of arrest, among others.

In the wake of numerous complaints about military justice during World War I, Congress enacted a new set of 121 Articles of War in 1920, which went into effect in 1921.[15] The new Articles of War adopted in 1920 were not revised again until 1948. The important changes to military justice proceedings in 1920 included requirements that general courts-martial consist of at least five commissioned officers; that separate trial judge advocates and defense counsels be appointed for each general and special courts-martial (defense counsels could be civilian or military); that thorough pretrial investigations be conducted in all cases; that the accused be given full opportunity to cross-examine witnesses and present evidence; and that a board of review, consisting of three officers from the Office of the Judge Advocate General, review all courts-martial. Concerns about undue (and unlawful) command influence under this system lingered until well after World War II, as a single commissioned officer could prefer charges against the accused, convene the court-martial, select the members of the court (including the defense counsel), and review the case.

Pre–World War I records of general courts-martial from Fort Riley are fragmentary and incomplete, making it difficult to reach comprehensive judgments about the ways in which the army used military legal instruments to regulate soldier sexuality. However, soldiers at Fort Riley seem to have been given relatively free rein to indulge in sexual activity, even with prostitutes and even when soldiers' sexual activities led to infection with venereal diseases, though the army appeared to draw the line at sexual activity or vulgar displays while in public, either at the fort or in nearby civilian areas. There seems to have been a general tacit acknowledgment by many in the army that—mostly save for concerns about venereal disease—sexual activity on the part of male enlisted personnel was a normal expression of their rough-and-tumble, working-class masculinity. Venereal infections certainly occurred throughout the period at Fort Riley, as the Annual Reports of the Surgeon-General of the Army and the existence of a venereal ward at the post hospital attested. However, soldiers received neither summary nor general courts-martial when they contracted venereal diseases, regardless of whether they received the required venereal prophylaxis. Several houses of prostitution existed in Junction City, Kansas, and soldiers patronized the women employed there. It appears that the soldiers were disciplined only if they attempted to bring these women onto the grounds of the fort or if they caused a public disturbance, either at one of the brothels or in another public space. While pre–World War I records of general courts-martial from Fort Riley are incomplete, army legal records for the two decades following the war are much more readily available, offering a more complete look at how the U.S. Army used military justice to regulate soldier sexuality after World War I. The relevant cases provide insight into a broad array of sexual transgressions by both white and black enlisted men, as well as noncommissioned and commissioned officers, across the two decades following World War I.

Lesser Criminal Offenses

While serious criminal offenses committed by enlisted men and officers were tried in general courts-martial, summary courts-martial provided a simple legal mechanism for trying relatively minor offenses. Unlike general courts-martial, which had elaborate judicial requirements and procedures, summary courts-martial usually consisted solely of the accused and a single commissioned officer, who functioned as prosecutor, defense counsel, and judge. Though the outcomes and punishments of summary courts-martial could generally not be appealed, they were subject to review by higher authority (usually a higher-ranking officer and legal specialist within the Office of the Judge Advocate General), who could dismiss or reduce—but not increase—the sentence administered.

Few records of U.S. Army summary courts-martial survive from the early decades of the twentieth century. Those that do are usually terse, providing little more than brief descriptions of the offenses and outcomes of the summary courts-martial. No transcripts of the proceedings were ever recorded. Summary court-martial records from Fort Riley are available for the period July 1904 through June 1910.[16] Despite the inherent limitations of summary court-martial records, this six-year period of records is sufficient to provide information on two dozen relevant courts-martial and a glimpse into how offenses of a sexual nature that the U.S. Army assessed to be relatively minor were adjudicated. Of the relevant twenty-four summary courts-martial, one of the soldiers charged was a sergeant; the remaining defendants were all privates or privates first class. Commissioned officers could not be brought to trial before summary courts-martial, and generally noncommissioned officers could not be brought before summary courts if they objected.[17] Though some

African American troops of the Ninth and Tenth Cavalry Regiments were stationed at Fort Riley during this period, all but one of the accused in these summary courts-martial were white. The cases analyzed here were mostly all charged as violations of the Sixty-Second Article of War, a kind of catchall article that specified punishment for "all crimes not capital . . . to the prejudice of good order and military discipline."[18] A few cases having a sexual component that involved failing to appear at the proper time for inspections and the like were charged as violations of the Thirty-Third Article of War.[19]

Of the two dozen relevant summary courts-martial in this period, nine explicitly involved prostitutes or bringing "disreputable" women or "women of bad repute" onto the post without permission.[20] The summary courts-martial involving prostitutes, or women the army deemed disreputable, concerned two types of cases: First were cases in which the soldier brought the woman onto the grounds of Fort Riley itself; the soldier was either observed walking around the post with the woman or was caught in flagrante delicto with her. Second were cases in which soldiers caused a public disturbance with the women in the nearby town of Junction City, Kansas (on a streetcar in one case and inside a bordello in the second). In three of the cases—two on post and one off post—race appears to have played a role, as the race of the women involved in these charges was specifically noted as "colored" or "negro." Presumably the women in the other cases were all white. The three cases involving African American women all resulted in convictions, and the soldiers were sentenced more harshly than those in cases involving white women. Convictions for disturbances involving white women almost invariably resulted in forfeitures of five dollars, while those involving black women resulted in a forfeiture of ten dollars in two cases and thirty dollars in the other. Additionally, two of these three judgments resulted in sentences of hard labor (for one month in one case and two months in the other). Admittedly, this is an extremely small number of cases, so definitive conclusions are impossible to draw. However, the results are suggestive of racial bias in sentencing, with white soldiers who were alleged to have consorted publicly with black women seemingly judged to be even more transgressive than those engaging in similar acts with white women. In both types of prostitute-related cases, the charges involved extremely public activities that would have brought embarrassment to the army because they took place in public areas, civilian or military, forcing the army to take official notice and pursue criminal charges.

Another nine summary courts-martial concerned infractions of the rules established to govern the behavior of patients in the post venereal ward of the hospital. These violations tended to involve smoking, gambling, eating, passing fruit into the venereal ward, or failing to appear for inspection, all of which were violations of standing orders for patients in the ward.[21] As with all types of summary courts-martial, nearly all venereally related cases ended in convictions, with many sentences being trivial (a forfeiture of fifty cents or one dollar for smoking or failing to appear for daily inspection) and much more significant sentences in two cases. In one of these, Private James Childers, a patient in the venereal ward, received fruit passed to him through a window by another private, Andy Kisch.[22] Kisch was convicted at a summary court-martial and sentenced to forfeit one dollar, while Childers was sentenced to a month of hard labor and ordered to forfeit ten dollars of his pay. These kinds of sentences support the idea that the army treated discipline for venereal patients seriously and clearly regarded venereal treatment itself as a kind of punishment, since soldiers not undergoing such treatments would have been able to indulge in petty luxuries, like smoking or eating fruit.

The remaining six cases covered a variety of other offenses. In a domestic violence case, the only one recorded at the post in this period, the accused (John S. Surber, a married private who would not have been allowed to reenlist) struck and kicked his wife on the cavalry parade ground.[23] While it may be that the incidence of domestic violence was, in fact, this low at Fort Riley, the fact that this was the only offense of this type charged in six years may suggest that because Private Surber attacked his wife in public, the army had no choice but to intervene. Had the beating occurred within the Surbers' quarters on post, it is possible there may not have been a summary court-martial for the action.

In another case, Private Michael Sefe was accused of making lewd remarks in front of women.[24] Unfortunately we have no record of the identity of these women; we only know that the alleged infraction occurred in Saint Joseph, Missouri, presumably while Sefe was on leave. There must have been an altercation in Missouri that elicited testimony or evidence against Sefe, since a formal complaint, likely by letter or telegram, would have had to be lodged against Sefe when he returned to Fort Riley. Whatever the specifics of the charge, the army seems to have taken it seriously, since Sefe was sentenced to forfeit ten dollars of his pay each month for three months (more than three-quarters of his total pay each month), which suggests an emphasis on maintaining a level of social propriety around women, at least of a certain social class, when their honor was besmirched in a public manner.

Two cases involved charges of indecent exposure, though the offenses were alleged to have occurred in extremely different contexts.[25] In one case, Private Jack Gallagher, a patient in the post hospital, exposed himself "in an indecent manner" in front of other soldiers (also patients in the hospital), caused a violent disturbance, and disobeyed a doctor's order to go to bed. Gallagher was convicted and given a sentence that was relatively harsh for a summary court-martial: he was sentenced to three months of hard labor and forfeited ten dollars per month of his pay (nearly all his pay). The second accused, Private Ernest Shaffer, was also convicted, but he had to forfeit only two dollars of his pay. Shaffer's offense was to expose "his person" (it is unclear whether Shaffer was accused of exposing his genitals or buttocks) in front of a train car's window, presumably in view of civilians. Clearly the army did not consider Shaffer's actions, though "indecent" and public, to be serious, as he received an extremely light sentence. Gallagher's exposure, though committed only in front of his fellow soldiers, was much more problematic, as it was accompanied by a violent disturbance and direct refusal of a commissioned officer's order.

Another case involved the possession of a pornographic photo (exact subject unknown), which was discovered during an inspection of Private Virginius Campbell's locker.[26] Soldiers were often given summary courts-martial for possessing contraband (most commonly food) in their lockers, and Campbell was not noticeably treated more harshly than others who possessed nonpornographic contraband. This would seem to indicate that possessing the pornographic photo was not considered an offense worthy of stricter punishment than a punishment for any other type of contraband material. It is, however, relevant that pornography was included in the list of contraband soldiers were forbidden to possess on base, presumably because it, like extra food or alcohol, had the potential to create discipline problems.

The final relevant case concerned a hospital orderly, Private Julius Sherman, who lay in the same bed as a patient, though the summary court ultimately attached no criminality to this action.[27] Before 1917—when the Articles of War were significantly revised for the first time since 1806—sodomy was not listed as a criminal offense in the *Manual for Courts-Martial*, the War Department's procedural manual for handling all matters related to military justice.[28] After 1917, Sherman could have been charged with assault with intent to commit sodomy, a violation of the Ninety-Third Article of War.[29] In Sherman's case, it seems clear that his explanation for why he lay down in the same bed as a patient—almost certainly one involving a nonsexual motive—was accepted. The army clearly did view two men lying down in the same bed to be a breach of discipline, however, indicating some level of concern about such activities. There were no other cases in which same-sex sexual activity was alleged between soldiers, or between a soldier and a male civilian, in Fort Riley's summary court-martial records in this period.

Marriage and Family Life at Fort Riley

"Married men in the Army are unquestionably a burden . . . so also are married officers," wrote George Shelton, an army official, in the Secretary of War's 1907 annual report.[30] Marriage—at least for commissioned and noncommissioned officers, as privates were not permitted to be married at enlistment—was a necessary burden. The army had to accept at least some marriages and families if it expected to retain experienced soldiers, and therefore it had to provide adequate pay and allowances to support these families. Some privates did marry, clandestinely and without the approval of their commanding officers, though they likely lived in common-law relationships more frequently than they did in formalized, legal marriages, especially in places like the Philippines and Hawaii, where such common-law relationships were more socially acceptable. The wives and children of noncommissioned officers generally lived on army posts; while formal education was often lacking, they were integrated into base social and professional life, though noncommissioned officers' careers could sometimes be made more difficult or even derailed by social missteps by their wives and children in interactions with officers and their families. Because of the relative cohesion and isolation of army life, it is not surprising that many male children of soldiers and officers went on to follow in their fathers' footsteps, choosing the army as a career.[31]

As a magazine writer in 1935 put it, the "sameness" and insularity of army garrison life for women and children created a kind of "world within a world" for army families.[32] They moved frequently, usually every few years, some to new homes in prosaic locations—like Fort Riley in Kansas—and some to more exotic, but not necessarily desirable, locales like Hawaii or the Philippines. Each army post came with ready-made friends, associates, and neighbors for the entire family, with whom they would pass many hours, on and off the job, often living in close proximity. Dinner parties and dances were common, along with polo and other equestrian pursuits for officers at cavalry posts like Fort Riley. Rich social networks, always carefully segregated by race and rank within the army, abounded at every post. Obligatory social calls and participation in communal events for officers' wives and families sometimes created frustrations and frictions of their own, however, as did the decorum required of officers' wives in public settings.[33] During the Depression, it became clear to the families of officers and noncommissioned officers alike that they possessed a level of financial and professional stability that their civilian peers lacked. The families of officers also found that with their army-provided housing on post came privileges that their middle-class salaries would not likely have afforded them in the civilian world: the army paid to maintain their residences, with maintenance and upkeep of homes and yards provided by the army and carried out by enlisted soldiers, some of whom earned extra money by working part time as officers' servants.[34] Additionally, army commissaries and post exchanges sold food and household goods at subsidized prices, and the army provided free medical and dental care. These benefits alone were luxuries often unaffordable to working-class or even middle-class families, especially during the Depression. As one officer's wife stated, "It was like a small elite club. We had a rich man's life on a small income."[35] While army life could feel stagnant and oppressive at times, and discipline (especially for enlisted men) harsh, it also offered constancy and a higher quality of life than might otherwise be available.[36] Many small army posts did not have schools—children there either went to local civilian schools or took classes offered by soldiers' wives—but larger, established bases like Fort Riley had schools on post. For the children of soldiers, the army became a way of life, and many army children married other army children.

Just as the army forbade married men from enlisting (or reenlisting) as soldiers, it also strongly discouraged junior officers from marrying.[37] In 1903, Major General Henry C. Corbin, Adjutant General of the Army, worked to establish policies preventing junior officers from marrying and married junior officer candidates from being commissioned. Other proponents of such policies alleged that married lieutenants were not as attentive to their duties as single men, as they were distracted by their wives and domestic concerns. Some single officers charged that the arrangement was unfair, as married lieutenants were given special privileges in housing and other matters.[38] Ultimately, Corbin was unsuccessful in pushing through this change in army policy, though the issue arose again in 1915 when the General Staff briefly considered barring second lieutenants from marriage. Once again it was asserted that marriage was too distracting and, perhaps more importantly from the army's perspective, "too expensive a luxury" because of the additional costs incurred by the army in housing and transporting the families of junior officers.[39] This effort too was unsuccessful, and while junior officers were unofficially but strongly discouraged from marrying, they were never legally prohibited from doing so.

The Family Life of Officers

As was common within the U.S. Army at the time, commissioned officers existed in a space within the army in which their personal lives and affairs were protected and kept apart from soldiers. This cut two ways: first, the intimate, family spaces of officers were protected from intrusion by enlisted men (few enlisted men had families or private domestic spaces); and second, the marital relationships of officers were held to be sacrosanct, with adultery and other marital transgressions punished by the army in keeping with American middle-class social mores of the period.

In 1922, Private George J. Meade was accused of climbing onto a window ledge and peering into the bedroom window of a captain and his family on post.[40] Meade was charged with a violation of the Ninety-Sixth Article of War, the final, catchall article of war, which covered "all disorders and neglects to the prejudice of good order and military discipline, all conduct of a nature to bring discredit upon the military service."[41] A Peeping Tom had been noticed by the captain and his wife the previous night, and several officers lay in wait outside their home to catch the perpetrator in case he returned. Meade was caught red-handed and offered no statement, evidence, or witnesses on his own behalf. He pleaded not guilty and was sentenced to be dishonorably discharged, to forfeit all pay, and to serve one year of hard labor. Because Meade chose to remain silent, he left no indications as to his possible motives, and there was no speculation offered in court.

Officers not only acted to protect each other's families and intimate spaces from enlisted men, they also policed the officer corps against sexually transgressive fellow officers. In 1936, First Lieutenant William B. Fraser was charged with committing adultery and conducting "highly improper correspondence" for six weeks with Rosanna Hitchings, the wife of Captain John L. Hitchings, a fellow officer at Fort Riley.[42] Fraser was charged with a violation of the Ninety-Fifth Article of War (like the Ninety-Sixth Article of War, this article covered all miscellaneous offenses that officers might commit), which made criminal any "conduct unbecoming an officer and a gentleman."[43] Fraser and Captain Hitchings had been friends, and Fraser visited the Hitchings' quarters on post on multiple occasions. On these visits, Hitchings "observed that the accused began to assume an attitude toward his wife indicating such a degree of intimacy as might cause scandal." On March 30, 1936, Hitchings ordered Fraser out of the house, "having reason to believe that [Fraser] had improper relations with his wife." Upon being asked why he had become romantically involved with Rosanna Hitchings, Fraser replied, "Well, there are some things a man just can't help doing."

Two weeks later, Hitchings discovered a packet of seven letters between his wife and Fraser. Hitchings again confronted Fraser and forced Fraser to agree to resign his commission. The letters clearly describe an illicit sexual relationship between the two, and there can be little doubt about the veracity of the allegations. In one letter, Fraser urged Rosanna Hitchings to cease having conjugal relations with her husband:

You must stop it [having sex with Captain Hitchings], and immediately. Get a divorce if you must, bring my name into it, anything. I'll throw my commission and everything else to hell if such a thing continues. It must sound somewhat hypocritical to hear those sentiments from me after the way you and I have done things; but between you and me there was love. Not so in Jack's [Captain Hitchings] case. It is a woman's prerogative to yield or resist as she wishes (and the same applied where you and I are concerned).

Rosanna Hitchings very reluctantly testified that she had indeed had a romantic affair with Fraser for at least three months and that they had sexual intercourse "on more than one occasion." She stated that her husband had initially agreed to a divorce but changed his mind when he discovered the letters. Fraser remained silent during his court-martial, offering no testimony in his own defense. Reinforcing the notion of a special, insular world of officers and their families, the prosecution reminded the court at the start of the trial, "We are trying this officer on . . . conduct not becoming an officer and a gentleman, for which there is no analogy in civil courts. That fact must be borne in mind at all times."

Fraser pleaded not guilty and was found not guilty to the specific charge of adultery—despite Rosanna Hitchings's testimony—but was found guilty to the lesser charge of "conducting highly improper correspondence." He was sentenced to be reprimanded, to be reduced on the promotion list one hundred files (since promotions were based on seniority by date of attaining rank, Fraser was made junior to the one hundred other officers below him in seniority), and to be restricted to post for three months. The reprimand, by Major General F. C. Bolles, Commanding General of the Seventh Army Corps, read, "That any officer in the Army should at any time or place conduct himself in such a manner as to make publication of his specific acts of misconduct an open door to scandal and disgrace, merits more punishment than can be adjudged by reprimand." As sentences for officers went, this was harsh, though it was not a dismissal from military service, which the court could have administered. The sentence reveals the opprobrium attached to infidelity and betrayal within the officer corps, but it also seems to indicate an even greater concern for the public scandal the relationship had instigated. The case, after all, led to the scandalous dissolution of a marriage (divorce was still uncommon in 1936), with the love letters removing any doubt as to the accuracy of the allegations. Despite this scandal, and Fraser's reduction on the promotion list, he went on to retire from the U.S. Army in 1959 with the rank of colonel.[44] This may be the most surprising result of the affair: one might reasonably expect that such a transgression would be career suicide for an army officer, but at least in Fraser's case, that was not true. The world war that would soon come and the need for experienced officers undoubtedly played a role in Fraser's longevity in the army.

The Family Life of Enlisted Men

The army also sought to enforce social norms regarding enlisted men's marriages and families, particularly when soldiers were accused of failing to support their wives and children, though it did so alongside its enforcement of the prohibition against the enlistment of married men. On enlistment, or reenlistment, soldiers were required to state that they had no wives or dependents (children or others dependent on them), and violators were court-martialed.[45] Until 1921, such men were charged with violating the Sixty-Second Article of War, the final, catchall article that covered all other offenses not covered by the preceding articles: "All crimes not capital, and all disorders and neglects, which officers and soldiers may be guilty of, to the prejudice of good order and military discipline, though not mentioned in the foregoing Articles of War, are to be . . . punished at the discretion of such court."[46] In the major revision of the Articles of War that came into effect in 1921, married men who enlisted in the army were charged with violations of the new Fifty-Fourth Article of War, which covered fraudulent enlistment. This article ordered that "any person who shall procure himself to be enlisted in the military service of the United States by means of willful misrepresentation or concealment as to his qualifications for enlistment, and shall receive pay or allowances under such enlistment, shall be punished as a court-martial may direct."[47]

Fort Riley witnessed two cases of enlisted men—both privates—who had lied to recruiters by claiming to be single and without dependents upon enlistment, one in 1918 and one in 1923. Both men pleaded guilty to the charges and were duly convicted. One, Private Henly C. Drinnon, was sentenced to ten days of hard labor but was allowed to remain in the service.[48] This was an unusually light sentence, and the reviewing authority criticized the court for its "inadequate" punishment and asked the court to reconsider Drinnon's sentence. The court reconvened and issued the same sentence, noting that "the country is now in need of all able bodied men who volunteer" because of U.S. intervention in the world war. The reviewing authority then approved the sentence. There is no indication that Drinnon had abandoned his wife, as was often the case, and he was caught only when he revealed his marital status to an army physician during a venereal inspection. Drinnon repeatedly stated his desire to remain in the army if at all possible during the trial. Had his offense been detected during peacetime, his sentence would have likely been harsher, and he almost certainly would have received a dishonorable discharge, as was commonly the case during peacetime courts-martial for similar offenses.

The other defendant, Private Charles A. Ennis (a.k.a. Charles A. McKenney), received a much more typical sentence for the offense: dishonorable discharge, forfeiture of all pay, and hard labor for three months.[49] The court recommended clemency, however, and after Ennis served three months of hard labor, the dishonorable discharge was set aside and he was permitted to rejoin his unit. Ennis, a balloon expert, was unusual in that he had previously served in the army and been discharged for "dependency": he financially provided for his parents and sister. Ennis reenlisted at Fort Riley under an assumed name because his mother did not want him to rejoin the army. Like Drinnon, Ennis was said to have excellent character and it was argued that his retention would "prove to the benefit of the Government after proper discipline has been effected." In both cases, the army sought to retain soldiers of good character, especially in time of war (in the case of Drinnon) or because of useful technical skills (Ennis's military ballooning expertise). The fact that both men had fulfilled their fiduciary responsibilities, rather than abandoning dependents, as was often the case in similar courts-martial elsewhere, no doubt contributed to their retention in the service.

Sexual Propriety and Harassment

Commissioned officers were not alone in being held to standards of sexual propriety, and enlisted soldiers were sometimes court-martialed for harassing civilian women. The two most obvious cases of offenses like this at Fort Riley involved two enlisted men—a private and a private first class—who wrote lewd, lascivious, or obscene letters to civilian women, one in 1921 and one in 1933.[50] Both were charged with violations of the Ninety-Sixth Article of War.

In 1921, Private Harry N. Greene was accused of writing three "vulgar and obscene" letters to Yvonne Davis, who was from Greene's hometown of Oxford, Massachusetts. Though Greene pleaded not guilty, he was convicted and sentenced to be dishonorably discharged, to forfeit all pay, and to serve six months of hard labor. Due to poor legal proceedings at his court-martial (Greene's identity was not properly established), Greene's sentence was eventually disapproved by the reviewing authority after he had served three months of it. He was then released from confinement and restored to duty. Greene's first letter to Davis began innocuously but included the line, "But waite till I get out god pity the first girl I get hold of she will sure think that hell has broke loose when she gets this old joy prong into her." Greene also requested that Davis provide him with the addresses of her female friends so that he could write to them. Davis responded to Greene's first letter in a friendly fashion, not mentioning Greene's vulgarity (or her friends' addresses), and he wrote again, this time including the line, "Say dear I wish you would come up here it is so lonesome and we could have such a good time together." He also told Davis of a purported recent sexual conquest, stating, "I did manage to pick up a married woman the other night that is about all a man can get around hear you can get a married one easier than a single one but it isn't the old hens I want it is the spring chickens." Davis's response was again friendly, and Greene wrote again, requesting that Davis provide him with a photograph of her in a bathing suit because he wanted to show it to his friends. Davis also described himself as "the best pussy bumper in the outfit I suppose you know what that means if you don't it means a man that always gets his tail when he goes after it." There is no indication that Davis found Greene's letters objectionable since she did not comment on the vulgarities or stop corresponding. The letters were discovered in Davis's possession by an employee of the Civic Protective Association (CPA)—a moral reform group that ran several homes for "wayward girls"—after the seventeen-year-old Davis had been turned over to the CPA by her father because of her "immoral tendencies" (the exact nature of which was left unspecified). Davis was committed to the CPA's State Farm for Women; her lengthy correspondence with Greene was described as "about the worst [the CPA] has ever handled" and "unspeakable," even though Davis's letters to Greene never actually included any sexually suggestive material. The CPA had contacted the American Red Cross because of its relationship with the U.S. Army, which then forwarded the letters to the army. In a lengthy cover letter accompanying the offending correspondence, Harry S. Sharpe, American Red Cross Field Director, stated that Greene's letters indicated "moral degeneracy" and that Greene represented a "danger to the community." Sharpe urged that the army undertake a full investigation, particularly to determine whether Greene had transported Davis or another woman across state lines "for immoral purposes," which would have been a violation of the federal Mann Act. Because of the high-profile intervention by two influential moral reform organizations, the army had little choice but to court-martial Greene. The army's investigation did not find that Greene had transported Davis across state lines, and it is unlikely that the two had even seen each other in person during the time of their correspondence.

The second case involving harassment of women was alleged to have occurred in 1933 when Private Willie Burns, an African American in the Ninth Cavalry, wrote a letter deemed "obscene, lewd, and lascivious" to Inez Dolan, the (white) wife of Second Lieutenant William C. Dolan at Fort Riley. In the letter, Burns, who is alleged to have used the pseudonym Jack Williams, stated, "Mrs. Dolan I would like to work for you. I will work for you free if you let me suck you. I will suck you any time you want." Burns was also alleged to have called Inez Dolan on the telephone on several occasions in an attempt to arrange a sexual liaison with her. Lieutenant Dolan had his wife meet Burns while Dolan, a captain (Fort Riley's Provost Marshal), and a sergeant observed from nearby concealment. Once Burns arrived to meet Inez Dolan, they took him into custody. Burns was alleged to have first had contact with Inez Dolan when he did some yard work for their neighbors on post, another lieutenant and his wife. This case clearly raised a host of sexual, racial, and class anxieties for Fort Riley's white officers, concerning as it did the unwanted romantic attention of a black enlisted man directed at a white woman who was married to a commissioned officer. Burns pleaded not guilty, though it is not surprising that he was convicted and sentenced to receive a dishonorable discharge, forfeit all pay, and serve five years of hard labor. The reviewing authority reduced Burns's sentence to three years; later, because of legal technicalities (an officer was involved in the proceedings who should not have been), the findings and sentence were vacated in their entirety and Burns was released and restored to duty.[51]

Venereal Disease at Fort Riley

The U.S. Army remained profoundly concerned about venereal disease among soldiers throughout the early twentieth century. It routinely rejected recruits who were found to be venereally infected. In the first two decades of the twentieth century, the army rejected 70–86 percent of all applicants each year for a multitude of causes, including physical ailments and criminal records. By 1904, venereal infection ranked as one of the top four reasons applicants were rejected and was the most common reason for the rejection of applicants in nine of twenty years during this period.[52] The army also sought to treat those soldiers who contracted venereal diseases during their military service. Army policy mandated venereal prophylaxis after sexual exposure. Note that army medical officers and civilian physicians of the early twentieth century used the term *prophylaxis* broadly, and differently from current usage, to describe a variety of measures they believed would prevent the onset of venereal diseases among soldiers after they had already had sexual contact with women who might have been infected. In a very real sense, the term *prophylaxis* is a misnomer, since it did not actually include measures—like condoms—that might have prevented infection from occurring in the first place. The army's prophylactic treatments were designed for intervention only after infection but before the onset of symptoms.

Soldiers at Fort Riley who contracted a venereal disease, whether or not they had taken venereal prophylaxis after exposure, were generally not punished, with one exception: soldiers who left Fort Riley without permission and subsequently contracted venereal diseases were punished for their infection in addition to whatever other charges they faced for leaving post without permission. In their court-martial specifications, each of these men was described as either deserting or going absent without leave (AWOL), a violation of the Fifty-Eighth Article of War, and committing acts of "illicit" sexual intercourse, neglecting to take prophylactic treatment, and contracting a venereal disease (in all cases, the specific disease was found to be "new" gonorrhea).[53] These sexual offenses were charged as violations of the general Ninety-Sixth Article of War. "New" gonorrhea was defined as a new diagnosis of venereal infection rather than a recurrence of a previously diagnosed venereal disease. The five men were all privates; one was African American, the remainder white. Four of the five pleaded not guilty; all five were convicted, given dishonorable discharges, required to forfeit all pay, and given a hard-labor sentence ranging from six months (in the case of Private Robert M. Hunter, the soldier who pleaded guilty at the outset) to two and a half years in one case (which was later remitted to eighteen months). The remainder of the accused received either one year or eighteen months of labor, which is similar to or slightly higher than punishments for desertion not involving additional charges for failing to receive venereal prophylaxis during this period.

One of the soldiers, Private Walter E. Mercer, deserted the morning after he was refused permission to marry by his commanding officer.[54] He was apprehended by civil authorities a few months later and returned to Fort Riley. Mercer was then medically inspected, apparently as a matter of course rather than as a result of a medical complaint by the soldier, and found to be venereally infected, with no record of his ever receiving prophylaxis. The soldier chose to remain silent during his court-martial, and so it is unclear whether he had gotten married during his absence from Fort Riley, or how he might have contracted gonorrhea. Another soldier, Private John A. Harrington, had a similar experience, though his possible rationale for desertion is unknown. He was described by his commanding officer and a sergeant in his unit as a "poor soldier," with no further details offered.[55] He remained absent from Fort Riley for six months until he turned himself in at Fort Leavenworth, Kansas. Harrington had stated that he believed he had contracted a venereal infection in Cumberland, Maryland, and had been treating the disease himself (unsuccessfully) with an over-the-counter remedy for several months.

The only soldiers who were charged with neglecting to receive venereal prophylaxis were those who had deserted or gone AWOL. It is difficult to believe that every other soldier at Fort Riley during this two-decade period took care to receive venereal prophylaxis; that was certainly not the case in other locales. It seems more plausible that this charge was used punitively, as an additional offense to be levied against those who deserted in order to increase their punishment, rather than as a means of encouraging prophylaxis. However, Private Clarence R. Smith—accused of having contracted gonorrhea as a result of "illicit sexual intercourse with a non-prostitute in Junction City, Kansas"—testified that he deserted because he did not believe that he had received proper venereal treatments at Fort Riley and went home to Arkansas to be tended by his mother and a local civilian physician.[56] Smith stated that before he left Fort Riley, his company commander had warned all the soldiers under his command that anyone failing to receive prophylaxis would face prosecution. In this light, it seems likely that, at least in Smith's case, army officials were simply following through on this threatened action.

Sodomy and Homosexuality

The 1917 revision to the army's *Manual for Courts-Martial*—which first introduced sodomy as an explicit offense—ushered in a series of new sodomy-related charges. Because there was no Federal Penal Code definition of sodomy, army courts-martial used the common-law definition of sodomy: "Sodomy at common law consists in sexual connection with any brute animal, or in sexual connection, per anum, by a man with any man or woman." The army went on to enlarge its definition of sodomy beyond that found in civil courts by noting explicitly that "penetration of the mouth of the person also constitutes this offense." Sodomy was thus an extremely broad category of offense: it could consist of bestiality, anal sex, or oral sex. There was no requirement that both parties involved in the offense be male; soldiers who had oral or anal sex with women were also guilty of sodomy. In its description of sodomy, the army made no attempt to distinguish between the active and passive participants in the act. "Both parties are liable as principals if each is adult and consents; but if either be a boy of tender age the adult alone is liable, and although the boy consent the act is still by force." In one important clarification—because it could often not be proved if ejaculation had occurred—the army noted that "penetration alone is sufficient." Army Regulation No. 40-105, which went into effect in 1921, created psychiatric screening standards for homosexuality that remained in effect until they were revised in 1941.[57] This regulation drew explicitly on then-prevailing psychiatric theories that considered same-sex sexual activity, often described as a form of "sexual psychopathy," to be symptomatic of grave physical, mental, and moral degeneracy, as well as effeminacy, which made such men unfit for military service.

Eight enlisted men, all privates, were charged with having committed or attempted sodomy at Fort Riley (violations of the Ninety-Third Article of War) between 1919 and 1938.[58] In one additional case involving a nine-year-old boy, a corporal was charged with sodomizing the boy, though he was also charged with a more general violation of the Ninety-Sixth Article of War.[59] Those soldiers charged with sodomy or attempted sodomy were all white, and all pleaded not guilty. Only two were acquitted entirely, though another was acquitted of sodomy but convicted of another charge. All six soldiers convicted of sodomy received dishonorable discharges and forfeiture of all pay. Five of the six received five years of hard labor (reduced to three years by the reviewing authority in one case), the maximum penalty allowed for sodomy, while the last received two years of hard labor. At Fort Riley, all these cases involved soldiers accused of having oral or anal sex—or attempting to have such sex—with each other, save for the two cases involving civilian boys. None were charged with having oral or anal sex with women, as occasionally occurred elsewhere.[60] As the historian George Chauncey has noted, the homosexual, as a deviant sexual actor, became increasingly identified and demonized throughout American society, mostly beginning in the 1920s,[61] so it is little surprise that the U.S. Army followed suit in its legal revisions and practices during this period. In no case were soldiers who were convicted of sodomy (oral or anal) with another man allowed to remain in military service; all were dishonorably discharged and usually received several years of hard labor.

The first postwar sodomy case, in 1923, involved two privates, Karl K. Ballenger and Melvin W. Oliver, who were both charged in a single court-martial of "wrongfully and feloniously engag[ing] in unnatural carnal intercourse with each other," with Ballenger accused of "penetrating per anum the person of [Oliver] with his penis."[62] The offense was alleged to have occurred in Ballenger and Oliver's quarters above the polo stables and was witnessed by three other soldiers, including a private, a private first class, and a corporal. The witnesses all agreed that Ballenger and Oliver had been roughhousing and rolling around on Ballenger's bunk when Ballenger ordered the other privates out of the room because he was going to get Oliver back for "double crossing" him in a minor disagreement over the cleaning of a saddle two days previously. The witnesses stated that they surreptitiously watched through a crack in the wooden wall as Ballenger turned Oliver on his stomach, pulled down both men's pants, used hair dressing as a lubricant, and struck Oliver on the shoulder when he initially resisted. Ballenger and Oliver flatly denied doing any more than playfully wrestling, and both attacked two of the witnesses' credibility, describing an environment in which all of the men involved in the case, accused and witness alike, frequently joked about or suggested having sex with each other, sometimes in a playfully threatening manner. Ballenger and Oliver stated that two of the witnesses had separately made "improper proposals" of sodomy to Oliver on previous occasions, one threatening him with a rifle while drunk. The court found the testimony of the witnesses credible, and the two accused were convicted, receiving identical sentences: five years of hard labor, dishonorable discharges, and forfeiture of all pay. As the reviewing authority noted, none of the witnesses saw actual penetration, which was a necessary element for a conviction on the charge of sodomy as with rape. The reviewing authority went on to add that penetration could be established circumstantially or by direct evidence, and because of the detailed testimony, penetration "reasonably may be inferred." One member of the court, a captain, urged clemency because of the conflicting testimony, the severity of the offense, and the improbability of the offense taking place in broad daylight in front of witnesses, but the convictions and sentences were allowed to stand.

In 1926, Private Claude C. Hunter was charged with committing sodomy "by feloniously and against the order of nature having carnal connection with Private Alfred T. Meyers by mouth."[63] Hunter and Meyers were both prisoners in the post guardhouse for various unrelated minor charges when the sodomy was alleged to have occurred. Hunter was seen by at least five other prisoners, all privates, to approach Meyers (who was lying on his bunk) just after lights out, talk quietly to Meyers for a few minutes, and then perform an act of oral sex on Meyers. Meyers was also called to testify and agreed that the act had occurred as described by the five witnesses. There appears to be no record of Meyers having been court-martialed for sodomy, which is unusual, since by Meyers's own testimony he consented to oral sex with Hunter, and had in fact "volunteered," and did not resist in any way. While this risky act was done after lights out, which would have offered some concealment, it was clearly not performed discreetly, since most of the prisoners had not yet fallen asleep and there was still some dim lighting in the room. It is unclear why Hunter would have approached and had oral sex with Meyers in such a public way—in full view of at least five other guardhouse prisoners—since the penalties for sodomy were so severe and must have been known by soldiers at

Fort Riley. One of the witnesses was asked whether there had been any discussion among the other witnesses of "framing" Hunter, which the witness denied, and Meyers was asked whether Hunter had ever caused him any problems, which Meyers also denied. The defense suggested that it was suspicious that all the witnesses used the same language to mention that they had heard a "smacking of lips," which the defense suggested was evidence of collusion. Hunter offered no testimony in his defense, though he pleaded not guilty, and was convicted and given the standard sentence of five years of hard labor, a dishonorable discharge, and forfeiture of all pay. As with all courts-martial, it is impossible to know whether there was collusion by witnesses to frame the accused; other than the inexplicably blatant, semipublic location of the alleged offense, there is no evidence in this case to suggest that Hunter was framed.

A later case, from 1938, involved Privates Harry H. Byerle and Glenn R. VanFleet.[64] The men were charged with sodomy "per anum." Three of their fellow privates alleged that the pair had been seen having anal sex (Byerle penetrating VanFleet) in a locked orderly room. The witnesses became suspicious that some "funny business" was going on when the accused were found in a locked room with the window shades pulled down, allegedly acting "nervous." When one of the witnesses knocked and the door opened, VanFleet's pants were pulled down. The first witness helped another private lift a third man up so that he could peer into the room through the transom, where he allegedly witnessed Byerle and VanFleet having sex. Upon questioning by a captain, Byerle admitted that he had committed the crime of sodomy, but only because he was drunk. One witness testified that a sergeant had told him that he had seen VanFleet in bed with another soldier and that "next time he saw him do anything like that he would report him." He was asked whether VanFleet had a reputation for being "sexually queer," and the witness testified that there were rumors to this effect.[65] Byerle also testified that VanFeet "had the reputation as being queer and had approached me several times when I was sober. I had always avoided him as not being worth associating with. I was drunk that afternoon and did not sober up until the next morning." VanFleet offered no testimony. The men were charged in separate courts-martial. Both men pleaded not guilty and were convicted. Byerle received a sentence of five years of hard labor (later remitted to three years of hard labor by the reviewing authority), a dishonorable discharge, and forfeiture of all pay; it seems to have made no difference to the court that Byerle claimed to be extremely intoxicated during the offense. VanFleet deserted two days after the investigation began and was apprehended only five months later. He was charged with the additional crime of desertion, which usually resulted in a sentence of a year of hard labor. Nevertheless, his sentence was less than Byerle's: two years of hard labor, a dishonorable discharge, and forfeiture of all pay. In this case the court desired to punish the active partner/penetrator to a greater degree, which is consistent with the findings of a study of sodomy convictions in the U.S. Navy in the early twentieth century.[66]

While most of the courts-martial for sodomy involved adult soldiers having sex with other soldiers, in two cases, soldiers were accused of having sex with underage boys. Though these boys could not legally consent to having sex, the accused were charged with committing acts of sodomy, rather than rape, which was used only in cases involving a female victim.[67] The first case involved Corporal Harold F. Hutchinson in 1919; the second involved Private Frederick D. Clark, who was court-martialed in 1927. In both cases, the accused pleaded not guilty but were nevertheless convicted and sentenced to dishonorable discharge, forfeiture of all pay, and five years of hard labor. In Hutchinson's case, the sentence was remitted by the reviewing authority because the victim's testimony was deemed "incompetent," due to the victim's age (the boy was nine years old), and therefore inadmissible. Hutchinson was freed and restored to duty. The alleged victim testified against Hutchinson, stating that he had been playing near a bridge near Fort Riley when Hutchinson approached him, lured him into nearby woods, and performed acts of oral and anal sex on the boy. The boy did not immediately tell anyone about what had happened, though a few weeks later, he confided in his twelve-year-old brother, who later told the story to adults. The boy was examined by a doctor several weeks after the crime was said to have occurred, but he found no evidence of injury on the boy (though the passage of time would seem to have been sufficiently long for the boy to heal from all but the most serious injuries). Hutchinson categorically denied ever having committed such acts and had an excellent service record to that point. The reviewing authority stated that such a crime was "the result of a pathological condition and it is highly improbable that such an act would be committed by a soldier whose record showed no prior commission of similar abnormalities." By the criteria laid out by the reviewing authority, this would have been an exceedingly difficult case to prove against Hutchinson, or, indeed, any similar offender, as either adult eyewitnesses would have had to be present or the boy would have had to immediately report the incident and have had injuries detectible by a physician in order for a conviction to be secured.

Private Clark was less fortunate than Hutchinson: the sentence and findings in his case were upheld and he served the entirety of his sentence. Clark was initially accused by a fifteen-year-old civilian boy, the nephew of a corporal stationed at Fort Riley, of seizing him and dragging him across railroad tracks and down an embankment, where Clark allegedly anally raped him.

During the course of the investigation, army investigators determined that there had been no struggle and that the boy had willingly accompanied Clark and participated in the anal sex. The boy's aunt and uncle examined him immediately after the incident and found evidence of "mucous" on the boy's rectum and undergarments. An army physician examined the boy soon thereafter and found no marks from the assault on the boy's body, though he did find "an abnormal dilation of his rectal muscles such as might have been caused by the habitual practice of sodomy." No other alternatives for the dilation were offered by the medical officers involved in the case, though his aunt stated that the boy had a chronic bowel problem that resulted in him frequently soiling himself. If true, this presented an alternative explanation for the boy's anal "dilation" and "mucous" that was considered by neither the army physician nor, seemingly, the court. Army investigators early on formed the opinion that the boy had made no effort to resist the assault and likely habitually engaged in sodomy, though no elaboration or concrete evidence of this was produced. Clark offered no testimony in his own defense and was convicted. From the court's perspective, there was sufficient evidence that sodomy had occurred, and Clark had committed a crime regardless of whether the boy had been a willing participant, since a minor could not legally grant consent.

The two sodomy cases that ended in acquittals involved, separately, Private Clifton R. Patterson, who was charged with trying to persuade Private Arthur D. J. Holloman to allow Patterson to "commit an unnatural act on the person of Holloman";[68] and Private Leslie L. Margerum, who was charged with, while a corporal (he was demoted once he was charged with sodomy), committing an assault on Private Herbert H. Patton with intent to commit sodomy.[69] In Patterson's case, Holloman testified that Patterson came into his bed one night and he "woke up with the sensation one has when he has intercourse with women." Holloman said that he then cursed at Patterson and pushed him away. Patterson then offered him some whiskey and said "Let's get some more," which Holloman also refused. Holloman also suggested that Patterson had previously offered him one dollar to assist with a chore, but that he suspected Patterson was really offering him money in exchange for sex. Three days after this alleged assault occurred, in an apparently unrelated matter, Patterson slashed another private's face with a razor blade for allegedly lying about him. Holloman came forward with his account after Patterson's arrest for the razor slashing. Patterson said that two days before the alleged sexual assault, he had accidentally sat on Holloman's bed after a dance before getting into his own bed. Patterson also suggested that Holloman had a grudge against him because of a disagreement over a woman that Patterson had danced with. In Patterson's defense, a sergeant testified that he had never heard anything to suggest that Patterson was a "sexual pervert of any kind," seeming to reiterate the idea that those who engaged in same-sex sexual activities were perverted, habitually engaged in such activities, and exhibited other characteristics or demeanors that could be readily detected. Despite the judge advocate's statement that the crime Patterson was charged with was "one of the most loathsome that can well be conceived," he was found not guilty of sodomy, though he was found guilty of the razor attack and sentenced to three months of hard labor and forfeiture of two-thirds of his pay during this confinement.

Private Leslie L. Margerum was also charged with attempted sodomy three years later, and he was likewise acquitted. Private Herbert H. Patton accused Margerum of approaching him while in his bunk and wrestling with him for ten minutes, attempting to place his penis in Patton's mouth all the while. In a legal review of the charges and investigation before the court-martial, W. G. Murchison, assistant adjutant, questioned the timing and location of the alleged incident, noting that it was said to have occurred in broad daylight in front of witnesses. Murchison noted that those "disposed to such acts of degeneracy" usually sought secrecy and privacy for their activities. He also suggested that since the incident was preceded by a "good-natured incident of wrestling . . . while the accused was clad in underclothes and[,] when some vulgar and suggestive language was used, had the aspect of suspected moral unnatural intimacy," a harmless act may have been misinterpreted by the alleged victim and witnesses. Murchison noted the accused's "excellent" conduct, stating that if Margerum were a "sexual pervert . . . such characteristics and disposition would have been previously shown and come to light." He also criticized the investigation for not considering the possibility of a "frame up" by the alleged victim and witnesses. Witnesses agreed that they had seen the wrestling, along with Margerum rubbing his penis on Patton's face as he said, "Look here, I'm teaching him to suck." Several witnesses also testified that Margerum was not well liked in his unit because he had a reputation as a bully. Margerum himself agreed that the wrestling had occurred as described, but he stated that it was good-natured fun, though he admitted to making at least two sexually suggestive statements. First, before the wrestling began, in an attempt to draw out Patton, Margerum remarked to another private, "Wouldn't it be fine if he [Patton] were a woman?" He also stated that during the wrestling, Patton had bitten him on the inner thigh and Margerum had said, "Well, kid if you want to suck I will let you do it." The court acquitted Margerum without comment, seeming to validate Murchison's argument that the incident consisted of little more than "good-natured wrestling" accompanied by vulgar, sexually suggestive language used by an unpopular bully, whose victim and comrades chose to ascribe sexual motives to his actions.

Charges of sodomy usually rested on the testimony of one or more witnesses to the alleged offense, since there was seldom physical evidence. Indeed, the outcome of these courts-martial often hinged on the credibility of such witnesses. Because verbal testimony by witnesses was so important, commissioned or noncommissioned officers were often called to testify as to the accused's character and performance as a soldier, though it is unclear how much such testimony helped to refute the testimony of those who claimed to have witnessed sodomy or attempts at sodomy. On a number of occasions, officers explicitly stated that there was a fundamental contradiction between good conduct as a soldier and "sexual perversion."[70] As awareness and stigmatization of same-sex sexual activity became more prevalent throughout American society,[71] such activity was increasingly perceived to be incompatible with the kind of martial masculinity fostered within the U.S. Army.[72] It is also impossible to know whether particular witnesses (individually or in small groups) had decided to "frame" other soldiers for sodomy. It would not have been difficult to do so, and many courts-martial called for cases involving sodomy considered the possibility. It is clear that on occasion some witnesses were disbelieved by the court, though witnesses who claimed to have been victims of attempted sodomy and were disbelieved by the court were not later court-martialed for perjury.

Sexual Violence toward Women

Cases at Fort Riley of sexual violence against women involved two kinds of victims and situations: rape or attempted rape of adult women (that is, women who were of the age of legal consent), and a case involving an alleged violation of the Mann Act, which prohibited the transportation of women across state lines for immoral purposes. Rape, like murder, was one of the very few capital crimes under the Articles of War, with the two crimes grouped together under the Ninety-Second Article of War.[73] Because federal law at the time did not define rape, the army adopted the common-law understanding of the crime: "the having of unlawful carnal knowledge of a woman by force and without her consent." The sex act did not have to be completed to be considered rape—"any penetration, however slight, of a woman's genitals is sufficient carnal knowledge, whether emission occurs or not." A husband could not commit rape against his wife, even if the wife did not grant her consent;

his marital privileges allowed him to legally have sex with his wife whenever he wished. In all other cases, women could be victims of rape: "The offense may be committed on a female of any age, on a man's mistress, or on a common harlot." Additionally, women who were mentally handicapped ("idiotic"), unconscious, asleep, or coerced to grant consent through violence or the threat of violence were all deemed unable to legally grant consent, and men who had sex with women under these circumstances were guilty of committing rape. The Ninety-Second Article of War made clear that "mere verbal protestations and a pretense of resistance do not of course show a want of consent, but the contrary, and where a woman fails to take such measures to frustrate the execution of the man's design as she is able to, and are called for by the circumstances, the same conclusion may be drawn." Women were thus required not simply to put up a token or verbal resistance to the sex act but to resist actively. The threshold was lower for younger women, in which case "the court will demand less clear opposition than in the case of an older and intelligent female." In practice, though it was technically a capital crime, soldiers who were convicted of committing rape were almost never sentenced to death during peacetime.[74]

Three cases of attempted rape, by a private and two privates first class, took place at Fort Riley between 1928 and 1936. One of the cases also involved a charge of indecent exposure.[75] In the first case, an African American private first class in the Ninth Cavalry, James Harris, stood accused of committing an assault on Argie Logan, an African American woman who was employed as a captain's servant on post, "with intent to commit rape . . . by taking hold of her, throwing her to the ground, and attempting to ravish her."[76] Harris pleaded not guilty and was acquitted. Harris was accused of accosting Logan as she walked across the parade ground and attempting to drag her off to a deserted area and rape her. She resisted and was eventually able to summon assistance from another soldier who was passing nearby. The alleged victim stated that she had known Harris for approximately fourteen years, as he was a friend of her ex-husband, who had also been a soldier in the Ninth Cavalry, though Harris and Logan had never previously been romantically involved—she was dating a corporal in the Ninth Cavalry at the time of the alleged assault. A witness testified that Logan had told him that she had been romantically involved with Harris, which she denied. From separate witness testimony, it is clear that Logan *was* assaulted, as she was seen on the ground, crying and being touched by an African American soldier who ran off when a passerby approached. A sergeant and two captains under whom Harris had served testified to his reliability and good character, and it seems that their testimony weighed more heavily than that of the victim. It is impossible to know why the court acquitted Harris—it did so without comment—but Harris's defense witnesses consistently portrayed him as a reliable soldier. Suggestions of a previous romantic relationship may have swayed the court. The races of both the alleged victim (black) and Harris's character witnesses (white) may have also played a role in the acquittal, though this is entirely speculative.

The second rape case at Fort Riley involved Private Lloyd W. Summers, who was charged with unlawfully entering the dwelling of Vivian Pearl, the wife of a private first class in Summers's unit, with intent to commit rape in 1934.[77] Summers was accused of entering Pearl's off-post apartment at night while her husband was ill on base and raping her. Summers had first expressed an interest in Pearl when he gave her a ride to visit her sick husband. She declined his advances, but he was alleged to have returned later that night with a pistol. Summers was heard separately telling two other soldiers that "if a big red headed guy in this troop [probably referencing Private First Class Troy Pearl, Vivian Pearl's husband, who had red hair] knew what happened last night . . . he, Summers, would be in a hell of a shape." Summers pleaded not guilty. He was initially found guilty, dishonorably discharged, and sentenced to forfeiture of all pay and hard labor for ten years. In an unusual ruling, the reviewing authority—Major General Johnson Hagood, Commander of the Seventh Corps Area—disapproved the findings and sentence without further comment, against the advice of his judge advocate, and ordered that the case be retried before a new court. An extremely lengthy retrial followed. This time, Summers was found not guilty of entering the dwelling for the purpose of committing a rape but was found guilty for entering in order to commit adultery. He received a relatively light sentence of hard labor for six months and forfeiture of ten dollars of pay per month for the same period. As Summers himself offered no testimony, the outcome of the court-martial essentially came down to the credibility of the alleged victim, Vivian Pearl, whom the defense portrayed as being of poor character. Two privates testified that they had visited the Pearls' apartment while Troy Pearl was away and "made love" to her (keeping in mind that in the 1930s this phrase did not imply that actual intercourse had taken place, as it was often used as a euphemism for sexual play that did not involve penetration and may have consisted of little more than kissing). The wife of another private testified, "[Vivian Pearl] had wanted me to date and she took dates so I decided that she was not the kind of girl for me to go with." Vivian Pearl was also questioned as to why she did not cry out during the alleged rape—she claimed Summers had a pistol, which at least two other soldiers had seen him carrying a few hours before the incident—why she took several hours to report the assault, and why she did not have herself examined by a physician, especially since she was pregnant. The defense also questioned why Summers would have had to commit a rape: "It is a fact as every officer is cognizant, that a good looking soldier, the owner of a car, would have no difficulty in finding plenty of women who would willingly consent to sexual intercourse with him." In disapproving the original sentence, the reviewing authority (Hagood) implied either that the sentence was too harsh or that the court's finding was entirely unwarranted. The second court accepted Hagood's implicit criticism of the original court and convicted Summers of a lesser offense, clearly choosing to disbelieve Vivian Pearl's version of events and judging that she had consented to sex with Summers, perhaps due to the adulterous character the defense had attempted to establish for her.

The last rape case occurred in 1936 and involved Private First Class Clarence G. Eberle, who was charged with committing an assault on Frances Cox, a sixteen-year-old girl, with intent to commit rape, by striking her "on the face and body with his hands" and appearing without his trousers in a public place "near Highway 40 and the Riverview Pavilion in a manner to bring discredit on the Military Service."[78] While Eberle, Private Earl Carver, and Cox were drinking beer at a bar, Eberle and Cox went outside to get some fresh air. When the pair did not return after forty-five minutes, Carver went outside and saw Cox fall to the ground, crying hysterically, her face, chest, and back bruised and bloodied. Eberle was lying in a weed-covered area nearby and was missing his pants. Carver then took Cox home, leaving Eberle where he lay. He was later discovered by a military policeman, a deputy sheriff, and another civilian. Cox testified that Eberle made "improper approaches and improper suggestions" and beat her when she refused his sexual advances. Eberle did not testify on his own behalf, though two privates acting as defense witnesses testified that they had seen Cox drunk before she was beaten, and one stated that she was not to be trusted. Perhaps most damningly to Cox's testimony, the defense introduced two letters that Cox had written to Eberle in which she professed to love him and discussed going on double dates with him and another couple without her parents' permission. She also instructed him in how to respond to her letters by using a false name and return address so that her parents would not know he had written to her. Eberle pleaded not guilty to the assault and attempted rape but guilty to the indecent exposure charge. He was found guilty of indecent exposure and assault, but not with intent to commit rape. Eberle was reduced to the grade of private and sentenced to forfeit his pay for six months and serve hard labor for the same period.

That Cox was beaten is not in question, given that multiple witnesses testified to her injuries and torn dress. The defense clearly established to the court's satisfaction that Cox had consented to Eberle's romantic advances, in keeping with the promiscuous character the defense had painted for her, though it is unclear why Eberle would have beaten her so badly for a reason other than her spurning his advances.

A final case of what might broadly be described as sexual violence (in the sense of nonconsensual or illegal sexual activity) was a case involving a violation of the Mann Act. In 1924, Private Jesse C. Davis, then aged twenty, was charged with desertion as well as transporting a twelve-and-a-half-year-old girl with whom he was acquainted from several public dances across state lines for "immoral purposes," which was a violation of the Mann Act (also known as the White Slavery Act)—legislation passed by Congress on June 25, 1910, in the wake of nationwide fears of an epidemic of "white slavery" and human trafficking—as well as a violation of the Ninety-Sixth Article of War.[79] After a lengthy trial, Davis was convicted and sentenced to dishonorable discharge and three years of hard labor. Davis was alleged to have taken the girl in his car to Omaha, Nebraska, where they stayed first in a hotel and then for about ten days in a boarding house, "indulging in sexual intercourse daily." On the stand, Davis provided a bizarre rationale for his actions: he stated that he had had a dream in which he married the girl, and because his dreams always came true, he asked the girl to marry him. She assented but told him that they could not do so in Kansas because of parental objections. In Omaha, Davis introduced the girl to his family as his wife. The defense introduced a group of witnesses designed to damage the girl's credibility, including the girl's teacher, all of whom testified to her "premature development" and "highly sexed nature." The teacher described her as an inveterate liar and "an abnormal child," then stated, "I cannot call her a child as she was so worldly wise [and] a woman of the world." She was also described as bragging to other girls about her "soldier beaus." A first lieutenant testified that he was familiar with the girl and she was a "prostitute type." The girl was also called to the stand, generally agreeing with Davis's account, except that she stated she had not wished to marry Davis and went with him only because her father had mistreated her. The defense argued that the girl was of the age of consent (twelve), and that the two were in a common-law marriage, which would have been legal in the states of Kansas and Nebraska. However, the court determined that no common-law marital agreement between Davis and the girl had existed, and so Davis was convicted of violating the Mann Act and the Ninety-Sixth Article of War.

The Sexual Economy of War at Fort Riley

In the early twentieth-century U.S. Army, ideas about marriage, family life, and sexual propriety were heavily entangled with prevailing notions about social class and gender relations. Enlisted soldiers who were married were not permitted to enlist or reenlist, and they were usually strongly discouraged from marrying while in the service. Their interactions with married or "respectable," middle-class women were also regulated by social conventions backed by the army's legal system. In several cases, soldiers were punished for making lewd or suggestive remarks to women verbally or in writing, and the army acted to punish the accused. It is impossible to discern the social positions of the women involved with certainty in some of the cases, but it seems clear that the army would not tolerate sexual improprieties committed against respectable, middle-class women by their enlisted social inferiors. In the one case of this nature involving a black soldier's lewd interactions with an officer's white wife, the soldier's actions seemed to elicit racial anxieties in addition to the social and gender concerns in the other cases, and he was punished severely. Despite these racial anxieties and the frequent presence of black soldiers stationed at Fort Riley (when they were not deployed elsewhere), there were not significant numbers of courts-martial involving sexual transgressions by black soldiers against whites.

Related to the issue of sexual propriety was the issue of invasions of privacy and the domestic spaces of commissioned officers by enlisted men. There were few cases of this at Fort Riley, unlike in Hawaii, which saw a large number of such cases, possibly because enlisted soldiers lived in much cruder quarters isolated from civilian habitations. The officer corps also acted to regulate itself in cases in which one officer violated the marriage vows of another through adultery. When these affairs became public or were brought to the official attention of the army by the offended party, the army charged the alleged adulterer as engaging in "conduct unbecoming an officer and a gentleman" and thereby creating a "scandal and disgrace" for the army as a whole. This offers strong support for the idea that officers were held to a very different standard of conduct from enlisted men, who were explicitly not considered "gentlemen," though they could be charged with conduct contrary to "good order and military discipline."

The army was also concerned with sexual activity that occurred outside marital relationships. While the U.S. Army sought to regulate prostitution via public health measures in order to control venereal disease among soldiers in locations outside the continental United States—in the Philippines, Hawaii, on the Mexican border, and in Europe during World War I—as well as around training camps during World War I, it does not appear to have ever attempted such a regime at Fort Riley. Prostitutes lived and worked in Junction City, Kansas, near the fort, and soldiers are known to have patronized these women, but the army never licensed or medically inspected these women. Soldiers did occasionally receive minor punishments when they brought such women onto the grounds of Fort Riley, were caught actually having sex with the women at the fort, or created public disturbances with them in civilian areas off-base. All of these offenses created embarrassment for the army and triggered criminal actions against the men, but none were given more than a token punishment for such offenses. It seems clear that the army tolerated soldiers at Fort Riley having sex with prostitutes as long as they observed at least a modicum of discretion and did not create public nuisances.

There is no evidence of significant outbreaks of venereal disease among soldiers at Fort Riley in the early twentieth century, unlike the experiences of the army when it deployed overseas to the Philippines, Hawaii, and Europe. Soldiers were medically segregated at the fort while they received their venereal treatments, but as long as they obeyed the regulations on how they should behave while in the venereal ward of the post hospital, they suffered no punishment other than confinement to the ward until their symptoms abated. The army did make it clear that time spent at the venereal ward was not a reward or vacation, and discipline there was carefully maintained, with violators receiving minor punishments for infractions. Soldiers at Fort Riley were almost never punished when they contracted venereal diseases, regardless of whether they had sought prophylaxis (as they were required to do by standing order). The apparent sole exception was when soldiers who had deserted or gone AWOL were captured: if they had contracted a venereal disease during their time away from Fort Riley, they were also charged with contracting a venereal disease. This policy suggests that the army's reaction was essentially punitive in nature.

With the changes to the code of military justice that made sodomy and same-sex sexual activity crimes within the army, it is no surprise that there were a number of charges of sodomy at Fort Riley during this period. It appears that in most of the cases of alleged sodomy—and in all the cases in which soldiers were charged with having sex with other soldiers—charges were brought against soldiers when their alleged sexual activities were witnessed by other soldiers who were not participating in the acts. As with cases of sexual violence, guilt or innocence in many cases of sodomy was difficult to determine objectively from physical evidence. Assuming that the soldiers who said they witnessed such activities were not colluding to falsely implicate the accused, the fact that witnesses viewed these activities in public areas of the fort and contacted officers to officially report what they had seen required that the army take such charges seriously and act to punish convicted transgressors. It is impossible to determine whether soldiers who participated in same-sex sexual activities in a more discreet fashion, perhaps while away from the fort while on leave, were less likely to be caught and court-martialed. In any case, there are no known courts-martial of such cases. All known sodomy cases involved soldiers who were said to have had sex with other men inside Fort Riley's facilities. In almost all cases, witnesses equated acts of sodomy with "sexual perversions" and in some cases expressed doubts as to the accused's having committed such acts because they had never before been perceived as a "sexual pervert." In several cases, serious doubt was cast on the guilt of soldiers who had previously been observed to have good character and be exemplary soldiers. To these witnesses, it was virtually impossible for good soldiers to also commit acts of sodomy. At least one case at Fort Riley also begins to cast light on a kind of vulgar set of working conditions for enlisted men in which sexually suggestive language, including frequent jokes and teasing about sodomy, which were, as agreed by all witnesses, common at the fort. This kind of rough, working-class ribaldry may have appeared to imply actual sexual contact to some middle-class observers.

Soldiers were seldom charged with rape or attempted rape at Fort Riley. In all of these cases, the character and morality of the woman who was alleged to have been raped was called into question by the defense and often led to acquittals for the accused. In several cases, multiple witnesses testified that the women were immoral, promiscuous, or had been romantically involved with the accused, casting doubt on the claims of the women that they had been raped. Rape is the only sexual offense that the Federal Bureau of Investigation tracked during this period. The FBI began tabulating and reporting on national crime rates of major crimes, including rape, defined as "forcible rape, statutory rape, assault to rape, and attempted rape" of women, in 1930. The national incidence of rape was approximately 2.6 per 100,000 population in 1930; the rate climbed dramatically by 1940, perhaps because of better reporting, reaching 13.7 per 100,000 population.[80] In 1918–1938, the period for which judicial data at Fort Riley is most complete, if we roughly calculate that there were 2,000 soldiers stationed at Fort Riley each year, the three courts-martial for rape during this period suggest that the overall incidence of rape at Fort Riley was 7.5 per 100,000 population.[81] Given the limited statistical data available, it is difficult to make direct comparisons between the incidence of rape at Fort Riley and that in the nation as a whole, except to say that in neither case was the crime reported as being frequently committed, and the few cases reported at Riley were probably not significantly different from the number reported by the civilian population at large in similar-size communities. There are also very few reported instances of what we might consider domestic violence at Fort Riley. Assuming that such incidents did take place on occasion, as long as they occurred in private homes, the army did not involve itself. In the only known case of such an offense, the soldier beat his wife on the cavalry parade ground, an extremely public space at the fort; the army had no choice but to intervene. The crime rates for sex-related offenses at Fort Riley are roughly in line with civilian rates, and the venereal rates are likely lower than comparable rates in the civilian populace, given the army's regular venereal inspections and prophylactic treatments.

Fort Riley offers a rich set of examples for the various ways in which soldiers experienced sexuality during their military service, as well as the ways in which the U.S. Army attempted to regulate these sexual experiences, and how it enforced these regulations and punished transgressors. This baseline set of experiences in a domestic American context serves, in many ways, as a useful counterpoint to the ways in which sexuality was regulated in overseas settings described in later chapters.

CHAPTER 2

"Benevolent Assimilation" and the Dangers of the Tropics

The American Occupation of the Philippines, 1898–1918

> Finally, it should be the earnest and paramount aim of the military administration to win the confidence, respect, and affection of the inhabitants of the Philippines by assuring them in every possible way that full measure of individual rights and liberties which is the heritage of a free people, and by proving to them that the mission of the United States is one of benevolent assimilation, substituting the mild sway of justice and right for arbitrary rule.
>
> —President William McKinley, "Benevolent Assimilation Proclamation," December 21, 1898
>
> The people of the United States want us to kill all the men, fuck all the women, and raise up a new race in these Islands.
>
> —U.S. soldier deployed to the Philippines in 1902

These two statements reveal starkly contrasting perspectives on the United States' early venture into empire. Publicly, President McKinley promoted a policy of "benevolent assimilation," in which American civilization would overcome barbarism, transforming the Philippines into a facsimile of the United States. The soldier, theoretically sent overseas to realize these ideals, privately asserted that his mission was instead to violently overturn Filipino racial and sexual order.[1] These contrasting notions highlight the conflicting means and ends of U.S. imperialism in the Philippines. During the American occupation, U.S. soldiers displayed many of the "uncivilized" traits imperialists attributed to Filipinos. U.S. soldiers learned to identify combatant and noncombatant Filipinos alike in highly racialized and sexualized terms, often perceiving Filipino women as racial inferiors and willing sexual partners—as well as sources of sexual contagion—and Filipino men as weak and effeminate. This view of Filipinos, and the set of associated sexual practices, contrasted sharply with U.S. moral reformers' concerns about American social purity and public morality. Throughout the Philippine-American War and subsequent occupation of the Philippines, U.S. Army officials continually struggled with navigating a path between domestic anxieties about sexual morality, soldiers' sexual practices, and problems related to health, sanitation, and military expediency.

The ink was barely dry on the Treaty of Paris, which ended the Spanish-American War, when the first shots were fired in the Philippine-American War.[2] The United States had paid Spain $20 million to relinquish its claims to the Philippines, but many Filipinos sought national independence, resisting American occupation as they had that of the Spanish. During this struggle, the U.S. Army deployed more than 126,000 soldiers to the Philippines, with troop strength peaking at approximately 74,000. The U.S. Army's strength averaged 13,000 men in the Philippines until the start of World War II, including more than 5,000 Filipinos recruited as Philippine Scouts.[3] The Philippine-American War officially ended in 1902, though a fierce insurgency raged sporadically until 1913. While U.S. officials continually reiterated their promise to bring "benevolent uplift" and "assimilation" to the Philippines, these goals barely masked an imperial mission that had profound racial, gender, and sexual overtones.[4] McKinley's evocatively titled notion of "benevolent assimilation" illustrates how paternalism can mask violent social and political policies.[5] Domestic American racial discourses called for such "assimilation" while also casting doubt that it could ever be realized. American advocates of imperial expansion perceived Filipinos as savage, childlike, and effeminate—and therefore in need of firm governance by the United States.[6] Major General Frederick Funston, a strong advocate of U.S. expansion in the Philippines who played a key role in the capture of Filipino nationalist leader Emilio Aguinaldo, described the Filipinos as "an illiterate, semi-savage people, who are waging war, not against tyranny, but against Anglo-Saxon order and decency."[7] Proponents of U.S. expansionism cast the conflict as a racial war that pitted civilization against savagery, a necessary imposition of American hegemony over a savage and uncivilized people. Racial ideologies and beliefs about the superiority of Anglo-Saxons to Filipinos permeated not just the arguments of those in favor of U.S. expansion into the Philippines but the arguments of those opposed to it as well.[8] Proponents of the U.S. occupation used such racial ideas to justify American intervention—and the imposition of American-style government and other institutions—in the Philippines, while many anti-imperialists, such as E. L. Godkin, founder of the *Nation* and editor in chief of the *New York Post*, openly expressed disdain for the "alien, inferior, and mongrel races" of the Philippines.[9]

American expansionists also asserted that the occupation of the Philippines would reinvigorate American masculinity, revitalizing a militarized ideal manhood badly in need of strengthening at the turn of the century.[10] These beliefs were predicated on the notion that white American men were suffering a "crisis of masculinity," and that martial endeavors could rebuild personal character and masculinity in an environment of gender and sexual anxieties. Scholars of masculinity have argued that these anxieties were brought about by the tremendous social and economic changes in turn-of-the-century America, including the growth of urbanization, the rise of modern bureaucracies and changing career paths for middle-class men, and the increasing intervention of American women in politics and public life, all of which challenged many middle-class white men's sense of security by reducing their sense of economic independence. Many in the United States became convinced that martial, imperial endeavors were good for the nation, not only because of their obvious strategic and economic benefits but also because they revitalized American men and rebuilt American masculinity. In this view, martial, masculine character was the very foundation of American democracy and a military adventure in the Philippines one of the few means available to rebuild American masculinity.[11]

Others remained skeptical that empire abroad, specifically in "tropical" areas, could be beneficial for white Americans, many seeing such places as dangerous sources of corruption and degeneracy.[12] Medical doctors frequently diagnosed whites living in tropical areas with "tropical neurasthenia." This was perceived as a psychological disorder with a bewildering array of physical symptoms, including fatigue, ennui, depression, various bodily aches and pains, loss of appetite, insomnia (or excessive sleep), and sexual disorders ranging from impotence to hypersexuality.[13] Some cast doubt on the very idea that whites could ever become fully acclimatized to tropical conditions, with one sociologist declaring that "in climatic conditions which are a burden to him; in the midst of races in a different and lower stage of development; divorced from the influences which have produced him . . . the white man . . . tends himself to sink slowly to the level around him."[14] An army doctor in 1905 lamented the lack of "innocent, wholesome, decent recreation" for soldiers in the Philippines, warning of "the climatic tendency of the tropics to lower the moral and intellectual standards of men and women," leaving soldiers vulnerable to the "vino joints [bars], gambling houses, brothels who throw open doors and welcome lonely Americans."[15] Many observers came to view venereal disease as a particular danger of places like the Philippines because tropical environments were highly eroticized in the minds of many Americans, who perceived tropical inhabitants as hypersexual beings, with local women thought of as aggressively sexual and indigenous men as effeminate and weak. This fate, they believed, awaited American soldiers who were sexually careless in the tropics.

Venereal disease rates among enlisted soldiers serving in the Philippines—averaging more than 14 percent per year throughout the 1910s—were commonly twice as high (or more) as those for soldiers serving in domestic posts.[16] One prominent anti-imperialist warned of syphilis-induced insanity when he wrote, "Consider what has been done to our soldiery, the youth of America, that have been sent to the Philippine islands. They have come home insane, diseased, without the power to serve their country or provide for themselves."[17] Other anti-imperialists were quick to latch onto the theme, with Senator Henry M. Teller (D-CO) stating, "I do dread the corruption of blood more than anything else." He went on to assert that "the greatest and most unavoidable danger to which these forces will be exposed . . . will be venereal diseases in their worst and most malignant form. . . . The exposure to the corruption of the young blood of the nation must be stopped."[18] He warned that Americans would be "cursed in our physical and mental and moral manhood" through venereal contamination from the Philippines, pointing to what he claimed was an epidemic of syphilis that had swept through Great Britain as a result of its imperial endeavors, an image that was taken up by other anti-imperialists.[19]

Public concerns about venereal disease among American soldiers often invoked images of contaminated blood, which resonated with white anxieties about miscegenation. Some anti-imperialists specifically played to these fears. An investigator sent to the Philippines by the Women's Christian Temperance Union reported back that "the women who consent to live with Americans are, as a rule, ignorant, lazy, and filthy in their habits, generally afflicted with some loathsome cutaneous disease, and it is hard to comprehend that an educated American, decently brought up, can live among dirty, frowzy natives, who have not one redeeming quality."[20] Senator Richard F. Pettigrew (R-SD) lamented that "the vigorous blood, the best blood, the young men of our land, will be drawn away to mix with inferior races."[21] Concerns about miscegenation were not limited to racial mixing in the Philippines. There were also considerable anxieties about "racial deterioration" within the United States because of its imperial ventures once American soldiers serving abroad returned home. Residents of the Philippines were not universally depicted as dangerous; Filipinas in particular were sometimes depicted in a positive, alluring fashion. One pro-expansion journalist stated, "The Philippine woman . . . is by no means unattractive. . . . She makes a good wife, a respected mother, and above all things, she is a woman. . . . I always feel encouraged when I see a woman who is wholly feminine."[22] Thus, a long-term military presence in the Philippines represented both an opportunity and a danger for white American men in the minds of some observers. The Philippines could serve as the proving ground for rebuilding American manhood, which many found to be in an increasingly precarious position by the turn of the century, but it could also pose a profound, nearly existential danger to those men deployed there, corrupting them mentally, morally, physically, and sexually.

U.S. Military Occupation and Prostitution in the Philippines

Administering an overseas territory was a new experience for the United States, and it looked to the British, French, and Spanish empires in designing its own colonial administration in the Philippines.[23] Though the United States inherited a Spanish colonial system in the Philippines, it did not simply copy Spanish or other imperial practices wholesale but rather attempted a new approach: progressive colonial administrations sought to reshape the Philippines (and Cuba and Puerto Rico) through a variety of social, political, economic, and civil engineering efforts, using U.S. domestic practices as models.[24] When they arrived in the Philippines, the Americans inherited a host of Spanish institutions and administrative infrastructure—a framework of colonial knowledge—that they gradually replaced with American knowledge as they learned from their own experiences and missteps, as well as from other imperial experiences, such as the British experience in Malaya.[25] As part of the U.S. "Americanization" of the Philippines, it drew on its long experience in governing Native American peoples, with many Americans and administrators arguing that ruling Filipinos was not unlike ruling Native Americans. Indeed, war in the Philippines was sometimes described as just another "Indian War." Not surprisingly, the four American military Governors-General of the Philippines (Wesley Merritt, Elwell S. Otis, Arthur MacArthur Jr., and Adna Chaffee) all had extensive experience in the Indian Wars.[26]

The sex trade was already thriving in the Philippines when U.S. forces arrived, prostitution having been legalized by the Spanish Governor-General in July 1897, and it increased dramatically as the American occupiers brought an influx of wealth with them.[27] Young, working-class women from the countryside provided a steady stream of domestic servants, laundresses, seamstresses, tobacco-factory workers, and other laborers for Manila and the provincial capitals, which functioned as magnets for the working class in the impoverished Philippine rural areas.[28] Once there, many young women found that prostitution offered a much more lucrative income than other employment, though it brought with it social stigmatization as well as the risk of violence and venereal disease.

The growing number of occupying soldiers increased the demand for prostitutes' services. U.S. enlisted soldiers were typically deployed to the Philippines for two-year periods. They were, on average, twenty years old, single, and in an environment where they had no familiarity with local language or customs. While officers were permitted to bring their wives and families with them to the Philippines, enlisted soldiers were not, and they frequently used prostitutes as a sexual outlet. Hundreds of foreign prostitutes, including Japanese, Chinese, Europeans, and Americans, entered the Philippines soon thereafter, though military authorities assured the U.S. public that no foreign prostitutes were permitted entrance.[29] Single women could disembark only if they had a passport, a sponsor, and employment papers, or if they tendered a fifty-dollar "tip" to colonial customs officials.

The withdrawal of Spanish military and police forces and the prospect of American occupation—along with the increased political turmoil before the United States could assert its dominance—significantly increased public sexual disorder. One observer fearfully noted of this period that "the orgies became so frightful that the Spanish families . . . began to lock up their houses and rent residences in other parts of the city. . . . Whole streets are filled with drunken soldiers, rioting, yelling Americans and half-naked women."[30] In September 1898, just one month after American forces captured Manila, Major H. W. Cardwell, the chief surgeon of the Second Division, reported that as soldiers became "habituated to the repulsiveness of the native women, sexual immorality [became] more common," along with outbreaks of syphilis and gonorrhea.[31]

After Spanish rule ended in the Philippines in August 1898, the newly proclaimed Philippine Republic authorized the continuation of the Spanish regulatory regime for prostitution in order to "prevent the contraction of syphilitic and venereal diseases."[32] The U.S. Army began to regulate prostitution almost as soon as American troops arrived. Special Order No. 19, issued by Brigadier General R. P. Hughes, the Provost Marshal General, on November 3, 1898, established both a clinic for the medical inspection of prostitutes and a hospital facility for the enforced treatment of infected prostitutes.[33] Prostitutes were required to report for regular medical inspections, for which they paid a nominal fee, and were issued identification cards and certificates indicating their state of health. The Board of Health (a civilian agency headed by army officers) and the Manila Police Department assisted the army's efforts.

Though the U.S. Army never attempted to prevent soldiers from coming into sexual contact with prostitutes in the Philippines, it did seek to impose a measure of control over the sexual behavior of soldiers by preventing them from coming into sexual contact with prostitutes who had been diagnosed with venereal disease. The army soon began on-site inspections of brothels and issued photographic identification cards to prostitutes. Inspected prostitutes were assigned serial numbers and issued a health certificate and inspection book; by 1900, these inspection books included a photograph of the owner, to counter the problem of prostitutes exchanging books. Army medical officers conducted the medical inspections, assisted variously by army hospital stewards and civilian Americans; army doctors reported on their activities to the Board of Health. These measures appeared to have little effect on overall venereal disease rates, however. For example, in a three-month period in 1900, of 542 registered prostitutes, 435 (80.3%) were detained and treated for venereal disease, with up to 161 prostitutes (29.7%) receiving treatment at one time.[34] Not all women working as prostitutes registered under the new regime, since most of the prostitutes inspected and "regulated" were those working in formal houses of prostitution. Many women worked part time as prostitutes outside brothels, sometimes even in their own homes. Prostitutes would commonly send for their female neighbors—seldom registered as prostitutes themselves—to assist when the number of American soldier clients outnumbered the available prostitutes.[35] The ubiquity of part-time prostitutes and prostitutes without a fixed worksite doomed any regime of surveillance and sanitary regulation to failure.

William Howard Taft, the first civilian Governor-General of the Philippines (1901–1903), viewed prostitution as "purely [an] army police measure [and a] military necessity."[36] Taft described his regulatory actions as Governor-General: "Each prostitute was required to have a certificate showing when the [medical] examination had taken place. By direction of the President and the Secretary of War . . . no fee is extracted from any prostitute, and a further change was contemplated when I left the Islands by which no certificates were to be issued. In other words, the effort is to diminish as much as possible the injuries from the evil without recognizing in any way the legality of the unlawful business."[37] Note that Taft was not speaking literally when he described prostitution as "unlawful." Prostitutes in the Philippines were registered with civilian authorities, and U.S. Army medical officers continued to supervise their regular medical inspections throughout Taft's tenure as Governor-General.

While Taft and some other U.S. officials may have found sanctioned prostitution in the Philippines morally distasteful, and noted its illegality under U.S. law, contrasting it with local ordinances in the Philippines, the public health program's very existence suggested they found prostitution necessary. Taft's remarks also make it clear that President McKinley and Secretary of War Elihu Root ordered changes in the way that army officials administered prostitutes to limit exposure to criticism.

The Philippines was not the site of the U.S. Army's first attempt to regulate prostitution. The army first medically inspected, treated, and licensed working prostitutes in Nashville, Tennessee, during the occupation of that city in the Civil War, beginning in 1863 and continuing through the end of the war.[38] The practice was deemed successful at reducing venereal disease infection among occupation troops, and it was repeated in Memphis, Tennessee, beginning in the summer of 1864. As in the Philippines, the prostitutes of these two Tennessee cities were issued licenses and examined by army doctors on a weekly basis. They were forcibly treated at army medical facilities established for this purpose when found to be infected. In reports of the Union army's practice after the war—using language eerily similar to that of later critics of Filipino sexual cleanliness—medical officers blamed Southern women for infecting Union soldiers, attributing the venereal infections solely to "evil congress with diseased women" and entirely absolving soldiers of responsibility for their actions. The Surgeon-General's Office seemed to view the sexual interactions between soldiers and prostitutes as inevitable, noting that "after the attempt to reduce disease by the forcible expulsion of the prostitutes had, as it always has, utterly failed, the more philosophic plan of recognizing and controlling an ineradicable evil has met with undoubted success."[39] Building on its experience with the medical regulation of prostitutes in order to control the spread of venereal disease in the Philippines, the U.S. Army would, under General John J. Pershing, undertake similar regimes on the Mexican border during the Mexican Expedition (1916–1917) and in France and Germany during and after World War I (1917–1923).

Domestic Responses to Army-Regulated Prostitution

The U.S. Army attempted to regulate prostitution in the Philippines with as little publicity as possible due to the potential backlash from the American public. The army's low-key approach led to its actions not being publicized inside the United States until June 27, 1900, when William B. Johnson, a correspondent for *Chicago New Voices*, a temperance newspaper, wrote an exposé entitled "The Administration's Brothels in the Philippines." The American League of Philadelphia reprinted the article in fall 1900 as a broadly circulated pamphlet entitled *The Crowning Infamy of Imperialism*.[40] Johnson decried the toleration of vice by the American military, using the issue to promote an anti-imperialist agenda based largely on the idea that the American imperial enterprise was having a deleterious effect on the morality of American men. A second, widely distributed article, the "Custer Henderson Letter," allegedly written by a young American soldier to his parents detailing sexual and other vices among soldiers in the Philippines, offered corroboration for Johnson's allegations of widespread vice.[41] The letter alleged, "There was brought here from China about eight hundred of the lowest type of Chinese women, and they are installed in houses, some for officers and some for private soldiers and each inmate pays a tax of $4 per week to the military authorities, which includes a license to sell wines and beer, and the worst of all is these houses are all decorated inside and out with the stars and stripes and at night the streets are a mass of howling, drunken, half-naked women and American soldiers."[42]

The letter—from the era of muckraking journalism—was designed to inflame the passion of moral reformers. It detailed in extremely racialized terms sexual escapades between presumably white American soldiers and racial "others"; public drunkenness and moral degeneracy, combined with "oriental standards of morality"[43] and sexual disorder; collusion between military authorities and procurers or slavers; and "worst of all," a debasement of the most important symbol of American ideals and patriotism, the American flag itself, which the author alleged was used to advertise debauchery.

The publication of these articles inspired influential social purity and moral reform organizations to contact the president, the Secretary of War, the Adjutant General, and various other government officials in a concerted letter- and telegram-writing campaign.[44] Activist organizations included national and state women's suffrage societies; temperance societies, including the Women's Christian Temperance Union, the nation's largest temperance society and largest women's organization; Protestant churches and clergymen; Christian social purity organizations, including the National Christian League for the Promotion of Social Purity; and individual Republican voters and donors. The State Department hired ten extra clerks to handle the influx of mail.[45] Letter writers used the issue of regulated prostitution as a springboard to discuss anti-imperialism, antimilitarism, temperance, morality, and venereal disease, all unified around the idea that the military occupation of the Philippines was leading to American moral degeneracy with the complicity of the U.S. military. As one U.S. anti-imperialist doctor indicated, the army had established "a system of nasty weekly medical inspections of hundreds of women by our army surgeons" so that "our officers and soldiers and sailors, and men and boys generally, might safely commit fornication and adultery, saving their bodies but destroying their souls."[46] Other physicians, such as U.S. Army Major Charles Lynch, advocated continuing the regulation regime, for without it, Lynch suggested, "venereal disease [would be] carried to innocent women and children in the United States, evil consequences which would follow unregulated prostitution here," presumably after American soldiers who contracted venereal diseases in the islands returned home and resumed sexual relations with their wives.[47]

Some local commanders allegedly went far beyond mere regulation of prostitution and other vices. The commanding officer at Jolo, Lieutenant Colonel Owen J. Sweet, became embroiled in controversy for allegedly organizing an elaborate system of prostitution "on the canteen plan."[48] This scheme was said to involve forty Japanese prostitutes, recruited by intermediaries on Sweet's behalf from Borneo and Singapore, who were placed in three brothels, two for enlisted men and one for officers. Army doctors regularly inspected both the prostitutes and Sweet's men. Soldiers had to show proof of recent medical inspection to enter the brothels, and each had an account with the brothels that was settled every payday. Note that the arrangement alleged here, like that in the Custer Henderson letter, retains a sharp class divide, with officers having sex with one set of prostitutes set aside for their use, and enlisted men having sex with another. Sweet denied these allegations completely, asserting that he had merely ordered regular inspections and surveillance of the bawdy houses in Jolo in an effort to contain and manage the vice already present.[49] Sweet received no punishment or censure, and army officers stationed at Jolo submitted written testimony stating that while the houses of prostitution did exist, the prostitutes were not in Sweet's employ and had been present before the arrival of the Americans.[50] Several officers in Sweet's unit stated that while U.S. soldiers and officers were permitted to patronize the prostitutes—contradicting other officers' statements—they were permitted to do so only if they had been given a clean bill of health by a medical officer first. Captain A. G. Cole stated that he "believe[d] that the toleration of these women not only promoted the health and contentment of the enlisted men, but also avoided unfortunate complications with the [M]oros outside the walled town, where our men would undoubtedly have gone in violation of orders," highlighting the widespread view among military authorities that U.S. soldiers would inevitably seek a sexual outlet.[51]

Debates between overseas expansionists and anti-imperialists became especially prevalent during the 1900 presidential campaign, as the Philippine-American War raged on. Anti-imperialists, many of whom were also moral reformers, were quick to latch onto the army's regulation of prostitution in the Philippines as a clear sign that the United States' presence and actions in the Philippines were both politically unadvisable and immoral. War Department and other government officials in Washington publicly denied any knowledge—apparently sincerely—of the kinds of regulated prostitution described in the letters of social purity activists. The Secretary of War responded to one letter in October 1900, "So far as this Department is advised no such conditions obtain as set forth in your letter."[52] In January 1901, the Adjutant General's Office in Washington, DC, telegraphed the commanding general in Manila, General Arthur MacArthur Jr., "Are houses of prostitution licensed, protected, or in any way encouraged by military authorities?"[53] MacArthur replied, perhaps disingenuously, the next day: "With reference to your telegram of 16th . . . houses of prostitution not licensed, protected, encouraged."[54] That houses of prostitution were not licensed was correct in a technical sense, though the women who worked in them were effectively licensed as individuals when they received their medical pass cards from army physicians. Had army physicians detected the presence of a venereal infection in the women, they would have been forced to stay in a venereal hospital under the supervision of the army until symptoms of their infection went away.

As a result of the domestic U.S. campaign against prostitution in the Philippines, the Adjutant General's Office directed MacArthur to issue a second, more elaborate statement intended for public release on February 4, 1901. He stated that "prostitution is not licensed in the Philippines," which was true, but MacArthur neglected to add that it was not illegal either, as it was within the United States, and that prostitutes did receive regular venereal certifications from army physicians that functioned as de facto licenses to engage in commercial sex work.[55] He briefly discussed the medical inspections by army doctors, describing this as part of the "sanitary regulations particularly necessary in the tropics" and emphasizing their military and medical necessity. MacArthur also asserted that "the average soldier is careless of his health, particularly on a foreign station, and every precaution must be taken to protect him." But MacArthur clearly had no intention of preventing the "average soldier" from engaging in sexual relations with prostitutes. He subtly cast the army's actions in a paternalistic light, claiming that the army was merely attempting to safeguard the health of American soldiers by regulating prostitution, since soldiers would naturally experience sexual danger in foreign lands. They could not be prevented from doing so, but the army had an obligation to protect them from the ill effects of their actions. MacArthur then noted that "every effort is made to maintain a high standard of true manhood in the young soldier."

MacArthur also issued General Order No. 101, which mandated biweekly venereal inspections of soldiers, with immediate treatment required for those found to be infected.[56] Medical officers were also instructed to place all women suspected of being infected under medical surveillance, with the aid of local authorities, to prevent further spread of disease. The U.S. Surgeon General's Office later noted that General Order No. 101 had been aimed at "detecting and giving early treatment to concealed cases of venereal disease" among soldiers and "was not intended primarily as a method of controlling the prevalence of the venereal diseases from the viewpoint of preventative medicine, but [was] a purely military measure for the purpose of increasing the efficiency of the Army."[57] This later view echoes earlier statements by army and War Department officials, as well as by numerous army medical officers, who were unswervingly pessimistic about ever being successful at preventing outbreaks of venereal disease among soldiers. Army doctors were never able to establish effective sanitary control over prostitutes, nor did the biweekly inspections prevent soldiers from becoming infected and further spreading disease between inspections.[58]

The Women's Christian Temperance Union accepted General MacArthur's offer to send a representative to the Philippines to conduct an independent investigation. Their emissary, a Protestant minister, Rev. A. Lester Hazlett, arrived in November 1901.[59] Hazlett had an extremely negative view of the Filipinas with whom American soldiers consorted, describing them as "native women of the lowest class . . . mostly drawn from canteen-keepers, camp followers, and prostitutes. A respectable native or Mestizo would not live with an American and would hardly marry one. . . . [The Filipinas are] ignorant, lazy and filthy in their habits."[60] Hazlett did support the army's position, however, stating categorically that prostitution had never been licensed in the Philippines during the U.S. occupation, though he acknowledged that there were forty-six brothels known to authorities in Manila, housing a total of 233 prostitutes.[61] Hazlett also reiterated the government's position in stating that prostitution was "not encouraged" and that known prostitutes were not permitted entry to American bases. During his trip to the Philippines, Hazlett also investigated the Sweet controversy, reporting that an unnamed enlisted soldier in the Hospital Corps at Jolo privately confirmed to him that Sweet had been responsible for importing prostitutes to Jolo for the exclusive use of the Americans stationed there.[62]

Because of the intense public debate in the United States about moral degeneracy among soldiers in the Philippines, the U.S. Congress investigated the medical inspection and potential licensing of prostitutes in Manila in February 1902. In congressional testimony, Governor-General Taft noted that while medical inspections had begun under military auspices and continued under colonial government authority, they had been recently discontinued; in any case, Taft stated, licensing of prostitutes had never occurred.[63] Taft indicated that medical authorities no longer issued medical certificates indicating a clean bill of health or charged a nominal fee for each inspection. Under Filipino law, prostitutes were still required to register with the Filipino government, undergo frequent and regular medical inspections, and be housed at a public hospital if found to be infected with venereal disease.[64] Interestingly, the day before Taft's testimony, February 19, Secretary of War Elihu Root ordered that "no fees be charged" to prostitutes for their venereal inspections and "no certificates of examination given" any longer. Medical inspectors would continue to "keep their own records of names, descriptions, residences, and dates of examination." Inspection was to continue "without the liability of a misunderstanding and the charge of maintaining a system of licensed prostitution."[65] While the timing may have been coincidental, it seems more likely that these policy changes made Taft's congressional testimony possible, offering the administration a kind of plausible deniability over its actions in the Philippines. Two of the major objections of U.S. social reformers to military regulation had been that army doctors charged fees for venereal inspections and kept records on individual prostitutes. Elimination of these practices the day before Taft's testimony obviated the need for congressional intervention.

U.S. civilian officials, swayed by moral reformers' ideologies, viewed prostitution primarily as a moral problem that could be solved by appealing to soldiers' moral principles. President Theodore Roosevelt issued a general order on March 18, 1902, warning soldiers deployed overseas of "the inevitable misery and disaster which follow upon intemperance and upon moral uncleanliness and vicious living."[66] This exhortation had so little effect on soldiers' sexual practices that it was reissued three years later, along with orders for military chaplains and medical officers to urge sexual temperance.[67] On the same day, Secretary of War Root issued Circular No. 10, ordering military commanders to set an example of moral living for enlisted soldiers, rather than simply warning them of the dangers inherent in immoral living.[68] Circular No. 10 went further, prescribing wholesome amusements to fill soldiers' free time. To this end, the army would supply military units with exchange stores in which they could gain access to goods, reading rooms, and gymnastic supplies.

Perhaps not coincidentally, also on March 18, the Manila Municipal Board issued Ordinance No. 27, "relating to vagrants, including mendicants, gamblers, and prostitutes." While it did not outlaw prostitution, it offered authorities a means of removing prostitutes from the streets (though not from brothels).[69] In mid-March 1902, Roosevelt also ordered that all American flags used by houses of prostitution for advertising purposes be removed.[70] Because of the timing of this set of new policy directives on the part of both the U.S. Army and colonial authorities, it seems likely that this represented a concerted effort on the part of the new Roosevelt administration to provide social reformers and critics of the army's policy with a nominal victory. By May 1902, what U.S. domestic social reformers called "regulated vice" had largely vanished from public view. The last Filipino guerrillas had just surrendered, and U.S. military operations ceased. In June, U.S. military government ended, and a civil government was established. The army's medical inspections of prostitutes continued in ways that attracted less attention from American observers; a practice that had been scandalous gradually became normalized as the U.S. Army's presence continued for decades in the Philippines.

Attempts to Contain and Eliminate Prostitution

While some military officers saw soldiers' patronage of prostitutes as a moral problem, others viewed it as sheer necessity. Major Ira C. Brown, surgeon and Acting President of the Board of Health in the Philippines, in a letter to the Acting Adjutant General and the Provost Marshal General, stated emphatically, "Houses of prostitution have become a necessity. When properly conducted, they are the safety of society. Medical men . . . are convinced that crime is lessened, virtue protected and the darkness that come[s] into the home greatly lessened. At this distance from home our people very often throw off the restrictions that society has placed upon them and the wom[a]n of easy virtue is sought; it is not unnatural, nor is it unusual; it is just a plain fact. This being so, it becomes our duty to surround this business with such safe-guards as will protect both parties to the contract; protect them from disease, I mean."[71]

Brown's views flatly gainsay the public statements of MacArthur, illustrating the contradiction between the U.S. government's public denunciations of prostitution and the private insistence by many officials that prostitution was necessary for the army. Brown also proposed the creation of a red-light district to contain the spread of prostitution and public drunkenness within a single district in Manila. Within this district, Brown sought to segregate prostitutes according to three racial categories: American prostitutes (of whom Brown noted the existence of twelve); Europeans (Brown recorded the presence of Russians, Austrians, and Italians); and a third class of "native" prostitutes.[72] American military authorities, through the Provost Marshal's Office, established the Gardenia District, largely according to Brown's scheme, after the presidential election in 1901. McKinley's opponent had been the vehemently anti-imperialist William Jennings Bryan, and military authorities had been concerned that their actions in the Philippines could bring opprobrium on the administration if publicized before the election.

By 1904, there were sixty licensed houses of prostitution in Manila.[73] Many of the prostitutes housed in these brothels were of Japanese, Russian, or American origin, though two houses were staffed exclusively by Chinese women. Each brothel housed an average of 5 to 7 prostitutes, with an estimated total population of 360 prostitutes working in brothels. Many additional prostitutes—primarily Filipinas—solicited customers on the street or worked out of their homes, which were not licensed. Japanese women made up the majority (roughly 210) of the prostitutes in brothels, 80–90 were Filipinas, and the remaining 60–70 prostitutes mostly originated from the United States or Europe. Doctors continued to inspect these sites on a weekly basis, segregating an average of 10 to 12 women per inspection (about 5% of the total) for venereal treatment.

One army doctor, Captain Weston P. Chamberlain, noted in 1905 that prostitutes "listed as clean probably contained some gonococci, and that those who were marked as infected nonetheless were patronized by soldiers."[74] He was undoubtedly correct on both counts, as there were no effective venereal cures before penicillin became available in the 1940s, though Salvarsan and Neosalvarsan (introduced in 1911 and 1912, respectively) had some effect on syphilis. Chamberlain's report thus illustrated two serious limitations of the army's campaign against venereal disease in the Philippines (and indeed, in other places it implemented similar regimes). First, the U.S. Army's medical officers did not have access to the kinds of medical technologies required to decisively detect or eradicate venereal diseases in either soldiers or their sexual partners.. Army doctors occasionally acknowledged the limitations of the available venereal tests and treatments, but their best efforts could never actually eradicate the venereal infections they found. The second limitation of the army's anti–venereal disease campaign was one of enforcement. The army could effectively license medically "safe" prostitutes by issuing certificates testifying to a clean bill of health, but it could not adequately enforce its requirement that soldiers patronize only prostitutes with a current certificate. If soldiers chose to have sex with women who did not have such a card, the army could not prevent them from doing so without creating a much more intrusive surveillance and enforcement apparatus, perhaps by having military police inspect brothels and streetwalkers, forcibly detaining individuals unable to produce certificates. While the army does not appear to have caught any prostitutes using forged medical inspection certificates in the Philippines, it is certainly possible that such forgeries were made, especially given the relatively simple nature of the inspection cards. Alternatively, it may be that such forgeries for infected prostitutes were unneeded because a failure to prominently display a current certificate may not have been a serious impediment to business.

The army's de facto medical inspection regime for prostitutes, which mostly went uncriticized in the American press, continued in the Philippines for the next decade until the onset of American involvement in World War I. Eventually reformers were able to force the Wilson administration to close the Manila red-light district in May 1917—"reluctantly," according to Governor Francis B. Harrison, who opposed the closure—as it did throughout the United States and other American-held territories through an executive order banishing such districts within ten miles of an army post.[75] Woodrow Wilson's executive order was part of a broader campaign to protect the morality of U.S. soldiers as they trained and prepared to enter World War I. Wilson created a new federal agency, the Commission on Training Camp Activities (CTCA), charging it, in part, with protecting newly mobilized soldiers from venereal disease and moral peril. The CTCA began its battle against immoral sexual behavior with an attack against prostitution and prostitutes, focusing on areas around military camps, which it perceived as the most blatant and clear-cut sources of venereal infection and sexual immorality. The CTCA's attack on prostitution met with significant success in eliminating red-light districts in many U.S. cities. On September 20, 1918, Brigadier General Robert K. Evans, the commander of the Philippine Department, issued an order prohibiting all military personnel and civilian government workers from "entering or residing in a house of ill-fame."[76] On October 16, 1918, the Gardenia District was cordoned off by police and the 230 Filipina, 122 Japanese, and 10 European and American prostitutes inhabiting the Gardenia's brothels were confined to their workplaces.[77] Over the course of the next two weeks, the foreign prostitutes were deported and the Filipina prostitutes were dispersed to other islands. The closure of these brothels, dance halls, and saloons did not, of course, put an end to prostitution in the Philippines, and because the red-light district was done away with, the entire city of Manila eventually became the site of prostitution, with U.S. soldiers continuing to patronize the now-dispersed prostitutes.

The Problem of Venereal Disease in the Army

Although individual generals and commanding officers may have objected on moral grounds to prostitutes, army leaders consistently stated that their primary concern was that sexual contact with prostitutes not harm soldiers through transmission of venereal disease, thereby diminishing the number of effective soldiers available to the army. One army doctor in the Philippines stated that soldiers' contraction of venereal disease was "most deplorable in extent and apparently uncontrollable."[78] Another despaired of ever controlling venereal disease in the Philippines: "The only effectual means under the sun would be to kill the women, or castrate the soldiers."[79] Venereal disease certainly was rampant among U.S. soldiers. From 1873 through 1898, the average annual venereal disease rate in the U.S. Army was 85.3 per 1,000 soldiers, meaning that 8.53 percent of regular army soldiers became infected with venereal disease annually. In 1899, the incidence of venereal disease within the U.S. Army as a whole increased to 138 (13.8%). The overall venereal disease rate continued to climb, with an average rate from 1899 through 1910 of 148.5 (meaning that 14.85% of all soldiers were infected with a venereal disease), representing an increase of 74.1 percent from the 1898 level. The primary change in army deployments in this period was the large-scale

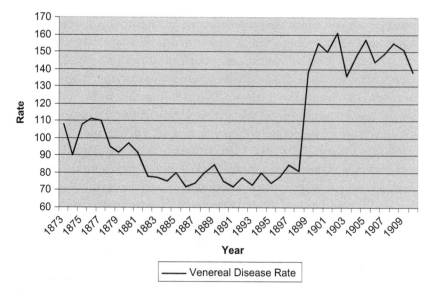

FIGURE 1. U.S. Army venereal disease rates, 1873–1910 (annual incidence per one thousand soldiers). Data from "Venereal Diseases and Alcoholism in the Regular Army in the United States," undated chart, AGO Docfile 1915426, filed with AGO Docfile 1045985, RG 94, NARA.

deployments to the Philippines. Figure 1 depicts the venereal disease rate trends from 1873 through 1910.

Venereal disease rates were even higher for U.S. units stationed in the Philippines. There, between 1908 and 1910, the venereal disease rate doubled. In acknowledging the venereal threat, Brigadier General George H. Torney, the Surgeon General of the Army, stated in 1910 that "the venereal peril has come to outweigh in importance any other sanitary question which now confronts the Army, and neither our national optimism nor the Anglo-Saxon disposition to ignore a subject which is offensive to public prudery can no longer excuse a frank and honest confrontation of the problem."[80] Torney recommended a series of countermeasures for decreasing the venereal infection rate. The War Department endorsed his plan in 1912, along with a new policy of stopping pay for soldiers during their venereal treatments. The Surgeon General's recommendations included the introduction of wholesome recreation facilities to lure soldiers away from sex; the creation of temperance societies within the army, since sex and alcohol were so frequently linked in the minds of reformers; lectures on sexual health focusing on the dangers of sex; and, perhaps most importantly, periodic venereal inspections of soldiers and increased availability of prophylactic packages.[81] These prophylactic packages, often described as "K-Packets," consisted of a glass syringe of chemicals packaged in wax paper that soldiers were to inject into the urethra after sex to prevent infection by syphilis.[82] Notably, they did not include condoms, which many American moralists believed would have only encouraged immoral sexual behavior.

Table 1 presents representative statistics on venereal disease infections in army garrisons in the Philippines for 1913 and the first half of 1914, a period for which extensive statistical data exist. A number of insights emerge from these data. First, the incidence of venereal disease infection for American units in the Philippines was the highest of any unit in the U.S. Army, and it only increased the longer units remained in the Philippines. In 1913, 14.4 percent of all U.S. soldiers stationed in the Philippines were infected. By the first six months of 1914, the average venereal disease infection rate of these units had increased to nearly 19.0 percent. This is in marked contrast with the venereal disease rates for U.S. units stationed within the borders of the United States, which were much lower: these rates were 8.2 percent in 1913 and 8.6 percent in 1914.[83] Second, the venereal disease infection rates for Philippine Scout units—military units composed of ethnically Filipino enlisted soldiers led by white American officers—were also much lower than the rates for American-only units. The average Scout unit infection rate in 1913 was 7.3 percent and fell to 6.6 percent by the first half of 1914. Why might this be the case? It may be that Filipino soldiers were kept under tighter, or at least different, standards

Table 1.   Annual venereal disease rates, U.S. Army units in the Philippines, 1913–1914 (annual incidence per 1,000 soldiers)

POST	TROOP TYPE AT POST, 1913	1913	JANUARY TO JUNE 1914	TROOP TYPE AT POST, 1914
Camp McGrath	American	273.47	355.42	American
Camp Stotsenburg	American	125.36	209.06	American
Fort Wint	American	60.61	197.37	American
Fort McKinley	American	210.93	233.94	American
Quartel de Espana	American	145.33	174.42	American
Headquarters, Santiago	American	136.26	108.11	American
Camp Connell	Scout	32.70	85.72	Scout
San Pedro	Scout	137.40	159.42	Scout
Warwick Barracks	Scout	13.22	60.61	Scout
Camp Eldridge	Mixed	165.32	215.47	American
Camp Gregg	Scout	84.25	74.07	American
Camp John Hay	Mixed	43.10	72.85	American
Camp Ward Cheney	Scout	97.94	214.30	American
Fort Mills	Mixed	63.81	140.82	American
Regan Barracks	Scout	72.73	280.37	American
Augur Barracks	Mixed	66.75	83.33	Scout
Camp Keithley	Mixed	39.82	37.04	Scout
Ludlow Barracks	American	55.29	20.73	Scout
Pettit Barracks	Mixed	21.51	15.62	Scout
Avg. of American posts		143.89	189.68	
Avg. of mixed posts		66.72	NA	
Avg. of Scout posts		73.04	66.07	
Avg. of U.S. posts (domestic)		**81.75**	**85.84**	

Sources: Data on Philippine posts taken from Surgeon General to the Adjutant General, "Rates for Venereal Disease in the Second Division," letter, November 19, 1914, AGO Docfile 2230647, filed with AGO Docfile 1045985, RG 94, NARA; data on U.S. domestic posts taken from Surgeon General to the Adjutant General, "Venereal Disease in the Army," table A, letter, September 30, 1915, AGO Docfile 2225425, filed with AGO Docfile 1045985, RG 94, NARA.

Notes: American posts are garrisons containing all-U.S. troops. Scout posts are garrisons populated by Philippine Scouts (units containing enlisted Filipinos led by white American officers). Mixed posts contain garrisons composed of both American and Scout units. By 1914, the character of many posts had changed; note, for example, that no mixed garrisons remained by 1914.

of discipline and were permitted fewer opportunities to have sex. They might have had less money to pay for prostitutes' services. They might have been less prone to engaging in sex for cultural or religious reasons. Those Philippine Scouts who did have the desire and opportunity to engage in sex also may have tended to have monogamous relationships with a single partner (for example, a steady girlfriend, fiancée, or wife) more frequently than occupying

Table 2.   Admissions of U.S. enlisted men in the Philippines for venereal disease, 1910–1922

YEAR	TOTAL ENLISTED STRENGTH IN PHILIPPINES	NUMBER OF ADMISSIONS FOR VENEREAL DISEASE	PERCENTAGE OF TOTAL ADMITTED
1910	17,370	3,700	21.3
1911	17,720	4,106	23.2
1912	17,764	3,380	19.0
1913	16,284	1,857	11.4
1914	15,273	2,192	14.4
1915	17,339	2,394	13.8
1916	17,159	2,058	12.0
1917	16,338	3,388	20.7
1918	13,363	1,601	12.0
1919	12,694	749	5.9
1920	17,869	2,089	11.7
1921	15,132	1,403	9.3
1922	**12,177**	**1,025**	**8.4**

Source: Serafin E. Macaraig, *Social Problems* (Manila: Educational Supply, 1929), 156–157.

Notes: The "percentage of total admitted" data do not necessarily reflect unique cases of infection; these data may include soldiers who were infected multiple times during a single year, though the extent of these recurring cases is impossible to determine from the source material.

American soldiers. Furthermore, army posts containing both U.S. and Scout units had even lower venereal disease rates (6.7% in 1913; there were no mixed garrisons by 1914). Discipline at these posts may have been higher due to a concern about the potential for conflict between American and Filipino troops, or American troops may have been less willing to patronize Filipina prostitutes when serving alongside Filipino soldiers.

Examining the available data on venereal disease rates for a longer period yields additional insights. Table 2 presents the number of soldiers admitted each year between 1910 and 1922 for venereal infections. The highest incidence rate occurred in 1911 (23.2%) and the lowest in 1919 (5.9%). This nadir is a dramatic decline from the previous year, though it is a unique occurrence; the incidence rate in 1920 (11.7%) climbed back nearly to the 1918 rate (12.0%). The low rate in 1919 may be attributed to the closing of Manila's red-light district in October 1918, which caused a temporary reduction in the number of available prostitutes. After a few months, however, prostitutes were able to re-establish themselves in less obvious venues. This is in marked contrast with the venereal disease rates for U.S. units stationed within the borders of the

United States, which were much lower; throughout the period, they averaged from 8.0 percent to 9.0 percent.[84]

Army doctors also recognized that white, African American, and Filipino soldiers suffered from venereal diseases at considerably different rates. For example, in 1906, white soldiers in the Philippines had a venereal disease infection rate of 30.9 percent, African American soldiers had a slightly higher rate of 32.2 percent, and Filipino soldiers in American service had the lowest rate of all, 6.3 percent.[85] This was at a time when the rate for white troops stationed in the United States was 15.9 percent and the rate was 15.0 percent for African American troops at domestic military posts.[86]

Venereal disease had profoundly debilitating effects on soldiers serving in the Philippines, causing more medical admissions among soldiers than any other disease, including malarial fevers, diarrheal diseases, typhoid fever, tuberculosis, and dengue fever, though it had a relatively low mortality rate.[87] It was also the largest cause of days lost to sickness of all diseases; indeed, venereal disease caused twice as many noneffective days as malarial fevers, diarrheal diseases, and dengue fever combined.[88] Additionally, venereal disease was the leading cause of discharges due to disability. Of the 1,364 men discharged for disability in 1906, for example, 165 (12.1%) were discharged for venereal disease infections.[89] Effective treatment for gonorrhea was not available until 1937 and syphilis until 1943, with the development of specific penicillins. Before these treatments became available, approximately 5–10 percent of adults contracting syphilis would eventually die from the infection; the mortality rate for unborn children contracting the disease from their mothers was much higher.[90] Limited treatments for syphilis were available to the U.S. Army starting in 1908, but they had little effect on overall venereal disease rates.[91]

Military Justice and Venereal Disease in the Philippines

Because the army was so concerned with controlling the spread of venereal disease among American soldiers in the Philippines, it is not surprising that it court-martialed soldiers for refusing to receive the medical treatment that army doctors ordered. At least eighty-five enlisted men (no noncommissioned or commissioned officers were medically inspected for venereal disease) were court-martialed for this offense in 1912–1918, nearly 95 percent of whom were convicted.[92] The average sentence for those convicted of refusing venereal treatments was just over six months of hard labor, in addition to forfeiture of all pay and receipt of a dishonorable discharge. A small number of convicted soldiers were permitted to remain in military service after serving a brief confinement at hard labor and/or forfeiting some pay, and some soldiers who refused treatment on multiple occasions received sentences of up to two years. The army reviewing authority occasionally chastised some courts for granting too lenient a sentence—generally those sentences involving just three or four months of hard labor—suggesting that the army sought to maintain a standard sentence of approximately six months of labor for this offense. The reviewing authority also complained that several of the acquittals should not have been granted, even returning one case to the court and requiring it to retry the case. In this case, the court reached the same acquittal verdict in its retrial, causing the reviewing authority to rebuke the court in a lengthy diatribe. In that instance, Major General James Franklin Bell described the members of the acquitting court as "either lacking[ing] sufficient intelligence . . . or . . . [being] too deficient in professional pride to comply" with Bell's obvious desire to convict the accused.[93] In another case, an acquittal was described as "a gross miscarriage of justice" and the defendant deemed "a menace to the health of his comrades" because he was venereally infected but allowed to remain free and in military service. No remark was made as to the sexual danger he represented to those women with whom he came into sexual contact.[94]

These courts-martial were generally brief and straightforward. Army physicians testified that they had prescribed a medical treatment they described as necessary (usually injections of mercuric salicylate), and the accused had refused to receive the treatment. Some of the accused were alleged to have even left camp and gone absent without leave to escape their physician's attention. The army invariably attempted to ascertain from the medical authorities whether the venereal diseases with which the accused were infected would "render [the men] unfit for military duty," and just as invariably the army doctors answered affirmatively. Frequently the infected men were described as "a danger to the community" and a "danger to the men in the barracks."[95] The doctors were questioned as to the potential danger of the treatment, and they assured the court that there was no danger to those receiving treatment, though the intramuscular injections were painful, and patients frequently complained of various side effects, including nervousness, anxiety, sleeplessness, and muscle and joint aches, among many other symptoms. One soldier, for example, had taken the mercurial treatments on several occasions and reported extreme fatigue, bleeding from the gums, softening of his teeth, and other side effects that left him extremely weak, in severe pain, and largely unable to move for a period of three days after each treatment. While he acknowledged that the army physician had told him that he would likely die of syphilis eventually if he did not receive treatment, the soldier said that he would rather forgo treatment than be weak and unable to move for three days out of each week, particularly since he would likely have to continue to receive the mercurial treatments indefinitely. He added, "This treatment is very hard on different people. It doesn't act the same way on every person who takes it. Some people can take it, and nothing bothers them at all. On other people it affects them so much that they have to go to bed; some of them."[96] Another soldier had been taking mercurial treatments for about one year for his syphilis, with no relief, and so he requested that he be prescribed Salvarsan, a new syphilis treatment that became available in 1910.[97] Two army doctors refused and seemed to strongly resent their patient's request for a new treatment. Salvarsan was, in fact, relatively effective in treating syphilis and did not have the same side effects that the mercurial treatment did, but it was new—and hence of unknown effectiveness to army doctors— and more expensive than mercuric salicylate. This soldier sought Salvarsan on the open market in Manila, and found it, but could not afford to pursue that treatment option. He then refused to continue pursuing mercurial treatments and was court-martialed like the rest.

Some men refused treatments because they said they did not have a venereal disease, though venereal patients were always given diagnostic tests.[98] The Wassermann test was given to detect syphilis, with positive test results necessitating a course of treatment. Other soldiers stated that they believed the treatment was "injurious to their health," despite being assured otherwise by army doctors, and claimed they had heard this from other soldiers or relatives, or had been told this by civilian physicians, or had read it in a magazine article or book.[99] In no case would the army accept soldiers' outright refusal of prescribed venereal treatments, no matter what the men's concerns about the treatments might be.

Same-Sex Sexual Activity in the Philippines

The U.S. Army was not just concerned about sex between soldiers and female prostitutes; it also sought to regulate sex between soldiers and between soldiers and male civilians. Before the end of World War I, attempts to regulate same-sex sexual activity within the U.S. military were erratic and tentative. The Articles of War of 1916, which went into effect on March 1, 1917, was the first substantial revision of military law in over a century. As discussed in chapter 1, it was the first legal document to directly address the potential for sodomy within the military.[100] The Ninety-Third Article of War prohibited assault with the intent to commit sodomy, which was defined as anal penetration of a man or woman by a man; both parties involved were equally guilty of the offense. In these new regulations, penetration of the mouth did not initially constitute sodomy. In the regulations that accompanied the revision of the Articles of War in 1920, however, *The Manual for Courts-Martial* redefined sodomy as anal or oral copulation between men or between a man and a woman.[101]

Relatively few records of courts-martial in the Philippines before World War I survive. Records of courts-martial in the Philippines for 1912–1917 are available, however, and show that even before sodomy was made a separate, explicit criminal offense under the Articles of War, at least thirty-one enlisted men (including six noncommissioned officers) were charged with sodomy. No commissioned officers were court-martialed for sodomy during this period. The vast majority of those charged were white, in keeping with the demographic makeup of the U.S. Army presence in the Philippines (more than 60% white during this period), though five African American soldiers were charged with such offenses, as was a single Filipino member of the Philippine Scouts. Given the approximate proportion of whites, blacks, and Filipinos in military service in the Philippines, one would expect that approximately nineteen of the accused would be white, two black, and ten Filipino. Clearly, blacks were charged at a rate more than two and half times their proportion of the military population, and Filipinos were charged only one-tenth of their expected percentage. Most of the cases (twenty-three of thirty-one) involved sex between soldiers, either consensually or nonconsensually. Note though that the issue of consent was not directly germane to the army; any sexual contact between men was considered sodomy. Because rape was defined as forcible sex with a woman, it was not legally possible for a soldier to rape another man. Seven of the remaining cases involved either civilian Filipino boys or men, most of whom were alleged to be male prostitutes,[102] and a single case involved a soldier alleged to have committed acts of oral sex on several U.S. Navy sailors.[103] The cases involving civilians often concerned soldiers who were caught in secluded public areas (parks and the like) at night by Filipino civilian police, who then turned the soldiers over to the U.S. Army for court-martial. In more than 20 percent of all the cases, none involving civilians, the prosecutor alleged that the acts of sodomy or attempted sodomy were nonconsensual. At least 65 percent of the courts-martial ended in convictions, most of which led to sentences of dishonorable discharge, forfeiture of all pay, and hard-labor terms of six months to six years. Cases involving the use of force or other injuries to the victims usually warranted stiffer penalties, though most of these cases' hard-labor terms averaged from six to eighteen months. In no case were men convicted of sodomy or attempted sodomy permitted to remain in military service. Acquittals usually resulted from cases in which the accused had previous records of good character and in which there were no third-party eyewitnesses or other evidence that the offense had been committed.

Because the nature of what the army—and American civil law—considered "sodomy" was both ambiguous and capacious, some courts-martial hinged on precisely what sex acts were alleged to have occurred or could be proved by the prosecution. Corporal Bryant Mowery's court-martial was one such case. He was accused of entering a civilian home while serving in the Philippines in 1915 "for the purpose of committing an unnatural crime, to wit, sodomy, upon the person of" Cipriano Maminta, a seventeen-year-old Filipino boy.[104] Mowery pleaded not guilty to the charge. The case began with testimony by the two civilian detectives who had initially arrested Mowery and Maminta. One of them had spotted Mowery following two Filipino bootblacks, who led him to an abandoned house "that had a reputation of being a place where bootblacks take soldiers to have indecent association with them." They found Mowery with "his pants unbuttoned and his penis in his hand" and Maminta hiding inside the house. They claimed that Mowery made a show of urinating after he saw the detectives, and he later claimed that the two bootblacks had told him they were taking him to a place where a drunk American soldier needed assistance. Maminta was examined by a medical doctor and found to have venereal cancroids around his rectum; his medical condition seems to have been used as evidence suggesting he was a prostitute. He was tried in a Filipino court before Mowery's court-martial, found guilty of committing sodomy, and because he was a minor, sentenced to serve a year in the Lolomboy Reform School.

Maminta was then called to testify as a witness for the prosecution, to which Mowery objected strenuously, describing the boy as having been convicted of an "infamous crime" and lacking in "sense [and] moral stamina," suggesting that Maminta was of such "moral turpitude" that he was an untrustworthy witness. This objection was not sustained and Maminta was allowed to give testimony. Maminta testified that Mowery had led him to the abandoned building, and when they arrived there, Mowery "unbuttoned his pants and drawers and held his penis out and told [Maminta] to masturbate his penis" just before the arrival of the detectives. When asked why he entered the building with Mowery, Maminta stated flatly, "We entered that building for the purpose of masturbation of the corporal's penis, but before we could do it the detectives came in." Maminta indicated that he had learned how to masturbate other men approximately two weeks before his arrest from some of his friends, and that he had done so on two other occasions before his arrest.

The definition of sodomy was raised in court, and the judge advocate read an extract from *Clark's Criminal Law*, second edition (1907), which he described as "a text book which is in use at the Army Service Schools, in the law department." There, sodomy was defined as

carnal copulation against the order of nature by man with man; or in the same unnatural manner with woman; or by man or woman in any manner with a beast. . . . Buggery is sodomy. . . . [This crime is] generally spoken of as the "abominable and detestable crime against nature." . . . Sodomy is named from the prevalence of the sin in the city of Sodom, which the Bible tells us was destroyed by fire because of its wickedness. . . . Both penetration and emission are necessary at common law, but in some jurisdictions there are statutes declaring proof of emission unnecessary. The act in a person's mouth is not enough. It must be per anum. Both parties are guilty, and consent is therefore no defense.

Mowery was then called to testify on his own behalf. He steadfastly held to his account that the two Filipino boys had found him in a bar where he had been drinking and urged him to follow them into the deserted house because they said there was an American soldier there who needed help. Once they arrived, one boy ran off and the other asked for a peso. Mowery said he refused to pay the boy after he failed to find an ailing soldier on the premises, then stopped to urinate behind the house when the two detectives entered the area and arrested Mowery and Maminta. Mowery said that he was not inspected by a police physician, but Maminta was, and the police doctor urged him to take venereal prophylaxis when he discovered Maminta's rectal chancres. Mowery refused, saying that he "did not need any of their medicine, that [he] had no call to use it." The defense then recalled to the stand one of the detectives and asked him the reputation of Maminta and other Filipino bootblacks. The detective replied, "Why, their general reputation, of newsboys and bootblacks, is not very good. We have arrested quite a number for the same thing [sodomy] at different places." The detective was then asked whether he had seen Mowery "in any position or any posture that would denote he was going to attempt or was attempting sodomy or buggery." He replied that Mowery "having his penis out looked very suspicious, although he was not actually in a position of committing sodomy" and that Maminta was not "in the position of recipient [of anal sex]." He later reiterated that there was no indication that Mowery "was going to commit an obscene act." As implausible as Mowery's story of why he was present at the deserted house with Maminta might have been, the evidence provided in court was clearly circumstantial and did not meet the definition of sodomy; he was acquitted by the court.

Some courts-martial for sodomy rehearsed the familiar trope that physical, mental, and moral "degeneration" of Americans was to be expected in the Philippines and other "tropical" areas.[105] This degeneracy was believed to result from whites being exposed to tropical heat, diseases, and sheer exhaustion, as well as close contact with other races. The devolution was seen to have medical, moral, racial, and sexual dimensions. Since American soldiers and civilians in the Philippines were cut off from civilized American surroundings, some feared that they would begin to emulate the presumably savage and degenerate Filipinos and other "tropical" races with whom they would come into contact. In its most extreme forms, degeneration was said to pose an existential danger, potentially leading to the complete collapse of American society if sufficiently large numbers of Americans succumbed to tropical temptations and then returned to the United States. Private George F. Goodfellow, for example, was charged with attempting to commit an act of oral sex on a fellow private and then deserting before he could be formally charged in 1913. Goodfellow pleaded guilty to all charges, essentially throwing himself on the mercy of the court. At his request, the judge advocate in the case made the following speech to the court, which is worth repeating in full as it illustrates all the familiar tropes:

Gentlemen of the court: you have before you a mere shell of a man. He is a wreck, mentally, physically and morally. The first fact you may ascertain by conversation with him, the second fact by your vision, and the third fact follows from his admission of an act so low and degraded that it is scorned by the lowest barbarians. But how came he thus? By heredity or environment. If the former, have pity on him for his heritage; if the latter let us consider what it has been. Eighteen months ago this man came to these islands, where many a stronger man has yielded to temptations that would be violently rejected at home,—at home, where there is the society of respectable women,—at home, where one escapes many petty tyrannies that may exist here. This tyranny or oppression may be fancy, but it surely existed in the mind of a man driven to his routine tasks during the midday heat hours in this torrid zone. Far better off the ignorant ta[o] [Filipino peasant], but not so ignorant as to court the midday sun, than the Anglo-Saxon who is forced, and not through emergency, to exposure which produces many terrible examples. One of these examples you have before you. A weak man, he became weaker. Not of the strong, he had no way to protect himself by a change of environment or a prescribed set of working hours. And at last so deep is he in the mire that he is willing to grasp at any act, however degraded, that will change his environment. Friendless and ill-advised, he immediately found himself a pariah and thoughtlessly added desertion to his other crime. But even to a pariah liberty is sweet, for in prison did not even Oscar Wilde say "That every day is like a year—a year whose days are long."[106]

This "tropical defense" failed to sway the court to mercy. Goodfellow was held responsible for his actions, receiving a sentence of dishonorable discharge and three years of hard labor, an even lengthier period of hard labor than was typical for such offenses.

In 1913, another enlisted man, Private Iseral Jones, was charged with "repeatedly attempt[ing] to satisfy his sexual instinct in a perverse manner, and . . . repeatedly urg[ing] on Private Harold M. Coon . . . unnatural proposals to this end" and, "without provocation, repeatedly threaten[ing] to kill" Coon.[107] Jones pleaded not guilty to both charges. During Coon's testimony against Jones, Coon stated that Jones had twice offered to perform oral sex on him, once in 1912 and once in 1913, threatening to kill Coon and commit suicide if Coon would not allow him to do so. According to Coon, the 1912 propositioning had resulted in Jones attempting to kill himself after Coon rejected his advances.

The case came to the army's attention in 1913 following Coon's recapture after he absented himself without leave from his unit because, he said, he was afraid for his life after spurning Jones's advances a second time. On being asked about Jones's sexual advances, Coon stated that Jones had said "he had never done anything like that [perform oral sex on a man], but he wanted to do it." Another private, Joseph K. Baumeister, a friend of Coon's, corroborated his account and stated that Jones had described himself as a "head artist." Baumeister was questioned at length about what Jones had "meant by that head artist business," eventually stating that Jones had said he wanted to "suck cock." The prosecution and multiple witnesses who were called to testify to Coon's character repeatedly described Jones as "immoral" and Coon as a "decent and respectable fellow" with "excellent character." The case seems to have hinged on the character of the two soldiers involved. The defense called several character witnesses (fellow enlisted soldiers), with one witness stating that Jones had "no immoral practices" and was "absolutely normal." Testifying on his own behalf, Jones flatly denied ever sexually propositioning Coon or anyone else, stating that he believed that the charges had been made in revenge for some past petty dispute between the two men, though he said they had been friends. Regarding the 1912 suicide attempt in which he had shot himself in the chest with a rifle, Jones explained that he "had been on a drunk and discouraged and was out of [his] head at the time being." When pressed further on his state of mind, he simply said that he had been "discouraged with life" but did not elaborate further.

The case appears to have been settled based on the testimony of the final witness, called to testify on behalf of the defense: Major William M. Roberts, an officer in the Army Medical Corps. Roberts had known and treated Jones for the past year, first meeting him when he was admitted to the hospital after his failed suicide attempt. Roberts seems to have made a special effort to look after Jones during his hospital stay and described Jones's character during his time at the hospital as "most exemplary." Roberts stated that he learned there had been "allegations of indecent proposals" and that he "wanted professionally to know the status of the case . . . so that [he] could form a professional opinion of the man's mental condition." After making an "exhaustive, unofficial, underground inquiry," he came to believe that there was "positively nothing" to the allegations. As a physician, Roberts was asked, "At what age would a man's unnatural sexual desires be likely to show themselves if at all?" Roberts replied that there are "two periods in a man's life in which sexual excitement is at its maximum, one is in the early stages when sexual development is being had—when the sexual nerve centers are being developed more or less under irritable conditions such as an excess blood supply, and again when a man is reaching the senile period when his nerve centers are deteriorating, when they are developing excitement; when they are deteriorating abnormally; in other words when the nerve centers become abnormal."

Roberts noted that, because Jones was thirty-six years old at the time of his court-martial, he "would not be of the age when he would develop such unnatural desires" and that such a development in middle age could only come about as a result of "some acute pathological process not in the normal course of a man's life." He elaborated that he thought a man would probably be "insane" if he did such a thing at Jones's age. Because Roberts had not observed "anything defective at all" with Jones psychologically, in Roberts's view the charges against him must be false. With that, the case came to an end and Jones was found not guilty of all charges. Roberts's testimony as a medical professional and amateur psychologist is consistent with a view espoused by many army medical and other officers in similar cases, that homosexual acts would only be committed by an individual whom they would consider insane. If the accused had never exhibited a history of mental instability or past pathological behavior, and no physical evidence of sexual activity other than a victim's testimony existed, then the army seems to have been willing to accept that the allegations were false in at least some cases.

Romantic Relationships, Marriage, and Family Life in the Philippines

The army appears to have discouraged marriage between U.S. soldiers and local women in the Philippines even more strongly and actively than it did elsewhere. Married men were not permitted to enlist (or reenlist) in the U.S. Army until 1942.[108] An article published in the *Army and Navy Journal* in 1905 expressed concern that "however indiscrete he may have been in the tropics, I trust the day may never come when an American officer may be induced by fear of a court-martial to escort as a wife into one of our Army posts, a diminutive, brown-skinned, ill-favored rice eater."[109] Despite these racial anxieties, the army officers who married Filipinas caused one fellow officer to complain that "many of the present and former officers of the Philippine Scouts have forgotten that they were white men, presumably white gentlemen."[110] An informal policy of discharging soldiers who married local women or who acknowledged paternity with them was eventually made official. In 1925, the army ordered that "white Americans married to natives will not be enlisted without approval of the department commander," which, presumably, would rarely be forthcoming.[111] Despite the legal and social sanctions, a significant number of enlisted men and officers cohabited with indigenous women, who were often described using the local term *querida*, throughout the American occupation.[112]

The army was serious about enforcing its ban on married men enlisting. In the Philippines from 1912 to 1918, twenty-three privates and one sergeant were accused of having lied to the army upon enlistment, claiming to be single when in fact they were married. All but four were convicted, most receiving dishonorable discharges and hard-labor sentences of three to six months, which was one of the lightest sentences meted out for convictions in general courts-martial at the time. This type of offense may have reflected the use of military service and enlistment as a means of escaping from domestic and marital responsibilities. In fact, the army generally learned of secret marriages when soldiers' wives contacted the War Department, usually to collect a portion of soldiers' earnings.

Officers were selected to overseas duty in the Philippines based on their rank, branch, and place on the foreign service list, from which replacement officers were drawn. Because the army retained a sizable presence in the Philippines from the Spanish-American War to World War II, most career army officers served at least one tour in the Philippines. Congress mandated two-year tours of overseas duty (officers could volunteer for a third year). The War

Department greatly resented this policy, not least because of the financial burden it placed on young, married junior officers and their families, who were forced to find rented rooms or houses for their families as they moved frequently throughout the islands as their duties required.[113] More senior married officers were permitted to bring their wives and families with them to the Philippines, and they often lived in army-furnished domiciles on or near U.S. Army posts. Officers' wives in the Philippines were expected to reproduce a cozy, American-style domestic setting for their husbands and children while participating in a host of social activities: teas, women's clubs, golf outings, charity functions, and the like. In the Philippines, as at all army posts domestic or overseas, officers and enlisted men lived in separate enclaves, with officers dining and dancing with their wives in Manila's luxurious Army and Navy Club or playing polo or golf, and soldiers, officially forbidden from marrying, often spending off-duty hours with local women with whom they lived or cohabited in "shack jobs," or carousing in town.[114]

Enlisted soldiers were normally barred from the on-base neighborhoods in which the officers lived. Courts-martial of enlisted men for intruding on married officers' living spaces suggest that enlisted men occasionally did just that. From 1912 to 1918, at least nine privates were court-martialed for invading the private domestic spaces of commissioned and noncommissioned officers and civilians in the Philippines. Most were charged with peering into windows of bedrooms or bathrooms (in at least one case using a ladder to peer into the window of a second-story bedroom), some with crawling under homes or cutting holes in walls to look into bathrooms. The locations where the offenses were alleged to have occurred were evenly divided between the homes of commissioned officers, the homes of noncommissioned officers, and the homes of civilians with no connection to the army. Cases of home intrusion for the purpose of larceny were treated separately by the army and are not considered here. An element of fear—involving class- or race-based anxieties—is evident in many of these cases.[115] In one case, for example, two African American privates were charged with "loiter[ing] around the homes of married noncommissioned officers . . . thereby terrifying the unprotected families."[116] In only two cases (both involving the homes of civilians) were the accused acquitted. In one case, the mother of a soldier convicted of being a Peeping Tom wrote to the President and Secretary of War protesting the "unjust" length of the man's sentence: eighteen months of hard labor. An army attorney was asked to review the case.[117] He noted that under U.S. Army regulations, there was no sentencing guideline for this type of offense, it being left entirely to the discretion of the court. He canvassed U.S. civil court systems and found that most such civilian convictions resulted in fines of approximately twenty-five dollars and sixty days of confinement. The attorney, without elaborating, suggested that "unquestionably an offense of this kind committed in the military service is of greater gravity because of the conditions under which our garrisons live and the more direct relations which individuals of the service sustain to each other." The exact meaning of this statement is left unclear, but the case involved a private who was alleged to have twice looked into the bathroom of a lieutenant's quarters and seen the lieutenant's wife there. It seems likely that the reviewer was alluding to the fact that officers and their families lived in close proximity to enlisted men and were therefore liable to come under the surveillance of men of a lower rank and perceived social class, even while engaging in intimate activities. The attorney did, however, allow that the accused man's sentence was probably excessive, and recommended that it be remitted to time served (approximately six months at that point). His recommendation was accepted by the Assistant Secretary of War.

The army also intervened in cases of violence between soldiers and their female sexual partners. From 1912 to 1918, three privates (one white, one black, and one Filipino) and one sergeant (white) were charged with committing acts of violence against women who were the sexual partners of the accused.[118] All were convicted. In three cases, the women were Filipinas (one was the wife of the Filipino soldier), while in the last the alleged victim was a white Army nurse. In this latter case, a white private was accused of breaking into the home of the nurse, a second lieutenant with whom he had apparently had a romantic relationship, and seizing her in his hands with the intent to harm her.[119] He received the harshest sentence of the four cases, a dishonorable discharge and five years at hard labor (later reduced to three years). The harshness of the sentence likely had to do with the fact that the private had committed an assault on an officer.

It was not only domestic spaces that were perceived to be threatened by enlisted soldiers in the Philippines but also the very persons of the wives of commissioned and noncommissioned officers, as well as some civilian women. In all, from 1912 to 1918, five African American privates and one white sergeant were charged with what we may, anachronistically, describe as sexual harassment of women. All were convicted. In some cases, it is difficult to assess exactly what the offending actions were. In one court-martial, a black private was accused of sending an "insulting and indecent letter" to an officer's wife asking her to meet him at his hotel room.[120] The exact contents of the letter were, oddly, never made public in the court-martial, and the letter itself was never entered into evidence, which was highly unusual. Nevertheless, the accused was dishonorably discharged and sentenced to six years of hard labor, though the sentence was reduced by the reviewing authority to two years.

In another case, two African American privates, Dora Jackson and Willie Waters, were charged with "in an insolent and unwarranted manner endeavor[ing] to force [their] presence and conversation on the wife of the major."[121] She found them "very disrespectful" when they approached her on a street and asked her who she was and what she was doing. She stated that their language was not "indecent or profane" but that it was "their attitude, their looks" that offended her. She was talking with some local Filipinos, who summoned the police when the major's wife became "afraid." Both the major and his wife were white. During the men's courts-martial, their race was never mentioned, and the major's wife's anxiety about conversing with the men was left unexplained. The two men did not deny speaking with the major's wife, though they did deny being intoxicated at the time. They were each convicted in a separate court-martial; both were dishonorably discharged, Jackson received one year of hard labor, and Waters three years.

In the only case involving a white soldier, Electrician Sergeant Jethro B. Bartham was alleged to have thrown confetti on the head and back of the neck of a white American woman who was the companion of an army second lieutenant at a public parade in Manila.[122] Specifically, Bartham was charged with "tak[ing] the liberty of addressing her in a manner inconsistent with military customs and the requirements of military discipline." Bartham did not deny having thrown the confetti and then drinking during the parade. He stated that he had been throwing confetti on many civilians throughout the day. He was convicted and sentenced to forfeit ten days of pay. The reviewing authority found the sentence "grossly inadequate" and disapproved the findings of the court, which, ironically, meant that Bartham received no punishment for his offense. This seems to have been a case involving a junior officer who was offended at the liberties taken by an enlisted man. While Bartham's actions appear to have been innocuous, the court sought to enforce the army's social stratification between officers and enlisted men.

African American Soldiers and Filipino Civilians

Large numbers of black soldiers served in the Philippines. All four of the army's black regiments—the Twenty-Fourth and Twenty-Fifth Infantries and the Ninth and Tenth Cavalries—were deployed to the islands, as were two additional black volunteer regiments raised in 1899 (the Forty-Eighth and

Forty-Ninth Infantry Regiments).[123] Long-term romantic relationships and marriages—in many cases, common-law marriages or marriages that had not been approved by the soldiers' commanding officers—were relatively common between African American soldiers and Filipinas. The historian Willard B. Gatewood Jr. has estimated that by 1903 at least five hundred black soldiers (out of about six thousand) had chosen to leave military service and remain behind in the Philippines with women they married during their tours of duty when their units returned home to the United States.[124] A black chaplain, George W. Prioleau, who served with the Ninth Cavalry, noted that "the soldiers of the old 9th Cavalry are on very friendly terms with the natives in fact, I believe it so wherever Negro soldiers are stationed on the island."[125] By June 1901, Prioleau had already performed three marriage ceremonies between African American soldiers and local women in the Philippines. One black soldier who served in the Twenty-Fifth Infantry recounted that twenty-five men in his regiment married Filipinas during their 1900–1902 service in the Philippines, and that the white soldiers of the Third Infantry left behind "fifteen deluded native women, their mistresses, [who] turned away in tears as the Artillery band played, 'The Girl I Left Behind.'"[126]

Many African Americans deployed to the Philippines expressed sympathy with the Filipinos, their desire for national independence, and their place in the new racial hierarchy imposed by the United States.[127] Some whites grew concerned about a growing rapport between at least some blacks and local Filipinos. The army attempted to replicate and enforce Southern-style segregation in the Philippines, including the creation and maintenance of segregated brothels for use by black troops.[128] William Howard Taft, the first American Governor-General of the Philippines, complained that black soldiers "got along fairly well with the natives, too well with the native women," resulting in "a good deal of demoralization in the towns where they have been stationed."[129] These misgivings aside, the four regular army black regiments were all eventually redeployed for an additional tour of duty to the Philippines as part of the army's normal deployment cycles.

A number of American officers agreed that "there was a natural bond between the rural Filipinos and the American Negro," which many African American soldiers stated they shared in letters home.[130] Race relations between American blacks and Filipinos were generally positive, certainly no worse and possibly better than those between whites and Filipinos. In 1902, when the first black army regiments deployed to the Philippines were returned home, there were several highly publicized cases of black soldiers abandoning wives and children in the Philippines. Some black soldiers resented the unfavorable media attention they received, complaining that they were being "held responsible for all the bastard children in the archipelago," and noted that many white soldiers also left wives and children behind.[131] This abandonment of wives and children in the Philippines was partially a product of army policy, which would not pay to transport Filipinas or their children to the United States, as well as domestic policies that made immigration for Filipinos difficult. One former soldier recalled a comrade, an Army Air Corps sergeant, who had married a Filipina and fathered six children during his deployment to the Philippines. The U.S. Asian Exclusion Act made immigration for the sergeant's wife nearly impossible, and their marriage would have been a violation of his home state's antimiscegenation law, so "he was doomed by his marriage to stay in the Philippines until he died."[132]

The Philippines and the Sexual Economy of War

Though many Americans initially perceived the Philippines as a highly beneficial strategic outpost following its acquisition by the United States, eventually the enthusiasm of even the most ardent supporters began to wane. Even Theodore Roosevelt worried in 1907 that the Philippines had become the U.S. "heel of Achilles." Seven years later, in a *New York Times* essay, Roosevelt explicitly excluded it from the list of Pacific territories the United States should be prepared to defend, arguing for the independence of the Philippines as a matter of expediency for the United States.[133] The Clarke Amendment, proposed in the U.S. Congress in 1916, would have guaranteed Filipino sovereignty by 1920 but was dropped before final passage. Many came to view the Philippines as a strategic liability for the United States after World War I, since U.S. presence there antagonized Japan.

Despite growing domestic sentiment that the American occupation of the Philippines might be more trouble than it was worth, the United States maintained an average of thirteen thousand soldiers in the Philippines for decades. The army's experiences before World War I revealed several tensions concerning its treatment of sexual issues. First, and perhaps most importantly, they illuminated the tension between the army's emphasis on "military necessity"—and the army's apparent reliance on regulated prostitution to mitigate the effects of venereal disease on soldiers—and the moral qualms of domestic reformers who abhorred any implicit endorsement of what they perceived as profound moral and physical dangers. The U.S. Army began a process of formally regulating prostitution in the Philippines, creating a political liability for the McKinley administration, stopping only when faced with considerable opposition from domestic sources, though informal medical regulation of prostitution continued throughout the army's occupation of the islands. During the actual Philippine-American War, 1899–1902, the U.S. Army's regulation of prostitution had become a source of scandal and public debate between American pro-expansionists and anti-imperialists. During the much longer-term occupation of the Philippines, the medical inspections continued in a far more discreet fashion and eventually became normalized. The army's experiences with the medical regulation of prostitution in the Philippines would lay the groundwork for similar experiences elsewhere during at least two other large-scale military expeditions: first, the punitive campaign against Pancho Villa undertaken by the U.S. Army on the Mexican border from 1916 to 1917, and second, the American intervention in World War I in both France and Germany.

Second, the racial makeup of both the islands themselves and the American military contingent, white and black, played on the racial anxieties the Americans brought with them to the Philippines, as individuals of different races and ethnicities interacted sexually. Filipinas were often treated as though they were generally sexually available to service soldiers' physical needs, but soldiers were not to marry these women or bring them (or the interracial offspring that sometimes resulted from these liaisons) back to the United States when their terms of deployment were over.

Third, the relative geographic remoteness of army posts in the Philippines, and the isolated enclaves of white American civilization they represented in a "dangerous," tropical locale, highlighted the concerns of some physicians and moralists alike, who feared that the tropical conditions present in the Philippines represented a source of physical, moral, and ultimately sexual danger to at least some white soldiers. Some feared that these men, deprived of American civilization and the company of respectable white women, might turn to sexual "depravity," including same-sex sexual activities. Homosexual activities, aggregated broadly under the military-legal category of "sodomy" and anathema to the army, were particularly feared in tropical areas like the Philippines. These activities were increasingly linked with effeminacy and mental instability, qualities deemed wholly unsuitable for army service.

Last, class divisions within the army between the officer corps and enlisted men are brought into particularly sharp relief in the Philippines. Enlisted men were forbidden from bringing their wives or female partners with them to the Philippines, though they were deployed to the islands for several years at a time. They were frequently denied permission from their commanding officers to marry local women. If they did marry while in the Philippines, they were forbidden by army regulation to reenlist, and their wives and children could not be returned to the United States on army transports. The difficulties of enlisted men who might seek to establish families or marital relationships acceptable to the army are in sharp contrast with those of the army's commissioned officers. Officers frequently brought their wives and families with them and were often provided quarters at army posts in the islands. When enlisted men intruded on these domestic spaces, here, as elsewhere, the army moved to punish them.

The unique racial, cultural, political, and geographic dimensions of the army's activities in the Philippines before World War I help highlight the U.S. Army's conflicted efforts to intervene in the sexual economy of war and address its concerns with controlling disease, purging sexual "deviants" from the ranks, and protecting the rank and class privileges of the officer corps while also taking into account the concerns of domestic audiences more interested in moral reform and anti-imperial efforts than in military expediency.

CHAPTER 3

"Come Back Clean"

Camp Beauregard and the Commission on Training Camp Activities in Louisiana, 1917–1919

> I may not leave for my children,
> Brave medals that I have worn,
> But the blood in my veins shall leave no stains
> On the bride or the babes unborn
> And the scars my body shall carry
> Shall not be from deeds obscene,
> For my will shall say to the beast, OBEY!
> And I will come back clean.
>
> —Ella Wheeler Wilcox, "Soldiers, Come Back Clean"

By the onset of American intervention in World War I, the Progressive movement had reached its pinnacle of influence in the United States. Progressives shared a commitment to reforming American government and society, with the desire for moral reform a unifying concern. Progressives tended to have great faith in the power of a reformed American state to impose sweeping, cleansing changes across all aspects of American society. They believed that public and private life were indivisible and that the state should do more to ensure the moral and social welfare of its citizens.[1] As the United States entered the war and began a massive military mobilization, ultimately inducting millions of American men into the army, many progressives began to express their anxieties about the threats American soldiers would face, not on the battlefield but in the training camps and red-light districts of American cities before they even deployed to Europe. While many were pessimistic about the moral perils conscripted soldiers would face during wartime, they were optimistic about the prospect that millions of young American men, inculcated with a newfound sense of morality, would help to socially and morally reform the nation after the war when they returned to civilian life. But first these newly inducted soldiers would have to be protected from and trained to resist the dangers posed by unbridled sexuality.

Such fears of moral and sexual danger, and federal efforts to mitigate them, played out in training camps like Camp Beauregard and surrounding communities like Alexandria and New Orleans, Louisiana. At Camp Beauregard, the army and federal officials intervened in the sexual economy of war in two chief ways: by teaching the army's new conscripts that sex posed great dangers to their physical and moral well-being, that their sexual desires could and in fact must be suppressed, and that sex with venereally infected women during the war was a betrayal of the nation; and by attempting to eliminate soldiers' access to prostitutes and other women who might be willing to have sex with them by doing away with red-light districts and imprisoning women suspected of being prostitutes or promiscuous. These efforts to eliminate "vice" near military bases were not universally accepted; military and civilian antivice efforts met with considerable local resistance in Louisiana, where there were many who had vested economic and other interests who benefited from continued access to prostitution. Soldiers and their sexual partners, commercial and otherwise, also strenuously resisted efforts to prevent them from engaging in sex, suggesting the impracticability of top-down programs designed to prevent individuals from having sex, as well as the unintended consequences of such programs, such as the tendency for vice to become harder than ever to manage and contain after red-light districts are eliminated.

Progressives' fears about the social and moral dangers of prostitution and venereal disease were intertwined with white, Anglo-Saxon, Protestant anxieties about changes in American society brought about, in large part, by increased urbanization and immigration. The presence of large numbers of nonwhite and mixed-race people in Louisiana and the stark differences in culture between Louisiana and New England, where most of the World War I–era moral reformers hailed from, posed additional significant challenges for would-be reformers. America's cities—such as New Orleans and Alexandria, Louisiana—harbored increasing numbers of working-class women from first- or second-generation immigrant families who enjoyed leisure time in public and behaved in ways counter to traditional norms of behavior.[2] All this provoked fear among some progressives and triggered calls for a variety of social reforms. Progressives believed that prostitution posed a moral and physical danger to American society, a "social evil," as it came to be widely described.[3] Concern and even fear fed on the perception that both prostitution and venereal disease were on the rise, especially in urban areas. A wave of reports, surveys, and studies promulgated by physicians and other medical "experts" on sexual behavior lent an aura of scientific rigor to the emotional and moral concern.[4]

This represented a profound change from the older, Victorian-era notion of prostitution as a "necessary evil," a kind of safety valve for civilized society.[5] As one vice commission reported, "[Sexual] vice is one of the weaknesses of men; it cannot be extirpated; if repressed unduly at one point, it will break out more violently and bafflingly elsewhere; a segregated district is really a protection to the morality of the womanhood of the city, for without it rape would be common and clandestine immorality would increase."[6] In one extreme example of such a view, prostitution was described as the "most efficient guardian of virtue," because it protected "respectable" or "virtuous" women from rape, adultery, and other threats to the sanctity of marriage.[7] Out of this notion arose the "regulationist" or "reglementarian" school of thought, beginning in the 1860s and 1870s, which sought to force prostitutes to register with civil authorities, place them under close surveillance and testing regimes by both police and physicians, and segregate their commercial activities to designated red-light districts.[8] The city of Saint Louis, Missouri, even created such a system of licensed brothels and medical inspections from 1870 to 1874.[9]

Progressive moral reformers strongly opposed reglementation. Calling themselves "social purity" activists, they sought to abolish prostitution altogether and eliminate the social conditions from which it arose by reforming the nation's morality.[10] Social purity advocates also sought the suppression of pornography and sexual education, among other goals.[11] Supported by a growing number of medical experts, they rejected the idea of sex as biologically necessary and came to see sex with prostitutes as being especially harmful. Reform groups helped to end the Saint Louis experiment with regulated prostitution and strongly resisted other attempts at reglementation. As the Chicago Vice Commission—one of many moral reform organizations established to study the twin problems of prostitution and venereal disease—stated in its 1911 report, "Prostitution is pregnant with disease, a disease infecting not only the guilty but contaminating the innocent wife and child in the home with sickening certainty almost inconceivable; a disease to be feared as a leprous plague; a disease scattering misery broadcast, and leaving in its wake sterility, insanity, paralysis, and the blinded eyes of little babes, the twisted limbs of deformed children, degradation, physical rot and mental decay."[12]

In 1917, public outcry arose over the moral conditions many believed army recruits would face during their military service. One mother of an inducted soldier wrote to President Woodrow Wilson, saying, "We are praying you will make camp life clean for boys [who] are willing to offer their bodies as sacrifice for their country, but not their souls."[13] The Wilson administration took such concerns seriously. Wilson's Secretary of War, Newton D. Baker, the progressive ex-mayor of Cleveland, required little convincing that the unprecedented level of conscription presented tremendous opportunities and dangers.[14] Casting his arguments in terms of rationality and social science, Baker suggested that the army's training camps be organized along the lines of the new urban spaces envisioned by progressive social reformers: not squalid, disorderly urban ghettos teeming with immigrants, as they imagined them, but orderly and clean planned communities. The army's thirty-two new training camps, each housing up to forty thousand soldiers, would keep the trainees busy with wholesome activities. "Wholesome recreation," Baker contended, "[is] the best possible cure for irregularities in conduct which arise from idleness and the baser temptations."[15]

Camp Beauregard, built just outside the small city of Alexandria, Louisiana, was one such camp. Camp Beauregard, Alexandria, and New Orleans—the closest large city where soldiers from Beauregard would travel—were all sites of intense surveillance regimes instituted by army and federal civilian officials to monitor soldiers' sexual activities. These efforts to observe and control inductees' sexual activities would have tremendous effects on prostitutes and other women with whom soldiers came into contact throughout Louisiana. The racial politics of Louisiana and the camp, host to white and black soldiers who would come into sexual contact with women of various races, served only to complicate the army's efforts. While the U.S. Army monitored the sex lives of soldiers and enforced army regulations pertaining to sexuality at Beauregard, it did not act alone. Because soldier sexuality and sexual "cleanliness" were of such great concern to many influential moral reformers, the War Department's newly created Commission on Training Camp Activities (CTCA) worked hand in hand with the army to enforce and expand sexual surveillance and law enforcement. Indeed, CTCA officials at Beauregard were more interested in antivice efforts than their military counterparts. Much of the army's and the CTCA's efforts at Beauregard focused on the dangers posed by prostitutes and "promiscuous" women, though both organizations acknowledged that their efforts could not prevent some army recruits from contracting sexually transmitted diseases. Soldiers found to have contracted venereal diseases were quarantined and treated before they could be sent off to war. Camp Beauregard offers a microcosm for examining the sexual concerns of the U.S. Army and federal officials during the American war mobilization effort, as the camp was a focal point for all of the debates and anxieties about the sexual activities of soldiers—and the feared effects of those activities on both soldiers' bodies and American society writ large—that swept through the United States during World War I.

The Creation of the Commission on Training Camp Activities

The U.S. Congress formally declared war on Germany on April 6, 1917. Just eleven days later, the Wilson administration created the CTCA, a federal agency run by civilians working under the auspices of the War Department.[16] The CTCA was assigned several linked goals. First, it would have overall responsibility for providing athletic training and wholesome recreation for soldiers during their stay in the training camps. Additionally, it would attempt to eliminate red-light districts near training camps and other military bases. While the CTCA tended to emphasize its training and recreation functions in the camps, the creation of "moral zones," as they came to be called, around the camps and the related campaign against vice quickly became the core of its work. In keeping with the doctrine of "social hygiene" espoused by many progressives, red-light districts were often discussed as sources of moral as well as medical contagion. As one official stated, "To drain a red-light district and destroy therefore a breeding place of syphilis and gonorrhea is as logical as it is to drain a swamp and destroy thereby a breeding place of malaria and yellow fever."[17] The head of the CTCA, Raymond B. Fosdick, a politically well-connected attorney and social reformer, promoted legislation for the elimination of red-light districts, believing that it "would eliminate many of the evils that attended the presence of our army on the Mexican border last summer [during the Mexican Expedition in 1916–1917]."[18] Secretary Baker had dispatched Fosdick to survey the moral conditions near the U.S. Army's camps there at the insistence of the American Social Hygiene Association.[19] The goal of the CTCA's program would be soldiers who were happy and healthy, physically and morally fit, well versed in athletic skills, and free from venereal disease and moral corruption. The CTCA anticipated a much larger role for itself than merely preventing a few manpower losses due to venereal disease. The protection of soldiers from venereal disease, many CTCA officials and other progressives believed, would also help the nation after the war. This project thus became an integral part of a much larger program of social engineering, the ultimate goal of which was a newly ordered "civilized morality" leading to a better, postwar American society. This new, progressive American society would be remade based on the moral ideals of a mostly white (and specifically Anglo-Saxon), Protestant, middle- and upper-class, urban, northeastern social movement.[20]

As was common throughout the Progressive Era, women were frequently depicted as being of two types in CTCA literature: "pure" women who, like mothers, sisters, and chaste sweethearts of soldiers, aided the nation's war effort, and "impure" women who sought to seduce soldiers. The latter spread moral corruption and venereal disease throughout the army, working either explicitly or implicitly as agents of the enemy.[21] Soldiers were urged to be inspired by the former while avoiding the latter at all costs. Social class played an important role in this thinking, which was carried over from older, nineteenth-century notions about female sexuality. Working-class women—especially African American women and white immigrants—were often considered by the middle class to be sexually active if not actively working as prostitutes; this kind of woman was considered to be fundamentally different from middle-class women, who were generally assumed to be chaste and virginal until marriage and then would remain sexually faithful to their husbands thereafter.[22] Prostitutes, though, were not the only women to fear; moral reformers were also greatly concerned about "patriotic girls," especially flappers, who were believed by some to be particularly licentious, throwing themselves at men in uniform and tempting them sexually. Fosdick described this latter type as "hundreds of young girls, not yet prostitutes, who seem to have become hysterical at the sight of buttons and uniforms."[23] These concerns were rooted in biological theories of crime prevalent at the time, which held that there were two types of criminals: "congenital defectives" who were biologically predisposed to commit crimes, and those lured into crime by their environment. Criminals of the former type were seen as incorrigible, while the latter were products of unfortunate circumstances and could be reformed.[24] There were some women—professional prostitutes, for example—who were often considered to be "untreatable," while others (for example, girls who were merely enamored by men in uniform out of a misguided sense of patriotism) behaved inappropriately and immorally due to these temporary conditions. Women in this latter category, the CTCA hoped, might be reformed through strenuous effort. CTCA officials and sex education experts cast the war not just as a physical battle against Germany but also as a symbolic battle in which American men would protect "pure" women from sexual depredations and channel their energies into the war effort rather than sex, while also being protected from immoral women on the home front. The progressive model of soldierly masculinity would be "red-blooded" and virile, yet virginal and sexually pure.[25]

With American entry into World War I and the creation of the CTCA, the moral and physical dangers of prostitution came to be seen as a domestic threat to the health of American doughboys and the very health of the nation.[26] By tackling vices such as prostitution, progressives were able to confront other perceived social hazards.[27] The prostitute—and the social evil she embodied—was now an internal enemy, to be battled as part of a comprehensive American war effort. Every American training camp became a potential battlefield. One concerned reformer warned, "If by throwing this army into France we defeat the German arms but destroy the moral health of the young men who make up that army, then most assuredly will we have done more to destroy the foundations upon which democracy rests than we can possibly do to protect them."[28] A woman asked Fosdick, "Is it inevitable that our troops (trained here under fine social and moral conditions) must be exposed in Europe to the French policy of 'laissez-faire' in all things sexual?"[29] In a sharp contrast with the horror experienced by many Americans when the venereal inspection regime instituted by the army in the Philippines came to light in 1900, by 1918, thirty-two states had passed laws requiring regular medical inspections of prostitutes.[30] These new laws were certainly not without their critics, but the growing social hygiene movement had clearly made its mark on both the public mind-set and domestic legislation.

The development of the War Department's so-called American Plan to combat prostitution called for the arrest of women working as, or suspected of working as, prostitutes within five miles of military encampments.[31] These women, upon their arrest, were to be medically inspected. In addition to whatever criminal penalties they might incur as a result of a prostitution conviction, if found to be venereally infected, they were sent to hospitals, reformatories, or work camps until they were "cured." During the course of the war, more than thirty thousand infected women were imprisoned. Those sent to "detention homes" spent an average of 70 days there, while those sent to reformatories stayed an average of 365 days.[32] Under the American Plan, no men, civilian or military, were arrested.

Not all army officers accepted the CTCA's views on sexual morality. A number of CTCA and YMCA officials reported that many officers "assume[d] the necessity of illicit relations and base[d] their talks to the men and their instructions on that assumption."[33] On at least a few occasions, the CTCA worked with the War and Navy Departments to take disciplinary action against such officers.

Neither was the CTCA's campaign to eliminate red-light districts universally welcomed in local communities.[34] Some local officials and others profited from the status quo, while some citizens feared that the influx of soldiers into their communities would lead to rapes of local "respectable" women as the supply of commercial sex dried up. As one citizen said in a letter to his mayor, "I'm going to buy a pistol, sir. For twelve years I've lived in this town and never felt the need to protect my two womenfolks. What do you suppose will happen when 40,000 virile, red-blooded young men come here to train for the army and find the segregated [red-light] district wiped out? I know; and I'm going to buy that pistol, sir, and do it now!"[35] The CTCA attempted to address this fear by pointing out that the incidence of rapes and assaults against women had not increased in communities after the closure of their red-light districts, though it continued to meet resistance to its antivice programs throughout the war.[36]

CTCA Policies and Practices

Major Bascom Johnson, of the army's Sanitary Corps, was made director of the Law Enforcement Division of the CTCA soon after the commission was founded. He immediately began an inspection tour of the training camps. An expert in the new progressive "science of moral engineering," Johnson had previously gained national prominence in closing down San Francisco's infamous Barbary Coast red-light district under the 1914 California Injunction and Abatement Act.[37] The CTCA sent uniformed and undercover investigators into the cities nearest all U.S. Army training camps during World War I. Their weekly reports chronicled the availability of alcohol and prostitutes for soldiers. Investigators spoke with large numbers of individuals—civilians, local government officials, soldiers, and army officers—to map out (literally in some cases) dens of iniquity. They did not name the soldiers they found at these sites, but they did identify civilian purveyors of sex and alcohol. CTCA investigators also assessed the moral conditions they found in these communities and the efforts of local governments to clean them up.

Moral and social reformers, as well as many army medical officers, perceived a significant link between the use of alcohol by soldiers and venereal diseases.[38] Alcohol use had been tolerated within the U.S. Army in the nineteenth century. The growing influence of temperance advocates led to the congressionally mandated closure of U.S. Army canteens (cafeteria-style restaurants that served alcohol) on military posts in 1899. Civilian contractors were permitted to continue to sell alcohol on bases for another two years until this loophole was closed by further congressional action. By 1903, the army's Medical Department recommended the total prohibition of alcohol on medical and moral grounds, a measure approved by Lieutenant General Nelson A. Miles, Commanding General of the Army. Soldiers were continually reminded of the dangers of alcohol consumption and the sexual dangers to which alcohol use could lead. Just as alcohol was often conceptually linked with venereal disease, venereal disease was also frequently coupled with immoral conduct and behavior.[39] Unlike some other diseases at the time, the causes of venereal diseases were clearly understood and linked in the minds of many social crusaders with lapses in moral judgment. Because preantibiotic medical treatments and prophylactic measures for venereal diseases were ineffective or even hazardous, many medical authorities saw complete sexual abstinence as the only effective means of avoiding infection. Though condoms were available, and widely promoted by the German army, many American moralists, including Secretary of the Navy Josephus Daniels, feared that promoting the use of condoms would corrupt troops' morals.[40]

Baker urged a strong moral component in soldiers' training, stating, "We are sending into this contest [World War I] Americans of culture and high ideals—worthy of the cause they are going to defend."[41] That the War Department placed such emphasis on moral indoctrination suggests a lack of confidence that soldiers would make morally correct decisions absent such training. Baker also urged a strong anti–venereal disease component to their training, cautioning that "there are things that soldiers can bring home that are worse than wounds." Baker termed this overall moral training for American soldiers "invisible armor," suggesting that it would protect them not from German bullets but from the many moral perils he believed they would face.[42] In its 1918 annual report to the Secretary of War, the CTCA proudly touted its accomplishments in the area of sexual education, which primarily focused on warning of the dangers of venereal disease.[43] It claimed that more than two million trainees had received lectures on venereal disease; 2.7 million copies of the pamphlet *Keeping Fit to Fight*, on the same theme, had been distributed to soldiers; and the companion film *Fit to Fight* had been widely shown at army training camps.[44] In many cases, the CTCA and the U.S. Army provided the first sex education that the soldiers had ever received, as it was not commonly provided in American schools at the time (and fewer than 18% of World War I enlistees had even attended high school, with many fewer actually graduating). The military saw itself as "demythologizing" sex for soldiers by bringing it into frank, open, public discourse.[45]

Soldiers were repeatedly cautioned to avoid sex. They were instructed that their masculinity did not require them to be sexually active, and in fact that it was manly to be chaste. The masculine ideal advocated for doughboys by the CTCA closely linked self-control over sexual impulses and venereal "cleanliness" with manhood. As *Keeping Fit to Fight* urged, "Will-power and courage go together. A venereal disease contracted after deliberate exposure through intercourse with a prostitute, is as much of a disgrace as showing the white feather [exhibiting cowardice]. . . . Every man can by self-control restrain the indulgence of the imprudent and reckless impulses that so often lead men astray, and he who thus resists is a better soldier and a better man than the man of weaker will who allows his bodily appetites to rule him."[46] Soldiers were bluntly warned to "shun illicit intercourse as you would the Plague."[47] "It is not true," said one lecture, "that the absence of previous sexual experience is any handicap to a man entering the married state. On the contrary, the man who comes to his bride as clean and as true as he expects that she will come to him will find the most perfect joy in the married state. All the sexual knowledge he requires he can readily secure from his family physician before marriage."[48] In a poem widely promulgated by the War Department, soldiers were urged to "come back clean" and pledge,

> The blood in my veins shall leave no stains
> On the bride or the babes unborn
> And the scars my body shall carry
> Shall not be from deeds obscene.[49]

Women were frequently depicted as both alluring and dangerous to men's health. "Does any red-blooded man feel any doubt of his ability to preserve his manhood though tempted by the alluring seductions of voluptuous and beautiful women in the whirl and excitement of the gay metropolis, or the fascinations that may come to you from delicate and devoted attentions in the solitude of remote billets?"[50] A fraternal organization's newspaper editorial titled "Shoot Them for Traitors" warned, "They say that nasty beasts in the shape of women have established abiding places near the cantonments and there spread their vile nets for Our Boys." It went on to add that "a German bullet is a blessing beside the thing she will give your boy."[51] The CTCA's *Keeping Fit to Fight* pamphlet warned, "If you go with a prostitute, you endanger your country because you risk your health, and perhaps your life. You lessen the man-power of your company and throw extra burdens on your comrades. You are a moral shirker."[52]

Fear was a common theme in the CTCA and army sexual education programs. As one doctor put it, "The sexual instinct is imperative"—reflecting a common belief in the irrepressibility of the male sex drive—"and will only listen to fear. Ninety-nine out of one hundred persons could be frightened into being good by the fear of evil consequences."[53] Giving in to sexual urges, the men were warned, could be a danger to their health. "Over-exercise or excitement of the sex-glands may exhaust and weaken a man. . . . The sex feelings are so powerful and the risk so great if they are turned loose, that it is common sense not to play with fire."[54] Indeed, by being abstinent, they were told, they would be fortifying their manhood: "Live strong and clean, and save every drop of your strength and manhood for the supreme experience. You have a right to demand this of yourself. Demand it. Secure it. By refraining from illicit intercourse you will defeat the deadly enemy and preserve your own manhood. . . . Sex organs do not have to be exercised or indulged in, in order to develop them, or preserve virility. Forget them, don't think about them, or dwell upon them. Live a good vigorous life and they will take care of themselves."[55] The CTCA likewise made appeals to the idea of military efficiency: "A man who is thinking below the belt is not efficient."[56]

The CTCA's sexual education program continually stressed that if soldiers failed to remain abstinent, they should immediately seek chemical prophylaxis from army medical officers.[57] These "prophylactic" treatments consisted of cleansing the penis with a mercuric solution; injecting into the urethra a protargol (silver salt) solution, which then had to be held inside the penis for several hours; coating the penis with calomel ointment; and then wrapping it with waxed paper, which also had to be left on for several hours. Such treatments were a somewhat controversial addition to the army's overall sexual education program, especially since many moralists believed that the availability of prophylaxis would only encourage illicit sex and increase the possibility of contracting venereal diseases. CTCA officials, like many progressives, were strong advocates of science and efficiency, so it is not surprising that the CTCA would advocate reliance on medical science to treat the venereal problem rather than rely solely on a sense of personal morality among soldiers. The powerful American Social Hygiene Association, a close ally of the CTCA, did, however, urge that soldiers be cautioned as to the potentially limited efficacy of venereal prophylaxis, lest they be too freely encouraged to engage in sexual relations with the mistaken belief that the army's physicians could readily cure any venereal infections they might contract.[58]

The CTCA lectured civilians who lived near army bases as well as soldiers on matters of sex, with one lecturer warning, "Girls must be made to realize that they bear a responsibility to the soldier and that their patriotic duty is to avoid weakening the soldier's devotion to his country's best interests by arousing his emotions to a pitch which will tend to divide that devotion."[59] A female CTCA lecturer asked American women, a new target for progressives' sexual education campaigns,[60] "Did you ever stop to ask yourself what might be the effect upon young men of the kind of clothes you wear? The too transparent waists, showing plainly all the underwear beneath, the dresses cut too low in the neck, the gowns that cling too closely to the figure—what are these but suggestions to young men to think only of the physical charms of these young feminine creatures, and of nothing else?"[61] These admonishments, of course, shifted the responsibility of sexual continence from the soldiers onto the civilian women who, while not considered prostitutes, still constituted a grave danger to American soldiers.

The CTCA's work extended well beyond sexual education; it also actively used its quasi–law enforcement powers to close down 110 red-light districts throughout the nation.[62] Thirty-five of these districts would have been shut down by the congressional mandate to eliminate all such districts within five miles of a military base or training camp, but the other 75—those outside the five-mile zone—were closed as a direct result of CTCA action. The goal of this program was not merely the elimination of the legally sanctioned institution of prostitution but rather "the eradication from the field of the prostitute herself."[63]

While the CTCA sought to mitigate or eliminate the deleterious effects of venereal disease, its work, and criticism of prostitutes, had a strong moral tone. The CTCA sought to reshape the attitudes of women toward sex and venereal disease. To this end, the CTCA produced many sex-education pamphlets and other materials targeted at women. In one such pamphlet, *Women's Share in a National Service*, the CTCA attempted to expose fallacious beliefs among women about sex and venereal disease. It denied, for example, that "sexual indulgence was a necessity for young men" and asserted that women "should know little of sexual matters—and never discuss them."[64] Instead, the CTCA stated that there was no necessity for either men or women to have sex and that it was dangerous to engage in "irregular sexual relations." The exact meaning of this term is unelaborated, but presumably it included all pre- and extra-marital sexual activities. As part of this effort, the CTCA fought hard against the conventional wisdom that prostitution was a "necessary evil" and actively sought to describe prostitution instead as "the ancient and unnecessary evil."[65] The CTCA also promoted the idea that women had a responsibility "to themselves . . . to their community, their country, and their future" to curb their sexual activities. "Desire," they were told, "is a fatal excuse."[66]

The CTCA was not just interested in making it more difficult for soldiers to come into contact with prostitutes. It was also concerned with reforming and rehabilitating women who had chosen to pursue a life of prostitution. To this end, it dispatched 150 female fieldworkers to military camps with the task of ensuring that women arrested for prostitution would receive venereal inspections and treatment if needed, and finding them alternative employment after they were released from arrest.[67] In cases in which no alternative work could be found, the women were sent to state work camps or farms, and the CTCA encouraged the creation of additional work camps in states where they

did not already exist.[68] Here, inmates performed agricultural or light industrial labor and received training in domestic chores (sewing, laundry, hand-
crafts, and the like) and a modicum of academics. They were also exposed to
middle-class culture, including the "humanizing and socializing effect of good
music."[69]

Camp Beauregard and CTCA Investigations in Alexandria, Louisiana

Camp Beauregard, like all thirty-two new army training camps constructed
in 1917, became the site of intense scrutiny and law enforcement action by
the CTCA as part of a broader program to address the concerns of moral reformers regarding the physical and moral dangers soldiers would face before
ever even deploying to Europe. Camp Beauregard's population reached its peak
in January 1918, when 24,661 soldiers were stationed there, with the camp's
population falling to a low point of just 4,173 in August 1918 after the Thirty-
Ninth Infantry Division left Camp Beauregard and deployed to Europe.[70] Most
of the troops sent to Beauregard were white southerners, mostly from Louisiana, with minorities from Mississippi, Arkansas, and the Panama Canal Zone
(this last group included 670 men described by the army as "Porto Ricans").[71]
Smaller numbers of African American men—fewer than 1,000 at the peak in
October 1918—also trained at Camp Beauregard in segregated units.[72] The civilian settlement closest to the camp was the relatively small town of Alexandria, Louisiana, located just over five miles away, whose population of 17,510 in
1920 was dwarfed by that of Camp Beauregard for much of the war.

Before the first CTCA official arrived in Alexandria, the presence of saloons
selling alcohol and "other evils"—meaning prostitution, available in Alexandria's
small red-light district—had already begun to alarm Charles H. Brough, the
governor of Arkansas.[73] A newly elected progressive, Brough wrote to Secretary Baker in July 1917 expressing concern that the six thousand Arkansan
National Guard soldiers who were about to be deployed to Camp Beauregard
would be exposed to vice during their training. Baker reassured Brough that
he planned to take action soon, stating that "the evil referred to will be eliminated."[74] Arkansas Representative William A. Oldfield also wrote to Baker, urging him to create a dry zone around the camp and to be mindful of the sexual
dangers that Arkansas's finest might face in Louisiana.[75] Baker passed Oldfield's
concern on to Fosdick, head of the CTCA, who assured Oldfield that the
CTCA, as part of the War Department, would protect the soldiers stationed

at Camp Beauregard "so far as is humanly possible from the moral dangers which have frequently attended military life in the past."[76] He went on to suggest that if the moral situation at Beauregard could not be brought under control, the camp would be moved. It is unclear how sincere this remark was, as moving a camp during wartime would have significantly delayed training and deployment and led to considerable political (and military) fallout.

Reports of the moral conditions in Alexandria began to pour into the CTCA even before significant numbers of soldiers had begun to populate Camp Beauregard. One civilian reformer who traveled to the area was aghast at the existence of a red-light district in town. This man, P. L. Gillett, a YMCA official who had served in China, described the situation: "For bald abandon and brazen shamelessness, Alexandria beats Shanghai, and we who have been living in the Orient have repeatedly heard that 'Shanghai is the most immoral city in the world.'"[77] Gillett also reported that soldiers on leave in Alexandria changed out of their uniforms before visiting the red-light district so that they would not be accosted by military police. In July, another social reformer conducted an investigation of Alexandria's red-light district, often referred to as the Line, describing the area as a small island containing roughly twenty houses of prostitution. Most were two- or three-story homes with large electric signs, each housing between six and ten prostitutes.[78] Camp Beauregard's provost marshal sent a small detachment of soldiers to guard the bridge to the island, but they had no authority over civilians and could not be sure who to stop and ask for identification. When the undercover investigator visited several of the Line's brothels, he reported that soldiers danced with and eventually went upstairs with prostitutes, some of whom were described by their madams as "French" or "perverts." While the exact meaning of these terms is unclear, in other contexts during World War I, the terms were used to describe prostitutes willing to engage in oral sex with clients.[79] The investigator noted that there was no visible prostitution in any part of town outside the red-light or "segregated district." He spoke with several officers and soldiers helping to construct Camp Beauregard. One officer expressed surprise that Alexandria had such a "fine [red-light] district." A soldier told him, "It's the finest [red-light district] I ever saw and I've hit them all. Wait until the men arrive, we'll take possession of this place." Confirming the social reformer's worst fear, the soldier added, "I'll bet every soldier boy will have a piece of —— to sleep with every night [redaction in original]."[80]

Bascom Johnson conducted the initial CTCA investigation of Alexandria, Louisiana, in early September 1917 as part of a national tour of all cities near army camps and naval ports.[81] Johnson immediately set up a meeting with both Major General Henry Clay Hodges Jr., commander of Camp Beauregard, and Alexandria city officials to discuss cleaning up the town "by amicable arrangement." The mayor of Alexandria, W. W. Whittington Jr., had, according to Johnson, promised that "if the city got the camp, they would clean up." At this meeting, the mayor proposed moving the red-light district so that it would be at least five miles away from the camp, but Johnson—supported by Hodges—said this was insufficient and that the district would have to be closed. The civilian officials objected to this because a local ordinance (No. 66) made prostitution legal within the district.[82] Johnson noted that this was a violation of federal law and began a series of additional meetings with local officials to ensure that the district would be closed. The City of Alexandria then passed another ordinance (No. 244) on September 4, 1917, repealing the earlier ordinance that legalized prostitution within the segregated district and making prostitution within Alexandria a misdemeanor punishable by a fine of ten to one hundred dollars.[83] To further "protect" the camp's soldiers, Hodges agreed to post guards to prevent soldiers from entering the city's "negro district," which the city engineer helpfully identified on a map.[84] Johnson was concerned that a new red-light district would be reopened outside town, and therefore in an area not geographically covered by city ordinances. He met with T. A. Carter, the Rapides Parish attorney, who hinted that the mayor and city commissioners were corrupt and would allow prostitution to continue in some clandestine manner. Carter pledged to do what he could to prevent this from happening.[85] Johnson was also concerned with rumors that married women in the town were of "low morals," a comment possibly related to the inferred ethnic heritage of many in the local population, which included many non-Anglo-Saxon immigrants and Creoles. He stated that he "came away with the very distinct impression that the whole moral tone of the town was lower than that of any city I visited except New Orleans." He concluded that Alexandria was in "the downward pull of legalized vice, and party to the demoralizing influence of New Orleans and the easy going attitude of the French population."[86] Johnson ended his report by noting that the city and its officials would require constant surveillance by the CTCA.

Several weeks later in September, a second CTCA investigator, George J. Anderson, who headed the CTCA's Section on Vice and Liquor Control, conducted a follow-up visit to Alexandria. Anderson reported that Alexandria's notorious red-light district had indeed closed just a few days before his visit, as required by the new legislation.[87] He noted that many of the men he questioned in town now had no idea where to find commercial sex workers. Several locals were in disbelief that the brothels had actually closed, but Anderson reported them all to be vacated. The prostitutes had left en masse, mainly via rail, for other cities, including Shreveport, New Orleans, and Houston. While the largest sex establishments had been closed, Anderson reported fleeting evidence that some prostitutes still worked in town, out of hotels or in rented rooms in boarding houses. Anderson met with the mayor during his visit and was not impressed, describing the mayor as "without the least moral backbone in these matters." During this interview, the mayor expressed his belief in the geographic segregation of prostitution, and noted that other local officials also favored it, but was willing to comply with federal requirements to maintain the economic benefits of having Camp Beauregard located near the town.[88] Anderson also met the local chief of police, in whom he had much more confidence, largely because the chief was opposed to prostitution. In the chief of police's view, the existence of the red-light district served to increase both the supply of and the demand for commercialized sex. The chief reported that one local prostitute, when he informed her that the district was to be closed, stated, "Well, I ain't sorry. If there'd never been a damned district, I'd never been a whore!"[89]

Johnson's and Anderson's visits paved the way for a permanent CTCA investigator to be stationed at Camp Beauregard. Starting in November 1917, First Lieutenant Thomas A. Larremore of the army's Sanitary Corps began a longer-term investigation of Alexandria. A staunch progressive who believed in strong federal antivice efforts, Larremore was pessimistic about moral conditions in town. When he arrived just two months after the closure of the red-light district, he found a number of prostitutes soliciting customers in the streets, both on foot and from automobiles, and there were rumors that more worked in city hotels.[90] A brothel, newly set up after the Line's closure, had just been raided by local police, and there were rumors of another elsewhere in town.[91] Larremore also noted the presence of a number of women around town who, while not overtly advertising themselves as prostitutes, were much more forward with and talkative to soldiers and other male passersby than he expected or was comfortable with. He suspected that many of these women were at least occasional prostitutes or "not above making a 'date.'"[92] Local police had made six arrests of prostitutes in both October and November, most of which resulted in convictions with some time served. The remainder of the women's sentences was suspended if they agreed to leave town and not return.[93]

By mid-December, Larremore noted an increase in prostitution in Alexandria and stated that he found local civilian authorities to be relatively uncooperative, ostensibly because they lacked the resources to root out prostitutes and illegal liquor sales. The chief of police in Alexandria sought to "pass the buck," as Larremore described it, by foisting the job of eradicating prostitution in Alexandria onto Camp Beauregard's military police (who did not have arrest powers over civilians), stating that his police would then arrest any civilians detained by the military police.[94] Questions over jurisdiction and allocation of police resources remained a continual struggle throughout the course of the war. But Larremore also implied that the local government's goals differed from those of the CTCA. "They are unwilling to interpret individual laws in favor of the [federal] government unless a person is guilty beyond the slightest shadow of a doubt. . . . People down in this country seem very unwilling to go after these women in a thorough and methodical way."[95] He went on to urge the passage of new federal legislation or the extension of the authority of military police or additional plainclothes investigators with arrest powers to combat prostitution.

Larremore and T. A. Carter, the local parish attorney, both interested in improving local antivice capabilities, sought to have soldiers from Camp Beauregard (military police or others) deputized and available to make arrests in Alexandria because of the limited number of local civilian police and deputy sheriffs. The judge advocate at Camp Beauregard, a National Guard soldier and civilian attorney from New Orleans, strenuously objected, citing the Posse Comitatus Act, passed in 1878, which substantially limited the ability of the federal government to use the military for law enforcement.[96] Larremore described a city in which prostitutes openly offered their services on the streets and in local restaurants and hotels, with the women usually taking their clients to local hotels to complete their sexual transactions. Larremore observed many of these interactions between soldiers and prostitutes himself, though he also developed an extensive network of informants, many of them middle-class women who lived in town, including the local postmistress. He worked closely with the commander of the camp's military police unit, whom he described as both eager and cooperative. Larremore found General Ira A. Haynes, the new commander of the Thirty-Ninth Infantry, the primary unit stationed at Camp Beauregard, to be less helpful than he had initially expected, since Haynes declined to provide any soldiers to assist in Larremore's investigations.[97] Undoubtedly Haynes had other manpower priorities in his preparations for deployment to France later in 1918. Clearly soldiers from Camp Beauregard engaged in commercial sex transactions with prostitutes, as prostitutes were observed working near the camp and soldiers were frequently seen in town with women known or suspected to be prostitutes. However, very few arrests of soldiers on prostitution-related charges were ever made, even when the women they were caught with were arrested as prostitutes.[98] One sergeant was arrested while engaged in sex with a prostitute at a hotel, but because of a procedural error and a seeming reluctance among civilian police and prosecutors to proceed with the case, no prosecution or court-martial ensued.[99] There was clearly a double standard operating in Alexandria, as elsewhere during the war, in which prostitutes were arrested when caught, while their male clients were hardly ever arrested or charged.

While most of the soldiers that CTCA officials reported as interacting with prostitutes were enlisted men, the CTCA also noted the involvement of some officers with the women. Larremore uncovered an officer (his name and rank unstated) who had been "holding intercourse" with a woman who lived in Alexandria, ostensibly working as a maid, and noted that other officers had been "having access" to this woman as well.[100] Another commissioned officer was placed under observation by the military police for his involvement with two prostitutes, but the case did not proceed for reasons that remain unclear.[101] A report of a lieutenant's wife who was rumored to be infected with syphilis and dating a sergeant smacked of little more than gossip and innuendo, as with many vice leads, and likewise did not amount to anything.[102] Two more officers were rebuked, though not court-martialed, one for cohabiting with a woman not his wife, and one for "holding occasional intercourse" with a woman carefully not described as a prostitute.[103] Though these matters were all separately brought to the attention of Camp Beauregard's chief of staff by a colonel, no courts-martial resulted, reflecting a difference in the behavioral standards and self-policing within the officer corps, as well as a lack of evidence and investigatory priority. Additionally, by December, at least some prostitutes had learned that if they told local law enforcement that they were officers' wives when questioned, they would be let go without arrest, as local officials were extremely reluctant to prosecute women they believed to be associated with military officers.[104]

CTCA officials stationed at Camp Beauregard also frequently commented on the character of the women they investigated, including those not believed to be actively engaged in prostitution. In following up on a lead provided to him by "Miss Herbert of the Patriotic League," Larremore discovered that a soldier at Camp Beauregard had impregnated a woman out of wedlock who was then living in Alexandria. While he did not consider the woman to be a prostitute, he considered her "equally to blame, for she is several years the older [than the soldier]."[105] At least three teenage girls followed soldiers from Arkansas to Louisiana.[106] In one of these cases, a sixteen-year-old girl from Little Rock followed a soldier to Alexandria and got a job as a restaurant cashier to be near him. She was forced out of town by local authorities and returned to Little Rock under the escort of a female YWCA worker. Her morals were questioned, though she denied being a prostitute. The other two girls were at least temporarily allowed to remain in town, though both CTCA and local police officials decided to keep them under surveillance because they suspected the girls might turn to prostitution. These anxieties about civilian women are in keeping with a common theme of concern regarding sexually predatory women who acted as independent sexual agents and might tempt soldiers, whom CTCA officials and others seemed to consider young, naïve, and impressionable. Larremore also criticized local women for having too much "facial adornment," as their use of cosmetics "seem[ed] so well nigh universal here that one can hardly use that as a distinguishing feature between the sheep and the goats."[107] Differing regional- and class-based ideas about the propriety of women's behavior seemed to provide at least one source of tension between progressive reformers and local southerners.

CTCA officials described a kind of hierarchy of prostitutes and brothels in Alexandria. Lowest on the list were African American prostitutes operating out of a part of town colloquially known as Niggertown. Soldiers sometimes traveled to this area in search of sex, particularly to an establishment that Larremore described as "a combination whore-and-assignation-house largely used by 'white niggers.'"[108] While Larremore left his exact meaning of that latter term unclear, he clearly held particular disdain for white soldiers who had sex with black women, and "flashily dressed" black women were universally suspected of prostitution.[109] Police raids of black saloons and other places that soldiers patronized for alcohol and sex seemed to take place on a weekly or biweekly basis.[110] Reflecting popular beliefs at the time among many whites that African Americans were disproportionately infected with venereal disease, one CTCA report estimated that as many as 70 percent of the blacks living in Alexandria were infected, without providing any support for such a claim. Alexandria's mayor placed particular blame on black females: "We have a large negro population and as you well know the female of this race are unmoral."[111] Given these views, it is not surprising that the CTCA particularly sought to prevent the (mostly white) soldiers stationed at Camp Beauregard from coming into sexual contact with local black women.

CTCA officials were interested in the physical, as well as the moral, well-being of the soldiers at Camp Beauregard. Larremore was concerned with the sexual education of soldiers, particularly lectures describing venereal disease and its prevention, and the medical inspections of soldiers' bodies for venereal disease. While Larremore was impressed with the training, enthusiasm, and cooperation of the army doctors at Camp Beauregard, other, nonmedical officers usually provided the sexual education for soldiers at the camp. Larremore sat in on some of these lectures because he wanted to "ascertain how perfunctory these had become," seeming to indicate he had already made up his mind. He was "a bit skeptical as to the sort of lecture some officers [he] ha[d] met would put forth."[112] Clearly, not all army officers shared the concerns of the CTCA regarding the importance of anti–venereal disease education and prophylaxis.

Larremore reported that venereal inspections occurred twice a month at Camp Beauregard and had detected only a small number of venereal infections; the last inspection performed before this particular weekly report detected only a single infection. However, he also noted that when another recent inspection had been performed unannounced, it had caught four additional venereal cases, "most of them long standing,"[113] probably indicating either that soldiers were becoming adept at concealing their venereal infections or that the inspection procedures themselves were deficient. In analyzing the camp medical records, he found that while venereal prophylaxis at the camp generally seemed to be effective, approximately 10 percent of those who contracted venereal diseases had also received prophylaxis treatments. This figure, if accurate, is better than that at other locations, particularly in Europe, during World War I.[114]

The CTCA was also interested in stamping out venereal disease among those civilians with whom soldiers from the camp might come into sexual contact. Its officials at Camp Beauregard sought to work with the U.S. Public Health Service and local officials to set up a venereal clinic to treat local prostitutes and others who might be infected. In fall 1917, Larremore caught a syphilitic bootlegger, which made him particularly concerned about the prevalence of venereal diseases "among the negroes" in Alexandria. It was unclear to CTCA officials whether the CTCA had the authority to require infected civilians to receive venereal treatments if they did not wish to do so.[115] (It did not; the CTCA only had direct jurisdiction over members of the military.)

While the CTCA got the City of Alexandria to end its legal endorsement of prostitution within a segregated red-light district, the agency's limitations also came into sharp relief: the red-light district was shut down and prostitution's formal legal umbrella removed, but prostitution as an institution around Camp Beauregard abided. Prostitutes continued to operate around the camp in a dispersed and clandestine fashion, tending to solicit clientele on the streets and in local hotels. As a CTCA report from April 1918 makes clear, "No great agitation under way to clean up tho' Police are still nibbling. . . . There seems no determined effort being made to rid Alexandria of 'home town girls.' Friday night, standing with the desk Sergeant of Police watching Cloud's saloon, a pair of 'the type' passed and the sergeant told me one of them was one who had recently outrun Miss Shields, the [CTCA's] Protective Officer, and made a getaway. He made no effort to catch her. She is said to be related by blood to one of the police."[116]

The episode highlights the philosophical and practical differences between supporters of the segregation of prostitution (that is, those who sought to maintain a controlled but legalized system of prostitution in a segregated area, as the mayor of Alexandria and other local elites did) and those who sought the complete elimination of prostitution (the majority progressive view, and the official position of the CTCA and the War Department). The situation was greatly complicated by the economic positions of those who favored the segregation of vice. While these individuals clearly received financial benefits from the continuation of a red-light district, they also perceived clear economic benefits from the presence of Camp Beauregard near the town, and they were forced to accede to the CTCA's demands, which also had the weight of federal law behind them. As the CTCA's 1918 annual report admitted, the nationwide closure of red-light districts had only forced prostitutes to relocate to "less convenient and more hazardous places," which, ironically, made rooting out the vestiges of prostitution all the more difficult. To combat this problem, the CTCA advocated eliminating the prostitute herself, rather than the institution of prostitution; the solution, it suggested, "lies in the eradication from the field the prostitute herself, and this is at present the leading feature of . . . activity."[117] By the end of the war, the CTCA had detained more than thirty thousand women, sending many to reformatories, workhouses, and camps; roughly half were judged to be prostitutes infected with venereal diseases.[118] The remaining fifteen thousand women were mostly considered to be in the somewhat nebulous category of "promiscuous girl."[119]

Venereal Disease at Camp Beauregard

Even with the aid of the CTCA, the U.S. Army was never able to prevent all sexual contact between soldiers at Camp Beauregard and women in the surrounding community, nor was it able to prevent all soldiers from becoming infected with venereal diseases during their time at the camp. When soldiers reported for duty in the army, within the first days or weeks of their induction, they were given a battery of medical tests. The army's physicians found that as many as 25 percent of all newly inducted recruits were infected with venereal diseases, and assessed that five-sixths of these cases were contracted before induction.[120] Two army doctors argued that "the amount of venereal disease contracted by the men after putting on the uniform is astonishingly small, while the amount of chronic venereal disease brought to the Army from civil life is a serious burden."[121] This made venereal treatment of army recruits

an immediate and top priority, but—despite the assurances of these two doctors that doughboys rarely contracted venereal diseases once they entered the
army—the army's ineffective prophylaxis efforts (that is, treatments administered after infection would have already occurred) remained the main thrust
of the army's overall anti–venereal disease campaign.

Camp Beauregard had its own base hospital, staffed by twenty-two army
physicians and 123 enlisted men working as nurses and orderlies.[122] These
medical personnel also provided support for Camp Beauregard's venereal
segregation camp, which housed all men found to be infected with venereal
diseases. (Men infected with other types of diseases were not so segregated at
the camp.) Venereal treatment at Camp Beauregard was described as using
"the usual methods,"[123] which included segregation in the separate venereal
camp, surrounded by barbed-wire fences policed by armed sentries.[124] In no
way was venereal segregation a leisurely duty assignment, and it was made
clear to all that soldiers diagnosed with venereal infections were "inmates"
and prisoners, and not merely medical patients. A prophylaxis station in
nearby Alexandria was considered but never constructed because it "was not
considered to be of sufficient value to be warranted."[125]

The venereal segregation area was originally designed to house up to two
thousand men at one time, though by the fall of 1918 (just before the Armistice was signed), the army planned to expand the facility to as many as six
thousand beds.[126] If the war had continued, the venereal segregation camp
would have included not just men who had become infected at Camp Beauregard but venereal cases returning home from Europe as well. Two thousand
beds at a camp that never housed more than twenty-four thousand soldiers
meant that army planners expected up to 8 percent of the men at Camp Beauregard to be infected with venereal diseases at any given time. This turned
out to be much higher than the actual rates experienced during the war. While
venereal diseases were detected in up to a quarter of new recruits at induction, relatively few of these men were segregated and made unavailable for
training because their old infections did not result in debilitating symptoms.
As table 3 demonstrates, venereal disease, while constituting a significant *perceived* threat, never resulted in large numbers of "noneffectives"—that is, men
who had to be placed in venereal segregation and thus made unable to perform their military duties at Camp Beauregard. Only in three months during
1918 did medical admissions for venereal infections reach 9–16 percent of all
medical admissions; for the remainder of the war, venereal admissions hovered around 2–4 percent of total medical admissions. In absolute terms, venereal admissions at Camp Beauregard were minimal. There were fewer than
2,100 men admitted for venereal infections at the camp, out of well over 30,000

men who passed through Camp Beauregard throughout the entirety of the war.[127] On a monthly basis, there were an average of 11.9 men per 1,000 (1.19% of the total) admitted for venereal diseases. In the worst month at Camp Beauregard for venereal admissions—August 1918, which included all the men who were unable to deploy to Europe with their comrades in the Thirty-Ninth Division because they were too sick—only 4 percent of the men at the camp were infected with venereal diseases. The CTCA believed that its anti–venereal disease training efforts to dissuade men from having illicit sex with women who might be infected with venereal diseases were effective. Superficially, the low venereal infection rates at Camp Beauregard would seem to bear this out. The Camp Beauregard rates were certainly lower than those of the American Expeditionary Forces in France during the war, the American forces in Germany immediately after the war, and U.S. Army units stationed in Hawaii and, especially, the Philippines. There were few African American men at Camp Beauregard, and this undoubtedly also improved Beauregard's statistics, as venereal disease rates were commonly higher among black soldiers than white soldiers. Regardless, it is apparent that venereal disease was not a seriously debilitating problem for the army at Camp Beauregard despite—or because of—the significant emphasis the army placed on anti–venereal disease efforts, though it is impossible to ascertain the degree to which the anti–venereal disease campaigns influenced venereal infection rates.

Accurately assessing venereal disease rates in the general American population in the first four decades of the twentieth century is difficult because neither the federal government nor any other organization undertook such studies on a national basis. The few studies that were done were generally sponsored by moral reform groups that reported significant venereal disease outbreaks as part of their efforts to attract greater public attention and support for moral reform, casting serious doubts on the credibility of these studies' findings. One such study in 1901 estimated that as many as 80 percent of American men in New York City had at one point been infected with gonorrhea, which the study considered the most prevalent disease in the adult male population. This study also estimated that 5–18 percent of adult American males were then currently infected with syphilis. A 1911 study of all men admitted to Massachusetts General Hospital found that 35.5 percent had gonorrhea. Reemphasizing the commonly held belief that prostitutes were the primary source of venereal contagion, studies from 1906 and 1914 estimated that 75–90 percent of New York prostitutes harbored venereal disease. Women's correctional institutions of the time reported that 70–80 percent of female inmates were venereally infected.[128] Venereal disease must have been relatively common in an era lacking any truly effective treatments for venereal disease

Table 3. Venereal disease rates, Camp Beauregard, Louisiana, 1917–1919

YEAR	MONTH	TOTAL ENLISTED MEN	TOTAL WHITE ENLISTED MEN	TOTAL BLACK ENLISTED MEN	TOTAL ADMISSIONS FROM ALL DISEASES, ENLISTED MEN	TOTAL ADMISSIONS FROM ALL VENEREAL DISEASES, ALL ENLISTED MEN	VENEREAL DISEASE ADMISSIONS AS % OF ALL DISEASE ADMISSIONS	% ALL MEN ADMITTED FOR VENEREAL DISEASE
1917	September	4,193	4,193	0	NA	77	NA	1.84
	October	7,007	7,007	0	NA	57	NA	0.81
	November	16,986	16,986	0	NA	165	NA	0.97
	December	19,279	19,279	0	NA	122	NA	0.63
1918	January	23,657	23,657	0	3,394	137	4.0	0.58
	February	20,821	20,821	0	2,354	109	4.6	0.52
	March	21,561	21,561	0	2,981	101	3.4	0.47
	April	19,349	19,349	0	3,100	137	4.4	0.71
	May	19,888	19,882	6	2,284	250	10.9	1.26
	June	18,980	18,967	13	1,824	165	9.0	0.87
	July	23,351	23,338	13	2,405	131	5.4	0.56
	August	4,001	3,987	14	1,025	160	15.6	4.0
	September	7,246	7,160	86	4,503	110	2.4	1.52
	October	9,001	8,003	998	3,046	43	1.4	0.48
	November	10,149	9,380	769	1,174	85	7.2	0.84
	December	7,805	7,564	241	752	17	2.3	0.22
1919	January	6,870	NA	NA	926	226	16.4	1.59
	February	5,229	NA	NA	319			
	March	1,809	NA	NA	115			
	April	192	NA	NA	9			
	May	73	NA	NA	2			
	June	37	NA	NA	3			
	July	20	NA	NA	0			
	August	0	0	0	0			

Sources: U.S. Department of War, Office of the Surgeon-General, *Annual Report of the Surgeon General, 1919* (Washington, DC: Government Printing Office, 1920), 1:132–135; U.S. Department of War, Office of the Surgeon-General, *Annual Report of the Surgeon General, 1920* (Washington, DC: Government Printing Office, 1921), 140, 145.

Notes: These percentages do not indicate the total number of men infected with venereal diseases at Camp Beauregard. That number is impossible to determine based on the camp's surviving medical records. It only indicates those men found to be both infected with venereal disease and in need of medical treatments that required them to be segregated from the other soldiers. These men experienced symptoms serious enough to prevent them from performing their duties and were thus considered to be "ineffectives."

or widespread acceptance of effective prophylactics, like condoms, but the statistics reported by moral reformers of the day must be read with great caution, as their studies lacked methodological rigor and were used tendentiously in attempts to influence public policy. Clearly, though, venereal diseases were prevalent in the United States in the early twentieth century, as the U.S. Army found that up to 25 percent of newly inducted soldiers in World War I were infected with one or more venereal diseases.

Military Justice at Camp Beauregard

Because soldiers were generally at Camp Beauregard for only a few months, there were relatively fewer opportunities for soldiers to commit offenses that could result in courts-martial. This was true for all types of offenses, sexual or otherwise. In fact, only three soldiers were court-martialed at Camp Beauregard between 1917 and 1919 for offenses that are obviously related to sexual matters.[129]

The worst fears of moral reformers and CTCA officials were embodied in the case of Sergeant Shay Vincent Danna, who was charged with "hav[ing] carnal knowledge of an unmarried female under the age of consent."[130] Rather than being depicted as a predatory, adult soldier who preyed on an innocent, underage girl, Danna—though found guilty—was portrayed by his defense as a kind of victim of what moral reformers considered a "promiscuous girl."[131] Danna pleaded not guilty but was convicted and sentenced to be reduced to the ranks (that is, made a private) and given one month of hard labor, an extremely light sentence for a statutory rape conviction.[132] The reviewing authority deemed this sentence too lenient but nevertheless approved it. The girl Danna was charged with raping, as well as her parents, testified that she was seventeen years old at the time of the offense (under Louisiana law, it was illegal to have sex with females under the age of eighteen). The girl stated that the intercourse was consensual. Danna testified that he met the girl at a dance, where she danced "unladylike." When he was giving her a ride home after the dance, Danna claimed, she kissed him and unsuccessfully attempted to seduce him. He went on a second date with her, during which, he alleged, she smoked cigarettes with him and attempted to seduce him a second time, which Danna said he also rebuffed. Danna stated that on the couple's third date he agreed to have sexual intercourse with her. After the act was completed, she told Danna that she was going to stay at a rooming house that night but that she only had thirty cents. He gave her two dollars, which lent an air of prostitution to the affair. Danna went on to state that, to him, she appeared to be twenty or twenty-one years old and that they never discussed her age. Danna also alleged that he had seen the girl riding around town with other soldiers on multiple occasions and that he had seen her kiss four soldiers other than himself. Danna also claimed that he had contracted a case of gonorrhea (for which he received venereal treatment at Camp Beauregard) as a result of his intercourse with the girl. Danna's commanding officer testified that his character was good, as part of the defense's strategy of casting the girl as a dangerous woman and a kind of sexual predator who essentially took advantage of Danna. Interestingly, Danna told an army investigator before his court-martial that he had had sex with her on several occasions and that he believed her to be both of legal age and "in commerce" (that is, a prostitute), though his court-martial testimony contradicted these statements.

As for the alleged rape victim in this case, the girl was reported by several people from her hometown of Shreveport, Louisiana, to have exhibited "waywardness." This waywardness apparently included drinking alcohol and having sexual relationships with several young men. She had been confined at the House of the Good Shepherd in New Orleans, a women's reformatory, before moving with her father to Alexandria, Louisiana, shortly before the incident took place. An army lawyer who reviewed the case noted that "the previous chaste or unchaste character of the woman in this prosecution of this kind is immaterial." Despite this, the case reviewer stated that "the court evidently took into consideration the appearance of the woman and her action, in rendering its award of punishment." It seems clear that the army was not willing to dishonorably discharge Danna, a typical peacetime sentence for similar offenses, on the eve of his deployment to Europe merely because he had had a sexual relationship with an "unchaste" woman, even if she had been under the age of consent.

The army also sought to protect some local civilian women—those deemed of good character—from soldiers at Camp Beauregard. Private Andrew L. Parham was charged with marking the picture of a female civilian, Thelma Whitcomb, "with lewd, obscene, vulgar, indecent, and suggestive references" and mailing the picture to her.[133] Parham allegedly wrote the following doggerel on the back of the photograph:

> Luck to the dove, flys [sic] above,
> an [sic] never sheds a feather,
> I like for your little shoes and my big boots,
> To lay under the bed together.

He was alleged to have stolen the photo from a fellow private, who had a romantic relationship with the recipient of the poem. Parham pleaded not guilty and was convicted, receiving what seems to be an unusually harsh sentence for an oblique, written sexual reference: a dishonorable discharge, forfeiture of all pay, and five years of hard labor. Though Major General Harry F. Hodges, the reviewing authority, commended the court for showing its disapproval of Parham's acts, he found the sentence too severe, as did the army attorney who reviewed the case, and noted that the evidence was entirely circumstantial and the offense relatively minor. In his formal review of the case, Hodges noted that Parham had "within him the capacity to become a well disciplined and well trained soldier." He reduced Parham's sentence to one year of hard labor, forfeiture of two-thirds of his pay during that year, and no dishonorable discharge, presumably to allow Parham to participate in the war effort after completing his sentence. Whitcomb, the victim and recipient of the letter in this case, was portrayed very differently from how the girl in the Danna case was depicted. Whitcomb was consistently described as a "decent girl," and her virtue was never called into question. Parham denied having written the poem and sent it to Whitcomb, stating that someone else in the unit must have committed the act. Nevertheless, he was convicted based on the accusations of some men from his unit who had already been deployed to France, handwriting similarities, and the fact that Parham's two years of formal education may have led him to spell in the manner used in the poem. Whitcomb's social class is difficult to determine, though she appears well dressed in the photo. There were oblique references to class differences between the two, with the court raising Parham's limited education on several occasions during the court-martial.

Many soldiers were treated for venereal diseases at Camp Beauregard, and all soldiers were required to receive venereal prophylaxis after they had been potentially exposed to venereal infection (that is, after they had sexual intercourse). No soldiers were court-martialed for contracting venereal diseases at Camp Beauregard. While some undoubtedly declined to receive prophylaxis—most soldiers reported the urethral mercuric solutions to be both uncomfortable and side-effect inducing—almost none were punished for refusing treatment, unlike in other locales, likely because the Beauregard soldiers were about to deploy to Europe during wartime. Private Harry Farley was the only soldier who appears in the court-martial records for refusing venereal treatment for his affliction. Along with several other charges involving insubordination, Farley was charged with refusing treatment for chancroids (a venereal disease).[134] He pleaded not guilty to all these charges but was convicted of all of them and sentenced to eleven months of hard labor, as well as forfeiture of two-thirds of his pay for this same period. The reviewing authority found this sentence inadequate but reluctantly approved it. Farley had a chancroid—a kind of ulcer caused by a bacterial infection transmitted via sexual contact—on his penis, and an army doctor (a lieutenant) sought to cauterize the ulcer. Farley refused in an extremely vocal way to receive the cauterization or an ice bag application, threatening to kill several doctors and orderlies if they laid hands on him ("If you put your hands on me you will die with your boots on"), and caused a great disturbance in the camp hospital. The doctor who treated Farley testified that Farley's anger was, he felt, caused not by pain but rather by anger that his venereal infection had been discovered. After Farley was placed under arrest in the camp hospital, he calmed down almost immediately, became cooperative with the doctor, and consented to the treatment. Farley testified in his own defense, stating that he had no recollection whatsoever of the incident, though a representative of the camp's Sanity Board testified that Farley had no mental problems or physical cause for a memory lapse. He was questioned as to how he contracted the chancroid. Farley said he believed he might have contracted it from a fall into contaminated water or mud. It is difficult to assess how much of Farley's punishment was assigned for contracting a venereal disease and how much was assigned because of the disturbance he caused, his refusal to obey a commissioned officer's order, and his public threats against the officer, a sergeant, and several orderlies. It seems apparent, though, that had Farley immediately consented to the prescribed treatment for his chancroid, he would not have been punished for being venereally infected, as no other soldiers at Camp Beauregard who contracted venereal infections—and there were hundreds—were punished for such an offense.

CTCA Investigations in New Orleans, Louisiana

Just as the CTCA conducted a series of investigations of the local prostitution and venereal conditions in Alexandria, Louisiana, it also operated in similar fashion in New Orleans. Its efforts there influenced local political structures to an even larger degree and affected significantly greater numbers of women. While New Orleans is approximately two hundred miles from Camp Beauregard, CTCA officials had significant concerns about soldiers from Camp Beauregard traveling to New Orleans while on leave to indulge in sexual activity. The army could have forbidden Beauregard's soldiers from traveling to New Orleans, but it would have incurred the burden of enforcing this regulation and soldiers' morale would have likely suffered from such a ban.

The city of New Orleans has a lengthy history of tolerating vice, with a rich culture of commercial sexuality. For many years it was called by critics the "Great Southern Babylon."[135] New Orleans's infamous red-light district, Storyville, also called the District, was well known and had a reputation as perhaps the largest red-light district in the nation.[136] Storyville was founded in March 1897 as a geographically and racially segregated district within New Orleans city limits where prostitution and other forms of vice would be legally permitted.[137] New Orleans and a host of other cities across the United States established such red-light districts to physically separate vice, particularly the sale of commercial sex and alcohol, from middle-class portions of the city and places where "respectable" white citizens might travel.[138]

While Storyville largely enjoyed popular support in New Orleans—from both clients and investors, who included many local elites—its critics sued the city in an effort to shut the district down. The case went before the U.S. Supreme Court in 1899, and Storyville's establishment was upheld.[139] In keeping with patterns of southern racial segregation, Storyville's brothels were for white clientele only, though black musicians and prostitutes worked in some establishments. Brothels were permitted to employ prostitutes of only a single race (that is, a brothel might employ white women or black women, but not both).[140] In February 1917, a second red-light district was established for the exclusive use of black clientele in New Orleans.[141]

Before the CTCA had even sent its first investigator to New Orleans, local moral reform organizations had already contacted the Commission, urging federal action. One such organization, the Citizens League of Louisiana, led by New Orleans attorney and businessman William M. Railey, was particularly vocal in opposing Storyville's continued existence.[142] The Citizens League was especially concerned about the effectiveness of the CTCA's involvement in New Orleans. Though the CTCA had succeeded in forcing Alexandria to close its red-light district by threatening to move Camp Beauregard and its twenty-five thousand soldiers if the city would not comply, New Orleans, a much larger city of 375,000, could not be so easily swayed, even by the federal government.[143]

In addition to using the political and social influence of its members, the Citizens League also maintained a body of vice investigators who, like CTCA officials, regularly visited New Orleans saloons and brothels and reported on the presence and activities of soldiers and sailors. The Citizens League was staunchly opposed to the administration of Mayor Martin Behrman and its associated political machine, which ran New Orleans.[144] The league also provided information to the CTCA on local political conflicts of interest on vice issues, as well as ownership of saloons and hotels used for assignations. The owners included the notorious Tom Anderson, the so-called mayor of Storyville, a state legislator who owned several of the largest and most popular brothels and saloons in the city.[145] The Behrman administration and New Orleans Police Department fought back against the Citizens League, charging the Citizens League's president, Railey, with libel for publicly alleging that many local houses of prostitution and bars enjoyed police protection.[146]

Race and class played important roles in the political and moral conflicts present in New Orleans, as the Behrman political machine relied heavily on the support of working-class whites, blacks, and individuals of mixed descent.[147] Behrman's political opponents, including social reform groups like the Citizens League, were primarily composed of middle- and upper-class whites. The issues of race and sexuality were complex in New Orleans, where a wide spectrum of racial categories was constructed and negotiated; race in New Orleans was not simply a matter of black and white. For example, the categories of "quadroon" (those with one-quarter African heritage) and "octoroon" (those with one-eighth African heritage) were prevalent in the city, with many octoroons able to "pass" as white. Octoroon women had a reputation in New Orleans as being sexually exotic and in high demand as sexual partners for many whites.[148] Additionally, whenever those involved in vice were not white, their precise racial categorization was usually mentioned by local reformers. For example, African Americans were always described as either "negro" or, more specifically, "quadroons," "octoroons," and the like.[149] The racial situation in the brothels of Storyville was equally complex. The availability of women of different racial and ethnic categories in the brothels of New Orleans allowed their clients (mainly white men) to traverse racial boundaries. Sex across color lines was a central attraction of Storyville, which consciously exploited New Orleans's romanticized history of sex between members of different races.[150] Though Storyville and the nameless black red-light district were "racially segregated," white men could visit the brothels in the black vice district. Of course, the reverse was not true.[151]

In August 1917, the CTCA's Bascom Johnson first traveled to New Orleans, meeting with a variety of local civilian officials and touring Storyville, which was, he reported, "going full blast."[152] In addition to part-time or itinerant prostitutes who worked as streetwalkers rather than out of brothels, there were 541 prostitutes registered officially with the New Orleans Police Department (426 white and 115 "colored") and 272 registered houses of prostitution. While these businesses were almost always racially segregated, the police did not maintain records of how many brothels employed women of each race.[153] Storyville's twenty city blocks were packed with brothels, saloons, gambling dens, and other businesses offering some combination of vices. Most houses of prostitution charged fifty cents or one dollar for intercourse (these places were called, colloquially, "cribs"), though more expensive establishments, some described as "veritable palaces," also existed.[154]

Unlike in Alexandria, where local officials quickly complied with government demands for reform after some initial, token opposition, the CTCA met considerable resistance from officials in New Orleans, particularly from Behrman.[155] The meetings between Johnson and Behrman did not go well, and Behrman fiercely rejected the idea that New Orleans should close its red-light district. Regarding the closing of Storyville, Behrman was famously reported to have said, "You can make it illegal, but you can't make it unpopular."[156] Initially, on War Department urging, local police kept uniformed soldiers and sailors out of Storyville, but as they could not prevent those dressed in civilian clothes from entering the district, and because not all houses of prostitution were in Storyville, this tactic was not especially effective.[157] In several cases, taxicab services and other local entrepreneurs provided civilian clothing for soldiers to rent specifically for venturing into Storyville.[158] Beyond this, Behrman and his administration were extremely reluctant to take further action to limit soldiers' access to prostitutes. Soon after his meetings with the CTCA, Behrman went on the offensive to save Storyville. Enlisting Louisiana's two senators, he met with Newton D. Baker, the Secretary of War, in Washington, DC, to argue for allowing the red-light district in New Orleans to remain open. Behrman advocated "a regulated and segregated district as the only sound method of police control."[159] The young Baker, a progressive and Wilson protégé, strongly supported the efforts of the CTCA to close down Storyville but was reluctant to interfere in local municipal affairs. He assured Behrman that Storyville would not have to be closed down unless soldiers were being admitted to the district.

Later in September, another CTCA official, George J. Anderson, arrived in New Orleans for a follow-up investigation. Anderson was assigned a single mission: to determine the extent to which soldiers and sailors had access to prostitutes in the red-light district.[160] He described the conditions he found there as "horrible," but he was also hopeful. "If the New Orleans district is closed it will have a far-reaching effect on the whole problem in the South. It is the last stronghold of the old regime."[161] While Anderson did not report seeing large numbers of uniformed soldiers in Storyville, the district was bustling with customers in civilian garb. He noted the prevalence of apparent collusion between local police and prostitutes, as well as persistent rumors that police officials owned some of the district's establishments and offered protection to the rest. He also reported on the widespread availability of prostitutes in the areas of the city surrounding Storyville, to which access was not at all controlled by local police or military police. Anderson, not surprisingly, urged the prompt closure of Storyville. By November, a CTCA investigator was permanently stationed in the city.

Bowing to renewed federal pressure, New Orleans did shut down Storyville in November, but CTCA officials and local reformers were still unhappy with the progress the city made in cleaning up vice. The dispute between the CTCA and the Behrman administration played out very publicly. Raymond Fosdick was quoted as saying that "the restricted area had been closed, it was true, but it was of no advantage . . . if prostitution were permitted to thrive across the street from the old stand."[162] Two days later, Fosdick denied the quotation, stating that he had full confidence in the New Orleans city government. He noted that they had been given thirty days to clean up vice in the city, a deadline that would not expire until December 13.[163] It is unclear under what circumstances the CTCA's ultimatum was issued, as no written records of such a dictate survive.

By mid-December, the CTCA's follow-up investigator reported mixed results in the suppression of prostitution in New Orleans.[164] While the lowest-priced brothels, the "cribs," had all been shut down, the higher-priced houses of prostitution were still open for business, though perhaps operating more discreetly than previously. One madam he interviewed said, "We were told [by police] to run but not let in any soldiers. No, we don't expect to be closed up because we are altogether different than the cheap cribs who had only soldiers and sailors for trade."[165] These still-open brothels, while perhaps disdaining enlisted customers, were still amenable to commissioned officers as customers, with a CTCA investigator reporting an establishment that had a number of first and second lieutenants as customers. He named these men in his report. He also reported an upswing in the number of prostitutes soliciting in the streets surrounding the former Storyville. These streetwalkers seemed to "strongly favor the uniformed men." In one of the few references to the availability of same-sex prostitution, one of the CTCA's investigators noted seeing eight black "fairies" soliciting. Their presence seemed to particularly alarm the investigator: "These creatures constitute a grave menace to soldiers and sailors," he opined.[166] "Fairies" were particularly alarming sexual "deviants" to many observers, as the language used by the CTCA investigator to describe them suggests, because these men tended to blur established gender conventions of dress and mannerism by emphasizing feminine characteristics, mannerisms, and speech. "Fairies" were usually not transvestites, though some sexologists at the time described them as a "third" or "intermediate sex."[167]

The CTCA triumph over Storyville led one official to claim, "Even that Gibraltar of commercialized vice, notorious not only to this continent but abroad, the New Orleans [red-light] district, which comprised 24 solid blocks given over to human degradation and lust and housing six to eight hundred women, has gone down with the rest."[168] Still, prostitution in the city did not cease. Houses of prostitution relocated elsewhere in the city, generally operating more discreetly and without the formal protection of the law, though almost always under police protection.[169] After Storyville was closed, the remaining brothels turned away men in uniform, though these men often continued the practice of renting civilian clothes by the hour specifically for the purposes of carousing.[170]

After the Armistice ended World War I in November 1918, the CTCA's work rapidly began winding down. By February 1919, a CTCA official reported, "It seems that word has gone out that New Orleans is 'good' and so they are flocking here from far and near."[171] He estimated that at least 2,500 prostitutes had returned to the city, though that estimate is significantly larger than the prewar prostitute population. When the CTCA was disbanded in 1919, its public health functions were turned over to other federal agencies, including the Interdepartmental Social Hygiene Board and the U.S. Public Health Service, while most of its antivice work was left in the hands of state and local law enforcement agencies. The army's nationwide war against prostitution had, like the rest of the American war effort, ceased, but it would be revived at the outset of World War II. The debates surrounding Storyville's closure encapsulate much of the broader story of attempts at "reform" and resistance. They also highlight the difficulty of successfully enacting meaningful, lasting reform in the face of concerted opposition.

Camp Beauregard, New Orleans, and the Sexual Economy of War

Camp Beauregard differed sharply in purpose and demographics from the other army communities examined in this project. It was originally created as a training camp for newly inducted soldiers who would deploy to Europe in a few months. The army did not plan for Camp Beauregard to be a permanent installation, though it became one after the war. Soldiers and officers did not bring wives and children with them during their brief stays at the camp, though some of the camp's training staff did bring families with them to Alexandria. Most of the men who passed through Camp Beauregard during the war years were not regulars in the U.S. Army. Some, but not all or even most, were National Guard soldiers, but few of the men sought to create a permanent life for themselves in the army. They enlisted or were drafted for the American war effort, hailing from various walks of civilian life, and almost all expected to return to their prewar lives, and civilian status, after the war. Many Americans perceived these men very differently from army regulars—enlisted men, at least—who even in 1917 were still considered to be socially and economically deficient by many middle-class and elite Americans. Men who made a career of the army before World War I were sometimes seen and treated by civilians as social outcasts and misfits, men who could not, for one reason or another, make it in civilian life.

But the men sent through Camp Beauregard were seen as doing their civic duty, willingly or not, by serving the United States in uniform in a time of war, risking their lives for the good of the nation. They were, in a very real sense, the pride of the nation. Many progressives viewed these draftees as men who could be transformed into moral paragons and who would then, in turn, help transform the nation after the war when they returned to their home communities. The army and the CTCA's experiences at Camp Beauregard, as well as in Alexandria and New Orleans, serve as powerful examples of how the army, in conjunction with civilian federal officials, sought to regulate the sexual activity of these soldiers and the American civilians with whom they came into contact. Both Alexandria and New Orleans were sites of resistance by local civilians to the federal government's attempts to impose new regimes of surveillance and control over sex. Not all Americans shared the progressives' morality or their fears about the dangers of unbridled access to sex. Prostitution in these cities' established red-light districts, especially in the expansive Storyville district, generated significant income for private citizens and some local officials and business leaders. There were major financial incentives for local investors and their political allies to keep these red-light districts open. Community standards of health and morality had never exerted much restraint over activities in these districts.

Much of the public debate surrounding the regulation of sexual activities around World War I training camps and bases was predicated on conflicting views on women and their potential for corrupting what were conceived of as morally and physically pure young men. Men involved in the sex trade, either as clients of prostitutes or as pimps, panderers, procurers, or owners of houses of prostitution, were rarely targeted by police action. The attention of law enforcement authorities focused almost solely on the women themselves. Many progressives claimed that these dangerous women, be they prostitutes or just promiscuous, represented threats not just to the men in uniform with whom they had sex but to the nation as a whole. Racial politics, too, seemed to play an important role in middle-class reformers' fears about sexually dangerous women in Louisiana, as did concerns about the potential for immoral sexual behavior among working-class whites. African American women (and men) were considered congenitally immoral and sexually promiscuous, as well as widely infected with venereal diseases. Many local black women were presumed by investigators to regularly solicit commercial sex from soldiers. And, of course, they were sometimes vectors for venereal disease. It was feared that soldiers would contract venereal diseases during their military service and, rather than "coming back clean," would return home and infect their girlfriends, fiancées, and wives, presumably "good girls" all, and potentially even infect the next generation of Americans, their unborn children. Just as importantly to many reformers, prostitutes and promiscuous women posed a moral threat to the soldiers by tempting them to engage in immoral sexual activity and, through them, tempting the country at large.

Army officials, some already sympathetic to the moral views of progressives, also worked to spread the anti–venereal disease message, if for no other reason than to prevent the medical disability of the army's soldiers. The worst predictions about the potential for venereal infections among soldiers did not come to pass at Camp Beauregard (or at any of the other training camps), and the rate of manpower losses due to venereal diseases was only a few percent, certainly lower than domestic peacetime rates and far lower than rates in the Philippines and Hawaii. The extent to which the army and the CTCA's anti–venereal disease measures were responsible in preventing wider outbreaks is impossible to judge with certainty, but it is clear that the venereal disease rates for soldiers in domestic training camps like Camp Beauregard were lower, perhaps considerably lower, than that of the U.S. population at large. This difference in debilitating venereal disease rates can probably be at least partially attributed to the army and CTCA campaign to educate soldiers about venereal diseases, scare them by emphasizing the dangers of sex, and physically prevent them from having easy access to prostitutes and other women willing to have sex with them.

CHAPTER 4

"Complete Continence Is Wholly Possible"

The U.S. Army in France and Germany, 1917–1923

> Sexual continence is the plain duty of members of the AEF [American Expeditionary Forces], both for the vigorous conduct of the war and for the clean health of the American people after the war. Sexual intercourse is not necessary for good health, and complete continence is wholly possible.
>
> —General John J. Pershing to the soldiers of the AEF

While the U.S. Army engaged in many significant deployments in the first four decades of the twentieth century, only one, the AEF sent to Europe during World War I, involved a major conventional war that required massive conscription and national military-industrial mobilization. U.S. intervention in World War I brought about the opportunity—and the perceived need—to intervene in the sexual economy of war on a vast, unprecedented scale during wartime. During the course of the American war effort, a total of 4,734,991 American men served in the armed forces. Of these, 2,810,296 were conscripted under the Selective Service Act of May 1917, the first comprehensive draft in U.S. history.[1] A considerable fraction of the total, 2,057,675 troops, actually served in Europe with the AEF during the war. At the time of the Armistice, when the AEF reached the peak of its numerical strength, there were 1,981,701 soldiers serving in Europe.[2] This was staggering growth for a Regular Army with a prewar strength of approximately 130,000 enlisted men and officers. A month after the Armistice effectively ended World War I, 225,000 American troops entered Germany, where they would remain until January 1923, to begin an occupation that would enforce the ceasefire, ensure demilitarization, and maintain social order. By mid-1919, the army's presence in the American zone of occupation had already fallen to 87,000, and by the end of 1919, fewer than 19,000 soldiers constituted the American Forces in Germany (AFG). By early 1922, fewer than 8,000 remained, and by the end of American occupation, a mere 1,100 soldiers made up the entire American occupation force.[3]

Just as World War I intervened dramatically in American civil life, so too did the U.S. Army intervene in new and increasingly widespread and significant ways in the sex lives of American soldiers during the war and subsequent occupation of Germany. The sexual economy of war at the outset of American involvement in World War I encompassed a variety of concerns of army and War Department officials, including how they might cope with an anticipated venereal epidemic and how to deal with expected problems from romantic fraternization between American soldiers and the European women they would encounter while deployed. Of these issues, the U.S. Army concentrated its efforts primarily on attempting to control the spread of venereal disease. In the minds of most medical experts and military planners, this meant intervening in local conditions of prostitution, since female prostitutes were most often blamed for the spread of venereal disease among men. Most, but certainly not all, of the army's interventions in the sexual behavior of American servicemen and their partners during World War I were attempts to regulate prostitution in order to mitigate the effects of venereal disease during training at domestic bases and deployment in Europe. Not since the Civil War had the U.S. Army attempted such a large and public intervention in the sexual behavior of its troops.[4]

The army believed that the development of romantic relationships between American soldiers and local women also warranted significant attention because these relationships had the potential to create discipline problems and complicate relations between the United States and its European hosts. It enacted a number of antifraternization regulations and other policies designed to limit the number of romantic relationships and marriages during and after the war. Though the army stated that it generally regulated sexual matters for reasons of military efficiency and discipline rather than out of moral concerns, it also sought to maintain the boundaries of social propriety in many sexual and social matters. The army expressed significant concerns regarding, for example, "acceptable" sex acts in which soldiers might engage, sexual harassment of civilian women through "indecent" proposals and language by soldiers, and the ways officers would comport themselves publicly.

The experiences of the AEF and the later AFG help illuminate the ways in which conceptions of masculinity and sexual propriety differed for the officer corps and enlisted men. In many ways, the prosecution of sex-related offenses during and immediately after World War I through the U.S. Army's General Courts-Martial reveals that commissioned officers were held to American middle-class standards of sexual propriety more frequently than enlisted soldiers, particularly in matters related to marriage and romantic affairs when in public. This represented a sharp break with the army's judicial practices in other times and places, where officers were seldom court-martialed for such offenses. Either enlisted men were not court-martialed for similar offenses as officers (such as consorting with prostitutes) while in Europe, or their offenses had to be accompanied by other crimes before the army officially took note. The army's class structure and bias are thus brought into stark relief by the army's legal treatment of World War I–era matters of sexuality.[5]

Because of fears of the potential for massive outbreaks of venereal diseases, as well as fears about promiscuous French women, the U.S. Army emphasized the theme of sexual abstinence in its troop education and indoctrination programs as never before. The military service of the mostly conscript American doughboys became charged with special meaning in the minds of many Americans, who saw these soldiers as physical and moral representatives of the nation. American moralists urged that they be strongly cautioned against sexual adventures in Europe, and institutionally, the army complied by incorporating sexual continence as a major theme in its indoctrination programs and anti–venereal disease policies and regulations.

The War against Venereal Disease in Europe

The U.S. Army was deeply concerned about venereal disease from the outset of its involvement in World War I. Four medical officers, led by Major (later Colonel) Hugh H. Young, who would head the army's newly formed urological department, accompanied General John J. Pershing and his headquarters staff on Pershing's ship to France in May 1917.[6] These medical officers immediately began a study of "the prevention and treatment of venereal disease in the English and French armies," with a goal of designing an anti–venereal disease regime for the American army. The AEF's sixth General Order, issued in July 1917, exclusively addressed policies for mitigating the effects of venereal disease within the U.S. Army.[7] It established prophylactic stations throughout France and mandated that all members of the AEF report to these stations for treatment within three hours of sexual exposure. It also dictated that men who contracted venereal diseases "through neglect" be court-martialed. Elaborate, detailed instructions were provided for the mandated prophylactic treatments, though army surgeons frequently complained about the inadequacy of the prophylactic stations under field conditions.[8]

The army combated venereal disease among soldiers not just through what it described as prophylaxis but also through the regulation of prostitution.

World War I was not Pershing's first encounter with regimes of regulating prostitution in areas outside the United States. He had been deployed to the Philippines for many years (1899–1903 and 1909–1912), witnessing the army's involvement in venereal inspections there, and more recently had led the U.S. Army's expedition against Pancho Villa on the Mexican border in 1916. Raymond B. Fosdick, then a YMCA official who later was asked to head the Commission on Training Camp Activities (CTCA), and Max J. Exner, a medical doctor, surveyed the conditions of prostitution around American encampments on the U.S.-Mexico border on behalf of a moral reform organization, submitting highly critical reports of what they found.[9] They described regular venereal inspections of all prostitutes every one to two weeks and multiple houses of prostitution set up by the army near each of its border camps, with at least one brothel near each camp reserved for exclusive use by officers. The women were charged two dollars for their inspections and then placed in brothels that were guarded by army sentries. Exner reported that "a military medical officer of high rank, in trying to show that prostitution was really quite limited, said 'I do not believe that there are more than 500 prostitutes in the city [near one camp].'"[10] Exner stated that he "rarely met an officer who did not take for granted that prostitution could not and should not be abolished. . . . Prostitution was deliberately provided by the officers on the assumption that it was necessary for the contentment and well-being of the men."[11] The attitude of army officers, according to another observer, was that "sissies were no use on the firing line. Soldiers must have women. They made poor soldiers if they did not have women."[12]

While on the Mexican border, Pershing was reported to have been concerned about the morality of regulated prostitution, but he attributed the high rate of venereal infection among soldiers to diseased Mexican prostitutes. Pershing ordered that the prostitutes accompanying American troops be segregated and placed "under the strictest military regulation," receiving venereal treatment from army physicians, as did soldiers who came into sexual contact with the women. Reformers were concerned that Pershing would take his attitude toward regulated prostitution—and the army's field-tested venereal prophylaxis program—with him to Europe as head of the AEF. "It would be most unfortunate to permit General Pershing," wrote Exner to Fosdick, "to take his contingent to Europe with any possibility of his continuing that sort of policy."[13] Concerned about Pershing's "laxness," reformers sought to sway him before his departure for Europe, and Young gave him and his staff a series of lurid lectures detailing the horrors of venereal disease during the voyage to France.[14] Young argued that, unlike the British and French militaries, which seemed resigned to relatively high venereal disease rates, the United States should look to New Zealand, which had instituted a major program to educate soldiers on the dangers of venereal disease, regularly inspected them for infections, and provided widespread chemical prophylaxis and condoms. Young's lectures, coupled with Pershing's own experiences, seem to have cemented the idea of a venereal disease–free U.S. Army in Pershing's mind.

The U.S. Army generally approached the control of venereal disease among soldiers of the AEF as a medical, rather than a moral, problem, though many army officials made moral judgments about the sexual activities frequently leading to venereal infection. As the Army Medical Department's postwar report stated, "The methods adopted for the control of venereal diseases in the American Expeditionary Forces were, excluding artificial immunization [which was not available for venereal diseases at the time], essentially the same as the methods applied in the control of other communicable diseases."[15] The AEF's Chief Surgeon, Colonel George Walker, suggested after the war, "There is no reason for sweeping condemnation or indictment concerning the sexual freedom taken by the soldiers. They were subjected to great stress of a kind entirely foreign to their experiences. . . . They were young, vigorous, and . . . were exposed to endless temptations so insistent that they could not be escaped."[16] Walker explicitly placed himself in opposition to many domestic moral reformers when he stated, "I am by no means of the opinion . . . that the introduction of medicinal prophylaxis to the public would be an 'immoral' thing or that . . . it would tend to increase illicit cohabitation."[17] Walker advocated the approach that the U.S. Army took to deterring extramarital sex and venereal infections by attempting to link sex with disease in the minds of soldiers, calling on medical officials to emphasize the "sordid danger of venereal infection and all of the degradation and suffering it may cause not only to him but those who are dear to him."[18] But Walker, like many army officials, was not sanguine about the success of such exhortations, and prepared to treat significant numbers of soldiers for venereal infections contracted in Europe.

Venereal Infection Prevention and Sexual Education

Almost immediately upon the arrival of the first American soldiers in France, U.S. Army physicians detected a significant outbreak of syphilis. Army leaders and medical experts quickly investigated and blamed French prostitutes for the outbreak.[19] Of the 146 licensed prostitutes in the port town of Saint-Nazaire, one of the largest ports used by American troops landing in France, 16 were found to be infected with syphilis. While some of these women were undoubtedly the source of some American soldiers' infections, the number of women found to be infected was not high enough to account for the out-break. On October 21, 1917, the army began to venereally inspect American troops before embarkation in the United States. American medical authori-ties were purportedly "somewhat surprised" at the number of cases of syphi-lis infections discovered before the troops left the United States. The army found that the rates of venereal infections among newly arriving members of the AEF varied tremendously. In October and November 1917, the average rate for all soldiers of the AEF was approximately 1.2 percent, though some units' rates were as high as 25–33 percent. Rates for black units were roughly four or five times as high as those of white units.[20] Contrary to the prejudices of some doctors and army leaders, the main vector of infection may have been from American soldiers to French prostitutes, rather than the other way around, but army leaders resisted that conclusion.

African American soldiers constituted approximately 10 percent of the AEF, but their race loomed large in the minds of U.S. Army leaders and at least some French civilians and officials when it came to matters of sexuality. For example, when the AEF placed the licensed houses of prostitutions in Saint-Nazaire off-limits to U.S. soldiers and civilians, the mayor and police officials protested. One of the mayor's arguments against the ban concerned the American "ne-gro stevedores." He believed "something must be done [to meet the sexual needs of the black soldiers], for the French would be in danger." He offered three "solutions" to the problem: "(1) That three houses of prostitution be opened for the negroes, (2) if this was not found to be satisfactory, that negro women be brought over from the United States to serve as prostitutes for these men; (3) that, if neither of the above suggestions could be accepted, all of the negroes be sent back to the United States."[21] Such was French anxiety about interracial sex between African Americans and French women. The mayor's anxiety was not, of course, that these men would have sex with French women who worked as prostitutes; he favored that. He was instead concerned about the possibility of sex between African Americans and French women who were *not* working as prostitutes.

French civil authorities were not alone in their anxieties about African American soldiers' sexual behavior. In December 1917, AEF officials required venereal prophylaxis for African American soldiers returning to camp, "with-out regard for possible exposure to venereal disease."[22] The army instituted this policy when officials became convinced that many black soldiers "under cover of darkness, got away [from camp] and had intercourse with white women in adjacent fields and houses. It became evident, therefore, that dras-tic measures would have to be employed."[23] This new policy stereotyped Af-rican Americans as "irresponsible," along with white men who returned to camp intoxicated. The army defended this practice because the incidence of venereal disease among African American soldiers was significantly higher than that among white troops. In the eighteen months the army tracked the venereal rates among soldiers stationed at the port of Saint-Nazaire, African American soldiers had an average annual venereal disease incident rate of more than 16 percent, compared with just over 5 percent for white soldiers.[24] Some months during this period, the African American rate climbed to five or six times the white rate, though the rates reached parity during one month and the African American rate fell to half the rate among white soldiers in June and July 1918.

Walker stated that "it was found impossible to induce the negroes to appear voluntarily for prophylactic treatment after exposure." As a rule, Walker stated, "the negro soldiers objected strenuously to prophylaxis for they regarded it with horrified suspicion."[25] The army attempted a number of measures to restrict the mobility of African American soldiers in the first months of the AEF's deployment but by December 1917 had settled on compulsory prophylaxis for African Americans. These measures had significant effects on both white and African American venereal disease rates. Before the prophylaxis for intoxicated whites and all African Americans was made compulsory, white soldiers had a rate of 15.4 percent and African Americans a rate of 64.2 percent. After the compulsory prophylaxis measures were put into effect, the white rate dropped to 3 percent and the African American rate to 6.4 percent. The measures thus cut the white rate by 80 percent and the African American rate by 90 percent.

Overall, venereal infection rates differed sharply between white and black soldiers in the AEF. While approximately 10 percent of all white soldiers contracted a venereal disease during the war, 58 percent of blacks did.[26] Several theories have been advanced to explain this sharp disparity: white physicians may have been prone to diagnosing a variety of ailments in blacks as sexual in origin because of racialized ideas about black male hypersexuality, for example. Also, while many whites who were venereally infected at induction were rejected for military service, most infected blacks were not, reflecting the prevailing idea that almost all blacks were venereally infected, and so they could not be disqualified solely for this reason. High venereal infection rates among African Americans also reflected the poor quality (or nonexistence, in some cases) of medical care available to them before their military service in the United States.

Sexual education was an important component of the U.S. Army's program to prevent the spread of venereal diseases among soldiers.[27] Mandatory sexual education during initial military training in the United States included viewing the film *Fit to Fight*, produced by the CTCA.[28] Walker and other progressive army medical officers had great faith in the power of sexual education. As Walker stated, "Educational measures will eventually prove effective, except in cases of utter depravity which, fortunately, are rare."[29]

By the end of the war, some army officials came to believe that perhaps sexual "depravity" was not as uncommon as they had once believed, and in fact might be learned from French prostitutes. AEF medical officers were concerned not only with the venereal diseases that American soldiers might contract from French prostitutes but also with the types of sexual practices in which they might engage while in France. Chief Urologist Walker stated that "practically all of the prostitutes were perverts, and they encouraged the men to use of [*sic*] unnatural methods. . . . American soldiers were very unwilling to engage in these practices at first, but later were inveigled into them."[30] He went on to say that "the majority of French prostitutes prefer abnormal to normal intercourse."[31] The army was oddly reluctant to elaborate in official documents on what "abnormal" sex acts might be. The Medical Corps was so concerned about the problem of sexual "perversion" that it dispatched an investigator into the field who interviewed 237 prostitutes, only four of whom were unwilling to practice "perversion."[32] The exact nature of the "perverse" sexual acts that so alarmed AEF medical officials is unclear, as it is never directly stated in their discussions. The veiled discussions seem to indicate that a wide range of sex acts were considered perverse, including oral sex, which was frequently described as the "French way."[33]

French women were often depicted as dangerous sexual predators in American sex education materials.[34] One AEF flyer warned, "You will be accosted many times by public women [a euphemism for prostitutes]. Venereal disease is prevalent among them and to go with them invites infection which will not only do you great bodily harm but will render you ineffective for the purpose for which you are in France. Dictates of morality, personal hygiene, and patriotism demand that you do not associate with such women."[35] An American civilian in France during the war asserted, "America has as much to fear from the French women of Paris as from Germany. The American Red Cross officials will tell you how much more deadly one has been to their organization than the other."[36] As one doughboy would later put it, "According to the lieutenant, we were in much danger of being raped the minute we put foot on French soil."[37]

The army frequently urged sexual abstinence during the war. In a bulletin for the soldiers of the AEF, Pershing said that "the practice of illicit indulgence in sexual intercourse will almost inevitably lead to venereal infection sooner or later" and that "sexual continence is the plain duty of members of the AEF, both for the vigorous conduct of the war and for the clean health of the American people after the war. Sexual intercourse is not necessary for good health, and complete continence is wholly possible."[38] The bulletin went on to add—naïvely and inaccurately—that "careful studies show that only a relatively small proportion of members of the AEF habitually indulge in sexual intercourse." Commanding officers were enjoined to "urge continence on all men of their commands" by using a program of "instruction, work, drill, athletics, and amusements" to fill soldiers' time and limit opportunities for sexual indulgence. Secretary of War Newton D. Baker echoed this call for abstinence and assured the women left behind by the doughboys in 1918 that he had never seen an American soldier who was not "living a life which he would not be willing to have mother see him live."[39] At the same time, however, the army also planned for venereal prophylaxis when soldiers strayed. The army's promotion of abstinence was ultimately unsuccessful. Whether through the commercial sex trade or romantic relationships in Europe, by the army's account, fully 71 percent of American soldiers had sexual relations of one kind or another while in service to the AEF.[40]

The army's preventative measures were not restricted to sexual education alone. It also attempted a variety of measures to prevent soldiers from ever coming into contact with prostitutes. Six weeks after the U.S. Congress declared war on Germany, it authorized the complete suppression of prostitution within a five-mile zone around all U.S. military camps and posts. When American forces began to deploy to France later in 1917, both the AEF's chief surgeon and its judge advocate's office investigated the possibility of enforcing such a prohibition, only to find that they were unable to do so under French law.[41] In France, prostitution was not considered a crime, though prostitutes were licensed—both those who resided in licensed houses of prostitution and those who solicited in public areas—and medically inspected weekly.[42] Women found to be infected were housed in special hospitals.[43]

Because most AEF troops arriving in France debarked at the French port of Saint-Nazaire, a seaport apparently housing a large number of prostitutes, the AEF undertook a study of prostitution there.[44] After finding the existing prophylactic stations to be inadequate and the prevalence of venereal disease to be higher than desirable, the AEF put additional measures into place to prevent American soldiers from patronizing local prostitutes. It restricted soldiers to base, declared all local houses of prostitution "out of bounds," and placed military police at the entrances of all local bordellos to prevent entry by servicemen.[45] In fact, a large area of the city of Saint-Nazaire that contained the houses of prostitution and grog shops was placed off-limits to U.S. soldiers in December 1917, a policy that was eventually replicated in many other French cities housing large numbers of American soldiers.[46] Local police and civil officials complained strenuously, arguing that "the number of rapes and attempts at seduction had never been so great" and that clandestine prostitution had spread throughout their communities.[47] In January 1918, the Chief Surgeon told Pershing that in Blois, army officers had arranged with the proprietress of a house of prostitution to admit only American soldiers, stationing a military policeman at the bordello to ensure compliance. Pershing expressed his strong disapproval of such an arrangement and ordered an immediate investigation. When the investigation showed that the report was accurate, he closed the brothel and punished the officers involved.[48]

Georges Clemenceau, French Premier and Minister of War, disapproved of the AEF's policies on prostitution and wrote to Pershing in February 1918 complaining that venereal disease had spread alarmingly among the French population as a result of the American prohibition because venereally infected soldiers were having sex with French women who were not prostitutes. He urged Pershing to reconsider the policy and once more allow American soldiers to patronize licensed houses of prostitution.[49] Clemenceau offered to establish "special houses [of prostitution]" for exclusive use by AEF troops to counter fears of venereally contaminated women, but this offer, of course, took no account of progressive moral aversion to prostitution.[50] An alarmed Baker told Fosdick, "For God's sake, Raymond, don't show this [Clemenceau's offer] to the president or he'll stop the war."[51] Subsequently, American, French, and British medical and sanitation officials held a joint conference on venereal policy in Paris in March 1918 to discuss the issue but could not reach a compromise. The AEF policy continued.[52] At this conference, Young and his subordinate, Major E. L. Keyes, maintained that the army's policies rested solely on scientific concerns about hygiene and not morality. "The Medical Department of the Army," he said, "is in no way concerned with the morals of the soldiers; its sole desire is to minimize the incidence of venereal disease."[53] Contradicting this, a YMCA official later asserted that "morality is an essential part of military efficiency and, hence, is a part of military policy."[54] This intertwining of concerns about morality, hygiene, and military efficiency was never fully disentangled in the minds of military or civilian officials. Moral reformers wanted the U.S. Army to promote their vision of chaste, virtuous soldiers throughout the AEF. Some officers shared this moral vision, while others emphasized pragmatic concerns or suggested the inevitability of sexual contact between American soldiers and European prostitutes. Official policies and public pronouncements continued to emphasize both moral and functional reasons for halting the spread of venereal disease throughout the war.

The army's preventative measures, instituted in December 1917, do appear to have had some impact on venereal disease transmission. Before the new measures were adopted, white troops permanently stationed at Saint-Nazaire had monthly venereal disease rates of 10–16 per 1,000 and African American troops had rates of 19–109. By January 1918, the rates had fallen to 2 per 1,000 among white troops and 11 per 1,000 among African Americans.[55]

Prophylaxis

As mentioned previously, World War I medical officers used the term *prophylaxis* to describe a variety of measures they believed would prevent the onset of venereal diseases among soldiers after they had already had sexual contact with women who might already be infected. These measures were not prophylactic in the modern sense, involving such interventions as condoms or spermicides, to which the army paid surprising little attention. Rather, Pershing, in conjunction with AEF medical and sanitation officials, continually emphasized postcoital venereal prophylaxis as the most important means of combating the venereal diseases that were prevalent among AEF soldiers. Four General Orders—nos. 6, 34, and 77 in 1917 and no. 32 in 1919—all provided detailed guidelines on how venereal prophylaxis was to be accomplished and required compliance from all members of the AEF.[56] The first, General Order No. 6, issued on July 2, 1917, established prophylactic stations and required all AEF personnel to report for treatment within three hours of exposure to venereal infection. How soldiers were supposed to know that they had been exposed to venereal disease was left unanswered. The implication seemed to be that all soldiers having sexual contact with women—certainly with prostitutes—would report for prophylaxis. Penalties were mandated for every case of venereal disease, regardless of whether the soldier had received prophylactic treatment. Men "contracting venereal disease through neglect" were to be court-martialed and sentenced to forfeiture of pay (the mildest sentence possible for convictions in general courts-martial).

General Order No. 6 was supplemented and elaborated on in two additional General Orders later in 1917. General Order No. 34 (dated September 9, 1917) reiterated the AEF's commitment to "insure temperance and to prevent the ravages of venereal diseases with their disabling consequences." It committed the AEF to providing additional sources of entertainment, athletics, and reading materials, as well as an enhanced program of sexual education "in which continence shall be advised and illicit intercourse with women discouraged. The dangers of venereal disease will be clearly presented and preventative measures discussed." It also mandated twice-monthly venereal inspections of soldiers and reiterated General Order No. 6's requirement for courts-martial for enlisted men who contracted venereal disease. General Order No. 34 stated that the penalty for officers contracting venereal disease was to include summary discipline by their immediate commanding officer, with a report issued to AEF headquarters. Last, it mandated that all infected soldiers be interrogated as to the source of their infection. The names of these women were to be turned over to French civilian authorities and the women incarcerated in municipal hospitals for prostitutes.

General Order No. 77 (dated December 18, 1917), promulgated just three months after General Order No. 34, repeated the previous emphases on venereal inspections and prophylaxis and established new procedures for "locat[ing] the habitations, rooms or apartments and sections of towns occupied by women engaged in prostitution" by a "military secret service" at all French ports of debarkation and other locations where American soldiers were stationed or billeted. These locations, once known, were to be placed "off-limits" to all AEF personnel. This was the first official notice of disapproval of the French system of legal and open houses of prostitution by any of the Allied militaries in France.[57] Troops were also to be inspected for venereal disease immediately upon their arrival in Europe before they were permitted to come ashore. Those found to be infected were to be sent to venereal camps for treatment.[58]

A supplementary AEF Bulletin, no. 54, issued the following year in August 1918, placed all houses of prostitution "off-limits" to soldiers, due to significant increases in the incidence of venereal diseases.[59] This order was ineffective at preventing sexual contact between American soldiers and prostitutes who did not work in the French-sanctioned houses of prostitution. No order was issued forbidding contact with streetwalkers "because of the difficulty in formulating one that would be practical," though a few such orders were issued by some local commanders, seemingly to limited effect.[60] There was clearly debate among army staff officers about the desirability and efficacy of placing French houses of prostitution off-limits to the AEF. As Walker noted, "It was the opinion of a large number of both line and medical officers that the regulated house of prostitution afforded the best solution to the venereal problem. They . . . were opposed to these places being put out-of-bounds." He went on to say, however, "To their credit . . . as a general rule, these orders [General Orders 34 and 77] were observed."[61]

Army physicians found that General Order No. 6 had a dramatically negative effect on soldiers' willingness to seek prophylactic treatment. That these orders had to be repeated and reemphasized several times offers

commentary on the level of compliance and effectiveness of the army's prophylactic measures. As reports filtered into the Chief Surgeon's Office, it
became clear that many men who contracted venereal diseases had failed to
take prophylaxis and that a significant proportion of those who had taken
prophylaxis still contracted a venereal disease, indicating serious failures in
the army's prophylaxis program.[62] To shore up the prophylactic regime, the
army issued new, enhanced guidelines for how prophylaxis was to be administered and mandated additional equipment to be issued to all prophylactic
stations.[63]

General Order No. 32, issued on February 15, 1919, addressed the sexual
health of the large numbers of soldiers preparing to return to the United States:

> The pride which every soldier in the American Expeditionary Forces feels
> in its achievement, and which the whole American nation shares, must
> not be marred by the return of anyone to civil life who, by his miscon-
> duct, has rendered himself incompetent to maintain that high standard
> of citizenship which America rightfully expects of her returning soldiers.
> The future health and welfare of our people demand that the soldiers
> of the AEF return to their homes as clean in person as they have been
> brave in battle. Those suffering from venereal disease will, therefore, be
> segregated and assigned to provisional organizations retained for labor
> purposes in Europe.

The order alluded to the rise in the number of venereal infections after the
Armistice, noting that many soldiers had been granted far more liberal leaves.[64]
It also amplified the AEF's policy that disciplinary procedures were mandatory for soldiers contracting venereal disease, whether or not prophylaxis was
taken by the infected soldier. As one AEF flyer given to troops about to go on
leave urged, "The United States Government is permitting you to go on leave,
NOT in order that you may SOW WILD OATS, but to give you an opportunity to
improve your health, and advance your education. . . . If you become intoxicated, associate with prostitutes, or contract a venereal disease, you are guilty
of a moral crime. . . . DO NOT LET BOOZE, A PRETTY FACE, A SHAPELY ANKLE MAKE
YOU FORGET!! THE AEF MUST NOT TAKE EUROPEAN DISEASE TO AMERICA. YOU MUST
GO HOME CLEAN!! [emphasis in original]."[65]

The army ultimately considered its prophylaxis campaign in Europe to be
largely successful. For the period August 22 through November 13, 1918, when
the members of the AEF were "with their organizations, under the disciplinary control of their respective commanding officers, and were familiar with
the location of the [prophylactic] facilities," there were 8,978 cases of venereal

diseases contracted, 34.1 percent of which were in men who had failed to take prophylaxis treatments after exposure. In the armistice period of January 2, 1919, through May 21, 1919, AEF soldiers contracted 17,282 cases of venereal disease, 41.6 percent of which were in men who had failed to take prophylaxis.[66] This is an alarming increase in the number of cases, especially since the number of U.S. soldiers remaining in Europe was decreasing every month. The army blamed this on a significant increase in the number of leaves of absence granted, which placed the men in situations in which they were not under the disciplinary control of their officers and may not have had ready access to prophylactic stations.[67] But this statistic also indicates that more than 58 percent of those who contracted venereal diseases during this period did receive prophylaxis and nevertheless became infected, confirming the inadequacy of army prophylactic measures.

Soldiers seemed to be less sanguine about the efficacy of the army's prophylaxis program than army medical officers. Using a large survey of AEF soldiers, the army initially assessed that 61 percent of men who contracted venereal disease claimed to have contracted the disease despite receiving prophylaxis. The army reduced this to 12 percent, stating that many of these so-called failures of prophylaxis happened because of "intoxication, incomplete, or hurried treatment, or treatment taken after three hours."[68] The army went on to state that of the total 242,000 prophylactic treatments administered throughout the AEF, only 1.3 percent of the treatments failed (that is, patients became infected with a venereal disease even though prophylaxis had been properly administered within three hours of infection).[69] Because the army believed that its prophylactic measures were largely successful, it attempted to ascertain why individual soldiers failed to comply with orders to receive prophylaxis. The army placed the blame solely on the soldiers, determining (in a separate survey) that the fault lay with the soldiers in 82 percent of the cases. The primary causes were "pure indifference" and "alcoholism."[70] Of the remaining cases, the army stated that the failure to take prophylaxis was mostly because soldiers (falsely, said the army) believed that prophylaxis would be completely ineffective if not taken within three hours of exposure, so soldiers who did not reach a prophylaxis station within this period did not bother to receive prophylaxis later. The army's own policy likely invited this interpretation by some soldiers because it frequently emphasized that prophylactic treatment needed to be taken within three hours of exposure. Still, the army wanted soldiers who had had sex to receive prophylaxis, even if it took them longer than three hours to arrive at the prophylaxis clinic.

Treatment and Segregation

When soldiers of the AEF were found to be venereally infected, if their units were currently deployed in training areas or quiet zones of the front, they were housed in their regimental infirmaries while receiving treatment. If their units were stationed in active combat zones, the infected men were sent to one of three "venereal labor camps" established at Saint-Nazaire, Nantes, and Coëtquidan.[71] This segregation had two purposes: to prevent the spread of venereal disease to other AEF soldiers (presumably through a shared female sexual partner, as AEF sanitation documents never expressed anxieties about homosexual transmission of venereal disease) and to reduce the time lost by men receiving medical treatments. At the largest of the three camps, Saint-Nazaire, the most severe cases were treated in a hospital ward with ninety-six beds, the rest housed in a stockade with room for four hundred patients. After October 1918, all patients, even those in the hospital ward, were required to perform at least some labor when not receiving medical treatment. White troops were quartered separately from black troops, and officers were housed separately from enlisted men.

The number of patients being treated at any one time at the venereal camps from September through December 1918 (the period for which the most complete records are available) ranged from a low of 142 to a high of 638, with an average of 373.[72] Patients remained at the segregation camps for an average of twenty-eight days, though the typical loss of workdays per patient was only five days because all but the sickest patients were required to perform at least some light-duty labor every day during their treatment.

The army was concerned about the morale of the venereal patients, owing to the "marked depression" observed among many of the men. On their admission to the camp, they were informed that "although they had contracted a venereal disease, they would not at any time be treated in any fashion that would bring discredit to them as individuals. Medical treatment was considered first and foremost."[73] As with almost all other army posts and camps, facilities for education, entertainment, and athletics were provided, including a moving-picture area and a building containing materials donated by the YMCA. Military discipline was maintained within the camps, with the interned soldiers formed into battalions, falling in for reveille, marching in formation, and receiving inspections each week. The army made it clear to soldiers that they were not prisoners: "At no time . . . was barbed wire of any character used as a means of confinement for men whose only reason for being in the camp was to secure treatment for venereal disease."[74] Nor were the infected considered morally hopeless cases or incapable of being rehabilitated.

Before discharge, patients were given "personal talks relative to their conditions" by medical officers and "every effort was made to encourage the men regarding their future careers."[75]

Postwar Anti–Venereal Disease Efforts in Germany

Just as in France, prostitution was legal in Germany before U.S. occupation, though it was regulated by the government.[76] Prostitutes were routinely examined and issued licenses if they did not exhibit symptoms of venereal diseases. Those practicing without a license faced legal penalties, including jail time and forced medical treatment. Until October 15, 1919, the only significant change the U.S. Army made to pre-occupation German civil procedures was to "merely [add] the expedient of deporting without trial such persons [German civilians] as seemed undesirable, and bringing them before a military court if they returned."[77] It otherwise generally allowed German courts and medical inspections of prostitutes to operate without interference.

The rate of venereal infection among soldiers increased dramatically the longer American forces remained in Germany. In the early months of 1919, the rate averaged 40 per 1,000 per annum, but by October the rate had increased more than tenfold to 422.65.[78] Army officials blamed the increase on the rescission of the AFG's antifraternization order in September 1919, the migration of French prostitutes into occupied Germany—further reminder that it was always French rather than German women who were feared as sexual dangers—and the arrival of new units to replace those demobilized at the end of the war.[79]

In October 1919, Headquarters, American Forces in Germany, issued Bulletin No. 34, "Vagrants and Juveniles," which changed procedures for handling prostitutes, venereally infected or otherwise.[80] This order defined one type of vagrant as "any woman who solicits or has illicit sexual intercourse with any person serving the United States or any associated government."[81] Women convicted of vagrancy in the newly established Vagrancy Court would be imprisoned for a minimum of two months and a maximum of six months, immediately inspected by an army medical sanitation officer, and confined for hospital treatment if found to be venereally infected.[82] In the October 1919 order, the army described its previous anti–venereal disease efforts as consisting of "medical examination of women; hospitalization of women suffering from venereal disease; prophylaxis for men; anti-fraternization regulations"; and later "deportation of undesirable persons."[83] The new order made prostitution itself a crime, while simultaneously making proof of actual prostitution unnecessary. The court only had to establish that the woman had had "illicit" sex with any American or Allied soldier or civilian employee of the American government. In establishing the Vagrancy Court and associated procedures, the army implicitly conceded its previous efforts, along with those of the German government, to have been inadequate. It correctly noted that medically examining and hospitalizing infected women did not appreciably protect against venereal disease and that existing prophylaxis procedures were likewise ineffective, since "statistics showed that half the men contracting venereal disease had taken prophylaxis." The antifraternization regulations, so the army now estimated, "prevented only the better class of women from associating with soldiers, and did not prevent the worst class of dissolute women from so doing." Deportation was likewise judged to be ineffective because of "lax procedures by German police officials."[84]

By the end of 1921, the AFG reported that it had managed to reduce the annual venereal disease rate among American soldiers from more than four hundred per one thousand at the peak of the problem to approximately one hundred.[85] After the occupation of Germany ended, the army concluded that the Vagrancy Court had been effective in lowering the number of new venereal infections among soldiers.[86] Still, the rate of venereal infection remained two and a half times greater during the occupation of Germany than it had been in France during the war.

Military Justice and Venereal Disease

In April 1919, Pershing learned that officers who contracted venereal diseases were not being court-martialed. He had told commanding generals on several occasions that "he wished [officers] to be court-martialed, as they deserved it more than enlisted men."[87] While Pershing approved a draft General Order making this punishment explicit and mandatory, he never issued it. It is unclear why he did not (surviving records do not shed light on the matter). The AEF's Chief Surgeon, in commenting on the draft order, noted only that "it is understood that he [Pershing] gave it careful attention and approval, but the general order was never issued."[88] A thorough search of the available AEF court-martial records revealed that just nine men (including three officers) were court-martialed for contracting venereal disease "through neglect" and six men (one an officer) were charged with refusing treatment for a venereal disease during either the war in France or the subsequent occupation of Germany.[89] Two of these men were charged with both offenses and are included in both totals. Five men were also charged with being absent without leave

(AWOL) and two with desertion, suggesting that the venereal charges may have been added for punitive purposes since deserting or being AWOL were more serious charges. That just thirteen men were charged with these kinds of offenses out of the more than two million men in the AEF suggests that these offenses were only very rarely punished through formal judicial proceedings. Though Pershing repeatedly ordered that all members of the AEF who contracted venereal diseases and failed to receive prophylaxis be court-martialed, there was clearly strong resistance by individual officers to the army's institutional pressures to formally punish venereal offenders.

The army used a functionalist rationale to court-martial one of the very few junior officers charged with a venereal offense. Second Lieutenant Leo A. Regan was charged with twice contracting venereal diseases "through his own misconduct . . . which thereby incapacitated him for the full and proper performance of his military duties."[90] The court went to unusual lengths to offer theories as to how Regan might have contracted acute gonorrhea through no fault of his own (for example, through sitting on a contaminated toilet seat) and also proposed that he could be suffering a recurrence of a case of gonorrhea contracted before his military service, though a medical officer testified that the case was acute and had been contracted at most two or three weeks before his examination of Regan. The court ultimately rendered the unusual verdict of nolle prosequi (we are unwilling to pursue) to one charge and not guilty to the other. While the defendant was acquitted, the court was chastised by the reviewing authority for "fail[ing] in its duty to convict because the second charge was established beyond a reasonable doubt." As the reviewing authority pointed out, it was clear that the members of the court believed the matter did not warrant a general court-martial but rather should have been handled as a disciplinary matter by Regan's immediate commanding officer, warranting no harsher penalty than a verbal reprimand or temporary restriction to post.

In another case, Second Lieutenant Hoyne Wells pleaded guilty to contracting a venereal disease and failing to receive prophylaxis and was dismissed from the service.[91] The reviewing authority, Major General J. G. Harbord, Commander, Services of Supply, recommended that the sentence be disapproved and Wells be restored to duty, stating that Wells "should not have his army career and general reputation blasted by such a sentence. . . . The notoriety of the trial in itself is greater punishment than has been found necessary to control similar offenses among enlisted men." Pershing accepted Harbord's recommendation.

These two cases in which officers of the AEF were court-martialed for contracting venereal diseases highlight the dramatic disparity between the harsh course of action Pershing ordered for venereal offenders and how these orders were executed within the AEF. It is clear that officers were not being regularly or frequently court-martialed for contracting venereal diseases, but this also held true for enlisted men. Penalties, when issued at all for these types of convictions, were minor, usually amounting only to a partial forfeiture of pay for several months. The threat of court-martial for contracting venereal diseases was an idle one. This fact seems to have been understood by most members of the AEF, and the threat likely had little effect on AEF soldiers' sexual behavior and compliance with the army's requirements for prophylaxis.

Pershing and Sexual Morality

The role of Pershing, as commander of the AEF, was so pivotal to how the U.S. Army treated sexuality during World War I that it is worth exploring his public statements and personal views and experiences in some detail.[92] While stationed in the Philippines, Pershing had evinced no concerns about the involvement of the U.S. Army in medically regulating prostitution there. During the Punitive Expedition in Mexico against Pancho Villa in 1916–1917, Pershing established a medical inspection program using U.S. Army physicians as health inspectors for the prostitutes who congregated near American encampments. "Everyone was satisfied," Pershing later said, "as the towns have been kept absolutely clear of that sort of thing [prostitution]. . . . The establishment was necessary and has proved the best way to handle a difficult problem."[93]

Pershing's public endorsement of a policy of abstinence for all soldiers of the AEF, as well as mandatory venereal treatments if they did engage in sexual activities while in Europe, was in sharp contrast with his experiences in the Philippines and on the Mexican border, as well as his personal life. Pershing's biographers agree that the general, a widower, had multiple sexual affairs during his time in France (it is unclear whether Pershing received the mandatory venereal treatments himself after these encounters). He had also been publicly accused of living with a Filipina *querida* (mistress) during his previous tour in the Philippines and fathering several "half-breed" children with her.[94] In France, Pershing struck up one particularly long-lasting sexual relationship with Micheline Resco, a Romanian woman (and naturalized French citizen) thirty-four years his junior.[95] Despite these personal relationships, Pershing remained publicly steadfast in urging that the soldiers of the AEF avoid all sexual contact with European women.

Aside from his continual advocacy of sexual abstinence for soldiers of the AEF during the war, Pershing was particularly concerned that demobilizing

soldiers would return to the United States infected with venereal disease. As
he toured units preparing to embark on transport ships for their return home,
Pershing gave a standard ten-minute speech to each unit. In this final speech
to his men, Pershing reiterated his hope for "the cleanest army in the world":
"May I say just one word about the moral side? . . . It should be our ambition
to maintain the splendid record for morality that has existed in the Army. . . .
It is my very great ambition that not a single case [of venereal disease] among
the American Expeditionary Forces shall arrive in the United States. I think
this is a goal that we all ought to work for."[96] During these visits, Pershing
would also often question the medical officers in each departing unit on venereal issues, with a typical conversation going as follows:

"How many cases of V.D.?"

"Only one, sir."

"One too many."[97]

Can Pershing's official positions on sexual behavior be reconciled with his
personal practice? Through his implicit endorsement of the army's regulated
prostitution programs during his years in the Philippines, as well as his establishment of a similar regime during the Mexican Expedition, Pershing evidenced a strong commitment to reducing the number of men rendered
combat ineffective due to venereal infections. But his efforts to mitigate (or
even eliminate altogether) the number of venereal cases in the AEF took on a
moralizing tone that had not been present in his earlier deployments. The context of World War I, and the vast conscription effort that had mobilized
young men from across American society, likely influenced Pershing's emphasis on abstinence and returning home pure. Before they were allowed to
board the homebound troopships, each division heard Pershing's sentiments
on the subject. "It is a proud thing to go back to our mothers, and our wives,
and our sisters and sweethearts," Pershing lectured returning troops, "[and]
be able to say that [we] belonged to an organization of two million men absolutely free from venereal disease and it will be the proudest thing in my life
if it can be done."[98] Young, Chief Urologist of the AEF, seems to have been a
major influence on Pershing's decision to adopt a policy emphasizing abstinence while also relying on mandatory venereal treatments in case of sexual
activity for the AEF.[99] Young traveled with Pershing on the first American transport ship bringing staff officers to France and gave a graphic presentation on
the effects of venereal disease to Pershing and his staff during the voyage. Once
in France, Young and Pershing met on a number of occasions, and Pershing
appears to have supported Young's anti–venereal disease efforts. It is difficult,
however, to entirely reconcile Pershing's stated policies on abstinence and sexual behavior within the AEF with his own activities during the war; such a

disparity must inevitably invite charges of hypocrisy. It should be noted, how-ever, that despite his position as commander of the AEF, and no matter his personal feelings or actions, Pershing was not solely responsible for an absti-nence policy for the AEF. Pershing's General Orders that emphasized and re-emphasized such a policy were important, to be sure, but the emphasis on sexual abstinence did not begin or end with him. The CTCA had initiated such a sexual education campaign independently of Pershing before he had even set foot on European soil.

Fraternization, Romantic Relationships, and Marriages with French and German Civilians

Though the AEF's anti–venereal disease campaign focused almost entirely on regulating prostitutes, not all sexual contact between AEF soldiers and Euro-pean women took place on a purely commercial basis. It is important to note that the very distinction between prostitutes and nonprostitutes often made by army officials and civilian moralists alike is problematic, particularly dur-ing the societal chaos of World War I, as these are almost entirely constructed (and contested) categories. For example, an impoverished French woman who received some money or food from an American soldier and later had sex with him might be variously considered a prostitute, a temporary sex partner, or simply the man's girlfriend. She might or might not self-identify as a prosti-tute, and her male sex partner might or might not consider their relationship a commercial one, to the extent that they conceived of the relationship in rigid terms at all. Army officials, and American moralists, might also have had differ-ing opinions of the woman's position and her relationship with the American soldier, shaped by a variety of factors, including their conceptions of the socio-economic classes of the individuals involved. Regardless, a significant number of American soldiers entered romantic relationships in Europe, either during the war or soon thereafter, with women the army did not consider prostitutes. This is unsurprising, given the army's policies intended to keep soldiers out of brothels. Shortly after the Armistice was declared in November 1918, the AEF edition of the *Chicago Tribune* published a short piece entitled "American or French Girls, which is best?" The responses from American doughboys poured into the newspaper for weeks.[100] Many of the soldiers praised the vir-tues of American women, but some strongly advocated French women as romantic partners, one officer stating, "If the American girl is jealous of the French girl today, she has good reason to be. . . . If [American] girls do not change and learn to be more attentive and appreciative of our men than they have been in the past, they are going to have more time for knitting. . . . The fellows . . . will go out with their little French girls when they want a really interesting evening."[101] Foreign women who would give American soldiers "a really interesting evening" were precisely the kind of women many Americans hoped to keep away from what the Wilson administration had been promoting as "the world's cleanest army."[102] American anxiety about intercultural romance was evident in the public outcry over a newspaper report suggesting that more than two hundred thousand American soldiers were planning to stay in Europe with their French wives and girlfriends rather than return to the United States.[103] The report was entirely unfounded and a retraction was printed four months later, but these incidents made visible the simple fact that many American soldiers were having intimate relationships with French, and later German, women during their military service in the AEF.

While the army was most concerned about the venereal effects of the commercial sex trade on U.S. servicemen and military operations, romantic relationships with local women abounded and had impacts on the military. As early as November 1917, one American journal reported on the rise of "Franco-Yanko Romance," noting that "the French girls like the American boys" and that such romantic relationships were becoming commonplace.[104] Though the AEF had made some halfhearted efforts during the war to segregate soldiers from French women, this was an impossible task. Billeting arrangements quartered some Americans with French families, French women worked in various administrative capacities with the AEF, and the soldiers moved freely about French cities and towns. By the end of the war, the AEF's own newspaper *Stars and Stripes* published ads for an English-French phrase book that promised "16 pages of snappy love stuff," including such phrases as "Where are you going, Bright Eyes? Where do you live?" and "When can I come see you?"[105]

The longer the AEF remained in France, the more requests for marriage between American soldiers and French women poured in. In June 1918, the AEF's Judge Advocate, W. A. Bethel, drafted a strong argument against granting permission for AEF soldiers to marry.[106] In Bethel's view, such marriages were "prejudicial to military interests . . . under present conditions." Marriage would, according to Bethel, only get in the way of winning the war. Bethel did, however, recognize that an outright ban was not possible under the existing legal framework. He recommended action "at the highest level," either in the War Department or by President Woodrow Wilson, to facilitate a ban. Bethel was certainly not alone in his opposition to marriage; his views coincided with those of many officers who refused many soldiers under their command permission to marry. As one veteran cavalry colonel put it, "When Pvt. W. asked permission to marry I refused . . . on the grounds that . . . we were over here to fight when the time came; and to spend the rest of the time getting ready for it and not to marry and raise families." The colonel was concerned about setting a precedent for marriage in his unit: "If Pvt. W. is allowed to marry this girl it will lead to a number of other cases just exactly like this. I have been through the whole thing twice before in Cuba and the Philippines."[107] Bethel acknowledged that "the matter of prohibiting marriage is a very delicate one" and that "marriage is a personal privilege with which the government, in general, has no right to interfere." He also thought that great care must be taken so as not to offend the French allies with a ban on marriage: "I think it is very important to make it clear . . . that there is absolutely no prejudice against matrimonial alliances between the American and French people. . . . Such restrictions are imposed [as] a military measure for the purpose of aiding both people in winning the war."

Pershing ultimately disagreed with the Judge Advocate's proposal, refusing to issue a blanket ban on marriages within the AEF. An outright ban, however, was unnecessary. In addition to withholding permission to marry, unit commanders could (and did) simply refuse to grant soldiers leave in order to attend marriage ceremonies, forcing the soldiers to go AWOL if they wished to marry, and face military discipline on their return. French civil law required potential marriage partners to present written documentation of identity and age (for example, birth certificates), which most American soldiers would be unable to supply, especially on short notice.[108]

Pershing issued an antifraternization order in November 1918, rescinded in September 1919, in an attempt to control sexual relations between U.S. soldiers and German women during the postwar occupation.[109] General Order No. 218 declared,

> During our occupation the civil population is under the special safeguard of the faith and honor of the American army. It is, therefore, the intention of this order to appeal directly to your pride in your position as representatives of a powerful but righteous nation, with the firm conviction that you will so conduct yourself in your relations with the inhabitants of Germany as will cause them to respect you and the country you have the honor to represent. . . . So long as a state of war continues, Germany remains enemy territory, and *there must be no intimate personal associations with its inhabitants* [emphasis added]. A dignified and reserved attitude will be maintained on your part at all times.[110]

The high incidence of prostitution in France and Germany and the venereal infection rate among soldiers throughout the American occupation suggest that the antifraternization order was less than successful.[111]

The AEF was persistent in its efforts to prevent the development of romantic relationships between African American soldiers and white French women. While white soldiers were often depicted in CTCA and AEF sexual education films, pamphlets, posters, and other materials as the potential victims of sexually predatory French women, army officials often seemed to consider black soldiers as sexually dangerous sources of corruption for white European women. Officials' efforts to prevent such corruption ranged from the petty orders and harassing regulations often described by black servicemen to more serious, public actions affecting entire units.[112] For example, in a Fourth of July celebration in which both black and white soldiers were invited by French locals, white officers objected to black troops' mingling with French women and held an impromptu public lecture on the need for racial segregation. The same colored unit, the Ninety-Second Infantry Division, was later restricted from traveling more than one mile from its base. Unofficially, white soldiers sometimes convinced French women that blacks were scoundrels and to be avoided. Officially, many army units took measures to prevent blacks from coming into contact with white women. For example, black soldiers in the 804th Pioneers were ordered "not to talk to or be in the company with any white woman, regardless of whether the women solicit their company or not."[113] Other army units drafted notices to local French communities—with limited compliance and effectiveness—ordering French women not to associate with African American soldiers.[114]

An AEF memo, dated August 7, 1918, and titled "Secret Information Concerning Black American Troops," sought to educate French military officials on the state of American race relations, warning the French not to "spoil the Negroes" and expressing particular concern over intimacy between black men and white women. The memo warned the French that "Americans become greatly incensed at any public expression of intimacy between white women with black men. They have recently uttered violent protests against a picture in the 'Vie Parisienne' entitled 'The Child of the Desert' which shows a [white] woman in a 'cabinet particulier' [private room] with a Negro. Familiarity on the part of white women with black men is furthermore a source of profound regret to our experienced colonials who see in it an overweening menace to the prestige of the white race."[115]

Charles R. Isum, an African American sergeant from the Ninety-Second Infantry Division, also complained of race-based problems that developed from his fraternization with white women in France.[116] He reported problems with "the southern rednecks who were in command of my division, brigade and regiment." A Ninety-Second Infantry Division order issued on December 26, 1918, instructed military police to "see that soldiers do not address, carry on conversation with, or accompany the female inhabitants of the area." The order applied only to the black soldiers of the division, as it was a divisional and not an AEF-wide order. Isum was arrested after attending a French wedding to which he had been invited. When the sergeant asserted his right to a court-martial rather than summary discipline (at the urging of his detachment commander, a white major from Massachusetts), he was threatened and intimidated. In the end, he escaped court-martial after several French civilians, including the town mayor, swore affidavits to Isum's character and good conduct at the party.[117]

The romantic relationships that developed between American soldiers and German women who were not deemed to be "of good character"—that is, prostitutes—were still problematic for the army. Civil affairs units were frequently required to function as interlocutors, tasked with adjudicating disputes between American soldiers and German civilians over issues of intimacy and personal relationships. One civil affairs report noted, "There was a general harassing of the girls and young women who had possibly been more or less intimate with the soldiers, which resulted in many family quarrels being brought to this office for settlement, but for lack of evidence showing any disrespect to the Americans, no action could be taken; in most cases it was only rivalry and jealousy on the part of those concerned."[118] German civilians also complained to the army about American men corrupting German women, with a frequent criticism being the amount of money that AFG soldiers had available to spend. One German stated bluntly, "Your soldiers have too much money. . . . Perhaps our girls can't be blamed so much, for, after many years of almost starvation, lack of proper clothing, etc., it seems nothing more or less than human to grasp the opportunity to get something to eat, better clothes and better living conditions, which are provided by the large amount of money which the American soldier has to lavish upon them."[119]

In several cases, Germans threatened fraternizing soldiers, and several American soldiers and their German lovers were said to have had their faces blackened by local men to humiliate them.[120] German women engaging in liaisons with Americans were also threatened with having their names published and distributed to unmarried German men. *Stars and Stripes* reported the *Bürgermeister* (mayor) of Trier as having said that "if any German girl is seen with an American soldier she would be an outcast and would not be allowed to marry on German soil."[121] Some German resistance to fraternization had a racial dimension, with one Berlin newspaper editorial stating, "It is not only an ignominious peace but a race shame that threatens our destruction. The danger exists less in the marriage itself than in the fact that there live German girls capable of such an idea. One of these base women may conclude her love pact, but we will refuse to admit such a couple to our society. We will fight by all means the infusion of blood from Negroes, Frenchmen, Indians, Tonkinese, Americans, and other bearers of that culture."[122]

On September 28, 1919, the AEF rescinded its antifraternization order, "with the hope that this would induce the soldiers to associate with the better classes of the civil population."[123] The army found itself unable to keep U.S. soldiers away from German women entirely and clearly preferred that soldiers associate with women who were not prostitutes and therefore, it believed, less likely to be infected with venereal diseases.

Despite attempts by both the Germans and the Americans to limit fraternization, a significant number of marriages resulted. The army did, however, place a number of impediments in the way of soldiers' marrying. On October 9, 1919, Major General Henry T. Allen, U.S. Commissioner in the Inter-Allied Rhineland High Commission, ordered that U.S. soldiers wanting to marry a German citizen must apply to the AFG General Staff for permission. Both parties must be "free of communicable diseases," and the woman had to prove her "good character." In the case of pregnancy, marriage was permitted, "provided an investigation proved the former good character of the girl."[124] In Allen's private journal (published in 1923 after his retirement), he confessed that he had intended to circumvent his own order and automatically disapprove all requests from soldiers below Grade 3 (Staff Sergeant), "otherwise it would not be long before a large percentage of this command would have wives."[125]

Allen was not alone in his concern. The AFG's postwar report stated bluntly that "in the large majority of cases marriage lowers the efficiency of the enlisted man. And it has been the common experience of military men that the larger the proportion of married soldiers in a military organization, the lower its efficiency," though it offered no data in support of this assertion.[126] It is clear that fears about the negative impact of marriage on military efficiency encompassed concerns about logistics—because of the limited billeting for married soldiers and transport capacity on ships returning to the United States—venereal disease, and lax discipline. Army officials also worried about soldiers marrying women of "ill repute," noting that prostitutes had flocked to the American area of occupation, attracted to American soldiers' relative affluence.[127]

The War Department disagreed with Allen's position on marriage, disapproving his order in a July 1920 letter and forcing the AFG to revise its marriage policy.[128] Under the new policy, soldiers wanting to marry had to place a one-hundred-dollar deposit with their commanding officer to defray the cost of their new wife's travel to the United States; soldiers under Grade 3 would have to leave the AFG; and the soldiers had to be of "very good" or "excellent" character. The number of applications accepted would depend on transportation capacity. These requirements still proved too onerous for at least some soldiers. In one 1922 case, an American staff sergeant was court-martialed for forging an endorsement from his commanding officer, which he presented to a local *Bürgermeister* in order to secure a legal marriage with a local German woman.[129] Despite these procedural obstacles, between October 1919 and January 1922, 1,527 U.S. soldiers requested permission to marry, and 767 (just over 50%) received approval to do so. This is a small proportion of the roughly quarter million American soldiers who served in the AFG at its peak. In the same period, European dependents of enlisted men traveled to America on U.S. transports: 782 women and 267 children.[130]

Certainly not all romantic relationships between American soldiers and German women resulted in marriage, even when pregnancies were involved. Illegitimate births helped create a sense of moral panic[131] among German civilians and caused what the army delicately termed "strained relations."[132] One local report noted an increase in the number of local illegitimate births from 12 in 1919 to 83 the following year. In Coblenz (the AFG's headquarters), American soldiers were blamed for 40–80 percent of the illegitimate pregnancies.[133] The army stated that in its area of occupation, there were 1,134 illegitimate births in 1920 and 863 in 1921, with alleged American parenthood in 36 percent and 42 percent of the cases, respectively. Of these cases, nearly 40 percent involving American soldiers occurred in the *Kreis* (County) Mayen area, where all soldiers were billeted with private families, instead of in barracks. More than 1.6 million German men died under arms during World War I (12.5% of all German men aged fifteen to forty-nine), creating a significant sex ratio imbalance after the war.[134] Given this postwar gender imbalance, it is not surprising that the relative lack of young German men of marriageable age meant that some German women turned to American soldiers as potential husbands. It is impossible to say how many illegitimate births there would have been in this area absent the American presence, though German civilians clearly placed most of the blame on the soldiers billeted in their homes and towns.

According to German law, fathers of children born in Germany were required to provide child support until the child reached the age of sixteen, though women had no legal recourse if the father failed to comply. As one German official wrote to the AFG officer in charge of civil affairs, "The assistance which is given to the children depends only on the free will of the soldiers concerned."[135] Many German women wrote to the U.S. Army attempting to force American soldiers to provide financial and other support for illegitimate children. The army would help locate the soldiers and point out to the men their "moral obligation," but it could not force the men to provide aid. The army stated that in about a quarter of the cases in which pregnant women approached the army for assistance, American soldiers agreed to make monthly payments to support the illegitimate children.[136] In some cases, the men denied responsibility and refused to pay child support, in which case the women were sometimes advised to take legal action against the men in U.S. courts. It is unclear, however, that any of the women could or did pursue this option.[137] Expectant mothers were not alone in contacting the army for assistance; local institutions such as the Infants Asylum in Coblenz also sought financial support, reasoning that since the American military was responsible for the increase in abandoned children, it was also financially liable for caring for the children.[138]

Ultimately, despite institutional and cultural impediments to marriage, more than five thousand American soldiers returned to the United States with European wives.[139] Demographically, those AEF soldiers who did marry while overseas tended to marry European women who were close to them in age and socioeconomic class, with the men usually a few years older than their brides, mirroring marriage patterns in the United States at the time.[140] The soldiers also tended to be disproportionately of foreign birth or parentage, even beyond the proportion of such men in the AEF. Despite domestic fears that these "war brides" would remain alien figures within their new communities in the United States, the women appear to have been entirely assimilated into American society, largely disappearing from the historical record.

Marriage-Related Offenses and Matters of Sexual Propriety

For those soldiers who were married, the army used its power to protect and enforce civilian social and legal norms surrounding the institution of marriage. At least thirteen married men were court-martialed for adultery. The specifics of the charges varied, but most were for either maintaining a female civilian mistress or registering at and occupying a hotel room with a woman who was not the accused's wife. Of these, nine were commissioned officers, one a civilian employee of the U.S. Army—who were subject to court-martial during the war—and one a first sergeant. Almost all were convicted and dismissed from the service.[141] One of the accused, a married private (and one of the very few enlisted men charged with a marriage-related offense), was acquitted of entering into an engagement and promising to marry a female civilian, as well as inducing the female civilian to come alone and unchaperoned into a military camp to meet him.[142] A married second lieutenant was charged with being AWOL, becoming drunk in a club, bringing a French woman to the club and getting her a job there, "causing comment by other officers and bringing discredit upon the military service," and writing a letter to his wife asking for a divorce.[143] This officer was acquitted of all charges except for being drunk in the club, without further comment by the court. He was dismissed from the service as a result of this conviction, a much harsher sentence than was generally given for a single count of drunkenness in public. While the second lieutenant's peers were unwilling to convict him for adultery, it appears that they were also unwilling to allow him to remain in military service because of the public scandal his behavior had caused.

An additional three men—two officers (a captain and a first lieutenant) and a civilian employee of the YMCA—were each court-martialed and convicted of "willfully and knowingly contract[ing] a bigamous marriage to the disgrace of the military service, knowing he had a legal wife living."[144] The men were dismissed from the service (in the case of the two officers) and sentenced to three years of hard labor (the first lieutenant) or five years of hard labor (the captain and the YMCA employee). In another court-martial, which the army—and the *New York Times*—seemed to consider a particularly sordid affront to traditional American values, Major Guy H. Wyman was court-martialed for intimidating his wife into granting him a legal divorce so that he could then marry a French woman he met while serving in the AEF. Wyman also legally adopted the French woman, only seven years his junior, so that he could secure free passage for her on an army transport from France to the United States after the war.[145] The matter came to a head when the major reneged on his alimony payments to his ex-wife. He was dismissed from the service in the wake of this public scandal. There were exceedingly few prosecutions for similar offenses in which there was no public scandal or outcry.

In almost all court-martial cases related to matters of sexual propriety, the accused was white. One case involving an African American officer, Second Lieutenant Thomas J. Narcisse, highlights racial anxieties regarding sex between African American men and white women.[146] Narcisse was charged with a wide range of offenses, from being AWOL, to falsely claiming to be part of the Military Police Corps, to failing to pay a debt. The bulk of the offenses with which he was charged, however, concerned his romantic correspondence with four white French women. He was charged with, "by persuasion and professions of affection, seduc[ing], debauch[ing], and carnally know[ing]" one of the women and corresponding for months with the others using "terms of endearment and affection." One of the letters was specifically cited as including the passage, "You little angel, why dont [sic] you write some-times. With love and best wishes to my dear little Renee, my little Reine [queen]." Narcisse was also charged with "feloniously ma[king] and publish[ing] a letter disparaging white Southern officers regarding his public romantic en-counters with white women with intent to hold up fellow officers to public shame, ridicule, and contempt." This letter purportedly written by Narcisse stated, in part, "All of the white officers from Alabama, Mississippi, Louisiana, and Texas, and other states of their kind, where they see me out walking with these white girls and holding such agreeable conversation, I think, it makes them sick." The court found Narcisse guilty of several offenses, including carrying on correspondence with the women and writing the letter about the white officers. He was found not guilty, however, of having sex with the women. He was sentenced to be dismissed from the service and serve ten years of hard labor, though this sentence was overturned by the reviewing au-thority. In an unusually long statement, the reviewing authority—in this partic-ular case, Pershing himself—overturned the charges in their entirety and noted, "The charges in this case breathe prejudice against the accused on ac-count of his color, and in the opinion of the confirming authority, the depar-ture from that judicial attitude which should regard all men as equal before the law was so marked as to render the trial of this accused unfair." Narcisse's sentence was disapproved and he was released from arrest.

Though the army represented its interventions in the sexual economy of war as promoting military efficiency and discipline, it clearly also sought to maintain a code of sexual and social mores and norms that extended well be-yond the letter of the law. It circumscribed, for example, "acceptable" sex acts that soldiers might engage in, defined sexual harassment of civilian women to include indecent proposals and language, and restricted the kinds of social interaction in which officers might engage, particularly when those officers were married or when the offenses resulted in public embarrassment. The army prosecuted servicemen for a broad variety of crimes involving sexual propriety, including many involving indecent proposals and lewd (sexual) lan-guage. These offenses were generally charged as violations of either the Ninety-Fifth Article of War ("conduct unbecoming an officer and gentleman") or the Ninety-Sixth (miscellaneous "disorders and neglects to the prejudice of good order and military discipline" or "conduct of a nature to bring discredit upon the military service"). "Disrespectful" interactions with women at so-cial events such as dinner parties were grounds for prosecution, as were en-gaging "in an exhibition dance with a woman under such circumstances as to bring discredit upon the military service" and discussing "immoral relations with women with enlisted men." Of the eight courts-martial that can clearly be identified as involving what twenty-first-century observers would term sexual harassment, all but two involved junior officers (the remaining cases involved a private and a corporal). All but one of the cases resulted in convictions (the final conviction was disapproved because of a legal technicality by the reviewing authority), and three resulted in dismissals from the service, one of the harshest sentences meted out to officers during this period. It is clear that the army took charges of sexual impropriety seriously, especially when committed by officers, at least on those occasions when the behavior took place in a public way that created a spectacle that risked damaging the army's reputation and relationship with local civilians.

The army's differing standards of sexual propriety for officers and enlisted men are made even clearer when courts-martial for prostitution-related offenses are considered. Only six enlisted men and a single noncommissioned officer (a corporal) were court-martialed for consorting with women the army alleged to be prostitutes, while forty-four commissioned officers were court-martialed for similar offenses.[147] Furthermore, all the enlisted cases generally included other, related offenses (for example, theft from the prostitute in several cases and abandoning a sentry post to visit a house of prostitution in another) that seem to have elevated the prostitution charges above the threshold the army could tolerate. Officers were court-martialed for being seen in public while in uniform with prostitutes (often described as "lewd and wanton women") drinking at cafés, boarding houses, or houses of prostitution. In several cases, officers were court-martialed for consorting with prostitutes while in the presence or company of enlisted men, but in none of these cases were enlisted men also court-martialed along with the officers.[148]

There appear to have been several aspects to the army's concern about the behavior of commissioned officers involving prostitutes or "lewd" women. The first concern was for officers who brought prostitutes into military quarters and engaged in boisterous behavior, usually involving alcohol, thereby creating a drunken, public spectacle of inappropriate sexual behavior in front of other American officers.[149] In the case of Captains Harry Cook and Charles H. Roche (court-martialed separately for the same set of offenses), the men were charged with bringing prostitutes into their barrack quarters "for immoral purposes," along with bottles of champagne (alcohol was not permitted in quarters), and lying to a major who asked the men whether they had women in their quarters. The men were caught and reported by fellow officers, convicted, and dismissed from the service.

The army's second concern involved officers who cohabited with a prostitute over an extended period of time, usually at a hotel or other public living space, in a manner that was visible to other officers and civilians, again creating a public spectacle.[150] For example, Captain Richard H. Erwin was accused of occupying a hotel room on at least eight occasions with a French woman who was not his wife. When called to testify on his own behalf, Erwin stated that he planned to divorce his wife and marry the French woman. He also stated that his intentions had been "pure and undefiled" toward the woman and that despite the fact that they slept in the same bed, no sexual intercourse had taken place. The court agreed with the prosecutor that no proof that sexual intercourse had taken place was necessary and that "when a man and a woman are together in the manner described in this case, that sexual intercourse does take place," finding Erwin's conduct to be "scandalous and disgraceful" and "to the discredit of the service." He was dismissed from the service.

The army's third main concern pertained to officers who entered houses of prostitution or other places in which enlisted men were present, often drinking and gambling with the enlisted soldiers before having sex with a prostitute, a clear breach of military discipline.[151] Captain John McKenzie was accused of entering a house of prostitution, associating with the women there (McKenzie's exact activities with the women were never discussed in his court-martial), and, most damningly in the eyes of the court, paying for three enlisted men also present to drink champagne and have sex with prostitutes. McKenzie, a career soldier who had served more than twenty years in the army as a private and sergeant before being commissioned on the eve of American intervention in Europe, was judged to be "morally unfit to hold a commission in the American army" and dismissed from the service. Captain Oscar T. Yates, another former enlisted soldier who was commissioned at the start of World War I, was accused of drinking with an enlisted soldier and a prostitute in a public café. He was convicted and dismissed from the service. First Lieutenant Levin I. Watkins was alleged to have donned a disguise in order to enter a house of prostitution after having been previously warned by a military policeman to leave an "off-limits" area. Watkins was intoxicated and created a public nuisance when he was caught a second time by the military police. He too was convicted and dismissed from the service. The commonality among these concerns was the spectacle of commissioned officers consorting with prostitutes in public in front of enlisted men. It is clear that officers were sometimes court-martialed for their interactions with prostitutes and other women "of ill fame" because they offended the sensibilities of their fellow officers who witnessed their behavior, and at other times because they engaged in activities the army deemed immoral in front of civilians and passersby. The army also acted to maintain the boundaries of social propriety between officers and enlisted men. When officers publicly violated these social norms—by drinking, gambling, or discussing sex with enlisted men, for example—the army acted rapidly and decisively to convict and dismiss the offending officers.

Commissioned officers were also court-martialed for behaving disrespectfully toward women in public in a variety of ways. One officer slapped the face of a female cashier.[152] Several more behaved disrespectfully toward women at dinner parties, including the wife of the American consul.[153] One discussed his "immoral relations with women" with enlisted men.[154] One was even court-martialed for publicly dancing with a woman.[155] While the total number of courts-martial involving matters of sexual propriety is relatively small, it is interesting that in almost all cases of adultery, bigamy, consorting with prostitutes, sexual harassment, and otherwise behaving disrespectfully toward women, those charged were almost exclusively commissioned officers. The record suggests significant differences in the ways that the U.S. Army thought about the marriages, sexual relationships, and public behavior of officers and enlisted men. There is clearly an element of class bias involved in these cases, with officers seemingly held to a higher standard of behavior, as it is difficult to believe that no enlisted men in the AEF committed any such acts of impropriety. In any case, enlisted men who did so were not court-martialed for such actions, though commissioned officers sometimes were. Commissioned officers seem to have been held to a higher standard of sexual propriety than enlisted men, at least when in public or when their actions came to light and caused scandal, speaking to a very different conception of how officers were supposed to behave—as "gentlemen," exhibiting a much more genteel model of masculinity than enlisted soldiers. In such cases, the army appears to have taken action not because of the particular actions in which some officers engaged but because the servicemen, especially officers, made a public spectacle of their behavior, which caused "scandal and disgrace to the military service."

Intentions and Goals of the Army's Sexual Interventions

The U.S. Army expended considerable resources to medically surveil and legally regulate the sexual activities of its soldiers and their partners in Europe. In some ways, it may seem surprising that the army was so interested in managing sexuality during wartime. The U.S. Army had three main areas of concern relative to sexuality. First was military efficiency. This had two major components: order and discipline; and able-bodiedness. The army sought to maintain what it described broadly as "military order and discipline," which encompassed a variety of expected and required behaviors and adherence to all army rules, regulations, and policies, as well as obedience to all lawful orders given by superiors within the military hierarchy. The army also desired that all soldiers be free from disease and physical incapacitations, so that they would be free to perform their duties.

A second broad area of concern for the army was diplomacy and geopolitics. In World War I, members of the AEF first deployed to France as allies and guests, and after the Armistice, the U.S. Army served in Germany until 1923 as representatives of an occupying power. Relationships with French and German civilians took place both at the official level (among leaders and officials) and at the unofficial level (between soldiers and citizens), all of which helped to continually negotiate the relationships between the United States, France, and Germany. The actions of individuals mattered greatly to the maintenance of these relationships between nations.[156] Additionally, the legal and cultural norms in Europe meant that the army dealt with sexual transgressions differently from how these issues were treated within the United States. While federal agencies, with the cooperation of the army, did establish a medical surveillance and incarceration program covering prostitutes and women considered to be potential prostitutes in areas around domestic army bases in the United States during World War I, the legal and cultural contexts in Europe permitted the army to create a much larger medical-legal framework for dealing with venereal disease and prostitution, despite some resistance by the French and German governments.

Last, various army officials repeatedly stated that the institution valued and promoted morality. The army and its leaders served their civilian masters, many of whom were progressives, deeply concerned with social and moral reform and ideologically invested in the use of statist institutions and legal practices to uphold perceived American moral traditions. Pershing's bulletins about the "clean health" of the nation were directed toward at least three audiences: the soldiers of the AEF, who were being urged to alter their personal behavior; the French and German civilians and leaders who hosted and interacted with American soldiers on a daily basis; and the American home front, encompassing a wide variety of interest groups, including the families of soldiers, moral and social reformers, and the Wilson administration itself, all of which were critical in maintaining political support for the war effort and the postwar occupation of Germany. For many progressives and other American observers, one dimension of the American war effort was protecting American servicemen from the "corrupt" influences of Old World Europeans. Some moralists were concerned that encounters between American "boys" and foreign temptresses would lead to sexual and moral decay. Many Americans conceived of the mainly conscript AEF in much sharper moral terms than they had the prewar professional U.S. Army. Professional, Regular Army soldiers were often stereotyped as rough, hard-drinking, sexually adventurous ne'er-do-wells. They did not elicit the same level of public concern over their sexual morality as the newly inducted doughboys. Engagement with the world and foreign affairs became increasingly important to Americans during this period, though many sought to forge a distinct national identity based on particular ideas about morality, with the U.S. Army as the instrument and recipient of this new American identity.

As an institution, the army needed to appear to be protecting American soldiers by policing their morals. This is evident from the numerous official policies, orders, medical directives, and courts-martial that sought to prevent illicit sexual contact and punish infractions. Some officers were no doubt earnestly trying to impose a progressive moral code on their fellow soldiers. Others clearly resisted too much intervention in sexual matters, seeming to adopt a "boys will be boys" attitude that embraced a virile conception of masculinity. The army sought to police the private sexual relations of soldiers and officers when these relationships resulted in either public disgrace for the army or venereal infections. When sexual matters spilled into public scandal—for example, when officers were caught publicly cavorting with prostitutes—or when soldiers became unable to perform their military duties because of venereal infections, the army took decisive action. As an organization, the AEF and the AFG remained internally divided on the extent to which a particular code of sexual morality should be imposed on soldiers or the sex lives of soldiers should be intruded on. So long as soldiers' sexual activities remained behind closed doors and did not cause overt problems for the army, such as scandals involving officers, pregnancies, and disease, they appear to have gone—officially—unnoticed.

The American experience in Europe brought with it many challenges to preexisting notions of sexuality—and Progressive Era medical and moral reform discourses—and increased the American government's concern with soldiers' sexuality. American soldiers and their European sexual partners complicated the debates between policymakers and critics by highlighting competing conceptions of acceptable sexual behavior and demonstrating the difficulties of regulating sexual behavior. These debates help explore the intersections between U.S. moral and social reform; concerns about disease and sexual danger; cross-cultural racial, class, and gender perceptions; and military efficiency.

CHAPTER 5

The "Racial (and Sexual) Maelstrom" in Hawaii, 1909–1940

> It is this being away from home that results in so many marriages between the men in military and naval service and the brunettes of Hawaii. . . . These girls find the romance the more thrilling because the boys are *haole* [white] and, perhaps, because they wear the uniform.
>
> —Sociologist Romanzo C. Adams

As in other locales, the U.S. Army in Hawaii was concerned about the problems that sex could cause for the institution, and it created a series of medical and legal interventions to mitigate the damage. These problems often occurred when soldiers' sexual misconduct was embarrassing or scandalous, or when it caused conflicts with local civilians in the communities surrounding the army's bases (for example, sexual harassment of local women or disputes with civilian men over women). Soldiers' sexual activities might also damage unit readiness, as in the case of soldiers who contracted venereal diseases. Sexual misconduct could create morale problems—for example, in cases of same-sex sexual activity, particularly when the activity was witnessed by others or was nonconsensual. The army was likewise invested in maintaining the privileges of commissioned officers and their families, which it sought to do in cases in which enlisted soldiers invaded the privacy of officers' and their families. This occurred with greater frequency at Hawaiian army bases than at other army posts, likely due to the relative remoteness of Hawaiian army bases from civilian communities. Hawaii, described as a racial and ethnic "maelstrom," is also useful for illuminating the complexities that differences in race and ethnicity brought to cases involving sexuality. Racial tensions—between native Hawaiians, the succession of various immigrant groups to the islands, and white and black soldiers—had a long history, developing as the army's presence in Hawaii grew over time.

In 1893, American and European settlers in Hawaii staged a revolution against Hawaiian Queen Liliuokalani and immediately sought Hawaii's admission to the United States.[1] President Grover Cleveland, a friend of the queen, rebuffed their efforts, allowing an interim Republic of Hawaii to govern the islands for the next five years. Under the Republic of Hawaii, the franchise was granted to 2,800 citizens, many of whom were employees of the Dole Pineapple Corporation. In 1898, President William McKinley urged annexation of Hawaii during the Spanish-American War, declaring the islands an important location for a military outpost in the Pacific, a request that Congress acceded to. Though the islands were granted self-governance in 1900, petitions for Hawaiian statehood were denied in 1903, 1911, 1913, and 1915; not until 1959 did Hawaii finally become a state.

For the first decade after annexation, the U.S. Army maintained a token presence of just over 200 troops in the islands. Soldiers lived in canvas tents and lean-tos at Camp McKinley, located in swampy terrain at Waikiki, on the island of Oahu. They cleared trees and coral, drained the swamp, and constructed roads.[2] Fear of Japanese invasion led the army to increase its presence in the islands beginning in 1909. By 1913, 7,100 troops were stationed there. That number reached 12,500 during World War I before falling back to 4,800 in 1920. Throughout the 1920s and early 1930s, army troop strength hovered around 15,000 in Hawaii (approximately 10% of all U.S. Army forces), increasing to 25,000 in 1940 as the United States slowly prepared for war with Japan.[3] Most of the soldiers who served in Hawaii before World War II were white. While the Ninth and Tenth Cavalry Regiments, both black units, passed through Hawaii on their way to and from the Philippines during this period, the only black unit stationed in Hawaii was the Twenty-Fifth Infantry Regiment (approximately 800 men), which was deployed to Hawaii from 1913 to 1918.

Most soldiers served on Oahu, the most populous island and site of both the capital city, Honolulu, and the U.S. Navy's Pearl Harbor installation, with the garrison divided into coastal defense and mobile units.[4] Coastal defense forts were constructed at Fort Ruger (Diamond Head), Fort DeRussy (Waikiki), Fort Kamehameha (Pearl Harbor), and Fort Armstrong (Honolulu Harbor), with Fort Weaver (located across the main channel from Fort Kamehameha at Pearl Harbor) completed in 1923. Mobile forces were headquartered at Fort Shafter (beginning in 1905) and Schofield Barracks (from 1908). After World War I, the army constructed three airfields: Wheeler Field (colocated with Schofield Barracks), Luke Field (on Ford Island at Pearl Harbor, transferred to the U.S. Navy in 1932), and Hickham Field, which replaced Luke Field.

Before World War II, army installations in Hawaii remained rudimentary and were not generally considered desirable postings. At Fort Kamehameha, officers were provided with three-bedroom homes with attached servants' quarters, but enlisted barracks were much more primitive. In 1927, one officer sent photographs of the barracks to the army's Inspector General, noting that it was "not reasonable to expect men to have pride in their service when they are required to live in such a hovel in a permanent post in peace time." One commanding general at Schofield Barracks frankly acknowledged to his troops that living conditions there "not only were a great injustice but rotten wrong." Conditions improved only slowly. Enlisted men were still housed in shacks when General Hugh A. Drum told congressional investigators in the 1930s that junior officers' quarters "compare[d] unfavorably with those of laborers on the adjoining sugar plantations."[5] Forts DeRussy and Ruger, much closer to Honolulu than Schofield Barracks, with better quarters, recreational facilities, and access to the city and beaches, were considered much better posts. By the late 1930s, the temporary wooden and canvas structures used to house most soldiers in Hawaii had been replaced by permanent concrete barracks with modern plumbing. Throughout the period, morale remained low, boredom and fatigue duty (manual labor performed by soldiers) were common, and luxuries scarce. While desertions in Hawaii were no higher than elsewhere—living conditions were poor but there was nowhere else to go, and few soldiers could afford passage back to the mainland—turnover among army units stationed in Hawaii was high. Large numbers of enlisted men and commissioned officers alike (approximately 40% of each) chose to leave the service in the 1920s and 1930s when reenlistment meant spending significant additional time in the islands.[6]

In addition to the often unsatisfactory living conditions, American soldiers and their families who were new to the islands were often surprised at the breadth of the racial diversity in Hawaii, and not infrequently made uncomfortable by it. In addition to the native Hawaiian and white communities living there, Hawaii saw far more immigration than most areas in the continental United States, as waves of immigrants from Asia and elsewhere—Chinese, Japanese, Filipinos, Pacific Islanders, Portuguese, Puerto Ricans, and others—arrived in Hawaii to work in the sugar, pineapple, and other local industries. By 1910, only 20 percent of Hawaii's total population was ethnically Hawaiian or white (excluding Puerto Ricans, Portuguese, and Spanish populations, who were not generally considered white at the time). This had slipped to 16 percent by 1920 and to less than 14 percent by 1930.[7] There were relatively few local social impediments to interracial relationships and marriages; by 1930, approximately 14 percent of Hawaiian residents were of mixed racial or ethnic origin.[8] U.S. citizenship had been extended to "all white persons [in Hawaii], including Portuguese, and persons of African descent, and all persons descended from the Hawaiian race . . . who were citizens of the Republic of Hawaii immediately prior to transfer [of sovereignty]" by the Hawaiian Organic Act enacted in 1900.[9] In the wake of the Chinese Exclusion Act of 1882, which suspended Chinese immigration to the United States because of nativist concerns, many other groups of the Pacific basin were legally declared nonwhite, including native Hawaiians in 1889.[10] A general order promulgated in Hawaii in 1919 stated that "such delicate subjects as . . . the race question, etc., will not be discussed at all except among ourselves and officially."[11] Officers' wives, who sometimes groused about being sent to a remote outpost far from friends and relatives,[12] were likewise cautioned to avoid public discussions of race: "The social implications of the mixture of the races in Hawaii are packed with dynamite, and waiting to explode in the face of the careless or unsophisticated newcomer."[13] As one army captain put it, there was "comparatively little racial animosity and prejudice except so-cially."[14] Not surprisingly, most army officers and their families created an all-white social environment for themselves, seldom straying from on-post entertainment facilities and segregated social clubs in Oahu. An "aversion . . . to the co-mingling of their children (particularly of girls) with the Oriental races" led to most children of officers being placed in private schools rather than the local, racially mixed public schools.[15]

Hawaiian demographics were also unusual in that there were significantly more men than women in the islands before World War II, due to the influx of large numbers of male laborers and, eventually, military personnel, as the U.S. Army and Navy began to grow in strength and bring tens of thousands of additional male soldiers, sailors, and civilian defense workers. By 1920, less than 18 percent of Hawaii's population was composed of women (of all races) aged fifteen and older. The female-to-male ratio had improved somewhat by 1930, when just over 24 percent of the population were females aged fifteen and over.[16] All of these unique conditions in Hawaii created an unusual cru-cible for army interventions in the sexual economy of war that played out with some continuities but more changes from how the army sought to regulate soldier sexuality in other locales.

Overview of Military Justice in Hawaii

Good U.S. Army court-martial data exist for Hawaiian bases from 1913 onward. This period witnessed nearly 550 courts-martial for sex-related offenses through 1940. Nearly 300 of these cases involved charges of same-sex sexual activity, some involving other soldiers and some civilians, some where the activity was alleged to be consensual and some where force was alleged. This is a much higher number of courts-martial of this type, in absolute and relative terms, than was present in the other case studies examined. Another 50 courts-martial concerned soldiers who refused venereal treatment from army physicians. Another 44 involved soldiers who were alleged to have invaded the privacy of officers' or civilians' quarters, usually by peering into windows or otherwise spying on the inhabitants' intimate affairs; this too represents a much higher number of this kind of charge. The remaining courts-martial covered a wide spectrum of offenses, from harassment of women to rape to a miscellany of offenses including adultery, bigamy, and indecent exposure, among many others. It is important to note that in all but 2 cases, the accused were enlisted soldiers or noncommissioned officers. While it is certainly possible that no other officers committed such offenses in these years, it seems more likely that officer offenses were handled differently, outside the formal system of courts-martial, as was often the case in other locales.

Interactions with Locals

Relationships between soldiers and locals were strained at times, with civilians' anxieties about the soldiers' treatment of women a source of conflict and concern for the army. One soldier recalled soldiers' relations with local civilians as "cordial but not familiar. . . . We knew that all the locals thought we were after their daughters or wives if we showed any attention." Another reported that civilian women in Hawaii were "just like the girls back home. If you have money to take them out they are all smiles [but] if you don't they don't want to be bothered with you." Unsurprisingly, poorly paid enlisted men often had difficulty competing on the dating scene, and many patronized prostitutes. The army was concerned about a perceived lack of adequate numbers of white Hawaiians, which "makes it difficult and often impossible for soldiers to find congenial associates, particularly girls, with whom to dance and amuse themselves, and they are frequently forced to go without congenial human association or else to consort with the vicious element present in cities."[17] In Hawaii, as at other army posts, enlisted soldiers had to seek their commanding officer's permission to marry local women, permission that was seldom, if ever, granted.[18] Soldiers were, of course, welcome to marry once their term of service was up, though this might entail a multiyear-long wait to legally marry if permission was not granted. In a study of marriage patterns of soldiers stationed in Hawaii in 1926–1927, 216 soldiers (all white, and representing approximately 1.5% of all soldiers stationed in Hawaii during that period) married local women.[19] Nearly 78 percent of these soldiers married women considered to be white, while the remaining 22 percent married women of Asian or mixed racial descent. These relatively common interracial marriages in Hawaii were rare—or even illegal—elsewhere in the United States. Hawaii had no antimiscegenation laws, unlike thirty U.S. states (the entire U.S. South and most of the states west of the Mississippi), and under civilian laws in Hawaii, there were no legal impediments to these interracial relationships.[20] As in the Philippines, soldiers stationed in Hawaii sometimes engaged in "shack jobs" (cohabitation with local women), which could lead to resentment from local civilian men, who, as agricultural laborers, usually made even less than the poorly paid soldiers. One native Hawaiian described soldiers as "cocky people" who "sometimes got nasty with our girls. So we always protected our girls."[21]

Race relations in Hawaii were not always placid, and the nexus of race and sex provided the impetus for at least one major incident in Honolulu in 1916.[22] African American soldiers from the Twenty-Fifth Infantry Regiment, a racially segregated unit of black enlisted men led by white officers, then stationed at Schofield Barracks in Hawaii, were entertaining members of the Ninth Cavalry Regiment (another black unit), which had stopped off in Hawaii while in transit to the Philippines. Members of both units traveled to Honolulu's Iwilei red-light district, where some white prostitutes refused the black soldiers as clients. The soldiers then proceeded to beat the women and wreck several of Iwilei's houses of prostitution. Military police broke up the riot, which resulted in many arrests of black soldiers, though no official punishments, with army investigators choosing to treat the affair as mostly just a misunderstanding. The way in which this incident was handled was in sharp contrast to the response to the infamous race riot in Brownsville, Texas, between black soldiers and white civilians ten years earlier, which resulted in the dishonorable discharge of 167 black soldiers in the Twenty-Fifth Infantry Regiment.[23] The army's history with the Brownsville riot, Hawaii's racial mix, the social class of the prostitutes, and the fact that no deaths resulted from the Hawaii riot were likely all factors that influenced the army's decision to handle this incident much more leniently.

The army also sought to maintain harmonious relations with civilians by prosecuting violations of the Ninety-Sixth Article of War ("conduct to the prejudice of good order and military discipline") that could be loosely defined as constituting sexual harassment. Soldiers committed these offenses through verbal interactions, inappropriate touching, or letters written to the women that the army deemed lewd, lascivious, or obscene. All but three men of the twenty-eight accused were convicted. This may seem surprising, given that in many of the cases, there were no witnesses to the offenses other than the women accusing the soldiers of inappropriate behavior, suggesting that the army took such charges seriously. Of those convicted, roughly half were dishonorably discharged and given up to two and a half years of hard labor, while the others—apparently those who committed what were deemed less serious offenses—received a few months of hard labor but were permitted to remain in the army. Interestingly, these cases do not appear to have involved the kind of offenses in which black soldiers' offhand comments or looks directed at white women were coded as criminal acts; only a single private accused of this kind of offense was African American. It is important to note that the victims involved in these cases varied significantly. Most of the cases concerned local civilian women with no discernible connection to the army, though eight cases involved women who were listed as wives of either noncommissioned or commissioned officers (most of whom lived on local army posts). Two additional cases involved female members of the Army Nurse Corps (who were both second lieutenants).

The case of Private Anderson Finchum is typical of the kind of sexual harassment that was not severely punished by the army.[24] A drunk Finchum was seen by two officers (a major and a captain) in downtown Honolulu harassing a woman by following her, calling to her, and grabbing at her clothing as she quickened her pace and tried to escape him. In court, one of the witnesses was questioned about the woman as to her race and station in life. She was described as white and "a respectable woman of medium walk in life." The court attempted to clarify this response by asking, "There was nothing about this woman's dress or appearance that would indicate any possibility that she was a street-walker or anything like that?" The major being questioned responded, "Oh! Not at all. She appeared to be a perfectly respectable woman." The captain who witnessed the harassment was also questioned about the race of the woman, and he responded that he thought she was "of mixed blood . . . nearly white" but was nevertheless "quite respectable." (The woman's identity was never known, as she hurried off as the officers were getting out of their car to stop Finchum from bothering her further.) Finchum defended himself by admitting that he was so drunk that afternoon that he had no recollection of accosting the woman. He was given four months of hard labor and a twenty-one-dollar fine but was not dishonorably discharged. The lengthy questioning of the two witnesses about the class and race of the woman accosted is notable, because it seems clear that the matter would have been treated very differently had the woman been visibly poor or of obvious nonwhite racial descent.

The actions of Private Robert E. Brown were considered much more serious.[25] Brown was charged with forcibly accosting Agnes Collins (a female civilian nurse at a local hospital) as she was walking home, threatening to destroy her reputation, breaking into her quarters and again threatening her, and stealing her jewelry after harassing her in a series of telephone calls. Brown is alleged to have told her, "You will make a fiend out of me. I'll show you I'll do everything to degrade you in your profession. I'll ruin your reputation." Brown and Collins had gone on a few dates before this incident, and Brown had proposed marriage, though Collins declined and broke off their relationship. Brown attempted to maintain the relationship in increasingly erratic and threatening phone calls. Collins had ended the relationship, in part, because she discovered that Brown was a soldier; he had concealed this fact from her at the start of their relationship, telling her that he was a civilian electrical engineer. While Brown did not offer any testimony in his own defense, his counsel presented him as a man who was infatuated with Collins: their disagreement was simply a lovers' quarrel, and Brown had never intended to carry out his threats to "degrade" Collins. Unlike in many other courts-martial for cases involving female victims, Collins's character and social status—as a white woman who worked as a civilian nurse—went unquestioned in court. The court clearly believed the matter serious, convicting Brown and sentencing him to a dishonorable discharge and five years of hard labor, which was reduced to two and a half years by the reviewing authority.

Interactions between soldiers and local women sometimes involved cases of sexual violence. The army generally seemed to take charges of rape or attempted rape seriously, based on the conviction rates and typical sentences for the offense. Twenty-four servicemen were accused of committing, or attempting to commit, rape in Hawaii during this period, eighteen of whom were convicted.[26] All those convicted were dishonorably discharged. The length of sentences of hard labor received by those convicted varied tremendously, with some soldiers receiving only a few months of hard labor (for some cases of attempted rape), while others received hard-labor sentences of five, ten, twenty, or thirty years, and in two cases, life sentences were handed down. Three of the soldiers, Privates James F. Brenties, Thurlow Dugan, and Shelby V. Hazelwood, were charged with participating in the gang rape of a female civilian in 1917, for which Brenties (but not Dugan or Hazelwood) was convicted.[27] Two other soldiers, Privates George B. Clark and Lyman J. Johnson, were also jointly charged with an attempted rape.[28] The remaining cases all involved soldiers who were alleged to have acted alone. Four of those court-martialed for rape or attempted rape were noncommissioned officers, all of whom seemed to receive very different court-martial outcomes from those of the enlisted men charged with similar offenses. Three of the noncommissioned officers were acquitted, and the last—convicted of attempted rape of a civilian—was granted an extremely light sentence and allowed to remain in the army as a private and serve just three months of hard labor. Most of the rape cases involved victims who were civilian women with no connection to the army. One case, however, involved a captain's wife; another involved a sergeant's wife; a third involved the female servant of an army captain who lived with the officer and his family; and a final case involved an attempted rape of a female army nurse (a second lieutenant).

The joint court-martial of Privates Brenties, Dugan, and Hazelwood is illustrative of rape cases in Hawaii during this period. The three were alleged to have come across a Japanese couple sitting in a park at night, grabbed the woman, and begun attempting to rape her. Her male companion ran for help and quickly returned with a group of American soldiers. Brenties was caught by this group trying to rape the woman, while his companions fled. The attack was as inexplicable as it was savage. It was unpremeditated and happened in a dark area, but one that was apparently not very remote, as the victim's companion was able to return quickly with help. On first approaching the couple, the soldiers shined flashlights in their faces and demanded to know what they were doing, implying that they were acting in an official capacity, probably attempting to intimidate immigrant civilians with military authority. The soldiers the civilian man approached for help did not hesitate to run to assist him in preventing the rape, despite the fact that he immediately told them that other soldiers were attempting to rape his companion. The defense did attempt to question the morality of the female victim, as seemed to be fairly routine in rape and sexual harassment courts-martial, asking whether she were a "harlot" and whether she and her companion had been having sex when they were accosted. The prosecution objected on the grounds that the questions were irrelevant, and the objection was sustained. Dugan and Hazelwood were acquitted because they could not be decisively identified by the witnesses. Brenties was dishonorably discharged and sentenced to twelve years of hard labor.

Cases involving violence did not always include allegations of rape. Thirteen soldiers were charged with offenses that can be broadly described as domestic violence. All but four were convicted, and those convicted served from six months to several years of hard labor; most were also dishonorably discharged. Race may have played a role in the way in which the army policed the domestic situations of soldiers, as four were African American. This was a disproportionately high percentage, given the small number of black U.S. Army soldiers deployed to Hawaii (who constituted less than 10% of the total U.S. force in Hawaii from 1913 to 1918). In one of the cases involving a black soldier, Private Joe Brown was charged with fighting with a woman whom he had been dating after she broke off their relationship.[29] The woman's lodging house, where the fight occurred, appeared to be a respectable establishment and was likely not a clandestine brothel, as were some lodging houses. The other residents were married couples, and Brown had told the lodging house owner that the woman was his wife. (They were not, in fact, married; she was married to someone else and convicted in Hawaiian civilian court of adultery for her affair with Brown.) However, in his testimony, Brown claimed that he argued with his ex-girlfriend, in part, because the female owner of the lodging house was "making a whore out of her . . . trying to make nothing but a white slave out of her in her place of business." Brown's choice of phrasing in his accusation is particularly interesting, given that he was African American, his girlfriend Hawaiian, and the lodging house owner white. The police were called, and Brown was arrested. The army convicted him, dishonorably discharged him, and sentenced him to five months of hard labor.

In another case, a white soldier, Private Charles H. McGarry, was accused of shooting and seriously wounding his girlfriend, Annie Flora, with the intent to kill her.[30] Flora said that just before she was shot, McGarry asked her to marry him and said other things that she claimed not to recall. McGarry stated that the two had been drinking heavily, and that she told McGarry to shoot her, a request with which he complied. Because there were no other witnesses to the pair's conversation before the shooting, it is almost impossible to accurately re-create the events leading up to the shooting or ascertain a true motive, though an alcohol-fueled argument, perhaps involving a rejected marriage proposal, seems likely. McGarry's explanation for shooting the woman was, in any case, entirely unconvincing, and he was convicted and sentenced to seven years of hard labor and a dishonorable discharge.

Just as the army was concerned about the sexual corruption of soldiers in France, going so far as to conduct an investigation into "sexual perversion," it also sought to enforce normative standards for the kinds of sex that soldiers could have with women in Hawaii. Two enlisted men, Privates Maurice Allard and James Stewart, were court-martialed for performing acts of oral sex on women.[31] Allard was acquitted, and Stewart convicted and dishonorably discharged, though he did not have to serve any time at hard labor. The circumstances surrounding Stewart's alleged offense are mostly unknown, since he declined to make a statement on his own behalf and no member of the court offered any specifics on the case. He was convicted and sentenced without comment. Allard's court-martial offered many more details. Allard was charged with performing cunnilingus on Rosa Cromley, whom the army described as a prostitute in Iwilei, the notorious Honolulu red-light district. Cromley is almost certainly the same alleged prostitute named two years earlier as Rosa Crumley in the court-martial of Private First Class Willie O. Hill and Sergeant Charles W. Manning.[32] Though subpoenaed, Cromley/ Crumley initially failed to appear in this court-martial. Allard was arrested by a civilian police officer inside the brothel where Cromley worked after being caught performing oral sex on her. The police officer had been summoned after a witness saw Allard doing "wrong business," as the policeman described it, with Cromley. The officer was asked to elaborate on exactly what he had witnessed, and he stated that he saw Allard "sucking the Porto [sic] Rican's cunt." (This exact phrase was used by four witnesses and the prosecutor to describe the alleged offense.) The sex act appeared, according to the policeman, to be consensual, if likely commercial, but since it was considered "deviant," Allard was arrested. Cunnilingus was considered a "crime against nature," like anal sex and fellatio, in the Territory of Hawaii at the time of Allard's arrest. Cromley had apparently arranged with the brothel's cook to summon a policeman when she signaled him via coughing because she knew that Allard was planning to perform oral sex on her. It is unclear why Cromley would have consented to the act, given her prior awareness of Allard's intent, if she did not want to do so. According to the cook's testimony, Cromley wanted to have Allard arrested for reasons that remain unclear. The court-martial went into recess and when it resumed, Cromley was produced as a witness. She described Allard as "try[ing] wrong things that a man can't do to a lady." Cromley testified that she had told Allard to stop several times, but he refused, telling her it would not hurt her. Cromley stated that she had heard of oral sex previously but had never engaged in it (Cromley would have well understood that cunnilingus was illegal in Hawaii as she gave her testimony). She mentioned that a previous client had also wanted to perform cunnilingus, and she had refused then as well because she feared it might injure her health. Another self-identified prostitute, Sylvia Lewis, was also called to testify. Lewis stated that Cromley summoned the police in order to get Allard arrested, which, Lewis claimed, was a standard "frame-up" well known to local prostitutes. Lewis alleged that Allard had wanted to stay the night with Cromley, but she sought to get rid of him so that she could engage in sex with additional clients. Lewis testified that whenever prostitutes wanted to get rid of soldier-clients—for any reason—they would threaten to summon the police and have them arrested for performing "unnatural acts." Allard's arrest may have been a frame-up to get rid of him, but four male witnesses, including the arresting officer, testified that they did witness Allard performing cunnilingus on Cromley. Another Honolulu policeman testified that this was a familiar tactic employed by local prostitutes and that Cromley was known to his department as a troublemaker who had stolen money from previous clients. A third policeman, who claimed he had himself been "framed" by Cromley for being drunk on duty, testified that he had previously heard Cromley suggest that a sailor perform oral sex on her. Allard testified on his own behalf, denying that he had performed cunnilingus on Cromley altogether. This complicated case rested entirely on the testimony of various witnesses, some of extremely dubious credibility. Since there was no physical evidence that the offense had occurred, the court acquitted Allard, taking his side against that of a prostitute and several denizens of Iwilei.

In addition to Private Joseph Arlington, whose charges will be discussed in greater detail later, four other soldiers were also charged during this period with (and convicted of) masturbation.[33] All were dishonorably discharged and served either two or three months of hard labor. While their labor sentences were light by army standards of the day, it is important to note that none of the accused was permitted to remain in military service. No doubt the public setting in which these offenses occurred weighed heavily in the decisions to charge and convict these alleged masturbators. The location of Private George R. Fox's alleged masturbation is unclear from the record, but Private George W. Rose was alleged to have masturbated in a "public and open manner," Private William Luby while he believed himself to be unobserved outdoors in a gulch, and Private Star Daly while in the guardhouse, detained there for an unrelated offense. The discussion surrounding Daly's case is particularly revealing of army attitudes toward masturbation. Masturbation, at least in these cases, was deemed a violation of the Sixty-Second Article of War, "conduct to the prejudice of good order and military discipline," which was often used as a kind of catchall category for offenses that were not otherwise specified in the Articles of War. Here, the prosecutor described masturbation as "[having] the natural tendency to incapacitate the mental powers and to reduce the physical abilities of those who indulge in that indoor sport," as well as "one of the surest ways to gain admittance to St. Elizabeth's [a mental hospital]." He went on to label masturbation as "conducive to moral degeneracy, because it undermines the very foundation of self-respect, and without self respect you cannot have respect for superiors and discipline." The fact that Daly had committed the act in front of witnesses was even worse, in the prosecutor's estimation, because it would encourage this "abominable practice" in others. The prosecutor also made a moral argument, noting that condemnation of masturbation "is mentioned in the Bible and . . . is condemned as an offense against every religious and social principle." This attitude toward masturbation, and the belief that masturbation had serious harmful physical, mental, and moral effects, especially on adolescents and young men, was common in Western Europe and the United States in the late nineteenth and early twentieth centuries, resulting in several decades of "masturbation panics."[34] An army physician, Captain Leopold Mitchell, was called by the prosecution and clearly expected to roundly condemn masturbation, though his testimony was more nuanced, perhaps even uncharacteristic of the period: "The man who masturbates as an isolated incidence, disregarding the circumstance of indecent exposure and public nuisance, I don't see that he has committed a crime nor an offense [sic]. Masturbation is a habit, or a vice, as you choose to call it, that is quite universal. It is common to both sexes and happens at all ages and is restricted to no color, creed, or religion that I know of. It is perhaps more common with the male than the female, and in early life. In its baneful effects I think there are none. A man who masturbates to excess does not send himself to the insane asylum from masturbating."

Mitchell went on to state that masturbation did not make a soldier "unfit for duty." Several of the men who witnessed Daly's alleged masturbation were called to testify. All stated that they had been offended by the sight of Daly's masturbation and that they did not want to serve with such a man. While Daly was convicted and originally dishonorably discharged and given a sentence of one year of hard labor, the reviewing authority, without further comment, reduced the labor sentence to two months, though it upheld the dishonorable discharge.

Invasion of Private Spaces

Throughout this period, soldiers were court-martialed for invading the private domestic spaces of officers or civilians, usually by peering in the windows of homes. Army prosecutors were careful to note that they believed these cases were not the result of soldiers carrying out surveillance for the purposes of breaking and entering; soldiers were charged with those kinds of offenses in other instances, but in forty-four courts-martial soldiers were charged with attempting to see women sleeping or undressing. In only seven cases were soldiers acquitted, one on a legal technicality. Twenty-eight of the thirty-seven convicted soldiers (76%) received dishonorable discharges and, on average, one year of hard labor. It is clear that the army took such charges seriously and sought to protect the wives, relatives, and female servants of commissioned and noncommissioned officers, as well as civilians living near Hawaii's army bases, from the prying eyes of enlisted soldiers, who were depicted as predators spying on and posing sexual dangers to the women they were accused of observing. Race seemed to play a role in these types of charges; in nine of the forty-four cases, the accused was African American, and all were convicted.

While African American soldiers may have committed a disproportionate number of these offenses in Hawaii, it could also be that racial anxieties about black men peering into the bedroom windows, or entering the private homes, of whites were the cause of at least some of these charges and the relatively higher conviction rate for black soldiers.

In three cases, the wives or other family members of army noncommissioned or commissioned officers were deemed to have been directly threatened by enlisted men. In one such case, Private Thomas Cherry was accused of peeping through the window of a married sergeant's home.[35] Cherry was black and the sergeant and his family were white; while race was not mentioned during the court-martial, the races of all those involved would have been apparent to the members of the court. Cherry was seen by multiple witnesses peering into the windows of a home, and he was said to have confessed that he had done so to see a woman who lived there.[36] Cherry, it was alleged, had previously looked through the bedroom windows of the home and made "vulgar remarks" and an "indecent proposal" to the sergeant's wife, though his identity had not been known before he was caught when he allegedly returned. Several pistol shots were fired at Cherry as he attempted to flee. Cherry escaped a beating when he was caught—a sergeant who lived nearby prevented the soldiers who caught Cherry from assaulting him. In his testimony, Cherry flatly denied that he had been peeping in the bedroom window, claiming he was just walking by the rear of the home, and stated that he had run when confronted because he was scared. Two character witnesses for Cherry were questioned regarding Cherry's "liking of women," clearly in an attempt to establish Cherry's sexual habits, but one witness denied any knowledge and the other would state only, "I suppose he likes women, the same as any other man." Because the prosecutor could not establish that Cherry was a sexual predator, he received a mild sentence of three months at hard labor, with forfeiture of two-thirds of his pay during confinement, and remained in military service.

In a separate incident, Private George J. Cornell was charged with lurking near his commanding officer's (a lieutenant colonel) quarters for the purpose of observing, by climbing a ladder and peering over a second-story bathroom curtain, a female houseguest undress in the bathroom and prepare herself for bed.[37] Cornell was convicted and sentenced to be dishonorably discharged, forfeit all pay, and serve three years of hard labor. The reviewing authority halved the hard-labor sentence because of a series of technical errors in the court-martial, including extensive use of leading questions posed to witnesses, improperly submitted evidence, and what a later legal reviewer noted as "circumstantial evidence," urging clemency for the accused. Cornell's face was not clearly seen by the lieutenant colonel's wife, and he seems to have been convicted on little more evidence than that he was tall (the Peeping Tom would have had to be over six feet tall to see through the window) and that he appeared "nervous" by sweating profusely when questioned. The perpetrator had also left a hat behind, though it was never definitively proved that Cornell was missing a hat. The prosecution brought up that Cornell had a "chronic case of syphilis," in an apparent attempt to establish his sexual deviancy. In an unsworn statement Cornell submitted to the court, he denied being a "moral pervert," stating that he had never been previously accused of being one, and that if he were a pervert, he undoubtedly would have been accused of being one before this case. In closing arguments, the prosecution emphasized the "moral rottenness of the crime," saying that it "shows the worst kind of moral degeneration" and that Cornell should be "most severely punished as a warning to others." The court sentenced Cornell to three years (later halved by the reviewing authority) of hard labor to be served at Alcatraz.

In the final case concerning the families of officers and unwanted voyeurs, African American Private Harold Leeper was accused of peering into the bedroom window of a first lieutenant and his wife.[38] Leeper was convicted largely because he was found in the area by another officer and had no satisfactory answer for why he was behind the officer's quarters. The prosecution also offered some evidence that Leeper had left a footprint in the soil of a flower pot, but the credibility of this evidence—a footprint made by a standard-issue army boot—seems to have been effectively questioned by the defense counsel. This shaky evidence led to Leeper's conviction (and three-year, hard-labor sentence) being overturned by the reviewing authority. As will be discussed later, however, this was not the last time that Leeper was charged with being a Peeping Tom.

Three more cases involved officers' female servants who were spied on or sexually harassed by enlisted men: those of Privates Samuel Anderson, James Hill, and Charles Ward.[39] Anderson, an African American in the Twenty-Fifth Infantry, was charged with attempting to break into the bedroom of a captain's female servant (who was also African American) through the window, addressing her with "obscene language" (he told the woman he wanted to kiss her), and then, when confronted, running away from an officer. Anderson was identified twice by the woman in lineups and was also recognized again by the officer who initially detained him before his escape. During a legal review of the case, the judge advocate general described the woman as "a rather good looking wife of a soldier, who might have, by her action, suggested she was approachable, although there is nothing positively shown against her character." Affidavits by several noncommissioned officers and their wives suggested the woman was "rather free and easy in her manner of conversation, and that such action might have suggested that she was approachable." This questioning of female victims' characters in army investigations was not unusual, though in this case, her character was not questioned in open court. Anderson received the unusually harsh sentence of a dishonorable discharge, forfeiture of all pay, and five years of hard labor, which is consistent with the kind of sentence often given for convictions of rape or violent attempted rapes. The Judge Advocate General recommended that the remaining unserved portion of Anderson's sentence be remitted because of the thinness of the evidence and uncertainty surrounding Anderson's motives and his relationship to the victim. The Assistant Secretary of War approved, and Anderson served approximately seven months of his sentence before being released. Hill, another African American soldier, was charged with loitering near a lieutenant's quarters, attempting to break into the officer's quarters in order to enter the bedroom of the lieutenant's Japanese maid/children's nurse, and giving money to the lieutenant's male Japanese servant to induce the maid to "have improper relations with him." Hill allegedly told the male servant that if the maid would not marry him, he would enter her bedroom one night and, presumably, rape her, though this was left unstated. In the final case, Ward was accused of peering into the tent of a nurse hired by an officer and "frightening and annoying" her. All three men were convicted. Anderson and Hill were given dishonorable discharges and sentences of five years and three years of hard labor, respectively (both later reduced to a single year). Ward, having committed what the court clearly deemed a minor offense, was allowed to remain in military service after serving six months of hard labor.

The bulk of these cases, however, involved not the wives or servants of officers living on army posts but rather civilian women living near army posts. The soldiers intruded on civilian homes, either by entering them for what the army determined were salacious purposes rather than theft or by peering in through windows for the purpose of observing women.[40] Two courts-martial illustrate these types of offenses. Private Harold D. Speares was charged with peering into the tent of a male civilian and his family by cutting through the fabric of the tent to try to access its interior.[41] While larceny could conceivably have been a motive, that was never mentioned as a possibility by anyone in the court-martial. The implication was that Speares was trying to gain access to the civilian's wife, who did not appear in court. Speares did not testify on his own behalf, so his motives are unknown. He was dishonorably discharged and sentenced to six months of hard labor.

In a separate case, two soldiers, Private First Class Willie O. Hill and Sergeant Charles W. Manning, were charged with battering down the door and entering the home of an elderly woman who lived on the grounds of Fort Shafter and washed clothes for soldiers.[42] A number of other soldiers, possibly as many as twenty, whose identities remained unknown, accompanied the two men. While the group broke or stole several small items, these petty thefts and vandalism were apparently not the goal of the incident. It came out during the course of the court-martial that the woman, Carmen Torrez, also sold alcohol illegally to soldiers. Some witnesses stated that they believed the sale of alcohol might have precipitated the attack, though the specifics of the dispute between Torrez and the soldiers remained unclear. Several officers testified as defense character witnesses, all expressing shock that Hill and especially Manning were involved in "this disgraceful affair," as one put it. All stated the men had "excellent" character, though two acknowledged that Manning occasionally drank to excess. Some of the soldiers accompanying Hill and Manning were also alleged to have dragged a young woman named Rosa Crumley,[43] who claimed to be working as Torrez's nursemaid, outside and into a nearby tent and raped her. Several soldiers who were familiar with both Torrez's house and the incident stated that Crumley was working as a prostitute out of Torrez's home (she apparently stayed there twice a month on paydays). Some of the soldiers may have gotten upset when she refused to see any more customers that night. Both Hill and Manning admitted to being at Torrez's home and drinking on the night in question but denied being present when the door was battered down and the remainder of the events unfolded. Torrez did not know the names of any of the other soldiers present at her home that evening, save Hill and Manning, and the court was unwilling to convict them. Both men were acquitted and returned to service, and no other soldiers were court-martialed for the incident. It is clear that the home was attacked, and though Crumley stated she had been raped, no one else during the court-martial pursued this line of questioning (since neither Hill nor Manning was alleged to have participated in the rape, it may not have been germane to their cases). This was a serious, extremely public incident, though the names of the other men involved in the affair were never publicized. It also seems clear that Torrez and Crumley had operated an unofficial bar and brothel on the grounds of Fort Shafter fairly openly for at least eighteen months. Since all the enlisted men at the fort knew of the arrangement, officers must have known as well. It is impossible to ascertain, but it seems likely that the army finally acted to shut down Torrez's operation after the court-martial because of the publicity surrounding the case. While the home in question was a private residence inhabited by civilians—Torrez and her son, who may have had some kind of mental disability—it clearly doubled as an illegal bar and brothel, and those activities seemed to have precipitated the attack.

Additionally, a soldier was charged with intruding on the private quarters of the Hawaiian Territorial Immigration Station, where immigrant workers stayed while awaiting residency permits and for which the U.S. Army provided security. Private James H. Kane was charged with entering the sleeping quarters of the immigration station and attempting to induce a female Portuguese immigrant to come outside with him, presumably for sexual purposes.[44] Sentinels at the station, including Kane, were not permitted in the sleeping quarters of the immigrants except in an emergency and were forbidden, by order of the Department Quartermaster at Fort Shafter, from conversing with the immigrants.[45] Several immigrants testified that Kane had twice entered the room, where approximately fifteen immigrants were sleeping, and attempted to summon the woman outside, though Kane denied doing so. The army clearly deemed discipline among the soldiers guarding the station a problem. Two weeks after Kane's court-martial, in August 1914, Corporal Benjamin T. Long was court-martialed for failing to perform his duties as head of the guard at the immigration station, twice leaving his post (and allowing other soldiers to do the same), allowing liquor to be brought into the station, and allowing soldiers—Kane among them—to enter the sleeping quarters of the immigrants.[46] Both men were convicted; given four and six months, respectively, of hard labor; and fined. Long was also reduced to the ranks (that is, made a private).

Several of the cases involved intrusions not into residences or dwellings but rather into private areas of public buildings where women might be seen in a state of undress. Private Joseph Arlington, for example, was accused of looking up women's skirts and masturbating under a baseball stadium grandstand,[47] and Private Harold Leeper was charged with hiding under a stage at the Infantry Amusement Hall and peering into the women's dressing room during a show and officers' dance.[48] The women alleged to have been viewed in various states of undress by Arlington and Leeper (both black soldiers) would have been the wives and girlfriends of white soldiers and officers. Arlington was charged with three counts of "conduct to the prejudice of good order and military discipline": peeping through a crack in the floorboards of the baseball grandstand "with intent to see up the clothes of ladies in the grandstand," having his penis out under the grandstand with intent to commit masturbation, and masturbating. Arlington pleaded guilty to the charges and, taking the stand in his own defense, stated, "I don't know what it was that come [*sic*] over me and made me want to do such a disgraceful thing." He went on to mention that he had promised his mother that he would do a good job in the army and that he had been sending her money. When further prompted by the defense counsel to elaborate on why he had done such a thing, Arlington stated,

"I don't know what it was. I hadn't had any intercourse with a woman and I felt awfully funny at the time." His commanding officer also testified to his good character and willingness to work hard in the unit. Arlington's testimony, vague though it was, apparently had a positive effect on the outcome of his court-martial. His sentence could have been much more severe, especially since Arlington was black and the women he watched while masturbating were white. He was dishonorably discharged and forfeited all pay but, unusually, received no hard labor.

In Leeper's second general court-martial for charges related to being a Peeping Tom, he was caught red-handed while crawling out from under a stage during a dance. He was charged with peering through a hole in the wall that he had created, allowing him visual access to the women's dressing room at the amusement hall. Leeper had apparently been hiding under the stage for a long period and had defecated there. Army officials knew that this area had been previously used for a similar purpose because they had discovered other holes drilled in the wall on a number of occasions and had made attempts to seal the holes but had never before caught anyone actually looking through them. During the closing remarks in this case, the prosecutor noted Leeper's previous general court-martial (discussed earlier in this chapter) and a special court-martial for similar offenses.[49] Leeper was described by the prosecutor as "not mentally straight. He has a perverted mind." The prosecutor continued to characterize Leeper as psychologically ill rather than violent, stating, "I find him more an unfortunate than a criminal." This court-martial convicted Leeper and sentenced him to dishonorable discharge, forfeiture of all pay, and six months of hard labor. Unlike Leeper's first general court-martial, this one was not overturned by the reviewing authority.

Venereal Disease in Hawaii

Since it had become an American territory in 1898, Hawaii was subjected to repeated but unsuccessful progressive attempts to outlaw prostitution. In 1909, a rail spur connecting Schofield Barracks and Fort Shafter (the main U.S. Army posts in Hawaii) with the Oahu Railway was completed, giving soldiers much easier access to Honolulu and its red-light district. Army physicians reported an almost immediate rise in venereal infections.[50] Starting in June 1909, the army mandated venereal inspections for all enlisted soldiers stationed at Schofield Barracks returning from leave. In the second half of 1909, 504 men voluntarily reported for prophylactic inspections and treatment, with only fourteen of these men later becoming venereally infected after prophylaxis.

This represented a 70 percent decrease in the number of infections from the first half of the year.[51]

An army memorandum published in 1911 repeated the familiar claim that "venereal diseases are contracted chiefly through sexual intercourse with prostitutes. . . . The only sure way to escape venereal diseases is to keep away from prostitutes."[52] The memo assured army personnel that "sexual intercourse is not necessary for the preservation of health and manly vigor." It also promoted the army's venereal prophylaxis program, saying that 95 percent of venereal diseases could be eliminated if men exposed to them received the army's treatment within a few hours of exposure. In 1911–1912 in the Philippine and Hawaiian Departments of the U.S. Army, a brouhaha arose over venereal prophylaxis.[53] An army surgeon had reported that Colonel Millard F. Waltz, commanding officer of the Nineteenth Infantry Regiment, which was then deploying to the Philippines via Hawaii, had refused to allow soldiers under his command to be subjected to venereal inspections when they left Hawaii because such inspections were "humiliating" and "impracticable."[54] Waltz's alleged order, in contravention to standing War Department policy, was brought to the attention of the Adjutant General's Office. Waltz flatly denied that he had forbidden venereal inspections, stating that he had only exempted married men and certain noncommissioned officers (sergeants) and, it went without saying, commissioned officers. Waltz said that he "believed it impracticable to make venereal prophylaxis compulsory, without requiring every man who had had opportunity to become infected, to be subjected to the treatment which would be humiliating to those men who had not exposed themselves to infection, as otherwise, the man's word would have to be taken upon the question of his exposure."[55] Waltz went on to claim that he had ordered that all men returning to the army transport ship who had been exposed to venereal infection return to the United States to receive venereal prophylaxis, and that 107 men from the regiment (of approximately 1,000 men total) had done so. Only two of the men who had received prophylaxis later contracted venereal diseases. By the time the unit arrived in Manila, however, there were thirty-five active cases of venereal disease in the regiment, and fifty more within the next three weeks. This suggests that many of the soldiers had contracted venereal diseases during their time in Hawaii. A failure to report for prophylaxis is probably not surprising, given the painful and humiliating nature of the treatments, which many soldiers seemed to perceive as a form of punishment or sanction by the physicians administering it, perhaps even a medicalized and extralegal form of judgment on individual moral lapses, though the army itself never described the treatments as such.

The War Department was particularly concerned with the venereal health of soldiers stationed in Hawaii and the Philippines, where army venereal disease rates were much higher than in units stationed within the continental United States. The department looked to British experience in India, where medical surveillance and venereal prophylaxis had proved successful in an imperial setting.[56] The Office of the Surgeon General conducted numerous studies and compared its record with those of other major world powers. (See Figure 2.)

In 1909, the U.S. Army found that its venereal disease rate was more than twice that of Britain, the European power with the highest incidence of venereal disease. The U.S. rate was triple that of Russia, six times that of France, nearly seven times that of Japan, and more than eight times that of Prussia. Army medical officers sought to explain these disparities and suggested two causes: the state of medical sanitary science and practice within each nation; and the geographic areas where each military was stationed. Prussia, in particular, was known for its advanced medical practices in combating venereal disease. The U.S. Army had adopted a serious program of medical prophylaxis only in 1908. Likewise, Russian, Japanese, and Prussian forces were not deployed outside their national boundaries on a large scale in 1909. Soldiers of those nations were less exposed to the high rates of venereal

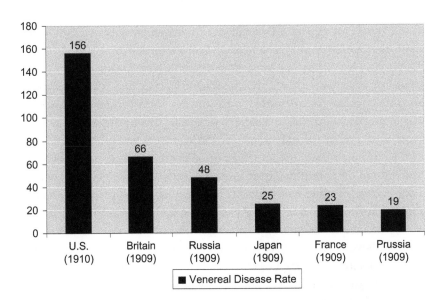

FIGURE 2. U.S. and foreign armies, comparative venereal disease rates (annual incidence per one thousand soldiers). Data from "Venereal Rates, American and Foreign Armies, Stations at Home," undated chart, AGO Docfile 1915426, filed with AGO Docfile 1045985, RG 94, NARA.

disease that British, French, and American soldiers often encountered in colonial settings.

Major General James Franklin Bell, commander of the Philippine Department, ordered that future commanding officers of units deploying across the Pacific cooperate with army medical officers in carrying out venereal treatments for diseases acquired in ports of call in Hawaii and elsewhere. Brigadier General George H. Torney, Surgeon General of the Army, concurred and ordered that all soldiers going ashore in Hawaii be warned of the dangers of venereal disease. He also ordered that those who went ashore in Hawaii and were exposed to venereal infection—that is, those who admitted to having sex while ashore—would henceforth be medically inspected "to detect concealed cases of venereal infection." Torney also suggested that those who did not report themselves for prophylaxis be punished in an unspecified fashion by their commanding officers. This policy was endorsed in March 1912 by the Secretary of War, who ordered that Torney's policies be carried out.[57] This took the form of War Department General Order No. 17, issued on May 31, 1912, which mandated that all men who had "expose[d] themselves to the danger of contracting venereal disease" report for prophylaxis immediately on their return to camp.[58] The General Order also required twice-monthly unannounced medical inspections of all enlisted soldiers, with the exception of "married men of good character," to ensure personal cleanliness and to provide an opportunity for "careful observation for the detection of venereal diseases." The army also issued a detailed set of instructions for exactly how this new program of venereal prophylaxis was to be carried out.[59]

Not only would venereal inspections be administered regularly throughout the army beginning in 1912, but four months later, the War Department sought to penalize, as a deterrent, men who contracted venereal diseases as a result of misconduct (that is, failing to receive treatment after exposure). The matter was formalized and extended in the War Department's General Order No. 31, which ordered that no soldier or officer would receive any pay while absent from duty "resulting from his own intemperate use of drugs, or alcoholic liquors, or other misconduct."[60] A subsequent section of the General Order clarified this coyly worded passage by stating that "venereal diseases not contracted in the line of duty, [are] within the purview of the statute quoted above." (The War Department did not clarify how a venereal disease might be contracted in the line of duty.) The explicit application of this General Order to commissioned officers, as well as enlisted soldiers, is at least symbolically important, though in practice officers were almost never charged with venereally related offenses.[61]

Refusal of Medical Treatment for Venereal Disease

As discussed in previous chapters, enlisted soldiers who had engaged in sexual contact with women other than their wives were ordered by army policy to report for venereal treatment within three hours of sexual contact. The army's standard treatment consisted of cleansing the penis with a highly toxic bichloride of mercury solution; injecting a protargol (silver salt) solution into the urethra, which could not be expelled for several hours; and coating the penis with calomel ointment.[62] Courts-martial for refusing such treatments began in November 1915 and continued through January 1918 and then abruptly stopped, with no more through 1940 in Hawaii. There were no courts-martial for refusing to receive treatment for a venereal infection in the years immediately before 1915 in Hawaii (and only one in 1915). This pattern of courts-martial clearly reflected conscious changes in army policy on how best to deal with the control and treatment of venereal infections among soldiers. For those few courts-martial for this type of offense that did occur, the evidence presented was usually clear and decisive: one or more army physicians (commissioned officers all) testified that they had diagnosed the accused as having contracted a venereal infection and that they had then prescribed a particular treatment regime for it. The physician witnesses would then state that they had ordered the patient to receive the treatment and that the soldier had refused what they, in their professional medical opinion, had deemed a necessary medical treatment. Therefore, the accused had refused a legitimate order by a superior. There was very little the accused could do to offer a convincing rebuttal to this testimony. Soldiers sometimes had noncommissioned officers under whom they served offer testimony in their defense, attesting to their good character and conduct, but these character witnesses seldom seemed to aid in mitigating the findings or sentences in the soldiers' courts-martial.[63] Of the forty-five courts-martial for this offense, all but one resulted in a conviction. In only one of these convictions was the accused permitted to remain in military service after serving his sentence. In all other cases, the convicted were given dishonorable discharges, forfeited all pay, and received up to two years of hard labor (the average sentence for hard labor was nine months).

When questioned about why they had refused treatment, soldiers often complained that they had received the venereal treatments previously and had suffered a variety of ill effects, such as chills, fevers, headaches, a variety of aches and pains (especially in the gums, legs, and joints), and sleeplessness. These side effects were so widely and consistently reported that it is difficult to believe that all those reporting them were lying. The penalties for refusing treatment were also consistently applied, and it had to have been known among soldiers that they would be court-martialed and almost invariably convicted if they refused further treatments. Army physicians were questioned about the reported side effects, and they were generally noncommittal as to their potential causes, stating that the venereal diseases themselves could conceivably cause these ill effects, and that in any case, there were no other treatment options available. Fears of the treatment were widespread; one doctor was asked, "You understand that among enlisted men there is a great deal of objection or antipathy to this treatment. Is that imaginary or is it due to a justified fear of the treatment?" The doctor replied, "I think some of it is imaginary and some of them are genuinely afraid. . . . I think [these men have] heard stories from other men who had the treatment and probably had severe reactions and had become so frightened that [they] did not wish to take the treatment [themselves]."[64]

In the sole case in which a soldier was convicted of refusing medical treatment for venereal disease but allowed to remain in military service, Private Frederick Poindexter pleaded guilty to refusing treatment on four occasions (Neosalvarsan once and mercuric salicylate three times), stating that he had previously received the treatments and had significant medical side effects from them—paralysis in the right leg, muscular spasms in the back, and sleeplessness—and had been in the hospital suffering from the previous side effects for 108 days.[65] Army physicians had told Poindexter that his condition was caused by venereal disease (which seems inconsistent with the known effects of common venereal infections), but he believed that the treatment was the cause. The court apparently sympathized with Poindexter, because his sentence was unusually light for a soldier who flatly refused venereal treatment.

Prostitution in Hawaii

Prostitution was illegal in Hawaii by territorial statute, just as it was on the mainland, but it also existed openly within clearly defined and regulated bounds.[66] Since the 1860 passage of the Act to Mitigate the Evils and Diseases Arising from Prostitution, prostitutes were registered with the Honolulu Police Department, with a nominal one-dollar-per-year fee charged.[67] Prostitutes were expected to report their income and pay income taxes. They were also expected to receive regular medical inspections for venereal diseases, paid for at their own expense, and faced incarceration for infection.[68] Houses of prostitution were not registered with local law enforcement (though their employees were registered as individuals), and allegations of routine police payoffs for each brothel abounded.[69] Additionally, registered prostitutes had their rights sharply curtailed during their work in Hawaii.[70] They were expected to work only at one of the brothels on Hotel Street, Honolulu's vice district near Chinatown, and could not change places of employment once hired. They were forbidden to leave the brothel after ten thirty at night or visit Waikiki Beach, public dances, bars, or "better class cafés" at any time. They were not allowed to ride in a taxicab with men, nor could they have a steady "boyfriend." Prostitutes were also enjoined not to marry soldiers or sailors. Violations of these rules meant a series of reprisals by the Honolulu Vice Squad, beginning with a warning and escalating to serious beatings, incarceration, and removal from the islands. This rigid system of expected behavior by prostitutes, enforced by the police, made it clear to the women, their male customers, and other Hawaiians exactly what the women's role was in the islands. Many locals believed that it was better that the prostitutes—many dark-skinned or lower-class white women—service men rather than have "respectable" (almost invariably white) women exposed to greater risk of rape or sexual assault.[71] This idea of prostitution as a "safety valve" harked back to older, Victorian ideas about men's irrepressible sexuality and a need for some women—that is, prostitutes—to satisfy these urges, lest greater social chaos result. It was also similar to the rationales provided for why legal prostitution was tolerated in France and Germany during the U.S. Army's service there. In Hawaii, these fears were brought about in part because of the gender imbalance in the islands due to the large number of male workers, soldiers, and sailors brought there, a demographic concern that was tremendously exacerbated during World War II and the military build-up in the islands from 1936 onward.[72]

Civilian moral reformers lamented what they considered to be the unduly pragmatic focus of the army's policies on prostitution and venereal disease in Hawaii. The 1914 Honolulu Social Survey stated that "the attitude of military authorities towards the question [of prostitution] is one mainly of solicitude for physical efficiency in the army. The sole object of the regulations seems to be to guard their men from disease."[73] In a 1925 report, the army encouraged soldiers to avoid disease-ridden prostitutes and instead patronize a "better class" of "white American women" who presumably took greater precautions against contracting venereal diseases. Soldiers were warned to avoid houses of prostitution with a "lower class of professional prostitute other than white. These places are filthy and are considered very dangerous as a venereal menace." Even worse than these women, according to the army's report, were "clandestine" prostitutes who were not venereally inspected and who operated out of automobiles and in public parks and rest areas. Their demographic composition was said to range from "white women of the 'Gold Digger type' to the lower class of natives."[74]

Local Hawaiians were concerned that as the army increased its presence in the islands, vice would also grow. The 1914 Honolulu Social Survey reported that "in proportion to their numbers, the increase in disorder and sexual vice has been less than expected," but "in the community it is a matter of common observation that prostitution has greatly increased since the coming of the army."[75] Before World War I, most organized prostitution in Hawaii was confined to the small, rough Iwilei dock district, which was shut down for the duration of the war.[76] After the war, new houses of prostitution were opened in the larger, more upscale Hotel Street district in Honolulu. Hotel Street later enjoyed tremendous expansion and unprecedented business during World War II with the massive influx of soldiers, sailors, and civilian defense workers brought to Hawaii as part of the American war effort.[77] Eventually, reformist territorial Governor Ingram Stainback ordered the closure of Honolulu's brothels on September 21, 1944. The U.S. military did not resist the order. Just as with the closure of Storyville in New Orleans during World War I, the closure of Hotel Street did not eliminate prostitution in Hawaii, though at least some prostitutes and madams left sex work and went on to other pursuits or returned to the mainland. Post–Hotel Street prostitution was simply driven underground, becoming dispersed and expensive. Male pimps and procurers came to play a much larger role in prostitution from that point forward.[78]

By the 1930s, the cost of hiring a prostitute was approximately three dollars for ten minutes for servicemen and two dollars for local civilian men. This would have represented a sizable amount of money to an enlisted soldier, but certainly not an unaffordable luxury; houses of prostitution had men—particularly soldiers—lined up on the streets on paydays.[79] In some brothels, servicemen and civilians used separate entrances and waiting areas, purportedly because some whites were uncomfortable seeing local Hawaiians, Filipinos, and other Asians visiting the same prostitutes as whites. This led them to believe that prostitutes were also segregated, though they were not.[80] Soldiers did not, of course, exclusively have sexual relationships with prostitutes in Hawaii; just as in the Philippines, "shack jobs," as they were derisively called, with local women, especially those of native Hawaiian or Filipino descent, were common among soldiers.[81] Shack jobs and soldiers' patronage of prostitutes—and the venereal infections that often came along with these interactions—were tolerated by the army because morale in Hawaii was a persistent problem, as chronicled in James Jones's semiautobiographical novel *From Here to Eternity*.[82]

Prostitution-Related Offenses

Unlike other venues, Hawaii saw no soldiers charged with having sex with prostitutes in the period under review. Two men were court-martialed in 1918 for "conducting and operating a disorderly house [brothel], thereby bringing discredit upon the military service," and one of the two men was also charged with "associating with a disreputable woman, thereby bringing discredit upon the military service."[83] The second man was also charged because he had been arrested by Hawaiian civil authorities while in bed with "a woman of immoral character at a disorderly house, thereby bringing discredit upon the military service."[84]

There were several cases of breaches of the peace, public nuisances, or violence involving prostitutes. For example, one African American soldier, Private John Manego, was charged with vandalizing a woman's home and threatening to kill her and hurt one of her female friends.[85] The victim, Beatrice Friedman, was a prostitute who had had a prior sexual relationship, presumably for pay, with Manego. She stated that she had refused to allow him into her home because she was afraid of "colored fellows," though she knew him and he had previously been inside the home. Friedman's friend and neighbor, a prostitute named Pansy Murphy, also alleged that she had been threatened by Manego because she did not "cater to them, to the Colored trade." A third prostitute, Sylvia Lewis, stated that she had been threatened by an unknown black soldier, whom she also refused to service, and that she and her fellow prostitutes were scared of "colored soldiers." Manego issued a statement saying that while he had been in Iwilei on the night the threats and vandalism had occurred, he had been unfairly accused in a case of mistaken identity, citing one witness who said, "As we all realize, these colored men all look alike." The court nevertheless convicted Manego, sentencing him to six months of hard labor.

The army sought to maintain certain bounds of social propriety in family matters, even for enlisted men. Two soldiers—Privates Charles E. Coleman and Isidore Abrahams—were court-martialed for marrying women alleged to be prostitutes, "to the scandal and disgrace of the military service."[86] Both were dishonorably discharged, with Abrahams receiving eighteen months of hard labor and Coleman six months (one year of Abrahams's sentence was later remitted by the Secretary of War). The large discrepancy between Coleman's and Abrahams's initial sentences is surprising, given that Coleman's conviction included a charge of striking and kicking his wife, as well as assaulting one of her female friends by ejecting her from their home. Abrahams's greater sentence may be at least partly explained because he was also charged with lying about his marital status; Coleman had also done this, but he was not charged for it. Coleman's defense counsel attempted to show that while his wife was a former prostitute, she was no longer employed in the sex trade after their marriage. As part of this testimony, Coleman testified that he did not believe his wife was a prostitute any longer because he had never contracted a venereal disease from her. Abrahams pleaded guilty, unlike Coleman, and stated that his wife was a former prostitute whom he loved and that she had pledged to renounce her former work and "lead a clean, decent life." He stated that he had lied to his commanding officer, a captain, about getting a marriage license and being married because he was "afraid to tell him," presumably because Abrahams knew that enlisted men were forbidden to marry without first receiving permission from their commanding officer. Abrahams had twice attempted to buy out the remainder of his military service, but his commanding officer had refused, despite Abrahams's having a good record of service in the army and a civilian job offer in Honolulu.

Sodomy and Same-Sex Sexual Activities

Sixty-four soldiers and two sergeants were court-martialed for engaging or attempting to engage in same-sex sexual activities from 1913 to 1918. All but eight were convicted and dishonorably discharged with forfeiture of all pay. Most also received some time at hard labor, ranging from a few months to five years, with an average sentence of two years. The lesser sentences of hard labor were generally those cases in which the accused only solicited sex, usually propositioning another soldier, but did not actually engage in sexual activity with another man. Because sodomy was not a violation of the Articles of War until 1917, same-sex sexual offenses before that time were usually charged under conduct to the prejudice of good order and military discipline, a violation of the Sixty-Second Article of War, with a specification that the accused had engaged in acts of "pederasty," "sodomy," "buccal coitus," or the like.

Prosecutions for sodomy or attempted sodomy in Hawaii increased dramatically after World War I, no doubt due in part to the army's 1917 revision to the *Manual for Courts-Martial*, which added sodomy as an offense. From 1919 to 1940, there were 229 courts-martial for sodomy or attempted sodomy in Hawaii. Not only did the frequency of prosecutions for sodomy increase, but the average sentence for sodomy or attempted sodomy convictions also increased from an average of 2 years to 3.3 years after 1918.[87] Fully 82 percent

(188) of these courts-martial ended in convictions. Interestingly, while no commissioned officers were court-martialed for sodomy in Hawaii during this period, 47 of the people charged with sodomy—more than one-fifth of the total—were noncommissioned officers. Of these, 79 percent were convicted.

The 1917 sodomy trial of Sergeant John Gaufin, Private William Myers, and Private Jesse W. Durham illustrates some of the complexities in these types of courts-martial. The three men were charged with jointly engaging in acts of sodomy, once between Gaufin and Myers and once between Gaufin and Durham.[88] Gaufin had recently transferred into the unit and, several witnesses claimed, rapidly gained a "reputation as a sodomist." The anonymous letter alleging this, written to the post surgeon, stated that several of the men serving under Gaufin had contracted gonorrhea from him. During the course of the investigation, Gaufin was inspected by the surgeon, but "his body show[ed] no evidence of being a sodomist and he was not infected with gonorrhea." Gaufin was apparently openly accused of the practice by several soldiers in public, which he jokingly accepted, saying that he was going to stop engaging in sodomy. A lieutenant under whom Gaufin served testified that he was one of the best noncommissioned officers the lieutenant had seen and that the rumors about Gaufin had been concocted by several other noncommissioned officers who were jealous of being passed over for promotion. Nevertheless, the three men were convicted and sentenced to be dishonorably discharged and to forfeit all pay; Gaufin received five years of hard labor and Myers and Durham four years each.

This case has an added poignancy because in 1970, Durham's son wrote to the Judge Advocate General's Office requesting that his father's case be reviewed. Durham's son wrote that Durham, in very poor health, had recently revealed to him that he and Myers had been "encouraged" by Gaufin, whom he described as "an individual with a perverted mind," to perform acts of sodomy on him. When they were caught, they were allegedly told "by older soldiers" that if they pleaded guilty, "nothing would happen to them, that only the sergeant would be transferred from the unit." Durham also stated that he and Myers had not wanted to be sent to France to fight. They had believed their guilty pleas would allow them to leave military service. Additionally, Durham had apparently told his friends and family that he had served time in prison for murder, rather than sodomy, hiding what he said was the truth of the situation for nearly fifty years. The Judge Advocate General's Office reviewed the case but declined to revise the legal findings. It is impossible to verify Durham's alternative version of the events, but if he was telling the truth, then the two young soldiers, anxious to escape wartime service, may indeed have been duped by Gaufin, then used as cat's-paws by Gaufin's jealous peers. Durham's lifelong lie about the reason for his imprisonment certainly speaks volumes to the social stigma associated with being a convicted sodomite.

The courts sometimes attempted to uncover the motives of the men accused of sodomy. Motives were usually difficult to determine, since the accused frequently declined to offer any testimony in their own defense, particularly in cases in which there were witnesses or physical evidence that would have likely led to convictions. While most of the sodomy cases in Hawaii during this period involved sex between soldiers, in one case, the accused, Private Charles Johnson, confessed to performing an act of oral sex on a local Hawaiian thirteen-year-old boy who shined shoes at Schofield Barracks in Honolulu. Johnson was caught in the act by four other soldiers.[89] Johnson had previously paid the boy for sex, though at no point was there a discussion of turning the boy over to Hawaiian civil authorities for punishment, nor was the boy's age made an issue. Johnson was asked by the defense counsel whether he was "addicted to this habit [sodomy]," and he answered in the affirmative. "Ever since I can remember," Johnson said. "I was born this way I guess. . . . I just can't help myself. It is my habit and my nature. . . . This boy tempted me and I had to give in. . . . Please have mercy on me as I can't do any better. I have been doing this ever since I can remember." In a closing statement, the defense counsel described Johnson as "not a pervert but an invert, a man who is incapable of doing anything else but what he has proven himself to do here, and I believe that no amount of punishment . . . will do him any good." This use of the term "invert" refers to the late nineteenth- and early twentieth-century idea of gender inversion, defined by sexologist Havelock Ellis as "sexual instinct turned by inborn constitutional abnormality toward persons of the same sex."[90] The defense counsel then requested that Johnson be confined not in a penitentiary but in "an institution for correction of degenerates." Johnson was found guilty and sentenced to be dishonorably discharged and receive a year of hard labor, but the reviewing authority reduced the sentence to a dishonorable discharge and a single month of hard labor.

Acquittals for charges of this nature usually resulted from cases in which there was only a single witness making an allegation with no supporting physical evidence. For example, Privates Harold Albert and Dewey Passmore were accused of engaging in an act of "pederasty" after a fellow soldier claimed he had heard heavy breathing when both men were sitting on Albert's bunk.[91] When questioned by the troop commander, Passmore confessed, but later recanted, stating that he had confessed simply to get out of military service after receiving word that several of his family members were ill and he had not realized that he would be court-martialed for the offense. Both men were acquitted and remained in military service. In a separate case, Private Harry J. Higdon was accused by Private Benjamin Jackson of soliciting sex on two occasions, a charge that Higdon flatly denied.[92] The two men knew each other, having worked together in the kitchen, and there was clearly a dispute over a loan of money. There was no evidence to support Jackson's accusation other than his own testimony, and Higdon was acquitted. In another case, two privates were witnessed having oral sex with each other, but because the court erred in not sustaining an objection, testimony about the case was deemed inadmissible by the reviewing authority and the convictions overturned.[93] Separately, Private Elmer E. Armstead was accused of allowing some unknown person to perform sodomy on him.[94] Two fellow privates claimed they came upon Armstead while he was asleep, with buttocks exposed and smeared with Vaseline. In Armstead's defense, his legal counsel described the charge of sodomy as a matter of "personal honor," trying to establish that Armstead was heterosexual. He called to the stand a soldier who had visited multiple houses of prostitution with Armstead, where both contracted venereal diseases. In his closing statement, the defense counsel stated, "I cannot find an example anywhere of a man who is addicted to the habit of sodomy being accustomed to going with women, and particularly to such a degree as to contract a venereal disease." Armstead was acquitted without further comment from the court, perhaps having been saved by his past sexual activities with women and venereal infection.

In a 1938 case at Schofield Barracks in Hawaii, Private James W. Sullivan Jr. was charged with seven counts of "commit[ting] the crime of sodomy, by feloniously and against the order of nature having carnal connection, with several other enlisted soldiers, by mouth."[95] Sullivan pleaded guilty to all seven counts and, unsurprisingly, was found guilty in each specification. In Sullivan's written confession given before the court-martial, he stated, "The accusation brought against me is true. I have been a sexual pervert ever since I can remember. I have had sexual relations with men of this organization [the Thirty-Fifth Infantry Regiment] for the past four (4) months. I have had these relations with at least ten (10) men." Sullivan was sentenced to be dishonorably discharged after serving five years of hard labor at the McNeil Island federal penitentiary in Washington State (the maximum sentence possible was thirty-five years, five years for each offense, to be served consecutively).

Though Sullivan pleaded guilty, the prosecution called as witnesses the four soldiers with whom Sullivan was accused of having sex (once with Private First Class Van B. Adams, twice with Private Emery G. Mabry, three times with

Private First Class Eugene A. Nicoletti, and once with Private First Class Brynlee I. Reese). All stated that the acts of sodomy had taken place, providing details on the exact places and times, and stated that penetration had indeed occurred (a necessary precondition for a conviction of sodomy). Each of the four men had provided written confessions before the court-martial began, and all offered virtually identical testimony. Each stated that he had been drunk when Sullivan asked him to go for a walk, that he had put his penis into Sullivan's mouth, that he would not have consented had he not been drunk, and that no money had changed hands. Mabry stated that this precise scenario had occurred on two separate occasions, and Nicoletti said that the same thing had occurred three times. Details varied only minimally; for instance, Adams noted that immediately after Sullivan took Adams's penis into his mouth, he lost consciousness. Nicoletti alleged that Sullivan had confessed to him, saying, "Do you know what I am? I am a cock sucker." Another soldier, Private First Class Robert T. Grady, testified that Sullivan had also approached him on two occasions offering oral sex, but that he had declined both offers, saying that once he "did not feel like having any sexual relations with Sullivan," and on the other, he "went out with Pvt Sullivan but [he] could not get in the mood for this act so [they] called it off."

Lieutenant Colonel William L. Starnes, an army psychiatrist, then testified as an expert medical witness. Starnes had interviewed and studied Sullivan at length, and he stated that he believed Sullivan should be classified as a "weak character" with homosexual tendencies by reason of a hereditary "constitutional misdevelopment." While Starnes said he believed Sullivan could have resisted this tendency by "super effort," he did not believe that Sullivan was capable of such a feat of willpower. He also described Sullivan as being "on the female side," and he stated that he believed Sullivan had "probably inherited more of the female sex than most of us do." Starnes stated that no medicine available could cure Sullivan, but that a psychiatrist might possibly be of assistance. He stated that he believed Sullivan to be incurable and that a long period of confinement would not be helpful in making Sullivan change his connection with this sexual deficiency. Starnes also noted that he had studied Sullivan with an eye toward assessing his sanity and stated that in his professional opinion, Sullivan was sane. Sullivan had also been examined after his arrest by another army psychiatrist, Lieutenant Colonel J. A. Rogers (who was not called to testify, though his diagnosis was presented as evidence). Rogers diagnosed Sullivan in the following way: "Constitutional psychopathic state; Sexual psychopathy, confirmed homosexual with fellatio practices. Not in line of duty. Existed prior to enlistment." Rogers also recommended that Sullivan be discharged if he were not tried by court-martial.

Sullivan then testified on his own behalf. Because Sullivan had already pleaded guilty to all charges, his testimony was offered to demonstrate "extenuating circumstances": the defense characterized Sullivan as a man who had been compulsively practicing sodomy, "a practice that ha[d] been steadily growing on him, since his days of puberty and for the succeeding fourteen years, without interruption and without realization that such practice was contrary to our every day concepts of decency. . . . [It is] a heinous practice that finally culminated in this affair [the court-martial]." Sullivan stated that he had been practicing sodomy since he was thirteen (he was twenty-seven at the time of the court-martial) and that the longest period he had been able to abstain from sodomy was one month. He reiterated that each of the seven acts of sodomy of which he was accused had taken place and that penetration had occurred in each. Additionally, Sullivan's defense attorney stated that Sullivan had admitted to him "frankly and in a well-behaved, straight-forward manner, of a hundred other similar instances with a hundred other soldiers of Schofield Barracks." Sullivan himself stated that he had had no problems finding willing sex partners while in the army. That was demonstrably true, since at least four other soldiers admitted they had had sexual contact with Sullivan, though all claimed they had only done so because they were intoxicated at the time and not responsible for their actions. None of these men were court-martialed or charged with having committed a crime, perhaps because the army accepted their explanations that they had been intoxicated to the point of near unconsciousness at the time, or because they were deemed less threatening to the integrity of the army because they had only received and not given oral sex, or perhaps simply because the army needed their cooperation to prosecute Sullivan and drum him out of the service. The case certainly suggests that Sullivan was understood very differently from the men with whom he had oral sex; their actions were treated as momentary lapses in judgment during alcoholic stupors in a setting where female sexual partners were mostly unavailable, while Sullivan was perceived as a congenital, perhaps even predatory, homosexual menace to the U.S. Army and its soldiers.

The army treated allegations of same-sex sexual activities by soldiers seriously. When there were multiple witnesses or physical evidence to corroborate such charges, courts-martial generally convicted the accused, almost always expelling them from the army and forcing them to serve an average of two or three years of hard labor. Such convictions often relied mostly or entirely on witnesses the courts found credible. Because courts-martial seldom commented on their verdicts, we have virtually no information on the deliberations or reasoning of the court officials. Courts seldom convicted based on flimsy, contradictory, or improbable testimony or lacking physical evidence.

The Sexual Economy of War in Hawaii

Hawaii has often been described as a racial melting pot or even a "racial mael-strom." Sexual relationships and marriages between individuals of different racial or ethnic groups were legally possible under the territorial laws of Hawaii and even socially acceptable in the islands during an era in which such relationships were illegal or socially unthinkable in much of the continental United States. While relations between the various ethnic and racial groups living in the islands were generally placid, with occasional notable exceptions, conflicts periodically arose, some of which pertained to sex. Fights between groups of soldiers and local civilian men of various races and ethnicities, of-ten over women, frequently had racial overtones. The demographic shortage of women for romantic or sexual encounters brought some of these conflicts about, as did disputes over equal access to prostitutes by members of differ-ent races. While there were no major racial problems in Hawaii during this period, relations among the races remained a constant issue with which army leaders had to grapple in Hawaii that was not present in other locales. Disputes between soldiers, white or black, and local men of various ethnici-ties over women remained a simmering concern for army commanders, as well as a cause of periodic flare-ups of violence. Racial consciousness was also present during nearly all courts-martial in which all those involved were nonwhite.

The U.S. Army was clearly concerned about establishing stable base com-munities in the Hawaiian Islands, a U.S. territory with its own system of laws and social mores, as it constructed new bases and increased existing facilities. Interactions between enlisted soldiers and local women, including "shack jobs" and prostitution, were often interracial, and racial, ethnic, and cultural differences frequently complicated matters for the individuals involved and the army as an institution when problems developed. Some of the more prevalent problems included disputes over access to prostitutes or financial disputes with prostitutes; disputes between soldiers and civilians over women; and cases of sexual harassment, domestic violence, and rape. Class differences also played a role in some cases of sexual harassment, when working-class enlisted soldiers interacted with women of higher social classes, or when sol-diers were alleged to have intruded on the private, domestic spaces of their social "betters," be they commissioned officers and their families or local ci-vilians. This latter problem—the invasion of private and domestic spaces by Peeping Tom soldiers, presumably for sexual titillation—does not seem to have been experienced to the same degree in other locations, foreign or do-mestic; if it did, the army never took notice of such incidents elsewhere. The army took such charges seriously, generally convicting the accused and sentencing them to what seem like lengthy terms of hard labor. The large number of such cases, far more than seen elsewhere, may have been due to the very different demographics of Hawaii and the relative inaccessibility of sexually available women (prostitutes or girlfriends) at some of the army's posts. At many army posts in Hawaii, especially those that were more isolated, most enlisted soldiers likely interacted socially with women only when on leave or on weekend passes, when they were permitted to leave their posts and visit local civilian communities. The army often chose to legally sanction soldiers for sexual misbehavior when their actions became public spectacles and threatened to embarrass the army as a whole. This is true for most categories of sexual misconduct leading to public spectacles (and therefore embarrassment for the army), including offenses like masturbation and indecent exposure, as well as cases in which soldiers publicly harassed women, especially when they were "respectable" women from the middle and upper classes.

The army was not concerned just about cases of sexual behavior that could publicly embarrass the institution; it was also concerned with sexual issues that could have effects on both unit readiness—venereal disease, which could incapacitate soldiers—and morale, including cases of sodomy, especially when the alleged acts were nonconsensual or committed in front of a significant number of witnesses. As in other locales, the army was anxious about the spread of venereal disease among soldiers in Hawaii, which it primarily blamed on soldiers' sexual contacts with local prostitutes. After venereal prophylaxis was made mandatory following sexual intercourse in the Hawaiian Department in 1912,[96] with violators threatened with courts-martial, the army took little further action to decrease venereal infections among soldiers in Hawaii. There is no evidence that a significant number of soldiers were ever punished for contracting venereal diseases or for failing to receive venereal prophylaxis or treatment. There were no major subsequent outbreaks of venereal disease that affected unit readiness in Hawaii, though soldiers continued to receive venereal prophylaxis and treatment for infections by army physicians. The army did little to help or hinder prostitution as an institution in Hawaii. If anything, the army seems to have condoned soldiers' visiting the medically inspected prostitutes allowed to operate with relative impunity by local civilian authorities. The army decisively cracked down on the small number of soldiers who attempted to work as pimps but took no action against those who merely patronized prostitutes as clients. While military police helped civilian police maintain order in Honolulu's red-light district, especially when large numbers of servicemen were present, they made no effort to prevent or even hinder soldiers from entering or patronizing brothels. They generally acted only to prevent outbreaks of violence or when intoxicated soldiers created public nuisances. While the army did not involve itself in the medical inspection of Hawaiian prostitutes as it had in the Philippines, the U.S. Army seemed content, just as it had in France and Germany, to allow local civilian authorities to create a de facto regulation of prostitution, which provided one of the few sexual outlets for many soldiers stationed in Hawaii.

More charges for sodomy and attempted sodomy, both quantitatively and proportionately, appear in Hawaii than in any of the other cases studied here. The army's increased interest in sodomy after World War I, and its decision to make such an offense an explicit violation of army regulations in 1917, helps explain the greater number of sodomy cases prosecuted. By the 1920s and 1930s, reflecting growing medical and psychoanalytic focus on homosexuality as a medical pathology, the army in Hawaii and elsewhere began to treat many of those accused of committing sodomy as psychopathic and unfit for military service. The army physicians who offered testimony in courts-martial sometimes suggested that certain individuals were congenitally predisposed toward moral weakness, which, they claimed, may have led accused soldiers to commit homosexual acts. The prevailing belief by other physicians and officers who testified seemed to be that same-sex sexual activity was situational, often brought about by overindulgence in alcohol. This implicit belief in "situational homosexuality," rather than congenital moral weakness, as the primary cause of some such acts did not prevent relatively harsh sentences of dishonorable discharges and up to several years of hard labor in federal penitentiaries. The moral weakness that was sometimes described as a cause of homosexual acts was only rarely mentioned in other sex-related cases (for example, almost never in cases of adultery, though it was sometimes mentioned in cases involving bestiality). The army seems to have particularly prosecuted cases in which same-sex acts were alleged to have taken place in public or semipublic areas in which there were multiple witnesses, or when soldiers were turned over to the army by civilian police after having been caught off base having sex with other men, or when violence or coercion was alleged. While most such cases involved two men who were alleged to have committed one or more consensual sexual acts together, some cases involved a single man charged with propositioning or actually having sex with many men,[97] and other cases involved multiple men who were said to have had sex with a single other man, usually involving force.[98] Regardless of the causes for the large number of sodomy cases in Hawaii, it seems apparent that same-sex sexual activities—or fears of such activity—had a significant presence at army posts in the islands. Civilian authorities closed Honolulu's red-light district for a few years, beginning in 1915, and at least one soldier noted in his memoirs that

Schofield Barracks almost immediately experienced an increase in same-sex sexual activity on post, which eventually elicited an order to keep lights on all night within the post barracks.[99] The newly restored edition of James Jones's semiautobiographical *From Here to Eternity* includes a number of scenes involving homosexuality among soldiers in Hawaii before and during World War II that had been cut from the original 1951 edition because of censorship and pornography concerns. These scenes include a soldier discussing having oral sex with a wealthy man in Hawaii for five or ten dollars, which "comes in handy the middle of the month," as well as an army investigation into homosexual activity.[100]

The army's anxieties about sexuality in Hawaii were similar in some ways to those at other posts—venereal disease was a continuous concern, and the army always acted to decisively punish those who caused public sexual scandals—but several new problems emerged in the Hawaiian Islands. The racial and gender demographics of Hawaii offered a unique set of challenges. Hawaii, an ethnically heterogeneous territory, contained large numbers of those considered to be nonwhite or of mixed parentage, creating an environment in which racial and ethnic lines were frequently blurred in sexual relationships. There were also relatively few adult women (of any race) living in Hawaii, which created a relative lack of women available to soldiers for noncommercial sexual interactions. Just as the U.S. Army encountered unique local legal and social conditions elsewhere—in the Philippines, France, and Germany—to which it had to accommodate, so too did it have to take into account local Hawaiian politics, the islands' legal status as a territory of the United States, and the local demographics. Additionally, African American soldiers composed a small percentage of the army's total presence in Hawaii but a disproportionate number of those charged with sex crimes, possibly reflecting institutional racism in selective prosecution, drawing on race-based fears of hypersexed black men. Likewise, the army's growing postwar belief that acts of sodomy were symptomatic of mental pathology, and hence completely incompatible with continued service in the army, are well illustrated here. This pathologized view of same-sex sex acts became increasingly solidified within the U.S. Army, as well as broader American society, setting the stage for how those engaging in such practices would be viewed throughout much of the twentieth century.

Conclusion

Ongoing Concerns with Soldiers' Sexualities and Sexual Cultures

> A soldier who won't fuck won't fight.
>
> —Unknown

This pithy but illuminating vulgarity has been variously attributed to Civil War generals J. E. B. Stewart, Philip Sheridan, and William T. Sherman, as well as World War II commander George S. Patton.[1] The statement is apocryphal but has nevertheless become part of the popular mythos surrounding the American military and its historic attitudes toward soldiers and sex. It appears, however, that this quotation has never been attributed to John J. Pershing, or to any other U.S. military leader during the early twentieth century, a period in American military history unusual for its encouragement of sexual abstinence by soldiers, at least during wartime. In the first four decades of the twentieth century, more so than during any other period in American history, the U.S. Army regulated practically all forms of sexual behavior and expressions by soldiers. While the U.S. Army in other times may have even encouraged a robust, virile, and even promiscuous heterosexuality in its soldiers—or at least looked the other way in a spirit of "boys will be boys"—it tried rather assiduously between 1898 and 1940 to regulate and at times prohibit almost all forms of sexual expression, ranging from the reprehensible (rape) to the harmless (masturbation).

The U.S. Army, in the decades immediately preceding and following World War I, did not focus solely on sexual abstinence, however; that policy was a product of the efforts of influential domestic moral reformers during the war years who were responding to the massive influx of middle-class, "respectable" young men into military service. These men, unlike those professional soldiers who chose to serve in the army during peacetime, were perceived as being morally and sexually vulnerable, in need of protection from the temptations of the flesh.[2] Many domestic reformers considered these draftees to be a potential source of moral renewal for the nation as a whole after the war—if they could be protected from sexual dangers and trained to reject sexual immorality.

Throughout the early decades of the twentieth century, the U.S. Army mandated that married men could not enlist or reenlist in the army. It inspected the bodies of soldiers and many of their civilian sex partners for venereal disease and required that both receive medical treatment when found to be infected. It prosecuted soldiers who refused such treatment. It punished soldiers whose sexual exploits led to public disturbances, or discipline or morale problems, or difficulties with local civilian communities. And, increasingly after World War I, the army sought to purge its ranks of men it classified as homosexuals. The U.S Army was initially interested in the sex lives of soldiers primarily for what it described as utilitarian reasons as it sought the smooth functioning of the organization, using its disciplinary and legal authority to enforce many regulations on sexuality for soldiers and their partners. Over time, though, the army took an institutional interest in cultivating particular kinds of masculine identities for soldiers.

This book has explored an integral but understudied dimension of how the United States mobilized and maintained its soldiery for its new missions of the early twentieth century. I have argued that the U.S. Army first attempted to gain control of almost all aspects of soldiers' sexuality—the ways that these aspects affected and interacted with the army and its attempts to regulate them constitute the "sexual economy of war"—and then tried to carefully manage and regulate that sexual economy to best fulfill the army's missions. In the process, it created a new kind of militant masculinity, one especially encouraged in enlisted soldiers. As a guiding principle, army leaders often used the notion of "military necessity" to shape their actions in controlling soldiers' sexuality. They stated they were concerned primarily with the army's operational effectiveness. They suppressed soldiers' sexual behaviors and expressions that they perceived as running counter to the good of the service or creating inefficiencies. They encouraged those aspects of sexual identity that the army believed benefited the service—for instance, hypermasculine demeanor and actions—eventually purging soldiers who engaged in same-sex sexual activities because these practices became linked, in the minds of officials, with effeminacy and mental disorders. The army's efforts, which took shape in very different ways, depending on the time period and geographic context, were continually, though rarely openly, resisted by many soldiers and their sexual partners, who sought sexual expressions that sometimes ran counter to the army's institutional goals. The result was a continual battle between the army, seeking to exert control, and individuals, seeking to assert agency, within the ever-contested sexual economy of war.

Army leaders often stated that they believed soldiers' sexual needs were irrepressible. On distant deployments, the army tended to allow soldiers to engage in sexual relations with local women, many of whom worked as prostitutes. I have argued that the army's actions went beyond mere toleration of sex with local prostitutes, showing how it actively created an environment in which soldiers could feel free to engage in sexual relationships with local women, generally without fear of significant consequences. The consensus within both the army and early twentieth-century American society was that prostitutes were the primary vectors of venereal contagion. Because of this, the army sought to limit the damage to military effectiveness that debilitating venereal infections might cause by medically inspecting, quarantining, and treating prostitutes believed to harbor such infections. Army leaders seldom discussed prohibiting soldiers from having sex with them altogether, however.

Some soldiers—officers and many older noncommissioned officers in particular—were married, and the experiences of their wives help shed light on the complicated ways in which the army perceived and dealt with women. Army leaders tended to categorize soldiers' female sexual partners according to their own prejudices. Officers' wives were mostly considered respectable. Enlisted men's working-class romantic partners were looked at askance, often seen as little more than undesirable distractions or burdens on the service. Unmarried women who interacted sexually with soldiers were almost universally considered to be prostitutes and sources of venereal contagion, however necessary they might have been deemed for meeting soldiers' "natural" sexual needs. The army's divergent views on the sexuality of officers and enlisted men help illuminate the disparities in class and rank inside the institution.

Over time, particularly after World War I, the army grew concerned about the possibility of homosexuality within the ranks. While these fears produced only sporadic investigations, they suggested considerable underlying anxieties, exhibited through the internal discussions of the problem as well as the significant resources expended to periodically root out offenders. The army, ever concerned that soldiers not behave effeminately, encouraged a kind of physically demonstrative, aggressive masculinity.

The U.S. Army appears to have had a number of goals for intervening in soldiers' sexuality in the various locales, foreign and domestic, where it deployed forces in the first four decades of the twentieth century. In many cases, several or all of these goals operated simultaneously, even harmoniously. In some instances, however, these goals worked at cross-purposes or otherwise complicated the army's efforts. For example, medical inspections of prostitutes helped to isolate women who might infect the soldiers but also gave tacit approval for soldiers to consort with those declared clean. These conflicts became especially apparent when the army's interventions conflicted with the concerns of politically influential domestic audiences. The first, and perhaps most important, of the army's goals for its regulation of sexual matters was to prevent the spread of venereal disease from making significant numbers of soldiers ineffective for duty and thereby causing a serious manpower problem. A second, related goal was to maintain good order, morale, and military discipline inside the army. A third goal was to enhance the public image of the United States and the U.S. Army by making its soldiers models of virtue and abstention. Fourth, the U.S. Army sought to use the broad category of regulated sexuality to construct, maintain, and reinforce class barriers and structures inside the army. The army's fifth goal was to maintain and encourage particular ideas about morality among soldiers. These ideas about sexual morality were heavily influenced by the concerns of influential moral reformers inside the United States, especially before World War I. Finally, the U.S. Army, particularly after World War I, sought to root out same-sex sexual activities within the army, which army leaders linked with "deviant" homosexual identities, effeminacy, and psychologically maladjusted personalities. This ultimately led to the creation of a "straight" army.[3] Understanding these goals helps shed light on how the army perceived a host of issues related to sexuality, what the effects of these perceptions were, and what kind of army, soldiers, and society the army hoped to create.

Goal: To Prevent Venereal Disease from Affecting the U.S. Army's Manpower and Readiness

The U.S. Army's early twentieth-century interventions in the sexual lives of soldiers and their partners most prominently involved efforts to mitigate, if not entirely eliminate, the effects of venereal diseases on army manpower. Because of the prevailing notion (in the army and within American society) that prostitutes were the primary source of venereal disease, the army frequently sought to attack venereal disease by medically regulating the prostitutes with whom soldiers came into contact or eliminating the possibility for such contact altogether. This created an inextricable linkage between the regulation of prostitution and venereal disease throughout the period.

Venereal disease did wreak tremendous havoc on the U.S. Army's manpower in the Philippines before World War I. In the twenty-five years before the U.S. occupation of the Philippines, the average annual hospital admission rate for venereal diseases in the U.S. Army as a whole was less than 9 percent, which was a high but manageable number for the army.[4] In 1899, the first year with significant numbers of U.S. troops deployed to the Philippines, the venereal disease admission rate immediately climbed to almost 14 percent. It climbed further to 15 percent the next year and held steady for the next decade. The venereal disease admission rates for army units in the Philippines were even higher. In some years, the annual venereal disease admission rate for the Philippine Department was more than 23 percent, with some units reaching nearly 36 percent.[5] Clearly, soldiers contracted venereal diseases in the Philippines at an alarming rate, far more than at any other station, foreign or domestic, during the first four decades of the twentieth century. The army sought to mitigate the effects of venereal disease on soldiers by medically inspecting and forcibly treating, if necessary, prostitutes and eventually American soldiers in the Philippines. The army's regulated-prostitution program had limited effects on the rate of venereal disease transmission to soldiers because there were no fully effective means available to treat venereal infections before the advent of antibiotics. The program soon came under tremendous criticism by domestic moral reform organizations, many of which were also sharply anti-imperialistic and used the issue of sexual immorality and excess in public debates to criticize the American occupation. Nevertheless, the army continued its program in the Philippines until World War I. During World War I, because the army feared that venereal disease rates would once again climb as a result of its new overseas deployments, it instituted similar regimes of mandated medical inspections of prostitutes in France and Germany with the cooperation of the French and German governments. American reformers were never entirely comfortable with such regimes but were forced to acquiesce to these policies as they were legally required under French and German law and widely accepted in France and Germany. Such medical inspection regimes were not tried in the continental United States because of domestic political resistance, though Pershing did implement such a program during the Pancho Villa Expedition on the Mexican-American border. A similar program was also implemented in Honolulu with the approval of local authorities.

Goal: To Maintain Good Order, Morale, and Military Discipline

After the army's seemingly all-pervasive desire to prevent large outbreaks of venereal disease from crippling its forces, the army's second major concern about sexuality seems to have been its tendency to erode what the army described as "good order, morale, and military discipline." Sex could, and often did, lead to an expansive set of outcomes that the army sought to avoid, including fights between soldiers and public disturbances. These conflicts could stem from a variety of factors, ranging from disagreements over sex partners, to cases in which one soldier sexually propositioned or had sex with another, to cases in which one soldier sexually harassed another's spouse. The most obvious, and most public, breakdowns in order and discipline occurred in two sexually motivated riots in Hawaii. The first took place in 1913 when twenty soldiers vandalized a clandestine brothel operating on the grounds of Fort Shafter,[6] and the second in 1916 when a large group of black soldiers rioted after white prostitutes refused to service them because of their race.[7] The army also prosecuted soldiers for disobeying a wide variety of direct orders on sexual matters. If, for example, a doctor diagnosed venereal infection in a soldier and ordered treatment, refusal to undergo the treatment could result in court-martial.

Goal: To Maintain and Enhance the Positive Public Image of the United States and the U.S. Army as an Institution

The U.S. Army found it politically expedient in the Progressive Era to cultivate an image of rectitude and morality. Professing and practicing sexual decorum promoted a positive image for the army and for the nation as a whole to domestic and foreign audiences. The army needed to maintain good relationships with local civilian communities around its bases, especially during World War I in France and later in Germany in the postwar occupation—it could not ignore the reactions of French and German populations and officials to individual soldiers' behavior, or to the army's policies. After all, the French were the U.S. Army's allies and hosts during the war, and the Germans were imagined as new future partners and allies after the war. The army was also forced to accommodate and incorporate existing French and German laws, policies, and cultures about sex in its own policies. To be sure, the U.S.

Army was able to effect some changes, such as declaring brothels off-limits to American soldiers in France and creating vagrancy courts for dealing with suspected prostitutes in Germany, but it could not unilaterally dictate how sexual matters would be regulated during the war or postwar occupation. Of course, these niceties did not apply to the Philippines, which the United States acquired after the Spanish-American War, essentially as part of the spoils of that conflict.

Disputes between soldiers and local civilians over sexual matters no doubt occurred in all the locales to which American soldiers were deployed, but they are mentioned most frequently in Germany and Hawaii. Problems between American soldiers and German civilians occurred most frequently when soldiers impregnated local women. While some soldiers took responsibility for their actions and either married or financially supported the women and infants, German civilians had little legal recourse when American soldiers abandoned their responsibilities, creating a public outcry during the occupation. Interactions between men of different racial and ethnic groups, as well as the relatively small number of adult women living in Hawaii, made these kinds of problems particularly prevalent in Hawaii.

Goal: To Create, Maintain, and Reinforce Class Barriers and Structures within the Army

The U.S. Army created and maintained sharp, class-based, hierarchical divides between commissioned officers and enlisted men throughout its history, and the early decades of the twentieth century were no exception.[8] U.S. Army officers and enlisted men of the early twentieth century maintained separate cultures within the army, a fact that had profound implications for all aspects of these men's lives, including the most intimate ones. Commissioned officers, for example, were only very rarely forced to submit to intrusive and demeaning venereal inspections of their bodies, unlike enlisted men, who would be court-martialed if they refused to submit to medical inspections and treatments. Officers and enlisted men received very different treatment under the military justice system and were subject to divergent sexual expectations, surveillance, and discipline. The varying experiences of officers and enlisted men and the different ways in which the army regulated their sexual lives help shed additional light on the army's separate cultures. These class structures included not only soldiers but also their wives, families, and sex partners; the army treated these associated civilians very differently depending on whether they were legally or emotionally bonded to officers or enlisted men.

The army imagined the sexualities of officers and enlisted men very differently and pursued two separate policies on marriage within the service. Officers (at least those who had served in the army for a few years) were often married, and their families formed close-knit communities at virtually all peacetime U.S. Army posts. Officers' wives were nearly always considered respectable women. Neither officers nor their families welcomed intrusion by enlisted men into their private spaces. Many older noncommissioned officers were also married, and their wives often accompanied them on deployments, though they formed their own family communities separate from those of officers. Enlisted men, however, were strongly discouraged from marrying and faced courts-martial if they were discovered to have married without permission. Thus, the sex lives of these different groups of men and their civilian sex partners were conceived of and regulated very differently by the army. These sharply divergent expectations and practices likewise led to different conceptions of masculinity for commissioned officers and enlisted men. Officers, for example, could violate the Ninety-Fifth Article of War, which made criminal any "conduct unbecoming an officer and a gentleman"; enlisted men could not.[9] The army required that officers behave themselves as "gentlemen" at all times, while enlisted men would certainly never be considered "gentlemen" at all.

There was also clearly a great deal of contact between officers' wives and enlisted men when no officers were present. Much of this contact stemmed from the fact that enlisted soldiers were frequently hired by officers to perform chores in and around the home. While officers were away, their wives supervised the soldiers' work. These interactions sometimes crossed a line, with officers' wives becoming scandalized at the remarks or insinuations made by soldiers. Soldiers found to have sexually harassed women, either the wives of officers or civilians, were generally punished severely and rarely allowed to remain in the army. Enlisted soldiers convicted of invading the intimate or domestic spaces of noncommissioned or commissioned officers and their families, usually as Peeping Toms, were also treated harshly.

Army officers were bound by a set of expectations regarding matters of social (and sexual) propriety to which enlisted men were generally not held accountable. Officers, at least while in Europe during World War I, faced legal reprisals for some kinds of sexual behaviors for which enlisted men were almost never prosecuted. For example, only six enlisted men and a single non-commissioned officer (a corporal) were court-martialed for consorting with women the army alleged to be prostitutes, while forty-four commissioned officers were court-martialed for similar offenses. Officers were court-martialed for their interactions with prostitutes because they either offended the sensibilities of their fellow officers or engaged publicly in activities the army deemed immoral. The army also acted to maintain the boundaries of social propriety between officers and enlisted men. When officers publicly violated these social norms—by drinking, gambling, or discussing sex with enlisted men, for example—the army could act rapidly and decisively to convict and dismiss the offending officers.

Goal: To Maintain and Encourage the Morality of Soldiers

Concerns about the morality of soldiers became especially significant during World War I, when the nation's massive military mobilization brought millions of civilian men from all walks of life into the army. These men were seen by many social and moral crusaders as being at risk of sexual and other temptations. World War I's influx of new soldiers coincided with the apex of the Progressive movement's influence. Many Progressives were deeply concerned about morality in general, and sexual morality in particular. They sought to use the powers of a newly energized federal government to push through sweeping legislation and policies to socially and morally reengineer the nation along particular middle-class, Protestant moral lines. The world war profoundly changed the very notion of what it meant to be a "citizen-soldier" of the United States, since now most able-bodied males could become soldiers. These men could be educated and trained in particular moral practices during wartime and then aid the nation in transforming and reforming itself morally after the war as part of the Progressives' larger social engineering efforts.

Because of fears that venereal disease would inundate the American Expeditionary Forces in France as it had in the Philippines, the U.S. Army, cooperating with federal civilian officials, engaged in a two-pronged attack on sexual immorality. The first effort focused on sexual education and indoctrination that strongly urged sexual abstinence, while the second sought to eliminate all red-light districts near training camps and bases and prosecute all prostitutes or "promiscuous women" who might prey on the soldiers. During World War I, particularly once soldiers were deployed to France, the army was also concerned that soldiers might not just have sex with French prostitutes but also engage in "perverse" or "deviant" sex acts with them, particularly oral sex. It is clear, though, that not all army officers wholeheartedly supported the wartime sexual abstinence policy, with at least some continuing to believe that soldiers' sexual needs were irrepressible and should be tacitly accepted by the army.[10]

Goal: To Root Out Homosexuality within the Army

Before the U.S. involvement in World War I, the U.S. Army focused narrowly on the physical act of sodomy in its legal practices, rather than on homosexuality as an identity of some soldiers.[11] While some army physicians—and occasionally other officers—who offered testimony in courts-martial suggested that certain individuals were congenitally predisposed toward moral weakness and this may have led accused soldiers to commit homosexual acts, more often, the prevailing notion within the army seems to have been that same-sex sexual activity was situational, often brought about by overindulgence in alcohol.[12] This implicit belief in "situational homosexuality" as the primary cause of such acts did not prevent relatively harsh sentences of dishonorable discharges and up to several years of hard labor in federal penitentiaries.

After World War I, the U.S. Army came to view the elimination of homosexuality within the service as a priority. American society, the medical and psychoanalytic communities, and the army increasingly took notice of homosexual practices and began to pathologize such activities.[13] In this new, postwar environment, same-sex sexual practices came to be seen as signifying an identifiable homosexual identity for those men who engaged in them. Homosexuality was increasingly perceived as being linked with psychiatric defects and effeminacy, neither of which was deemed acceptable for soldiers. While these fears about the dangers of homosexuality produced only sporadic investigations, they suggested considerable underlying anxieties, and the resources expended to periodically root out offenders were significant. These efforts produced a considerable number of courts-martial for men charged with various offenses related to sexual contact with other men. Despite the growing sense that men who were sexually attracted to other men were mentally deficient or effeminate—and therefore poor soldiers—without some evidence of physical, sexual acts, soldiers suspected of being homosexuals were not charged. The army seems to have developed in this period a new perception of homosexuality, which it then projected onto soldiers accused of some behaviors that were previously treated less seriously.[14]

Uncovering Underlying Sexual Cultures within the U.S. Army

Examining the sexual economy of war within the U.S. Army is, most obviously, helpful for understanding the kinds of normative sexualities and sexual lives that the army promoted for officers, enlisted men, and their families and sex partners. These sexual expectations, prevalent during the Progressive Era, included abstaining from sex before marriage, not indulging in extramarital sex, and refraining from "deviant" forms of sexuality, which included activities as varied as masturbation, same-sex sexual activities, and oral sex, among many others. But the U.S. Army, and individual army commanders and policymakers, did not simply adopt such sexual norms without alteration for the army. Army practice, particularly when it medically inspected prostitutes as a precondition of their consorting with American soldiers, deviated from the norm desired by American moralists. Most senior leaders of the army believed that the sexual desires of soldiers, especially those deployed abroad without wives, were irrepressible. Medically inspected prostitutes, according to this way of thinking, would thus provide the sexual outlet that best served the army's interests. It is equally clear that exploring the sexual economy of war can help uncover not only the army's desired set of sexual practices and enforcement mechanisms for promoting such practices but the underlying sexual cultures within the army as well. Courts-martial are extremely useful for what they reveal about the types of behaviors that the institution considered so transgressive that they had to be formally and publicly prosecuted. The language used to describe the offenses in these cases can also illuminate much about how the offenses were conceived of at the time. But in many of the courts-martial examined in this study, the specifics of the individual cases are far less interesting than what the cases reveal about life inside the army, or what may be better described as the "underlife" of the institution.[15]

Many soldiers, including those at domestic bases like Fort Riley, as well as soldiers deployed outside the United States to the Philippines, Europe, and Hawaii, seem to have been given relatively free rein to indulge in sexual activity with women, even prostitutes. This tolerance was usually extended even when soldiers' sexual activities led to infection with venereal diseases, though army regulations usually required soldiers to submit to postcoital prophylaxis from army physicians. The army went beyond merely tolerating prostitution (and soldiers' patronage of prostitutes) and seems to have essentially condoned it. It generally only acted to mitigate the harmful effects of venereal disease on troop readiness. The army appeared to draw the line at public displays of sexual activity or vulgar displays of a sexual nature, either on army property or in nearby civilian areas. The primary exception to this fairly tolerant official attitude arose in World War I, during which the army cooperated with civilian officials who took significant measures to limit the ability of soldiers to have sex while in domestic training camps.

Enlisted men were forbidden to marry before enlistment, or to reenlist if married, though they did sometimes marry, with or without the approval of their commanding officers. They also sometimes formed common-law relationships, especially in places like the Philippines and Hawaii, where such relationships were more socially acceptable. Relationships like this also existed at bases in the United States, such as Fort Riley, where they tended to be tacitly accepted among working-class Americans. Married couples, both officers and enlisted, socialized among their peers, married and single, and there were a number of cases in which soldiers entered into sexual relationships with their fellow soldiers' wives. These men, officers and enlisted soldiers alike, were charged with committing adultery when their situations became known to the army.

A large degree of homosociality is to be expected in a largely same-sex institution like the U.S. Army, but some of the activities routinely described by soldiers seem to have had what can only be described as sexual undertones.[16] For example, soldiers were known to sometimes sleep in the same bed or bunk; criminality was not always attached to such acts, though they were unusual enough that when such cases became officially known to the army, an investigation or court-martial could result.[17] Soldiers seem to have engaged in a fair amount of behavior generally deemed unproblematic—wrestling, horseplay, and roughhousing—but that sometimes took on sexual elements, especially when accompanied by vulgar banter and sexual teasing, or when conducted by soldiers in a state of undress. These kinds of activities occasionally led to courts-martial when they were interpreted by observers or the authorities as having crossed a line of acceptable behavior. These activities also lend credence to the suggestion in recent historiography in queer history that sexual diversity and blurred conceptions of homosexuality and heterosexuality were apparent in the early decades of the twentieth century.[18] Additionally, a culture of drunkenness and alcohol abuse appears to have permeated the army. It was usually tolerated, unless it brought on other problematic behavior, some of it sexual. Soldiers were thus fairly free—with some notable exceptions—to indulge in the kinds of sexual practices they wished, generally so long as they did so discreetly and did not bring public attention to their activities from civilians or fellow soldiers, who may have disapproved, or officers, who may have felt obliged to take official notice of proscribed activities.

Final Thoughts

I have argued that the U.S. Army became increasingly interested in regulating almost all aspects of soldiers' sexuality in order to help fulfill the needs and missions of the army as a whole. It found that it could not ignore sex and thus had to choose carefully when and how to intervene in the sex lives of soldiers and their partners. These interventions were sometimes the result of muddled or conflicting views on sexual practices and morality. The army's public attempts to gain control over soldiers' sex lives, and the sexual regulatory apparatus it established to implement these policies, also served the army's interests by appealing to domestic constituencies interested in using the military as a tool of broader moral and social reform, as well as civilian communities near army bases overseas that were concerned about the potential for sexual dangers and disruptions posed by soldiers.

Beyond the regulation of sexuality within the U.S. Army lies a vast terrain of sexual practices and behaviors in which soldiers and their sex partners engaged that this research has only begun to uncover. Delving much more deeply into the personal materials and literature produced by those who served in the army during this period will undoubtedly yield further insights about the subterranean sexual cultures that existed within the U.S. Army of the early twentieth century.

NOTES

Introduction. Society, Sexuality, and the U.S. Army in the Early Twentieth Century

Epigraph: Felix Frankfurter to Newton Baker, August 15, 1917, Newton D. Baker Papers, Library of Congress, Washington, DC, quoted in Allan M. Brandt, *No Magic Bullet: A Social History of Venereal Disease in the United States since 1880*, expanded ed. (New York: Oxford University Press, 1987), 99.

1. William B. Johnson, *The Crowning Infamy of Imperialism* (Philadelphia: American League of Philadelphia, 1900).

2. "The Custer Henderson Letter," Custer Henderson, Thirty-Third U.S. Volunteer Infantry Regiment, Manila, to Albert J. and Margaret T. Henderson, Saint Bernice, Indiana, September 16, 1900, Adjutant General's Office [hereafter AGO] Docfile 343790, RG 94, National Archives and Record Administration, Washington, DC [hereafter NARA].

3. Kristin L. Hoganson, *Fighting for American Manhood: How Gender Politics Provoked the Spanish-American and Philippine-American Wars* (New Haven, CT: Yale University Press, 1998), 188.

4. Major Charles Lynch to president, Board of Health, May 18, 1901, File 2039-13, Box 246, RG 350, NARA.

5. Quoted in Henry Parker Willis, *Our Philippine Problem: A Study of American Colonial Policy* (New York: Henry Holt, 1905), 257.

6. Catherine Lutz, ed., *The Bases of Empire: The Global Struggle against U.S. Military Posts* (Washington Square: New York University Press, 2009); Maria Höhn and Seung-sook Moon, eds., *Over There: Living with the U.S. Military Empire from World War Two to the Present* (Durham, NC: Duke University Press, 2010); Cynthia H. Enloe, *Maneuvers: The International Politics of Militarizing Women's Lives* (Berkeley: University of California Press, 2000).

7. Ian R. Tyrrell, *Reforming the World: The Creation of America's Moral Empire* (Princeton, NJ: Princeton University Press, 2010); Nancy K. Bristow, *Making Men Moral: Social Engineering during the Great War* (New York: New York University Press, 1996), 8–11.

8. Paul A. Kramer, "Power and Connection: Imperial Histories of the United States in the World," *American Historical Review* 116, no. 5 (December 2011): 1348–1391; Brian McAllister Linn, *Guardians of Empire: The U.S. Army and the Pacific, 1902–1940* (Chapel Hill: University of North Carolina Press, 1997).

9. Richard S. Faulkner, *Pershing's Crusaders: The American Soldier in World War I* (Lawrence: University Press of Kansas, 2017); Nancy Gentile Ford, *Americans All! Foreign-Born*

Soldiers in World War I (College Station: Texas A&M University Press, 2001); Edward M. Coffman, *The Regulars: The American Army, 1898–1941* (Cambridge, MA: Belknap Press of Harvard University Press, 2004), 142–201.

10. Alan R. Millett, Peter Maslowski, and William B. Feis, *For the Common Defense: A Military History of the United States of America from 1607 to 2012*, 3rd ed. (New York: Free Press, 2012), 683.

11. Jennifer Keene, *Doughboys, the Great War, and the Remaking of America* (Baltimore: Johns Hopkins University Press, 2001); Edward M. Coffman, *The War to End All Wars: The American Military Experience in World War I* (Madison: University of Wisconsin Press, 1968, 1986); David M. Kennedy, *Over Here: The First World War and American Society* (New York: Oxford University Press, 1980).

12. David J. Pivar, *Purity and Hygiene: Women, Prostitution, and the "American Plan," 1900–1930* (Westport, CT: Greenwood, 2002); Nancy K. Bristow, *Making Men Moral: Social Engineering during the Great War* (New York: New York University Press, 1996); Noralee Frankel and Nancy S. Dye, eds., *Gender, Class, Race, and Reform in the Progressive Era* (Lexington: University Press of Kentucky, 1991).

13. Jeffrey T. Sammons and John H. Morrow, Jr., *Harlem's Rattlers and the Great War: The Undaunted 369th Regiment and the African American Quest for Equality* (Lawrence: University Press of Kansas, 2014); Chad L. Williams, *Torchbearers of Democracy: African American Soldiers in the World War I Era* (Chapel Hill: University of North Carolina Press, 2010); Adriane Lentz-Smith, *Freedom Struggles: African Americans and World War I* (Cambridge, MA: Harvard University Press, 2009).

14. David F. Trask, *The War with Spain in 1898* (New York: Macmillan, 1981).

15. Stephen E. Bosanac and Merle Jacobs, eds., *The Professionalization of Work* (Whitby, ON: De Sitter, 2006); Keith M. MacDonald, *The Sociology of the Professions* (London: Sage, 1995).

16. Surgeon General to the Adjutant General, "Rates for Venereal Disease in the Second Division," November 19, 1914, AGO Docfile 2230647, filed with AGO Docfile 1045985, RG 94, NARA.

17. Philippa Levine, *Prostitution, Race, and Politics: Policing Venereal Disease in the British Empire* (New York: Routledge, 2003); Philip Howell, *Geographies of Regulation: Policing Prostitution in Nineteenth-Century Britain and the Empire* (Cambridge: Cambridge University Press, 2009).

18. George Chauncey Jr., "Christian Brotherhood or Sexual Perversion? Homosexual Identities and the Construction of Sexual Boundaries in the World War I Era," in *Hidden from History: Reclaiming the Gay and Lesbian Past*, ed. Martin Bauml Duberman, Martha Vicinus, and George Chauncey Jr. (New York: New American Library, 1989), 294–317.

19. E. Anthony Rotundo, *American Manhood: Transformations in Masculinity from the Revolution to the Modern Era* (New York: Basic Books, 1993); Gail Bederman, *Manliness and Civilization: A Cultural History of Gender and Race in the United States, 1880–1917* (Chicago: University of Chicago Press, 1995); Amy S. Greenberg, *Manifest Manhood and the Antebellum American Empire* (Cambridge: Cambridge University Press, 2005).

20. Rotundo, *American Manhood*, 225–226.

21. Bederman, *Manliness and Civilization*, 170–215.

22. Donald L. Mosher and Mark Sirkin, "Measuring a Macho Personality Constellation," *Journal of Research in Personality* 18 (1984): 150–163; Leonard L. Glass, "Man's Man / Ladies' Man: Motifs of Hypermasculinity," *Psychiatry* 47, no. 3 (1984): 260–278; Donald L. Mosher and Silvan S. Tomkins, "Scripting the Macho Man: Hypermasculine Socialization and Enculturation," *Journal of Sex Research* 25 (1988): 60–84.

23. U.S. Department of War, *Regulations for the Army of the United States, 1913 Corrected to 1917* (Washington, DC: Government Printing Office, 1917); Nancy L. Goldman, "Trends in Family Patterns of U.S. Military Personnel during the 20th Century," in *The Social Psychology of Military Service*, ed. Nancy L. Goldman and David R. Segal (Beverly Hills: Sage, 1976), 119–134; U.S. Army, *The Army Family* (Washington, DC: Chief of Staff, U.S. Army, 1983), 2.

24. William Leuchtenburg, "Progressivism and Imperialism: The Progressive Movement and American Foreign Policy, 1898–1916," *Mississippi Valley Historical Review* 39, no. 3 (December 1952): 500–501.

25. Ruth Rosen, *The Lost Sisterhood: Prostitution in America, 1900–1918* (Baltimore: Johns Hopkins University Press, 1982), xiii, 39–41; Barbara Meil Hobson, *Uneasy Virtue: The Politics of Prostitution and the American Reform Tradition* (Chicago: University of Chicago Press, 1990); Mara L. Keire, *For Business and Pleasure: Red-Light Districts and the Regulation of Vice in the United States, 1890–1933* (Baltimore: Johns Hopkins University Press, 2010).

26. David J. Langum, *Crossing over the Line: Legislating Morality and the Mann Act* (Chicago: University of Chicago Press, 1994).

27. David F. Musto, *The American Disease: Origins of Narcotic Control*, 3rd ed. (New York: Oxford University Press, 1999).

28. John D'Emilio and Estelle B. Freedman, *Intimate Matters: A History of Sexuality in America*, 2nd ed. (Chicago: University of Chicago Press, 1997), 239–249; Peter G. Filene, *Him/Her/Self: Sex Roles in Modern America*, 2nd ed. (Baltimore: Johns Hopkins University Press, 1986), 131; Langum, *Crossing over the Line*, 165–166.

29. Alfred C. Kinsey, Wardell B. Pomeroy, and Clyde E. Martin, *Sexual Behavior in the Human Male* (Philadelphia: W. B. Saunders, 1948); Alfred C. Kinsey et al., *Sexual Behavior in the Human Female* (Philadelphia: W. B. Saunders, 1953).

30. Jonathan Engel, *American Therapy: The Rise of Psychotherapy in the United States* (New York: Gotham Books, 2008); Jennifer Terry, *An American Obsession: Science, Medicine, and Homosexuality in Modern Society* (Chicago: University of Chicago Press, 1999); John Demos, "Oedipus and America: Historical Perspectives on the Reception of Psychoanalysis in the United States," in *Inventing the Psychological: Toward a Cultural History of Emotional Life in America*, ed. Joel Pfister and Nancy Schnog (New Haven, CT: Yale University Press, 1997), 63–78.

31. Michel Foucault, *The History of Sexuality*, vol. 1, *An Introduction* (New York: Vintage Books, 1990), 43.

32. Engel, *American Therapy*, 7, 298; Ronald Bayer, *Homosexuality and American Psychiatry: The Politics of Diagnosis* (Princeton, NJ: Princeton University Press, 1987), 21–27.

33. Sigmund Freud, *Three Essays on the Theory of Sexuality*, trans. James Strachey (New York: Basic Books, 1962), 133.

34. Jeffrey S. Davis, "Military Policy toward Homosexuals: Scientific, Historical, and Legal Perspectives," *Military Law Review* 131 (Winter 1991): 73.

35. "Report of Sanitary Conditions in the Provinces of Rizal, Laguna, Cavite, and Batangas, by Dr. Lionel A. B. Street, Special Medical Inspector, Covering the Year 1902," in U.S. Department of War, *Fourth Annual Report of the Philippine Commission, 1903*, pt. 2 (Washington, DC: Government Printing Office, 1904), 215; Ira C. Brown, surgeon and Acting President, Board of Health, to the Acting Adjutant General and the Provost Marshal General, May 16, 1900, AGO Docfile 475016, filed with 343790, RG 94, Entry 25, NARA.

36. David R. Roediger, *The Wages of Whiteness: Race and the Making of the American Working Class*, rev. ed. (London: Verso, 2007); Michael H. Hunt, *Ideology and U.S. Foreign Policy* (New Haven, CT: Yale University Press, 2009), 77–81.

37. Chad C. Heap, *Slumming: Sexual and Racial Encounters in American Nightlife, 1885–1940* (Chicago: University of Chicago Press, 2009), 114–129; Michael Omi and Howard Winant, *Racial Formation in the United States: From the 1960s to the 1990s*, 2nd ed. (New York: Routledge, 1994).

38. Margot Canaday, *The Straight State: Sexuality and Citizenship in Twentieth-Century America* (Princeton, NJ: Princeton University Press, 2009).

39. Elizabeth Lutes Hillman, *Defending America: Military Culture and the Cold War Court-Martial* (Princeton, NJ: Princeton University Press, 2005); Eugene R. Fidell, Elizabeth L. Hillman, and Dwight H. Sullivan, eds., *Military Justice: Cases and Materials* (Newark, NJ: LexisNexis, 2007).

40. Michael Hussey, "'Do You Know What It Means When a Man Uses Another Man as a Woman?': Sodomy, Gender, Class, and Power in the United States Navy, 1890–1925" (PhD diss., University of Maryland, College Park, 2002), esp. 103–147.

41. William M. Reddy, *The Navigation of Feeling: A Framework for the History of Emotions* (Cambridge: Cambridge University Press, 2001).

42. Jennifer Terry, "Theorizing Deviant Historiography," *differences* 3 (Summer 1991): 55–74; Ann Laura Stoler, "Colonial Archives and the Arts of Governance," *Archival Science* 2 (2002): 87–109.

1. "Conduct of a Nature to Bring Discredit upon the Military Service"

Epigraphs: U.S. Department of War, *A Manual for Courts-Martial, Courts of Inquiry, and of Other Procedure under Military Law*, approved by the U.S. Congress on June 4, 1920, and effective February 4, 1921 (Washington, DC: Government Printing Office, 1920).

1. J. P. Clark, *Preparing for War: The Emergence of the Modern U.S. Army, 1815–1917* (Cambridge, MA: Harvard University Press, 2017); William A. Dobak and Thomas D. Phillips, *The Black Regulars, 1866–1898* (Norman: University of Oklahoma Press, 2001).

2. William A. Dobak, *Fort Riley and Its Neighbors: Military Money and Economic Growth, 1853–1895* (Norman: University of Oklahoma Press, 1998).

3. W. F. Pride, *The History of Fort Riley* (Fort Riley, KS: U.S. Army Cavalry School, Book Department, 1926); U.S. Department of the Army, *Fort Riley: Its Historic Past* (Washington, DC: Government Printing Office, 1984).

4. Willard B. Gatewood Jr., *"Smoked Yankees" and the Struggle for Empire: Letters from Negro Soldiers, 1898–1902* (Urbana: University of Illinois Press, 1971), 7–8.

5. Nancy K. Bristow, *Making Men Moral: Social Engineering during the Great War* (New York: New York University Press, 1996), 230.

6. Alfred W. Crosby, *America's Forgotten Pandemic: The Influenza of 1918* (Cambridge: Cambridge University Press, 2003).

7. U.S. Department of War, *Annual Report of the War Department*, multiple vols. (Washington, DC: Government Printing Office, 1898–1941).

8. Quoted in Bristow, *Making Men Moral*, 164–165.

9. Quoted in ibid., 166.

10. Bristow, *Making Men Moral*, 166.

11. Ibid., 168.

12. David A. Schlueter, "The Court-Martial: An Historical Survey," *Military Law Review* 87 (1980): 129–166, esp. 144–158.

13. Ibid., 155.

14. Ibid., 156–157.

15. Ibid., 157–158.

16. Fort Riley summary courts-martial, July 1904–June 1910, RG 393, Entry 3017, Part 1, Boxes 9–13, NARA. Relatively few records of summary courts-martial survive from this period, though copies are usually still maintained within individual soldiers' personnel records. However, without access to overall unit records of summary courts-martial, it would be impossible to know which soldiers received summary courts-martial. Note though that roughly 80 percent of army records for soldiers discharged from 1912 to 1960 were destroyed in the 1973 fire at the National Personnel Records Center in Saint Louis, Missouri, which means that no records survive for most of these cases.

17. U.S. Department of War, *A Manual for Courts-Martial, Courts of Inquiry, and Retiring Boards, and of Other Procedure under Military Law*, rev. ed., 1901 (Washington, DC: Government Printing Office, 1902), 72. By 1901, summary courts-martial had almost entirely replaced garrison and regimental courts-martial for relatively minor infractions, and the field officers' court had been abolished entirely.

18. Article 62 reads, "All crimes not capital, and all disorders and neglects, which officers and soldiers may be guilty of, to the prejudice of good order and military discipline, though not mentioned in the foregoing Articles of War, are to be taken cognizance of by a general, or a regimental, garrison, or field officers' court-martial, according to the nature and degree of the offense, and punished at the discretion of such court." Ibid., 106–107.

19. Article 33 reads, "Any officer or soldier who fails, except when prevented by sickness or other necessity, to repair, at the fixed time, to the place of parade, exercise or other rendezvous appointed by his commanding officer, or goes from the same, without leave from his commanding officer, before he is dismissed or relieved, shall be punished as a court-martial may direct." Ibid., 100.

20. Summary court-martial records of Private Jerry De Gray, February 17, 1910, RG 393, Entry 3017, Part 1, Box 13, NARA; Trumpeter Richard Finney, June 24, 1907, RG 393, Entry 3017, Part 1, Box 11, NARA; Sergeant Raymond H. Gilbert, January 15, 1909, RG 393, Entry 3017, Part 1, Box 13, NARA; Private William Heator [spelling of last name uncertain due to handwriting], April 29, 1910, RG 393, Entry 3017, Part 1, Box 13, NARA; Cook Matheny Lee, February 28, 1905, RG 393, Entry

3017, Part 1, Box 9, NARA; Private Bernard McCoy, November 9, 1905, RG 393, Entry 3017, Part 1, Box 10, NARA; Private Theodore Shurmyer, November 17, 1904, RG 393, Entry 3017, Part 1, Box 9, NARA; Private John Smith, December 8, 1908, RG 393, Entry 3017, Part 1, Box 12, NARA; and Private Ray W. Smith, June 25, 1905, RG 393, Entry 3017, Part 1, Box 10, NARA.

21. Summary court-martial records of Private James Childers, March 30, 1908, RG 393, Entry 3017, Part 1, Box 11, NARA; Private Thomas J. Kerns, November 2, 1909, RG 393, Entry 3017, Part 1, Box 13, NARA; Private Andy Kisch, March 31, 1908, RG 393, Entry 3017, Part 1, Box 11, NARA; Private Thomas B. Lally, June 15, 1909, RG 393, Entry 3017, Part 1, Box 12, NARA; Private George Lawrence, January 27, 1909, RG 393, Entry 3017, Part 1, Box 12, NARA; Private First Class Elmer Logan, March 12, 1910, RG 393, Entry 3017, Part 1, Box 13, NARA; Private First Class Dilworth M. McClellan, June 25, 1910, RG 393, Entry 3017, Part 1, Box 13, NARA; Private John S. Surber, October 23, 1909, RG 393, Entry 3017, Part 1, Box 12, NARA; and Private William J. Vopasek, October 23, 1909, RG 393, Entry 3017, Part 1, Box 12, NARA.

22. Summary court-martial records of Private James Childers and Private Andy Kisch.

23. Summary court-martial record of Private John S. Surber.

24. Summary court-martial record of Private Michael Sefe, October 13, 1908, RG 393, Entry 3017, Part 1, Box 11, NARA.

25. Summary court-martial records of Private Jack Gallagher, March 12, 1908, RG 393, Entry 3017, Part 1, Box 11, NARA; and Private Ernest Shaffer, July 24, 1907, RG 393, Entry 3017, Part 1, Box 11, NARA.

26. Summary court-martial record of Private Virginius Campbell, June 27, 1905, RG 393, Entry 3017, Part 1, Box 10, NARA.

27. Summary court-martial record of Private Julius Sherman, February 20, 1906, RG 393, Entry 3017, Part 1, Box 10, NARA.

28. U.S. Department of War, *Manual for Courts-Martial* (1902).

29. U.S. Department of War, *A Manual for Courts-Martial, Courts of Inquiry, and of Other Procedure under Military Law* (Washington, DC: Government Printing Office, 1918), 252–272, esp. 271–272.

30. Office of the Chief of Staff, "The Army as a Life Occupation for Enlisted Men," appendix B in *Annual Report of the Secretary of War, 1907* (Washington, DC: War Department, 1907), 78.

31. Edward M. Coffman, *The Regulars: The American Army, 1898–1941* (Cambridge, MA: Belknap Press of Harvard University Press, 2004), 133–138.

32. "Who's in the Army Now?," *Fortune*, September 1935, 136.

33. See Coffman, *Regulars*, 251–252, 255–256, for examples of these social problems and expectations.

34. Ibid., 251.

35. Quoted in ibid., 259.

36. For more discussion of army life in the 1920s and 1930s, see Coffman, *Regulars*, 168–176, 247–259, 320–323, 345–348.

37. See ibid., 168, for more discussion of the debates over married junior officers in the early twentieth century.

38. *Army and Navy Journal*, January 3, 1903; October 8, 1904; October 29, 1904; and August 26, 1905.

39. *Army and Navy Journal*, April 24, 1915.

40. Court-martial record of Private George J. Meade, Court-Martial 152433, RG 153, Entry 15B, National Archives and Record Administration, College Park, MD [hereafter NARA II].

41. U.S. Department of War, *Manual for Courts-Martial* (1920).

42. Court-martial record of First Lieutenant William B. Fraser, Court-Martial 205138, RG 153, Entry 15B, NARA II.

43. U.S. Department of War, *Manual for Courts-Martial* (1920).

44. Fraser also married two years after the court-martial, in 1938, though it is unclear whether the woman he married was Rosanna Hitchings. Fraser eventually had two children with his wife. Edward L. Daily, *We Remember: U.S. Cavalry Association* (Paducah, KY: Turner, 1996), 114–115.

45. U.S. Department of War, *Regulations for the Army of the United States, 1913 Corrected to 1917* (Washington, DC: Government Printing Office, 1917). This is discussed further in Nancy L. Goldman, "Trends in Family Patterns of U.S. Military Personnel during the 20th Century," in *The Social Psychology of Military Service*, ed. Nancy L. Goldman and David R. Segal (Beverly Hills: Sage, 1976); and U.S. Department of the Army, *The Army Family* (Washington, DC: Chief of Staff, U.S. Army, 1983), 2. These men were usually detected when the men's wives contacted the U.S. Army or War Department notifying them of the situation and demanding a share of past wages.

46. U.S. Department of War, *A Manual for Courts-Martial, Courts of Inquiry, and Retiring Boards, and of Other Procedure under Military Law*, rev. ed., 1908, corrected to August 1910 (Washington, DC: Government Printing Office, 1910).

47. The Fifty-Fourth Article of War was explicitly defined as only applying to enlisted men. Five criteria were established that had to be proved to the satisfaction of the court for a conviction:

    (a) The enlistment of the accused in the military service as alleged.

    (b) That the accused willfully misrepresented a certain fact or facts regarding his qualifications or disqualifications for enlistment, or willfully—that is, intentionally—concealed a disqualification, as alleged.

    (c) That enlistment was procured by such misrepresentation or concealment.

    (d) That under such enlistment the accused received either pay or allowances, or both, as alleged.

    (e) Where a soldier enlists without a discharge (see A. W. [Article of War] 28), the proof should include the fact that at the time of the alleged enlistment the accused was a soldier, and that the enlistment was entered into without a regular discharge from the former enlistment.

U.S. Department of War, *Manual for Courts-Martial* (1920).

48. Court-martial record of Private Henly C. Drinnon, Court-Martial 110371, RG 153, Entry 15B, NARA II.

49. Court-martial record of Private Charles A. Ennis (a.k.a. Charles A. McKenney), Court-Martial 156610, RG 153, Entry 15B, NARA II.

50. Court-martial records of Private Harry N. Greene, Court-Martial 144715, RG 153, Entry 15B NARA II; and Private First Class Willie Burns, Court-Martial 200734, RG 153, Entry 15B, NARA II.

51. One might expect that in a case like this, with a reversal of punishment by a reviewing authority, which at least some officers familiar with the case might have regarded as a miscarriage of justice, some form of extralegal punishment by Burns's superiors might have taken place. If it did, no records of such an action survive.

52. Coffman, *Regulars*, 97.

53. Court-martial records of Private John A. Harrington, Court-Martial 209019, RG 153, Entry 15B, NARA II; Private Robert M. Hunter, Court-Martial 203243, RG 153, Entry 15B, NARA II; Private Walter E. Mercer, Court-Martial 188240, RG 153, Entry 15B, NARA II; Private Harold R. Shaffer, Court-Martial 210086, RG 153, Entry 15B, NARA II; and Private Clarence R. Smith, Court-Martial 210679, RG 153, Entry 15B, NARA II.

54. Court-martial record of Private Walter E. Mercer.

55. Court-martial record of Private John A. Harrington.

56. Court-martial record of Private Clarence R. Smith.

57. Allan Bérubé, *Coming Out under Fire: The History of Gay Men and Women in World War Two* (New York: Plume, 1990), 12–14.

58. Court-martial records of Private Karl K. Ballenger, Court-Martial 157500, RG 153, Entry 15B, NARA II; Private Harry H. Byerle, Court-Martial 209387, RG 153, Entry 15B, NARA II; Private Frederick D. Clark, Court-Martial 179231, RG 153, Entry 15B, NARA II; Private Claude C. Hunter, Court-Martial 172345, RG 153, Entry 15B, NARA II; Private Leslie L. Margerum, Court-Martial 153259, RG 153, Entry 15B, NARA II; Private Melvin W. Oliver, Court-Martial 157500, RG 153, Entry 15B, NARA II; Private Clifton E. Patterson, Court-Martial 126888, RG 153, Entry 15B, NARA II; and Private Glenn R. VanFleet, Court-Martial 210235, RG 153, Entry 15B, NARA II.

59. Court-martial record of Corporal Harold F. Hutchinson, Court-Martial 119938, RG 153, Entry 15B, NARA II.

60. In practice, as analysis of courts-martial in the other case studies shows, soldiers who had anal sex with women or who received oral sex from women were rarely charged with sodomy, though there were a few courts-martial in which soldiers who were alleged to have performed oral sex on prostitutes were tried for this offense, suggesting that the army found cunnilingus to be an especially deviant sex act.

61. George Chauncey Jr., *Gay New York: Gender, Urban Culture, and the Making of the Gay Male World, 1890–1940* (New York: Basic Books, 1994); George Chauncey Jr., "Christian Brotherhood or Sexual Perversion? Homosexual Identities and the Construction of Sexual Boundaries in the World War I Era," in *Hidden from History: Reclaiming the Gay and Lesbian Past*, ed. Martin Bauml Duberman, Martha Vicinus, and George Chauncey Jr. (New York: New American Library, 1989), 294–317.

62. Court-martial records of Private Karl K. Ballenger and Private Melvin W. Oliver.

63. Court-martial record of Private Claude C. Hunter.

64. Court-martial records of Private Harry H. Byerle and Private Glenn R. VanFleet.

65. This line of questioning was stricken from the record as hearsay.

66. Michael Joseph Hussey, "'Do You Know What It Means When a Man Uses Another Man as a Woman?': Sodomy, Gender, Class, and Power in the United States

Navy, 1890–1925" (PhD diss., University of Maryland, College Park, 2002). There are no comparable studies of the U.S. Amy during this period.

67. Court-martial records of Private Frederick D. Clark and Corporal Harold F. Hutchinson.

68. In a separate incident that was also tried during this court-martial, Patterson was also charged with assaulting Private Mattie B. Hubbard with a razor by cutting Hubbard on the face and neck. Patterson was found guilty of the assault but not attempted sodomy. Court-martial record of Private Clifton E. Patterson.

69. Court-martial record of Private Leslie L. Margerum.

70. For example, see W. G. Murchison, Assistant Adjutant, to Judge Advocate, Seventh Corps Area, "Charges against Leslie L. Margerum, R-328256, Company A, 9th Engineers," letter, July 5, 1922, court-martial record of Private Leslie L. Margerum.

71. Jonathan Engel, *American Therapy: The Rise of Psychotherapy in the United States* (New York: Gotham Books, 2008), 7, 298; Ronald Bayer, *Homosexuality and American Psychiatry: The Politics of Diagnosis* (Princeton, NJ: Princeton University Press, 1987), 21–27.

72. E. Anthony Rotundo, *American Manhood: Transformations in Masculinity from the Revolution to the Modern Era* (New York: Basic Books, 1993), 222–246; Gail Bederman, *Manliness and Civilization: A Cultural History of Gender and Race in the United States, 1880–1917* (Chicago: University of Chicago Press, 1995); Amy S. Greenberg, *Manifest Manhood and the Antebellum American Empire* (Cambridge: Cambridge University Press, 2005).

73. U.S. Department of War, *Manual for Courts-Martial* (1920).

74. In the case studies discussed here, the only convicted rapists who were ever sentenced to death were in France during World War I.

75. Court-martial records of Private First Class Clarence G. Eberle, Court-Martial 205791, RG 153, Entry 15B, NARA II; Private First Class James Harris, Court-Martial 184039, RG 153, Entry 15B, NARA II; and Private Lloyd W. Summers, Court-Martial 201736, RG 153, Entry 15B, NARA II.

76. Court-martial record of Private First Class James Harris.

77. Court-martial record of Private Lloyd W. Summers.

78. Court-martial record of Private First Class Clarence G. Eberle.

79. David J. Langum, *Crossing over the Line: Legislating Morality and the Mann Act* (Chicago: University of Chicago Press, 1994); court-martial record of Private Jesse C. Davis, Court-Martial 159710, RG 153, Entry 15B, NARA II.

80. Federal Bureau of Investigation, *Uniform Crime Reports*, 1930–1940, 2010, http://www.fbi.gov/about-us/cjis/ucr/ucr. For comparison, the annual national rape rate from 1991 to 2010 averaged 34.2 per 100,000 population.

81. The exact strength at Fort Riley varied throughout the period, but 2,000 is a reasonable approximate.

2. "Benevolent Assimilation" and the Dangers of the Tropics

Epigraphs: President William McKinley, "Benevolent Assimilation Proclamation," December 21, 1898, quoted in Stuart Creighton Miller, *"Benevolent Assimilation": The American Conquest of the Philippines, 1899–1903* (New Haven, CT: Yale University Press, 1982), frontispiece; Robert E. Austill to Herbert Welsh, June 17, 1902, correspondence,

Box A, Herbert Welsh Collection, Historical Society of Pennsylvania, quoted in Kristin L. Hoganson, *Fighting for American Manhood: How Gender Politics Provoked the Spanish-American and Philippine-American Wars* (New Haven, CT: Yale University Press, 1998), 187.

1. Joshua Gedacht, "'Mohammedan Religion Made It Necessary to Fire': Massacres on the American Imperial Frontier from South Dakota to the Southern Philippines," in *Colonial Crucible: Empire in the Making of the Modern American State*, ed. Alfred W. McCoy and Francisco A. Scarano (Madison: University of Wisconsin Press, 2009), 397–409; Glen Anthony May, "Was the Philippine-American War a 'Total War'?," in *Anticipating Total War: The German and American Experiences, 1871–1914*, ed. Manfred F. Boemeke, Roger Chickering, and Stig Förster (Cambridge: Cambridge University Press, 1999), 437–457, esp. 454; Paul A. Kramer, *The Blood of Government: Race, Empire, the United States, and the Philippines* (Chapel Hill: University of North Carolina Press, 2006).

2. Warwick Anderson, *Colonial Pathologies: American Tropical Medicine, Race, and Hygiene in the Philippines* (Durham, NC: Duke University Press, 2006); Julian Go and Anne L. Foster, eds., *The American Colonial State in the Philippines: Global Perspectives* (Durham, NC: Duke University Press, 2003); Michael Salman, *The Embarrassment of Slavery: Controversies over Bondage and Nationalism in the American Colonial Philippines* (Berkeley: University of California Press, 2001).

3. U.S. Department of War, *Annual Report of the War Department*, multiple vols. (Washington, DC: Government Printing Office, 1902–1940).

4. Richard E. Welch Jr., *Response to Imperialism: The United States and the Philippine-American War, 1899–1902* (Chapel Hill: University of North Carolina Press, 1979), esp. 101–116; Paul A. Kramer, "Power and Connection: Imperial Histories of the United States in the World," *American Historical Review* 116, no. 5 (December 2011): 1348–1391.

5. Matthew Frye Jacobson, *Barbarian Virtues: The United States Encounters Foreign Peoples at Home and Abroad, 1876–1917* (New York: Hill and Wang, 2000), 176.

6. See Hoganson, *Fighting for American Manhood*, 138–140.

7. Quoted in H. W. Brands, *Bound to Empire: The United States and the Philippines* (New York: Oxford University Press, 1992), 58.

8. Jacobson, *Barbarian Virtues*, 230–231; Paul A. Kramer, "Empires, Exceptions, and Anglo-Saxons: Race and Rule between the British and U.S. Empires, 1880–1910," in Go and Foster, *American Colonial State*, 43–91.

9. Quoted in Jacobson, *Barbarian Virtues*, 231.

10. E. Anthony Rotundo, *American Manhood: Transformations in Masculinity from the Revolution to the Modern Era* (New York: Basic Books, 1993), 222–246; Ann Douglas, *The Feminization of American Culture* (New York: Noonday, 1998); Joe Dubbert, "Progressivism and the Masculinity Crisis," *The Psychoanalytic Review* 61 (Fall 1974): 433–455.

11. Americans were not alone in viewing imperial adventures as a source of revitalization for the nation. Rudyard Kipling's poem "The White Man's Burden" exhorted the United States to expand its empire while warning of the costs. Rudyard Kipling, "The White Man's Burden," *McClure's Magazine*, February 1899. British colonel Sir G. S. Clarke recommended that the United States take up imperial responsibilities as a means of improving its national character and building manhood,

telling American readers, "To India we owe in great measure the training of our best manhood. India makes men." He went on to add that imperial responsibilities create a "high ideal of manhood. . . . The empire, with all its anxieties and burdens, is now more than ever producing men." G. S. Clarke, "Imperial Responsibilities a National Gain," *North American Review* 168 (February 1899): 129–141, quotes on pages 137–138.

12. Bobby A. Wintermute, *Public Health and the U.S. Military: A History of the Army Medical Department, 1818–1917* (New York: Routledge, 2011), 121–156; Hoganson, *Fighting for American Manhood*, 191–192.

13. Charles E. Woodruff, *The Effects of Tropical Light on White Men* (New York: Rebman, 1905); W. W. King, "Tropical Neurasthenia" (presented at the annual meeting of the American Society of Tropical Medicine, Philadelphia, March 24, 1906), *Journal of the American Medical Association* 46, no. 20 (1906): 1518–1519; Anna Greenwood, "Looking Back: The Strange History of Tropical Neurasthenia," *Psychologist* 24, no. 3 (March 2011): 226–227.

14. Benjamin Kidd, *The Control of the Tropics* (New York: Macmillan, 1898), 50.

15. "Manila's Greatest Need," *Army and Navy Journal*, August 12, 1905.

16. Data on Philippine posts taken from Surgeon General to the Adjutant General, "Rates for Venereal Disease in the Second Division," letter, November 19, 1914, AGO Docfile 2230647, filed with AGO Docfile 1045985, RG 94, NARA. Data on U.S. domestic posts taken from Surgeon General to the Adjutant General, "Venereal Disease in the Army," table A, letter, September 30, 1915, AGO Docfile 2225425, filed with AGO Docfile 1045985, RG 94, NARA. Comparisons with venereal disease rates among American civilians are difficult to make because there were few governmental efforts to assess overall rates across American society. The few studies available generally only attempted to assess the rates of specific hospitals or urban areas. These studies must be analyzed cautiously because of their methodological limitations and their biased sponsors, which were generally moral reform organizations that sought to create a public outcry over venereal epidemics. Allan M. Brandt, *No Magic Bullet: A Social History of Venereal Disease in the United States since 1880* (New York: Oxford University Press, 1985), 12–13, 31.

17. George S. Boutwell II, speech, October 24, 1902, George S. Boutwell II Papers, Massachusetts Historical Society, Boston, quoted in Hoganson, *Fighting for American Manhood*, 188.

18. Henry Moore Teller, *The Problem in the Philippines, Speech of Hon. Henry M. Teller, of Colorado, in the Senate of the United States, February 11, 12, and 13, 1902* (Washington, DC, 1902), 4989.

19. Judith R. Walkowitz, *Prostitution and Victorian Society: Women, Class, and the State* (Cambridge: Cambridge University Press, 1980).

20. A. Lester Hazlett, *Affairs in the Philippine Islands: Hearings before the United States Senate Committee on the Philippines, Fifty-Seventh Congress, First Session, on Jan. 31, Feb. 1, 3–8, 10, 14, 15, 17–20, 25–28, Mar. 3–6, 11–13, 17–20, 1902* (Washington, DC: Government Printing Office, 1902), 1736–1738.

21. Richard F. Pettigrew, *The Course of Empire* (New York: Boni and Liveright, 1920), 181.

22. Phelps Whitmarsh, "In Pampanga Province," *Outlook*, February 17, 1903, 399.

23. Julian Go, "Introduction: Global Perspectives on the U.S. Colonial State in the Philippines," in Go and Foster, *American Colonial State*, 23; Daniel T. Rodgers, *Atlantic Crossings: Social Politics in a Progressive Age* (Cambridge, MA: Belknap Press of Harvard University Press, 1998); Ann Laura Stoler, "Intimidations of Empire: Predicaments of the Tactile and Unseen" and "Tense and Tender Ties: The Politics of Comparison in North American History and (Post) Colonial Studies," in *Haunted by Empire: Geographies of Intimacy in North American History*, ed. Ann Laura Stoler (Durham, NC: Duke University Press, 2006), 1–22 and 23–70.

24. Wintermute, *Public Health*, 154–156.

25. Donna J. Amoroso, "Inheriting the 'Moro Problem': Muslim Authority and Colonial Rule in British Malaya and the Philippines," in Go and Foster, *American Colonial State*, 118–147.

26. Go, "Introduction," 8–9; and Anderson, *Colonial Pathologies*, 57–58.

27. Luis C. Dery, "Prostitution in Colonial Manila," *Philippine Studies* 39, no. 4 (1991): 486; Ian R. Tyrrell, *Reforming the World: The Creation of America's Moral Empire* (Princeton, NJ: Princeton University Press, 2010), 137.

28. Ken De Bevoise, *Agents of Apocalypse: Epidemic Disease in the Colonial Philippines* (Princeton, NJ: Princeton University Press, 1995), 69, 75.

29. Andrew Jimenez Abalahin, "Prostitution Policy and the Project of Modernity: A Comparative Study of Colonial Indonesia and the Philippines, 1850–1940" (PhD diss., Cornell University, 2003), 286–287; De Bevoise, *Agents of Apocalypse*, 86–87.

30. William B. Johnson, *The Crowning Infamy of Imperialism* (Philadelphia: American League of Philadelphia, 1900), 3.

31. U.S. Department of War, Office of the Surgeon-General, *Annual Report of the Surgeon General, 1899* (Washington, DC: Government Printing Office, 1898–1941), 136.

32. John R. M. Taylor, *The Philippine Insurrection against the United States, 1899–1903: A Compilation of Documents with Notes and Introduction*, 5 vols. (Pasay City, Philippines, 1971–1973), 3:194–195, quoted in De Bevoise, *Agents of Apocalypse*, 86; also discussed in Abalahin, "Prostitution Policy," 284–285.

33. Abalahin, "Prostitution Policy," 290–294.

34. Major Charles Lynch, Surgeon and Member, Board of Health, to President, Board of Health, May 18, 1901, AGO Docfile 343790, RG 94, NARA.

35. Major Ira C. Brown, Surgeon and Acting President, Board of Health, to the Acting Adjutant General and the Provost Marshal General, May 16, 1900, AGO Docfile 475016, filed with AGO Docfile 343790, RG 94, NARA.

36. "Report of Sanitary Conditions in the Provinces of Rizal, Laguna, Cavite, and Batangas, by Dr. Lionel A. B. Street, Special Medical Inspector, Covering the Year 1902," in U.S. War Department, *Fourth Annual Report of the Philippine Commission, 1903*, pt. 2 (Washington, DC: Government Printing Office, 1904), 215.

37. Taft to Dr. David D. Thompson, April 12, 1902, 10–11, Taft Papers, quoted in Dery, "Prostitution in Colonial Manila," 487.

38. Wintermute, *Public Health*, 204–205.

39. U.S. Surgeon-General's Office, *The Medical and Surgical History of the War of the Rebellion, 1861–65* (Washington, DC: Government Printing Office, 1888), 6:891, 894.

40. Johnson, *Crowning Infamy of Imperialism*.

41. "The Custer Henderson Letter," Custer Henderson, Thirty-Third U.S. Volunteer Infantry Regiment, Manila, to Albert J. and Margaret T. Henderson of Saint Bernice, Indiana, September 16, 1900, AGO Docfile 343790, RG 94, NARA. Henderson later denied ever having written the letter in question to his parents, even though his parents issued a notarized statement certifying the authenticity of the original letter. In his denial, Henderson stated the letter attributed to him was a forgery and that he had not been in Manila on the date the letter was alleged to have been written, having been on detached service with the Philippine Scouts in Balanga at the time. Henderson enclosed an affidavit signed by several dozen of his fellow soldiers testifying that he had indeed been on detached service with them and that he had never expressed the opinions attributed to him in the original letter. Custer Henderson to commanding officer, Thirty-Third U.S. Volunteer Infantry Regiment, December 24, 1900, AGO Docfile 352921, filed with AGO Docfile 343790, RG 94, NARA.

42. "Custer Henderson Letter."

43. Paul A. Kramer, "The Darkness That Enters the Home: The Politics of Prostitution during the Philippine-American War," in Stoler, *Haunted by Empire*, 377.

44. AGO Docfile 343790, RG 94, NARA; Abalahin, "Prostitution Policy," 304–309; Tyrrell, *Reforming the World*, 136–145.

45. David J. Pivar, "The Military, Prostitution, and Colonial Peoples: India and the Philippines, 1885–1917," in "History and Sexuality," special issue, *Journal of Sex Research* 17, no. 3 (August 1981): 256–269.

46. Hoganson, *Fighting for American Manhood*, 188.

47. Major Charles Lynch to President, Board of Health, May 18, 1901, File 2039-13, Box 246, RG 350, NARA.

48. Johnson, *Crowning Infamy of Imperialism*; Abalahin, "Prostitution Policy," 302–304; De Bevoise, *Agents of Apocalypse*, 88.

49. Lieutenant Colonel Owen J. Sweet, Twenty-First U.S. Infantry Regiment, to the adjutant general, February 7, 1902, and Adjutant General's Office to Colonel Andrews, memorandum, February 17, 1902, AGO Docfile 417937, filed with AGO Docfile 343790, RG 94, NARA; Kramer, "Darkness That Enters the Home," 366–367.

50. Second Lieutenant James A. Moore, Twenty-Third U.S. Infantry Regiment, to adjutant, Twenty-Third U.S. Infantry Regiment, March 7, 1902; Second Lieutenant John W. Norwood, Twenty-Third U.S. Infantry Regiment, to Adjutant, Twenty-Third U.S. Infantry Regiment, March 7, 1902; and Major W. A. Nichols, Twenty-First U.S. Infantry Regiment, to Commanding Officer, Twenty-Third U.S. Infantry Regiment, March 10, 1902, all in AGO Docfile 417937, filed with AGO Docfile 343790, RG 94, NARA. Nichols also noted, "Every large city recognizes the necessity for such houses [of prostitution] as a protection to the good women from violence, and for the health of the community."

51. Captain J. L. Hines, Quartermaster, Twenty-Third U.S. Infantry Regiment, to Adjutant, Twenty-Third U.S. Infantry Regiment, March 20, 1902, and Captain A G. Cole, Commissary, Twenty-Third U.S. Infantry Regiment, to Colonel J. M. Thompson, Twenty-Third U.S. Infantry Regiment, March 12, 1902, AGO Docfile 417937, filed with AGO Docfile 343790, RG 94, NARA.

52. Acting Secretary of War to Lillian Stevens, October 8, 1900, AGO Docfile 343790, RG 94, NARA.

53. Adjutant-General's Office, Washington, DC, to MacArthur, Manila, telegram, January 16, 1901, in *Correspondence Relating to the War with Spain Including the Insurrection in the Philippine Islands and the China Relief Expedition, between the Adjutant-General of the Army and Military Commanders in the United States, Cuba, Porto Rico, China, and the Philippine Islands, from April 15, 1898, to July 30, 1902* (Washington, DC: Government Printing Office, 1902), 2:1246.

54. Ibid., 1247.

55. Major General Arthur MacArthur to adjutant general of the army, February 4, 1901, AGO Docfile 343790, RG 94, NARA.

56. General Order No. 101, issued May 21, 1901, RG 350, Entry 2039, Box 246, NARA II.

57. Major General C. R. Reynolds, "Summary of the History of the Control of Venereal Disease in the United States Army," December 7, 1937, quoted in De Bevoise, *Agents of Apocalypse*, 91.

58. De Bevoise, *Agents of Apocalypse*, 91–92.

59. See Rev. A. Lester Hazlett, "A View of the Moral Conditions Existing in the Philippines," AGO Docfile 417937, filed with AGO Docfile 343790, RG 94, NARA. In MacArthur's February 4, 1901, letter, he invited social reformers to "be given transportation to Manila, where they will be afforded every opportunity to see things as they are." Major General Arthur MacArthur to Adjutant General of the Army, February 4, 1901, AGO Docfile 343790, RG 94, NARA.

60. Hazlett, "View of the Moral Conditions," 5.

61. Ibid., 6. Hazlett cites the racial breakdown of the prostitutes as follows: 124 Japanese, 72 Filipinas, 14 Americans, 12 Russians, 3 Romanians, 2 Italians, 2 Europeans of nonspecific origin, and 1 each from Australia, Hungary, Spain, and Turkey.

62. Rev. A. Lester Hazlett to Adjutant General and Secretary of War, March 24, 1902, AGO Docfile 417937, filed with AGO Docfile 343790, RG 94, NARA. Because of the conflicting testimonies of alleged eyewitnesses, it is impossible to satisfactorily ascertain whether Sweet had directly employed prostitutes and was personally profiting from the enterprise, or whether he was merely aware of the prostitutes in Jolo and oversaw their medical inspections, as was done everywhere else in the Philippines.

63. Taft's testimony of February 20, 1902, is directly quoted and discussed at much greater length in Henry Parker Willis, *Our Philippine Problem: A Study of American Colonial Policy* (New York: Henry Holt, 1905), 254–257.

64. Ibid., 257.

65. Elihu Root to Luke Wright, February 18, 1902, RG 350, Entry 2039, Box 246, NARA II, quoted in Kramer, "Darkness That Enters the Home," 395.

66. Assistant Adjutant General, Circular 10, March 18, 1902, quoted in *Army and Navy Journal*, March 29, 1902.

67. Brian McAllister Linn, *Guardians of Empire: The U.S. Army and the Pacific, 1902–1940* (Chapel Hill: University of North Carolina Press, 1997), 128.

68. Abalahin, "Prostitution Policy," 313.

69. Ibid., 314.

70. Kramer, "Darkness That Enters the Home," 394.

71. Major Ira C. Brown, Surgeon and Acting President, Board of Health, to the Acting Adjutant General and the Provost Marshal General, May 16, 1900, AGO Docfile 475016, filed with AGO Docfile 343790, RG 94, NARA.

72. Brown made no mention of Japanese or Chinese prostitutes, though other sources indicate their presence in large numbers. It seems apparent that Brown made no distinction between Asian women of different nationalities, in this case Japanese, Chinese, and Filipina women, classifying them all equally as "natives." Just four years after Brown's initial survey of prostitutes, Japanese women apparently made up the majority of prostitutes officially known to Filipino authorities.

73. Details on the scope of legal prostitution in Manila in 1904 are found in Willis, *Our Philippine Problem*, 257–259.

74. Weston P. Chamberlain to Surgeon General, June 24, 1905, RG 112, Entry 26, Folder 72605-31, NARA.

75. Francis Burton Harrison, *Origins of the Philippine Republic: Extracts from the Diaries and Records of Francis Burton Harrison*, ed. Michael Paul Onorato (Ithaca, NY: Cornell University Press, 1974), 110.

76. Dery, "Prostitution in Colonial Manila," 482.

77. Abalahin, "Prostitution Policy," 346–347.

78. R. H. R. Loughbrough to CG, PD, Sub: Annual Report, District of Luzon, June 30, 1913, RG 395, Entry 3676, NARA, quoted in Linn, *Guardians of Empire*, 128.

79. Quoted in De Bevoise, *Agents of Apocalypse*, 90.

80. Quoted in Brandt, *No Magic Bullet*, 98.

81. Brandt, *No Magic Bullet*, 97–98.

82. K-Packets were first introduced in the Philippines in 1910 on a small scale, and while they appeared to reduce the overall venereal disease rate briefly, they had no long-term effects. The army's Surgeon General attributed this inefficacy to noncompliance with medical instructions. The standard venereal treatments during this period relied primarily on injections of salicylic mercury, both subcutaneously and via the urethra, but were not particularly effective and often caused serious side effects. Wintermute, *Public Health*, 208; Brandt, *No Magic Bullet*, 11–12, 114.

83. Surgeon general to the adjutant general, "Venereal Disease in the Army," table A, letter, September 30, 1915, AGO Docfile 2225425, filed with AGO Docfile 1045985, RG 94, NARA.

84. Data on Philippine posts taken from Surgeon General to the Adjutant General, "Rates for Venereal Disease in the Second Division," letter, November 19, 1914, AGO Docfile 2230647, filed with AGO Docfile 1045985, RG 94, NARA. Data on U.S. domestic posts taken from Surgeon General to the Adjutant General, "Venereal Disease in the Army," table A.

85. William S. Washburn, "Health Conditions in the Philippines," *Philippine Journal of Science* 3, no. 4 (September 1908): 274.

86. Ibid., 276.

87. Ibid., 271, 274.

88. Ibid., 272.

89. U.S. Department of War, Office of the Surgeon General, *Annual Report of the Surgeon General* (Washington, DC: Government Printing Office, 1907).

90. De Bevoise, *Agents of Apocalypse*, 71.

91. Abalahin, "Prostitution Policy," 329–330.

92. Good court-martial records from the Philippines (as for most other locales) only survive from 1912 onward. Records from 1898–1911 either are only available

for some units during brief intervals during this period or are entirely unavailable, making comprehensive analytic judgments on the army's judicial practices before 1912 impossible.

93. Court-martial record of Private Frank Sephus, Court-Martial 78089, RG 153, Entry 15, NARA.

94. Court-martial record of Private Harry C. Holmes, Court-Martial 101479, RG 153, Entry 15B, NARA II.

95. These quotations are taken from the court-martial record of Private Robert W. Anderson, Court-Martial 87698, RG 153, Entry 15, NARA, though similar or identical statements are common to many courts-martial for cases involving refusal to receive venereal treatment.

96. Court-martial record of Private Frederick Cole, Court-Martial 90757, RG 153, Entry 15, NARA. The court seemed to find Cole's testimony sympathetic, as it gave Cole the extremely lenient sentence—as acknowledged by the reviewing authority—of merely forfeiting ten days of pay.

97. Court-martial record of Private William Rae, Court-Martial 103326, RG 153, Entry 15B, NARA II.

98. See, for example, the court-martial record of Private Robert W. Anderson, Court-Martial 87698, RG 153, Entry 15, NARA.

99. For an example of this excuse, see the court-martial record of Private Edward W. Tolle, Court-Martial 79694, RG 153, Entry 15, NARA.

100. Jeffrey S. Davis, "Military Policy toward Homosexuals: Scientific, Historical, and Legal Perspectives," *Military Law Review* 131 (Winter 1991): 55–108.

101. Ibid., 73.

102. Court-martial records of Sergeant Harry B. Ernst, Court-Martial 85853, RG 153, Entry 15, NARA; Sergeant George F. Smith, Court-Martial 86042, RG 153, Entry 15, NARA; Private Claude C. Grubb, Court-Martial 87257, RG 153, Entry 15, NARA; Private James C. Rasmussen, Court-Martial 91267, RG 153, Entry 15, NARA; Private James B. Fitzgerald, Court-Martial 92542, RG 153, Entry 15, NARA; Corporal Bryant Mowery, Court-Martial 94453, RG 153, Entry 15, NARA; and Private Desmond G. Fitzgerald, Court-Martial 102511, RG 153, Entry 15B, NARA II.

103. Court-martial record of Private Arthur Coleman, Court-Martial 92103, RG 153, Entry 15, NARA. Coleman was black, and the unnamed sailors white.

104. Court-martial record of Corporal Bryant Mowery.

105. Hoganson, *Fighting for American Manhood*, esp. 180–199; Kramer, *Blood of Government*, 149–151; Warwick Anderson, "Immunities of Empire: Race, Disease, and the New Tropical Medicine, 1900–1920," *Bulletin of the History of Medicine* 70 (Spring 1996): 94–118; Anderson, *Colonial Pathologies*, 74–103 (physical deterioration), 130–157 (mental and moral degeneracy).

106. Court-martial record of Private George F. Goodfellow, Court-Martial 81230, RG 153, Entry 15, NARA.

107. Court-martial record of Private Iseral Jones, Court-Martial 84918, RG 153, Entry 15, NARA.

108. U.S. Department of War, *Regulations for the Army of the United States, 1913 Corrected to 1917* (Washington, DC: Government Printing Office, 1917); Nancy L. Goldman, "Trends in Family Patterns of U.S. Military Personnel during the

20th Century," in *The Social Psychology of Military Service*, ed. Nancy L. Goldman and David R. Segal (Beverly Hills: Sage, 1976), 119–134; U.S. Department of the Army, *The Army Family* (Washington, DC: Chief of Staff, U.S. Army, 1983), 2.

109. Quoted in Linn, *Guardians of Empire*, 126.

110. W. D. Ketcham to secretary, GS, "The Use of Native Military Forces in the Philippine Islands," March 26, 1918, OCS 1183, RG 165, NARA, quoted in ibid, 126.

111. PDN, Standing Orders No. 600–750, in *Personnel: Recruiting for the Regular Army*, October 19, 1925, 300.4, PF-PD, RG 18, NARA, quoted in Linn, *Guardians of Empire*, 126.

112. Linn, *Guardians of Empire*, 126–127.

113. Ibid., 66–67.

114. Ibid., 115.

115. Of the sixteen courts-martial for these types of charges, one case involved African Americans, five Filipinos, and the remainder whites.

116. Court-martial record of Private Lewis Fambro, Court-Martial 79866, RG 153, Entry 15, NARA.

117. Court-martial record of Private Alford A. Amber, Court-Martial 94929, RG 153, Entry 15, NARA. See especially Judge Advocate General E. H. Crowder to the secretary of war, memo, June 7, 1916.

118. Court-martial records of Private Ollie B. Amos, Court-Martial 92725, RG 153, Entry 2, Box 130, NARA; Private Chalason, RG 153, Entry 2, Box 149, NARA; Private Robert J. McCord, RG 153, Entry 2, Box 149, NARA; and Sergeant Charles W. Kearse, Court-Martial 86978, RG 395, Entry 2071, Box 1.

119. Court-martial record of Private Robert J. McCord, RG 153, Entry 2, Box 149, NARA.

120. Court-martial record of Private George Williams, Court-Martial 84909, RG 153, Entry 15, NARA.

121. Court-martial records of Private Dora Jackson, Court-Martial 79819, RG 153, Entry 15, NARA; and Private Willie Waters, Court-Martial 79824, RG 153, Entry 15, NARA.

122. Court-martial record of Electrician Sergeant Jethro B. Bartham, Court-Martial 90790, RG 153, Entry 15, NARA.

123. Willard B. Gatewood Jr., *"Smoked Yankees" and the Struggle for Empire: Letters from Negro Soldiers, 1898–1902* (Urbana: University of Illinois Press, 1971), 240.

124. Ibid., 15–16.

125. Chaplain George W. Prioleau, Ninth Cavalry, letter to the editor of the *Colored American* (Washington, DC), dated June 1901, published July 13, 1901, reprinted in ibid., 300–303.

126. Private Rienzi B. Lemus, Twenty-Fifth Infantry, two letters to the editor of the *Richmond (VA) Planet*, the first dated March 14, 1902, and published April 26, 1902, the second dated April 17, 1902, and published May 3, 1902, both reprinted in Gatewood, *"Smoked Yankees,"* 312–316.

127. Gatewood, *"Smoked Yankees,"* 4–6, 242–244.

128. Ibid., 244.

129. Quoted in ibid., 243.

130. Quoted in Linn, *Guardians of Empire*, 60.

131. Quoted in ibid., 60–61.

132. Charles Ray Willeford, *Something about a Soldier* (New York: Random House, 1986), 61.

133. Quoted in Kramer, *Blood of Government*, 356.

3. "Come Back Clean"

Epigraph: Ella Wheeler Wilcox, "Soldiers, Come Back Clean," RG 165, Entry 393, Box 19, Document 12535, NARA II. The poem was apparently originally published in the *Chicago Evening American* before receiving the endorsement of Secretary of the Navy Josephus Daniels and being reprinted in pamphlet format by the Department of War in 1917.

1. Ian R. Tyrrell, *Reforming the World: The Creation of America's Moral Empire* (Princeton, NJ: Princeton University Press, 2010); Nancy K. Bristow, *Making Men Moral: Social Engineering during the Great War* (New York: New York University Press, 1996), 8–11.

2. Ruth Rosen, *The Lost Sisterhood: Prostitution in America, 1900–1918* (Baltimore: Johns Hopkins University Press, 1982), xiii, 39–41; Allan M. Brandt, *No Magic Bullet: A Social History of Venereal Disease in the United States since 1880*, expanded ed. (New York: Oxford University Press, 1987), 7–8, 16, 20–21; Mary E. Odem, *Delinquent Daughters: Protecting and Policing Adolescent Female Sexuality in the United States, 1885–1920* (Chapel Hill: University of North Carolina Press, 1995).

3. Brandt, *No Magic Bullet*, 31–32, 72.

4. Brandt, *No Magic Bullet*, 8, 57.

5. Rosen, *Lost Sisterhood*, xi, 13, 38–50.

6. Quoted in Rosen, *Lost Sisterhood*, 5.

7. Quoted in ibid., 5.

8. Brandt, *No Magic Bullet*, 35–36.

9. Marilyn E. Hegarty, *Victory Girls, Khaki-Wackies, and Patriotutes: The Regulation of Female Sexuality during World War II* (New York: New York University Press, 2008), 195–196n22; John C. Burnham, "Medical Inspection of Prostitutes in America in the Nineteenth Century: The St. Louis Experiment and Its Sequel," *Bulletin of the History of Medicine* 45 (May 1971): 203–218.

10. David J. Pivar, *Purity Crusade: Sexual Morality and Social Control, 1868–1900* (Westport, CT: Greenwood, 1973).

11. Rosen, *Lost Sisterhood*, 11; Alexandra M. Lord, *Condom Nation: The U.S. Government's Sex Education Campaign from World War I to the Internet* (Baltimore: Johns Hopkins University Press, 2010).

12. Chicago Vice Commission, *The Social Evil in Chicago: A Study of Existing Conditions with Recommendations by the Vice Commission of Chicago* (Chicago: Vice Commission of Chicago, 1911), 25–26.

13. Caroline Bunker to Woodrow Wilson, June 18, 1917, RG 165, Box 586, NARA II, quoted in Brandt, *No Magic Bullet*, 57.

14. Bristow, *Making Men Moral*, 4–5.

15. Newton D. Baker, *Frontiers of Freedom* (New York: George H. Doran, 1918), 231.

16. Bristow, *Making Men Moral*, xvii, 8.

17. Quoted in Brandt, *No Magic Bullet*, 72.

18. Quoted in ibid., 59.

19. Bristow, *Making Men Moral*, 5.

20. Ibid., xvii–xviii.

21. Brandt, *No Magic Bullet*, 67; Bristow, *Making Men Moral*, 45–50, 93–98.

22. Mary Louise Roberts, *What Soldiers Do: Sex and the American GI in World War II France* (Chicago: University of Chicago Press, 2013), 190.

23. Quoted in Bristow, *Making Men Moral*, 113.

24. Barbara Meil Hobson, *Uneasy Virtue: The Politics of Prostitution and the American Reform Tradition* (Chicago: University of Chicago Press, 1990), 85–86.

25. Brandt, *No Magic Bullet*, 68–69; Bristow, *Making Men Moral*, 19–23.

26. Rosen, *Lost Sisterhood*, 33.

27. Brandt, *No Magic Bullet*, 8–9.

28. "Statement of One of the YMCA Divisional Secretaries," unpublished manuscript, undated, RG 112, Box 5179, NARA II, quoted in ibid., 97.

29. Mrs. J. W. Broughton to Raymond B. Fosdick, September 7, 1917, RG 165, Box 585, NARA II, quoted in Brandt, *No Magic Bullet*, 97.

30. Brandt, *No Magic Bullet*, 85–86.

31. David J. Pivar, *Purity and Hygiene: Women, Prostitution, and the "American Plan," 1900–1930* (Westport, CT: Greenwood, 2002).

32. Rosen, *Lost Sisterhood*, 35; Brandt, *No Magic Bullet*, 88–89.

33. Quoted in Brandt, *No Magic Bullet*, 68.

34. Gary Krist, *Empire of Sin: A Story of Sex, Jazz, Murder, and the Battle for Modern New Orleans* (New York: Crown, 2014); Emily Epstein Landau, *Spectacular Wickedness: Sex, Race, and Memory in Storyville, New Orleans* (Baton Rouge: Louisiana State University Press, 2013).

35. Quoted in Brandt, 80.

36. Bascom Johnson, "Eliminating Vice from Camp Cities," *Annals of the American Academy of Political and Social Science* 78 (1918): 60–64.

37. Brandt, *No Magic Bullet*, 73; James W. Ceaser, "What Kind of Government Do We Have to Fear?," in *Politics at the Turn of the Century*, ed. Arthur M. Melzer, Jerry Weinberger, and M. Richard Zinman (Lanham, MD: Rowman and Littlefield, 2001), 86–87.

38. Bobby A. Wintermute, *Public Health and the U.S. Military: A History of the Army Medical Department, 1818–1917* (New York: Routledge, 2011), 189–218; John C. Burnham, *Bad Habits: Drinking, Smoking, Taking Drugs, Gambling, Sexual Misbehavior, and Swearing in American History* (New York: New York University Press, 1993); Brandt, *No Magic Bullet*, 72.

39. Wintermute, *Public Health*, 202–203.

40. Lord, *Condom Nation*; Aine Collier, *The Humble Little Condom: A History* (Amherst: Prometheus Books, 2007).

41. Quoted in Bristow, *Making Men Moral*, 12.

42. Quoted in ibid., 14–15.

43. Commission on Training Camp Activities, *Report of the Chairman on Training Camp Activities to the Secretary of War, 1918* (Washington, DC: Government Printing Office, 1918), 9.

44. Brandt, *No Magic Bullet*, 61–62.

45. David M. Kennedy, *Over Here: The First World War and American Society* (New York: Oxford University Press, 1980), 187–188.

46. Commission on Training Camp Activities, *Keeping Fit to Fight* (Washington, DC: Government Printing Office, 1918).

47. "Lecture to Troops," unpublished manuscript, December 1917, p. 21, RG 165, Box 418, NARA II.

48. Ibid., 12.

49. Wilcox, "Soldiers, Come Back Clean."

50. "Lecture to Troops," 23–24.

51. "Shoot Them for Traitors," *Pythian Guest*, December 1917.

52. Commission on Training Camp Activities, *Keeping Fit to Fight*.

53. Abraham Wolbarst, "Discussion," *Transactions of the American Society for Sanitary and Moral Prophylaxis* 3 (1910): 34.

54. Commission on Training Camp Activities, *Keeping Fit to Fight*, 6–7.

55. "Lecture to Troops," 21–22.

56. "Syllabus Accredited for Use in Official Supplementary Lectures on Sex Hygiene and Venereal Diseases," unpublished manuscript, February 1918, RG 165, Box 433, NARA II.

57. Bristow, *Making Men Moral*, 30–35. As has been mentioned previously, the term *prophylaxis* was used at this time to indicate medical interventions and treatments after exposure to venereal disease, usually within a few hours of sexual contact, and before symptoms became evident. The term was almost never used to indicate treatments or technologies (like condoms) that would have prevented venereal infections from occurring.

58. Ibid., 35.

59. "Lecture to Women," undated manuscript [1918?], p. 2, RG 62, Box 437, National Archives and Records Administration, Washington National Records Center, Suitland, MD, quoted in Brandt, *No Magic Bullet*, 83.

60. For more on sexual education for women during this period, see Brandt, *No Magic Bullet*, 27–31.

61. Mrs. Woodallen Chapman, *A Nation's Call to Young Women*, Commission on Training Camp Activities pamphlet (Washington, DC: Government Printing Office, 1918), quoted in Brandt, *No Magic Bullet*, 82.

62. Commission on Training Camp Activities, *Report of the Chairman*, 11.

63. Ibid.

64. Commission on Training Camp Activities, *Women's Share in a National Service* (Washington, DC: Government Printing Office, n.d., ca. 1918).

65. George J. Anderson, *Making the Camps Safe for the Army* (Washington, DC: Government Printing Office, 1919), 5, 7.

66. Commission on Training Camp Activities, *Women's Share*.

67. Commission on Training Camp Activities, *Report of the Chairman*, 13.

68. Ibid., 16; Commission on Training Camp Activities, *Committee on Protective Work for Girls* (Washington: Government Printing Office, 1917).

69. Commission on Training Camp Activities, *Report of the Chairman*, 16.

70. Population statistics of Camp Beauregard and Alexandria, Louisiana, quoted in Bristow, *Making Men Moral*, 230.

71. These "Porto Ricans" or Panamanians were rarely discussed in army reports and do not seem to have been perceived as representing a particular kind of racial or sexual category or threat in the same ways that African American soldiers sometimes were. U.S. Department of War, Office of the Surgeon-General, *Annual Report of the Surgeon General, 1919* (Washington, DC: Government Printing Office, 1920), 1:127.

72. Ibid., 1:127–128, 132–135; U.S. Department of War, Office of the Surgeon-General, *Annual Report of the Surgeon General, 1920* (Washington, DC: Government Printing Office, 1921), 140, 145.

73. Bristow, *Making Men Moral*, 104–106, 110–112.

74. Charles H. Brough to Newton D. Baker, telegram, July 21, 1917, RG 165, Entry 395, Box 1, Alexandria, Louisiana, Folder, NARA II; Newton D. Baker to Charles H. Brough, telegram, July 25, 1917, RG 165, Entry 395, Box 1, Alexandria, Louisiana, Folder, NARA II.

75. William A. Oldfield to Newton D. Baker, July 25, 1917, RG 165, Entry 395, Box 1, Alexandria, Louisiana, Folder, NARA II.

76. Raymond B. Fosdick to William A. Oldfield, July 31, 1917, RG 165, Entry 395, Box 1, Alexandria, Louisiana, Folder, NARA II.

77. P. L. Gillett to W. E. Adams, August 12, 1917, RG 165, Entry 395, Box 1, Alexandria, Louisiana, Folder, NARA II.

78. P. K. [full name unknown], "Alexandria, La.," report, July 26, 1917, RG 165, Entry 395, Box 1, Alexandria, Louisiana, Folder, NARA II. Locals used the euphemism "going over the bridge" for patronizing the establishments in the red-light district. The area even had its own local telephone exchange (1600) for the thirteen houses of prostitution with telephones there. George J. Anderson, "Supplementary Report No. I on Alexandria, La.," CTCA document, September 22, 1917, pp. 2–3, RG 165, Entry 395, Box 1, Alexandria, Louisiana, Folder, NARA II.

79. Elizabeth Clement, *Love for Sale: Courting, Treating, and Prostitution in New York City, 1900–1945* (Chapel Hill: University of North Carolina Press, 2006), 80, 116; Heather Lee Miller, "The Teeming Brothel: Sex Acts, Desires, and Sexual Identities in the United States, 1870–1940" (PhD diss., Ohio State University, 2002), 202–207.

80. P. K., "Alexandria, La.," 2.

81. Bascom Johnson, "Preliminery [*sic*] Report on Alexandria, La.," CTCA document, September 2–4, 1917, RG 165, Entry 395, Box 1, Alexandria, Louisiana, Folder, NARA II.

82. Alexandria, Louisiana, Penal Ordinance No. 66, introduced and approved September 4, 1917, complete text reproduced in ibid., 4.

83. Alexandria, Louisiana, Penal Ordinance No. 244, introduced and approved September 4, 1917, complete text reproduced in Johnson, "Preliminery [*sic*] Report on Alexandria, La.," 3.

84. Johnson, "Preliminery [*sic*] Report on Alexandria, La.," 4.

85. Ibid., 5.

86. Ibid.

87. Anderson, "Supplementary Report No. I on Alexandria, La.," 2.

88. One of the local madams met with the mayor for nearly an hour just before Anderson's visit with the mayor. Ibid., 4–5.

89. Ibid., 6.

90. Prostitutes' use of automobiles to travel around town and near Camp Beauregard to locate customers and elude police and other investigators became common after the elimination of the red-light district. For more on the role of automobile-using prostitutes, see First Lieutenant Thomas A. Larremore, "Report of Thos. A. Larremore, 1st Lt., San. Corps, Natl. Army for Week Ending 12/1/17," RG 165, Entry 395, Box 1, Alexandria, Louisiana, Folder, NARA II.

91. First Lieutenant Thomas A. Larremore, "Report of Thos. A. Larremore, 1st Lt., San. Corps, Natl. Army for Week Ending 11/24/17," p. 1, RG 165, Entry 395, Box 1, Alexandria, Louisiana, Folder, NARA II.

92. Ibid., 3.

93. Larremore, "Week Ending 12/1/17," 4–5.

94. First Lieutenant Thomas A. Larremore, "Report of Thos. A. Larremore, 1st Lt., San. Corps, Natl. Army for Week Ending 12/15/17," p. 10, RG 165, Entry 395, Box 1, Alexandria, Louisiana, Folder, NARA II.

95. Ibid., 2.

96. Larremore, "Week Ending 11/24/17," 8, 14.

97. Larremore, "Week Ending 12/15/17," 3, 9.

98. First Lieutenant Thomas A. Larremore, "Report of Thos. A. Larremore, 1st Lt., San. Corps, Natl. Army for Week Ending 12/8/17," p. 3, RG 165, Entry 395, Box 1, Alexandria, Louisiana Folder, NARA II.

99. Larremore, "Week Ending 12/1/17," 5.

100. Larremore, "Week Ending 12/15/17," 4.

101. Larremore, "Week Ending 12/1/17," 5.

102. Ibid., 6.

103. First Lieutenant Thomas A. Larremore, "Report of Thos. A. Larremore, 1st Lt., San. Corps, Natl. Army for Week Ending 12/23/17," p. 7, RG 165, Entry 395, Box 1, Alexandria, Louisiana, Folder, NARA II.

104. Ibid., 4.

105. Larremore, "Week Ending 12/15/17," 4.

106. Larremore, "Week Ending 12/8/17," 3–4.

107. Larremore, "Week Ending 12/1/17," 5.

108. Larremore, "Week Ending 12/15/17," 4.

109. See, for example, Larremore, "Week Ending 12/8/17," 5.

110. Ibid., 3.

111. Alexandria, Louisiana, mayor W. W. Whittington Jr. to Senator Robert F. Broussard (D-LA), September 3, 1917, RG 165, Entry 395, Box 8, Alexandria, Louisiana, Folder, NARA II.

112. Larremore, "Week Ending 12/15/17," 12.

113. Ibid.

114. Larremore, "Week Ending 11/24/17," 9.

115. Larremore and camp medical officers were particularly concerned that a large number of the local African American population, men and women alike, were infected with untreated venereal diseases. Ibid., 10; Larremore, "Week Ending 12/15/17," 12.

116. First Lieutenant Thomas A. Larremore, "Report of Thos. A. Larremore, 1st Lt., San. Corps, Natl. Army for Week Ending 4/14/18, on Camp Beauregard and Vicinity," RG 165, Entry 393, Box 51, Document 24961, NARA II.

117. Commission on Training Camp Activities, *Report of the Chairman*, 11.

118. Bristow, *Making Men Moral*, 129.

119. For more discussion of the category of the "promiscuous girl," see Bristow, *Making Men Moral*, 113–119.

120. Brandt, *No Magic Bullet*, 77.

121. William F. Snow and Wilbur A. Sawyer, "Venereal Disease Control in the Army" (presented at the Section on Preventive Medicine and Public Health at the Sixty-Ninth Annual Session of the American Medical Association, Chicago, June 1918), *Journal of the American Medical Association* 71, no. 6 (1918): 462.

122. Frank W. Weed, *Military Hospitals in the United States*, vol. 5 of U.S. Surgeon-General's Office, *The Medical Department of the United States Army in the World War*, ed. M. W. Ireland (Washington, DC: Government Printing Office, 1923), 619.

123. U.S. Department of War, Office of the Surgeon-General, *Annual Report of the Surgeon General, 1919*, 1:125–141.

124. Colonel W. F. Lewis, M. C., U.S. Army, to the Surgeon General, U.S. Army, Washington, DC, November 5, 1918, "Sanitary Inspection," Camp Beauregard, Alexandria, LA, cited in Weed, *Military Hospitals*, 162.

125. Lieutenant Colonel William G. Schauffler, M. C., Sanitary Inspector, Thirty-Ninth Division, "Medical History of Camp Beauregard, Alexandria, Louisiana, September 1917 to May 1918," Record Room, Sergeant General's Office, 314.7 (Camp Beauregard) D, cited in Weed, *Military Hospitals*, 162.

126. Weed, *Military Hospitals*, 162.

127. It is difficult to determine with certainty the total number of soldiers who spent at least some time at Camp Beauregard, though 30,000 is a conservative, if possibly too low, estimate.

128. Brandt, *No Magic Bullet*, 12, 13, 31.

129. The relevant cases are the following: court-martial records of Sergeant Shay Vincent Danna, Court-Martial 107501, RG 153, Entry 15B, NARA II; Private Harry Farley, Court-Martial 108030, RG 153, Entry 15B, NARA II; and Private Andrew L. Parham, Court-Martial 118280, RG 153, Entry 15B, NARA II.

130. Court-martial record of Sergeant Shay Vincent Danna.

131. Bristow, *Making Men Moral*, 113–119.

132. Had Danna been a civilian, he could have received a sentence of up to ten years of hard labor for such an offense, which would have been considered a felony under Louisiana state law. Louisiana Revised Statutes 14:80, Part V, Offenses Affecting the Public Morals, Subpart A, Offenses Affecting Sexual Immorality, 1. Sexual Offenses Affecting Minors.

133. Court-martial record of Private Andrew L. Parham.

134. Court-martial record of Private Harry Farley.

135. Alecia P. Long, *The Great Southern Babylon: Sex, Race, and Respectability in New Orleans, 1865–1920* (Baton Rouge: Louisiana State University Press, 2004), 1–5; Herbert Asbury, *The French Quarter: An Informal History of the New Orleans Underworld* (1936; repr., New York: Old Town Books, 1989).

136. Al Rose, *Storyville, New Orleans, Being an Authentic, Illustrated Account of the Notorious Red-Light District* (Tuscaloosa: University of Alabama Press, 1974).

137. Ibid., 192–193.

138. Long, *Great Southern Babylon*, 103.

139. Rose, *Storyville*, 185–190; Thomas C. Mackey, *Red Lights Out: A Legal History of Prostitution, Disorderly Houses, and Vice Districts, 1870–1917* (New York: Garland, 1986), 176–184.

140. Rose, *Storyville*, 67.

141. Ibid., 194–203.

142. Long, *Great Southern Babylon*, 110–111.

143. William M. Railey to Raymond B. Fosdick, September 6, 1917, RG 165, Entry 395, Box 5, New Orleans, Louisiana, Folder, NARA II.

144. Long, *Great Southern Babylon*, 109–110.

145. William M. Railey to Raymond B. Fosdick, September 12, 1917, p. 3, RG 165, Entry 395, Box 5, New Orleans, Louisiana, Folder, NARA II; William M. Railey to Raymond B. Fosdick, November 19, 1917, RG 165, Entry 393, Box 17, Document 11915, NARA II.

146. "Railey Expose Causes Charge of Libel," undated newspaper clipping from a New Orleans newspaper enclosed with William M. Railey to Raymond B. Fosdick, October 12, 1917, RG 165, Entry 395, Box 5, New Orleans, Louisiana, Folder, NARA II.

147. Edward F. Haas, *Political Leadership in a Southern City: New Orleans in the Progressive Era, 1896–1902* (Ruston: Louisiana Tech University, 1988).

148. Long, *Great Southern Babylon*, 6–7, 37–39.

149. As an example, the prominent local madam Lulu White was almost always referred to as a "negro" in reports about her activities, and she was often said to run an "octoroon house," staffed by female prostitutes of one-eighth African heritage. William M. Railey to Raymond B. Fosdick, December 4, 1917, p. 1, RG 165, Entry 395, Box 5, New Orleans, Louisiana, Folder, NARA II.

150. Long, *Great Southern Babylon*, 203.

151. Ibid., 194–196.

152. See untitled report accompanying Bascom Johnson to Raymond B. Fosdick, August 27, 1917, RG 165, Entry 395, Box 5, New Orleans, Louisiana, Folder, NARA II.

153. Ibid.

154. P. K. [full name unknown], untitled CTCA report on the conditions in New Orleans, covering the period December 19–21, 1917, undated [likely December 22, 1917], RG 165, Entry 395, Box 5, New Orleans, Louisiana, Folder, NARA II.

155. Behrman was a Democratic politician who served as mayor from 1904 to 1920, when he was defeated by Andrew McShane, who ran on a reform platform to clean up municipal corruption and machine politics. Behrman ran against McShane in 1925, defeating him, though Behrman died less than a year into his fifth term in office.

156. Quoted in Rose, *Storyville*, 182.

157. William M. Railey to Raymond B. Fosdick, October 27, 1917, p. 1, RG 165, Entry 395, Box 5, New Orleans, Louisiana, Folder, NARA II.

158. William M. Railey to Raymond B. Fosdick, October 6, 1917, p. 1, RG 165, Entry 395, Box 5, New Orleans, Louisiana, Folder, NARA II; William M. Railey to Raymond B. Fosdick, October 27, 1917, 6.

159. Behrman quoted in Newton D. Baker to Raymond B. Fosdick, September 2, 1917, RG 165, Entry 395, Box 5, New Orleans, Louisiana, Folder, NARA II.

160. George J. Anderson, "Supplementary Report No. I on New Orleans, La.," CTCA document, September 25, 1917, RG 165, Entry 395, Box 5, New Orleans, Louisiana, Folder, NARA II.

161. Ibid.

162. "U.S. Threatens Drastic Action on N.O. District," December 1, 1917, *New Orleans Item*.

163. "Flat Denial Fosdick of N.O. Attack," December 3, 1917, *New Orleans States*. The *New Orleans Item* stood by its original report in an undated article published after Fosdick's denial. "Correspondent Wrote What Mr. Fosdick Said," undated article, *New Orleans Item*, RG 165, Entry 395, Box 5, New Orleans, Louisiana, Folder, NARA II.

164. J. S. [full name unknown], untitled CTCA report on the conditions in New Orleans, covering the period December 19–21, 1917, undated [likely December 22, 1917], RG 165, Entry 395, Box 5, New Orleans, Louisiana, Folder, NARA II.

165. Ibid., 1.

166. Ibid.

167. George Chauncey Jr., *Gay New York: Gender, Urban Culture, and the Making of the Gay Male World, 1890–1940* (New York: Basic Books, 1994), 47–63.

168. Anderson, *Making the Camps Safe*, 6.

169. Rose, *Storyville*, 166–181.

170. Long, *Great Southern Babylon*, 227–228.

171. Quoted in Bristow, *Making Men Moral*, 195.

4. "Complete Continence Is Wholly Possible"

Epigraph: John J. Pershing, AEF Bulletin 54, August 7, 1918, in Center of Military History, U.S. Army, *United States Army in the World War, 1917–1919*, vol. 17, *Bulletins, GHQ, AEF* (Washington, DC: Center of Military History, U.S. Army, 1992), 82.

1. Precise statistics on the U.S. Army and AEF during World War I vary slightly by source. See U.S. Provost Marshal General, *Second Report of the Provost Marshal General to the Secretary of War on the Operations of the Selective Service System to December 20, 1918* (Washington, DC: Government Printing Office, 1919), 226–229; Leonard Porter Ayres, ed., *The War with Germany: A Statistical Summary*, 2nd ed., with data rev. to August 1, 1919 (Washington, DC: Government Printing Office, 1919); Marvin A. Kreidberg and Merton G. Henry, eds., *History of Military Mobilization in the United States Army, 1775–1945* (Washington, DC: Center of Military History, U.S. Army, 1984), 246–252; and U.S. Department of Defense, Statistical Service Center, *Principal Wars in Which the United States Participated: U.S. Personnel Serving and Casualties* (Washington, DC: Government Printing Office, 1957).

2. American Battle Monuments Commission, *American Armies and Battlefields in Europe: A History, Guide, and Reference Book* (Washington, DC: Government Printing Office, 1938), 507.

3. Douglas F. Habib, "Chastity, Masculinity, and Military Efficiency: The United States Army in Germany, 1918–1923," *International History Review* 28, no. 4 (December 2006): 738–740.

4. Thomas P. Lowry, *The Story the Soldiers Wouldn't Tell: Sex in the Civil War* (Mechanicsburg, PA: Stackpole Books, 1994), 104–105; Bobby A. Wintermute, *Public Health and the U.S. Military: A History of the Army Medical Department, 1818–1917* (New York: Routledge, 2011), 204–205; Darla Brock, "Memphis's *Nymphs Du Pave*: 'The Most Abandoned Women in the World,'" *West Tennessee Historical Society Papers* 50 (1996):

58–69; Jeannine Cole, "'Upon the Stage of Disorder': Legalized Prostitution in Memphis and Nashville, 1863–1865," *Tennessee Historical Quarterly* 68, no. 1 (March 2009): 40–65; James B. Jones Jr., "A Tale of Two Cities," *North and South: The Magazine of Civil War Conflict* 10, no. 5 (March 2008): 64–70.

5. Kevin Adams, *Class and Race in the Frontier Army: Military Life in the West, 1870–1890* (Norman: University of Oklahoma Press, 2009); Edward M. Coffman, *The Regulars: The American Army, 1898–1941* (Cambridge, MA: Belknap Press of Harvard University Press, 2004).

6. Hugh H. Young, *Hugh Young: A Surgeon's Autobiography* (New York: Harcourt, Brace, 1940), 264–271; George Walker, *Venereal Disease in the American Expeditionary Forces* (Baltimore: Medical Standard, 1922), 1, 46–47.

7. General Order Number 6 (Headquarters, AEF), July 2, 1917, in Center of Military History, U.S. Army, *United States Army in the World War, 1917–1919*, vol. 16, *General Orders, GHQ, AEF* (Washington, DC: Center of Military History, U.S. Army, 1992), 11–12.

8. Weston P. Chamberlain and Frank W. Weed, *Sanitation*, vol. 6 of U.S. Surgeon-General's Office, *The Medical Department of the United States Army in the World War*, ed. M. W. Ireland (Washington, DC: Government Printing Office, 1926), 938–949.

9. Max J. Exner, "Prostitution in Its Relation to the Army on the Mexican Border," *Journal of Social Hygiene* 3 (1917): 205–219.

10. Ibid., 210.

11. Ibid., 218, 210.

12. Frederick Palmer, *Newton D. Baker: America at War*, 2 vols. (New York: Dodd, Mead, 1931), 1:298.

13. May J. Exner to Raymond B. Fosdick, May 26, 1917, RG 165, Box 575, NARA II, quoted in Allan M. Brandt, *No Magic Bullet: A Social History of Venereal Disease in the United States since 1880*, expanded ed. (New York: Oxford University Press, 1987), 99.

14. Young, *Hugh Young*, 301–333.

15. Chamberlain and Weed, *Sanitation*, 899.

16. Walker, *Venereal Disease*, 40.

17. Ibid., 40–43.

18. Ibid., 41.

19. Pershing, AEF Bulletin 54, August 7, 1918, 17:82. Here, under the section "Facts about Venereal Disease," it is stated that "the greatest source of venereal infection is the regulated and inspected house of prostitution" and that "venereal infection is highly prevalent among unregistered 'clandestine' prostitutes, and exists to-day to an increasing degree in social classes hitherto little suspected. The practice of illicit indulgence in sexual intercourse will almost inevitably lead to venereal infection sooner or later."

20. Walker, *Venereal Disease*, 77–81; Chamberlain and Weed, *Sanitation*, 908.

21. Chamberlain and Weed, *Sanitation*, 906.

22. Ibid., 953.

23. Walker, *Venereal Disease*, 122–123.

24. Chamberlain and Weed, *Sanitation*, 954; Walker, *Venereal Disease*, 32–33.

25. Walker, *Venereal Disease*, 32, 122.

26. Brandt, *No Magic Bullet*, 116.

27. Michael A. Imber, "The First World War, Sex Education, and the American Social Hygiene Association's Campaign against Venereal Disease," *Journal of Educational*

Administration and History 16, no. 1 (1984): 47–56; Alexandra M. Lord, *Condom Nation: The U.S. Government's Sex Education Campaign from World War I to the Internet* (Baltimore: Johns Hopkins University Press, 2010).

28. Lord, *Condom Nation*, 29.

29. Walker, *Venereal Disease*, 45.

30. Ibid., 85.

31. Ibid., 225.

32. Ibid., 223–231.

33. Brandt, *No Magic Bullet*, 119.

34. Susan Zeiger, *Entangling Alliances: Foreign War Brides and American Soldiers in the Twentieth Century* (New York: New York University Press, 2010), 22–27.

35. "Advice to Soldiers in Paris," *Social Hygiene* 5 (January 1919): 111–112.

36. Quoted in Brandt, *No Magic Bullet*, 108.

37. George Browne, *An American Soldier in World War I*, ed. David L. Snead (Lincoln: University of Nebraska Press, 2006), 43.

38. Pershing, AEF Bulletin 54, August 7, 1918, 17:82.

39. Quoted in William L. O'Neill, *Everyone Was Brave: The Rise and Fall of Feminism in America* (Chicago: Quadrangle Books, 1969), 190.

40. Walker, *Venereal Disease*, 101.

41. Chamberlain and Weed, *Sanitation*, 899.

42. At least some AEF medical observers had grave reservations about the quality of French venereal inspections of prostitutes. The inspections were reported to last an average of less than one minute (an insufficient time for a thorough inspection) and often used the same speculums for all women inspected, which increased the likelihood of transmission of diseases to uninfected women. Walker, *Venereal Disease*, 84–85, 90–93.

43. Chamberlain and Weed, *Sanitation*, 900–902.

44. Ibid., 902–914.

45. Ibid., 903–906. Note that in at least some cases, military police either were found to ignore orders to prevent other troops from accessing the houses of prostitution or were caught taking bribes from either soldiers or the prostitutes themselves. Walker notes that the military police units' venereal disease rates were the highest of any units in France. Walker, *Venereal Disease*, 82–83.

46. General Order No. 77 (General Headquarters, AEF), December 18, 1917, required that the prohibition on prostitution be applied at all stations housing AEF soldiers.

47. Chamberlain and Weed, *Sanitation*, 909. See also Walker, *Venereal Disease*, 93–96.

48. Walker, *Venereal Disease*, 48–49, which includes a transcript of Pershing's memo on the issue. The exact punishment for the officers is undisclosed, but additional research has not turned up a court-martial for the officers, so the punishment was likely relatively mild, probably consisting of a verbal reprimand.

49. Georges Clemenceau to Pershing, "Hygiene of Allied Troops," letter, February 17, 1918, in Chamberlain and Weed, *Sanitation*, 910.

50. Brandt, *No Magic Bullet*, 105.

51. Raymond B. Fosdick, *Chronicle of a Generation: An Autobiography* (New York: Harper, 1958), 171.

52. The conference is discussed in detail in Walker, *Venereal Disease*, 49–51.

53. H. H. Young and E. L. Keyes, "Reply to Simonin," unpublished manuscript, undated, p. 28, Thomas Parran Papers, Library of the School of Public Health, University of Pittsburgh, quoted in Brandt, *No Magic Bullet*, 106.

54. Luther H. Gulick, *Morals and Morale* (New York: Association, 1919), 48.

55. Chamberlain and Weed, *Sanitation*, 905.

56. General Orders Number 6 (Headquarters, AEF), July 2, 1917; Number 34 (Headquarters, AEF), September 9, 1917; Number 77 (Headquarters, AEF), December 18, 1917; and Number 32 (General Headquarters, AEF), February 15, 1919, all in Center of Military History, U.S. Army, *United States Army*, 16:11–12, 71–72, 144–146, 656–657.

57. Walker, *Venereal Disease*, 65.

58. Ibid., 197–213.

59. AEF Bulletin 54 (General Headquarters, AEF), August 7, 1918, in Center of Military History, U.S. Army, *United States Army*, 17:82.

60. Walker, *Venereal Disease*, 68–69.

61. Ibid., 73.

62. Ibid., 9.

63. Ibid., 9–13.

64. Walker, *Venereal Disease*, 52.

65. "Something to Think about for Men Going on Leave," mimeograph, April 12, 1919, RG 120, Box 5259, NARA II, quoted in Brandt, *No Magic Bullet*, 109.

66. Chamberlain and Weed, *Sanitation*, 949.

67. Ibid., 950.

68. Walker, *Venereal Disease*, 16–17; Chamberlain and Weed, *Sanitation*, 952.

69. Walker, *Venereal Disease*, 31–32.

70. Ibid., 14–16; Chamberlain and Weed, *Sanitation*, 950.

71. Memoranda from Services of Supply, Office of the Surgeon, Base Section No. 1, July 30 and November 28, 1918, in Chamberlain and Weed, *Sanitation*, 965–969. Exact venereal treatments are described in great detail in Walker, *Venereal Disease*, 115–121.

72. Chamberlain and Weed, *Sanitation*, 969–973.

73. Ibid., 978.

74. Ibid., 979.

75. Ibid.

76. Headquarters, American Forces in Germany, Office of Civil Affairs, U.S. Army, and I. L. Hunt, *American Military Government of Occupied Germany, 1918–1920: Report of the Officer in Charge of Civil Affairs, Third Army and American Forces in Germany* (Washington, DC: Government Printing Office, 1943) [hereafter Hunt], 144.

77. Ibid., 145.

78. Ibid., 146.

79. Habib, "Chastity, Masculinity, and Military Efficiency," 745.

80. Hunt, 148–149.

81. Ibid., 148.

82. Ibid.

83. Ibid., 149.

84. Ibid.

85. [Philip H. Bagby], *American Representation in Occupied Germany, 1920–21* (Washington, DC: Government Printing Office, 1921), 2:396.

86. "It is a fact that the venereal rate slowly but steadily decreased after its [the Vagrancy Court] establishment." Hunt, 150.

87. Walker, *Venereal Disease*, 54–57.

88. Ibid., 54.

89. Historian David M. Kennedy has suggested that the U.S. Army "met[ed] out stern punishment to soldiers suffering from venereal disease," but while this was urged in several general orders, it is not borne out by army judicial records. David M. Kennedy, *Over Here: The First World War and American Society* (New York: Oxford University Press, 1980), 187.

90. Court-martial record of Second Lieutenant Leo A. Regan, Court-Martial 116607, RG 153, Entry 15B, NARA II.

91. Court-martial record of Second Lieutenant Hoyne Wells, Court-Martial 121878, RG 153, Entry 15B, NARA II.

92. The definitive biography of Pershing remains Frank Everson Vandiver, *Black Jack: The Life and Times of John J. Pershing*, 2 vols. (College Station: Texas A&M University Press, 1977), though many additional details are included in Donald Smythe, *Pershing, General of the Armies* (Bloomington: Indiana University Press, 1986). More recent, though less comprehensive, biographies include Jim Lacey, *Pershing* (New York: Palgrave Macmillan, 2008); and Gene Smith, *Until the Last Trumpet Sounds: The Life of General of the Armies John J. Pershing* (New York: Wiley, 1998).

93. Quoted in Vandiver, *Black Jack*, 2:662.

94. The Filipina in question, Joaquina Bondoy Ignacio, was said to have lived with Pershing in a cottage for two years and had two children with him, one of whom died in a cholera epidemic in 1902. In a private letter to Pershing, Guy Preston, an old friend and fellow army officer who had served with Pershing in the Philippines, wrote, "You know the course of our lives in the old days was such as to suggest the possibilities that the statements might have some foundation in truth." The exact meaning of this remark is unclear, though it is suggestive. Smith, *Until the Last Trumpet Sounds*, 92–93; Zeiger, *Entangling Alliances*, 240n11. In addition to Micheline Resco, discussed later in the text, Pershing was also sexually involved with Elizabeth Hoyt and Dorothy Canfield Fisher, among others, during World War I. Vandiver, *Black Jack*, 2:1008; Lacey, *Pershing*, 124.

95. Pershing and Resco's relationship was well established and known to all close friends, family members, and Pershing's immediate subordinates. For more discussion of the Pershing-Resco relationship, see Smythe, *Pershing, General of the Armies*, 296–301; Vandiver, *Black Jack*, 2:814–816, 995, 1007–1008, 1017, 1031, 1063; and Lacey, *Pershing*, 124–125. The pair maintained their long-distance, common-law relationship until Pershing's death in 1948, though it is known that Pershing was not entirely faithful to Resco and carried on several shorter-term affairs over the course of the next three decades. The day after Pershing's death, his son hand-delivered a final letter from Pershing to Resco affirming his heartfelt affections. While some of Resco's detractors have claimed that Pershing continued the relationship only out of fear that Resco would go public, the letters and telegrams between the two, preserved in their entirety, make it clear that Pershing had strong feelings for Resco, and vice

versa. Smythe, *Pershing, General of the Armies*, 296–301. One later biographer has claimed, without citation, that Pershing and Resco secretly wed in 1946, but no other biographies confirm this. Lacey, *Pershing*, 125. During the war, Pershing used several of his staff officers to arrange liaisons with Resco (and other women), traveled incognito to meet Resco, and developed an elaborate code for communicating romantic matters discreetly in letters and telegrams. The affair with Resco caused a minor scandal when it resulted in Pershing's breaking off his engagement to Anne "Nita" Patton, the sister of Pershing's subordinate, George S. Patton Jr. On Pershing's relationship with Nita Patton, see Vandiver, *Black Jack*, 2:606, 658, 698, 1008; Lacey, *Pershing*, 80, 97, 124; Smith, *Until the Last Trumpet Sounds*, 141, 148, 168–169, 225; and Smythe, *Pershing, General of the Armies*, 296. In an attempt to rekindle the relationship, Nita Patton traveled to France immediately after the Armistice was declared, but she was rebuffed by Pershing in no uncertain terms. Nita Patton immediately returned to the United States and asked her family to never mention the matter again. Pershing's sexual practices over the years may have caused additional problems: one of Pershing's biographers notes that Pershing had contracted gonorrhea "twice in his younger days and knew the effects of such disease." Smythe, *Pershing, General of the Armies*, 250.

96. John J. Pershing, speech at Brest, France, January 1919, quoted in Smythe, *Pershing, General of the Armies*, 251.

97. Quoted in Smythe, *Pershing, General of the Armies*, 250.

98. John J. Pershing, speech to officers of the Seventy-Seventh Division at Sable, France, February 24, 1919, quoted in Vandiver, *Black Jack*, 2:1001.

99. For Young's lengthy discussion of his efforts to influence Pershing to adopt what came to be the AEF's policies on venereal disease and prostitution in France, see Young, *Hugh Young*.

100. The article and letters columns are discussed in detail in Zeiger, *Entangling Alliances*, 11–12.

101. *Stars and Stripes*, November 22, 1918.

102. Brandt, *No Magic Bullet*, 96.

103. "Cupid's Success in A.E.F.," *New York Times*, January 30, 1919, 3.

104. "Franco-Yanko Romance," *Literary Digest*, November 10, 1917, 46–50.

105. *Stars and Stripes*, April 4, 1919, 6.

106. W. A. Bethel, Judge Advocate, AEF, to General Pershing, "Marriage of American Soldiers to French Girls," memorandum, June 18, 1918, RG 120, Entry 594, Box 22, NARA. Bethel's memo is further discussed in Zeiger, *Entangling Alliances*, 29–32.

107. Quoted in Lieutenant Colonel Albert B. Kellogg, "Marriages of Soldiers, Report for the Historical Section of the Army War College," July 1942, p. 5, RG 165, Entry 310C, Box 74, NARA.

108. Zeiger, *Entangling Alliances*, 32–33.

109. Erika Kuhlman, "American Doughboys and German *Fräuleins*: Sexuality, Patriarchy, and Privilege in the American-Occupied Rhineland, 1918–23," *Journal of Military History* 71 (October 2007): 1077–1106.

110. Quoted in Habib, "Chastity, Masculinity, and Military Efficiency," 740.

111. Ibid., 748–749.

112. Discussed at length in Arthur E. Barbeau and Florette Henri, *The Unknown Soldiers: Black American Troops in World War I* (Philadelphia: Temple University Press, 1974), esp. 114–115, 142–145. See also Zeiger, *Entangling Alliances*, 25–26.

113. Quoted in Adriane Lentz-Smith, *Freedom Struggles: African Americans and World War I* (Cambridge, MA: Harvard University Press, 2009), 100.

114. Ibid.

115. Memo discussed in Barbeau and Henri, *Unknown Soldiers*, 114–115, 142–145, and reprinted in its entirety as "A French Directive," *Crisis* 18 (May 1919): 16–18.

116. Charles R. Isum to W. E. B. Du Bois, May 1919, W. E. B. Du Bois Papers, University of Massachusetts–Amherst, Reel 7, Frame 980, in Jennifer D. Keene, *The United States and the First World War* (Harlow, UK: Longman, 2000).

117. The soldier stated that he received an honorable discharge, and while I have not viewed Isum's service record (assuming it survived the 1973 National Personnel Records Center fire), there is certainly no evidence in AEF court-martial records to suggest that he was ever court-martialed.

118. U.S. Army, "Office of Civil Affairs Report, Kreis Berncastel, Germany, May 18 to September 3, 1919," RG 120, Military Government, Box 1, Folder 21, NARA.

119. U.S. Army, "Weekly Report, Coblenz, to AFG, December 20, 1919," RG 120, Civil Affairs, Miscellaneous, Folder 36, NARA.

120. *Amaroc News*, May 5, 1919, 1; *Amaroc News*, July 18, 1919, 1. German resistance to American fraternization is discussed in Kuhlman, "American Doughboys and German *Fräuleins*," 1089.

121. *Stars and Stripes*, December 20, 1918, 8.

122. Quoted in *Amaroc News*, July 18, 1919, 1.

123. Hunt, 150.

124. [Bagby], *American Representation*, 2:45.

125. Henry T. Allen, *My Rhineland Journal* (Boston: Houghton Mifflin, 1923), 78.

126. [Bagby], *American Representation*, 2:45.

127. Ibid., 43–44.

128. Ibid., 46.

129. The soldier successfully married before his court-martial and was only lightly punished by the court (he had to forfeit two-thirds of his pay for three months). Court-martial record of Staff Sergeant Cosmos J. Rose, Court-Martial 151810, RG 153, Entry 15B, NARA II.

130. [Bagby], *American Representation*, 2:48.

131. Here I use Stanley Cohen's term "moral panic" to indicate a "condition, episode, person or group of persons [that] emerges to become defined as a threat to societal values and interests." The term is intended to suggest not irrationality or a lack of control on the part of German civilians but rather a set of expressions of intense concern about an issue that was perceived as threatening the social order. Stanley Cohen, *Folk Devils and Moral Panics: The Creation of the Mods and Rockers*, 3rd ed. (London: Routledge, 2002), 9.

132. This moral panic is discussed further in Kuhlman, "American Doughboys and German *Fräuleins*," 1099–1103, and was evidenced by the large number of German newspaper articles and editorials written on the topic, as well as the many letters and visits to army headquarters by German civilians concerned about the pregnancies. The

term "strained relations" is used in the title of a lengthy appendix discussing the problem of illegitimate births in [Bagby], *American Representation*, 2:53–65.

133. The name of the German city of Koblenz was spelled Coblenz before 1926. [Bagby], *American Representation*, 2:50–55.

134. Jay Winter, "Some Paradoxes of the First World War," in *The Upheaval of War: Family, Work, and Welfare in Europe, 1914–1918*, ed. Richard Wall and Jay Winter (Cambridge: Cambridge University Press, 1988), 27.

135. [Bagby], *American Representation*, 2:55–56.

136. Ibid., 50.

137. Discussed further in Kuhlman, "American Doughboys and German *Fräuleins*," 1100.

138. In response to this particular request, the AFG assisted in finding additional space to house the children. This and similar cases are discussed in ibid., 1100–1101, 1103.

139. Zeiger, *Entangling Alliances*, 13.

140. Ibid., 65–70.

141. One of the few who was convicted of twice registering at a hotel with a woman not his wife but was not dismissed from the service had his sentence of being confined to post and forfeiting one-third of his pay for the same period described as too "lenient" by the reviewing authority, though it ultimately approved the sentence. Court-martial record of First Lieutenant T. J. Butler, Court-Martial 125229, RG 153, Entry 15B, NARA II.

142. Court-martial record of Private Earl R. Caldwell, Court-Martial 134223, RG 153, Entry 15B, NARA II.

143. Court-martial record of Second Lieutenant David J. Andrews, Court-Martial 120511, RG 153, Entry 15B, NARA II.

144. Court-martial records of Captain William Wallace Leathe, Court-Martial 118533, RG 153, Entry 15B, NARA II; First Lieutenant Anton H. Boekee, Court-Martial 134535, RG 153, Entry 15B, NARA II; George Wallace Guthrie, RG 153, Entry 2, Box 159, NARA II.

145. Court-martial record of Major Guy H. Wyman, Court-Martial 150087, RG 153, Entry 15B, NARA II. The case became nationally infamous and was reported in the *New York Times*. "Major Who Married French Ward Guilty," *New York Times*, November 10, 1921. This case was not the first time Wyman had marital problems that led to courts-martial (or received national attention); he was court-martialed in 1908 because he had reported that he was single when in fact a previous divorce in 1905 was never completed. Court-martial record of Lieutenant Guy H. Wyman, Court-Martial 57993, RG 153, Entry 15, NARA; "Army Lieutenant Denies His Marriage," *New York Times*, August 10, 1908. After his dismissal from the army, Wyman began styling himself "Colonel" Wyman, claimed to be retired from the army, became a Florida real estate developer, and went on to found the town of Navarre, Florida, with his new French bride (Wyman named the town he founded after his bride's home region of France). The pair were later divorced, and Wyman shot and killed her during an altercation, though he was not charged for her death.

146. Court-martial record of Second Lieutenant Thomas J. Narcisse, RG 153, Entry 2, Box 154, NARA.

147. There were approximately twenty enlisted men in the AEF for every officer. We would expect that officers would thus constitute roughly 5 percent of all the accused, rather than 86 percent.

148. See, for example, the court-martial records of Major Robert J. Bates, Court-Martial 121984, RG 153, Entry 15B, NARA II; First Lieutenant James W. Cullen, Court-Martial 120953, RG 153, Entry 15B, NARA II; and First Lieutenant Theodore F. King, RG 153, Entry 2, Box 168, NARA.

149. Examples of such cases include the court-martial records of Captain Harry Cook, Court-Martial 125740, RG 153, Entry 15B, NARA II; and Captain Charles H. Roche, Court-Martial 125739, NARA II, RG 153, Entry 15B.

150. Examples of these cases include the court-martial records of Captain Richard H. Erwin, Court-Martial 120532, RG 153, Entry 15B, NARA II; and Captain William F. Wiscombe, Court-Martial 113130, RG 153, Entry 15B, NARA II.

151. Examples include the court-martial records of Captain John McKenzie, Court-Martial 130940, RG 153, Entry 15B, NARA II; First Lieutenant Levin I. Watkins, Court-Martial 129085, RG 153, Entry 15B, NARA II; and Captain Oscar T. Yates, Court-Martial 120534, RG 153, Entry 15B, NARA II.

152. Court-martial record of Captain John J. Deeming, Court-Martial 146785, RG 153, Entry 15B, NARA II.

153. Court-martial records of First Lieutenant Bledsoe Kelly, Court-Martial 134350, RG 153, Entry 15B, NARA II; and Major Malcolm M. Kilduff, Court-Martial 124768, RG 153, Entry 15B, NARA II.

154. Court-martial record of Second Lieutenant Benjamin H. Simons, Court-Martial 131649, RG 153, Entry 15B, NARA II.

155. Court-martial record of Captain William R. Fleming, Court-Martial 138610, RG 153, Entry 15B, NARA II.

156. Other scholars have pointed out that sexual relationships between soldiers and local civilians could sometimes rise to the level of diplomacy during and after the Cold War. Katharine H. S. Moon, *Sex among Allies: Military Prostitution in U.S.-Korea Relations* (New York: Columbia University Press, 1997).

5. The "Racial (and Sexual) Maelstrom" in Hawaii, 1909–1940

Epigraph: Romanzo Colfax Adams, *Interracial Marriage in Hawaii: A Study of the Mutually Conditioned Processes of Acculturation and Amalgamation* (New York: Macmillan, 1937), 124.

1. J. Kēhaulani Kauanui, *Hawaiian Blood: Colonialism and the Politics of Sovereignty and Indigeneity* (Durham, NC: Duke University Press, 2008); Gary Y. Okihiro, *Island World: A History of Hawai'i and the United States* (Berkeley: University of California Press, 2008); Noenoe K. Silva, *Aloha Betrayed: Native Hawaiian Resistance to American Colonialism* (Durham, NC: Duke University Press, 2004); Matthew Frye Jacobson, *Barbarian Virtues: The United States Encounters Foreign Peoples at Home and Abroad, 1876–1917* (New York: Hill and Wang, 2000).

2. Brian McAllister Linn, *Guardians of Empire: The U.S. Army and the Pacific, 1902–1940* (Chapel Hill: University of North Carolina Press, 1997), 69.

3. U.S. Department of War, *Annual Report of the War Department*, multiple vols. (Washington, DC: Government Printing Office, 1902–1941); Hawaii and Philippine

Department annual reports; and Mark S. Watson, *Chief of Staff: Prewar Plans and Preparations* (Washington, DC: Historical Division, Department of the Army, 1950), 16, 474; all quoted in Brian McAllister Linn, *Guardians of Empire: The U.S. Army and the Pacific, 1902–1940* (Chapel Hill: University of North Carolina Press, 1997), 253–254.

4. A good summary of the construction of the various U.S. Army installations in Hawaii can be found in Linn, *Guardians of Empire*, 70–72.

5. Quoted in ibid., 71–72.

6. The army's retention problems in Hawaii are discussed further in ibid., 63–64.

7. U.S. Census Bureau, *Outlying Territories and Possessions: Number and Distribution of Inhabitants, Composition and Characteristics of the Population, Occupations, Unemployment, and Agriculture* (Washington, DC: Government Printing Office, 1932), 48.

8. Adams, *Interracial Marriage in Hawaii*, 18.

9. Rubin Francis Weston, *Racism in U.S. Imperialism: The Influence of Racial Assumptions on American Foreign Policy, 1893–1946* (Columbia: University of South Carolina Press, 1972), 72.

10. Jacobson, *Barbarian Virtues*, 195–196.

11. Quoted in Linn, *Guardians of Empire*, 123.

12. Harry A. Franck, *Roaming in Hawaii: A Narrative of Months of Wandering among the Glamorous Islands That May Become Our 49th State* (New York: Frederick A. Stokes, 1937), 115–116.

13. Nancy Shea, *The Army Wife*, 4th ed. (1941; New York: Harper and Row, 1966), 257–258.

14. Quoted in Linn, *Guardians of Empire*, 123.

15. Quoted in ibid.

16. U.S. Census Bureau, *Outlying Territories and Possessions*, 60.

17. Quoted in Linn, *Guardians of Empire*, 125–127.

18. Franck, *Roaming in Hawaii*, 116.

19. Hawaiian divorce rates were nearly twice as high as those within the continental United States, which Adams attributed in part to the relatively high rate of local marriages between soldiers and sailors stationed in Hawaii and local women. Adams, *Interracial Marriage in Hawaii*, 127–128, 209–211.

20. Beginning with California in 1948 and continuing through 1967, fourteen states repealed their antimiscegenation laws. The remaining sixteen states' antimiscegenation laws were not struck down until the U.S. Supreme Court decision in *Loving v. Virginia*, 388 U.S. 1 (1967), declared such laws unconstitutional. Jonathan Peter Spiro, *Defending the Master Race: Conservation, Eugenics, and the Legacy of Madison Grant* (Burlington, VT: University Press of New England, 2009).

21. Quoted in Linn, *Guardians of Empire*, 126.

22. *Army and Navy Journal*, January 29, 1916, and February 5, 1916. For more discussion of the riot, see Edward M. Coffman, *The Regulars: The American Army, 1898–1941* (Cambridge, MA: Belknap Press of Harvard University Press, 2004), 132–133. For one white perspective on the broader issue of race in Hawaii from the mid-1930s, see Franck, *Roaming in Hawaii*, 260–286.

23. On the 1906 Brownsville race riot and its aftermath, see John D. Weaver, *The Brownsville Raid* (New York: W. W. Norton, 1970), which prompted a new U.S. Army investigation of the affair.

24. Court-martial record of Private Anderson Finchum, Court-Martial 80665, RG 153, Entry 15, NARA.

25. Court-martial record of Private Robert E. Brown, Court-Martial 98795, RG 153, Entry 15, NARA.

26. Twenty-one of those charged were white, the remaining three black. Three of the accused were corporals and one a sergeant; the rest were privates.

27. Court-martial record of Privates James F. Brenties, Thurlow Dugan, and Shelby V. Hazelwood, Court-Martial 102689, RG 153, Entry 15B, NARA II (all tried in the same court-martial).

28. Court-martial records of Private George B. Clark, Court-Martial 88074, RG 153, Entry 15, NARA; and Private Lyman J. Johnson, Court-Martial 88073, RG 153, Entry 15, NARA.

29. Court-martial record of Private Joe Brown, Court-Martial #85378, RG 395, Entry 2061, Box 1, NARA.

30. Court-martial record of Private Charles H. McGarry, Court-Martial #89055, RG 395, Entry 2061, Box 1, NARA.

31. Court-martial records of Private Maurice Allard, Court-Martial 90802, RG 153, Entry 15, NARA; and Private James Stewart, Court-Martial 98572, RG 153, Entry 15, NARA.

32. For more on Cromley/Crumley, see court-martial record of Private First Class Willie O. Hill and Sergeant Charles W. Manning, Court-Martial 83218, RG 153, Entry 15, NARA (both tried in same court-martial). Note that her first and last names were spelled with several variants in both courts-martial, making the proper spelling of her name impossible to determine.

33. Court-martial records of Private Star Daly, Court-Martial 98384, RG 153, Entry 15, NARA; Private George R. Fox, Court-Martial 83851, RG 153, Entry 15, NARA; Private William Luby, Court-Martial 166116, RG 153, Entry 15B, NARA II; and Private George W. Rose, Court-Martial 92069, RG 153, Entry 15, NARA.

34. Thomas W. Laqueur, *Solitary Sex: A Cultural History of Masturbation* (New York: Zone Books, 2003); Alan Hunt, "The Great Masturbation Panic and the Discourses of Moral Regulation in Nineteenth- and Early Twentieth-Century Britain," *Journal of the History of Sexuality* 8, no. 4 (April 1998): 575–615.

35. Court-martial record of Private Thomas Cherry, Court-Martial 93135, RG 153, Entry 15, NARA.

36. Cherry was noticed because another sergeant's home nearby was being watched because that sergeant had received a written threat that someone was going to burn down his residence. Cherry was not implicated in this threat, and his case seems to have been an entirely unrelated matter. The note read, in part, "I love your wife and will kill her to keep you from fucking and sucken [sic] her cunt."

37. Court-martial record of Private George J. Cornell, Court-Martial 119909, RG 153, Entry 15B, NARA II. The woman's relationship to the lieutenant colonel was never established in the court-martial and is unclear. She was apparently a married woman and they did not share a surname.

38. Court-martial record of Private Harold Leeper, Court-Martial 83059, RG 153, Entry 15, NARA. This court-martial took place on October 22, 1913; Leeper was charged with another sexual offense six months after this court-martial, which will be discussed later.

39. Court-martial records of Private Samuel Anderson, Court-Martial 81719, RG 153, Entry 15, NARA; Private James Hill, Court-Martial 85938, RG 153, Entry 15, NARA; and Private Charles Ward, Court-Martial 89238, RG 153, Entry 15, NARA.

40. Examples of these kinds of courts-martial include court-martial records of Private First Class Willie O. Hill and Sergeant Charles W. Manning (both tried in same court-martial); Private Harold D. Speares, Court-Martial 86180, RG 153, Entry 15, NARA; and Private First Class Joseph L. Rippard, Court-Martial 102036, RG 153, Entry 15B, NARA II.

41. Court-martial record of Private Harold D. Speares.

42. Court-martial record of Private First Class Willie O. Hill and Sergeant Charles W. Manning (both tried in same court-martial).

43. This is the same local prostitute mentioned in the court-martial record of Private Maurice Allard, Court-Martial 90802, RG 153, Entry 15, NARA. Note that her first and last names were spelled with several variants in both courts-martial, making the proper spelling of her name impossible to determine.

44. Court-martial record of Private James H. Kane, Court-Martial 86516, RG 153, Entry 15, NARA.

45. Lieutenant Colonel B. F. Cheatham, Commanding Officer, Fort Shafter, "Guard at Territorial Immigration Station and Navy Yard," order, July 1, 1914, in court-martial record of Corporal Benjamin T. Long, Court-Martial 86703, RG 153, Entry 15, NARA. Discipline problems and sexual disorder at the immigration station had been previously reported: in March 1914, Cheatham reported to the Commanding Officer at Fort Shafter that a passing captain had seen a corporal and a private with a "native woman" in their tent at the station.

46. Court-martial record of Corporal Benjamin T. Long.

47. Court-martial record of Private Joseph Arlington, Court-Martial 93121, RG 153, Entry 15, NARA.

48. Court-martial record of Private Harold Leeper, Court-Martial 85471, RG 153, Entry 15, NARA. This court-martial took place on April 24, 1914. Leeper had been convicted in October 1913 of peering into the bedroom of a first lieutenant and his wife, discussed previously, but that conviction had been overturned by the reviewing authority for a legal technicality and Leeper had returned to military service.

49. No records of this special court-martial appear to have survived, though his personnel record would likely contain some information on that trial and conviction with six months of hard labor. The personnel record would be unlikely to contain a complete transcript of the trial, assuming it survived the 1973 fire at the National Personnel Records Center.

50. Henry I. Raymond, "Prophylaxis under G.O. #31, War Department, 1912, for the Hawaiian Department," *Military Surgeon* 34, no. 2 (February 1914): 134–139.

51. C. F. Morse, "The Prevalence and Prophylaxis of Venereal Diseases at One Military Post," *Military Surgeon* 27, no. 3 (September 1910): 268–273.

52. Memorandum accompanying Deane C. Howard, *Venereal Prophylaxis* (Washington, DC: Association of Military Surgeons, 1911), AGO Docfile 131060, RG 94, Entry 25, NARA.

53. AGO Docfile 1881219, RG 94, Entry 25, NARA.

54. Waltz had served in various units and capacities in the U.S. Army in the Philippines, first as a captain and major from 1899 to 1903 and later as a colonel from 1911 to 1912, as was typical of army officers in the period. George Washington Cullum, *Biographical Register of the Officers and Graduates of the U.S. Military Academy at West Point, New York since Its Establishment in 1802*, ed. Wirt Robinson, supplement, vol. 6A, *1910–1920* (Saginaw, MI: Seemann and Peters, 1920), 256.

55. AGO Docfile 1881219, RG 94, Entry 25, NARA.

56. On the positive example of Great Britain's anti–venereal disease campaigns in the military, see, for example, Office of the Surgeon General of the U.S. Army to the Office of the Chief of Staff of the U.S. Army, "Prevention of Venereal Diseases," memorandum, April 8, 1912, filed with AGO Docfile 1045985, RG 94, Entry 25, NARA.

57. War Department, Office of the Chief of Staff, to acting adjutant general, memorandum, March 5, 1912, AGO Docfile 1881219, RG 94, Entry 25, NARA.

58. War Department, General Order No. 17, May 31, 1912, enclosed with AGO Docfile 1045985, RG 94, Entry 25, NARA.

59. War Department, Office of the Surgeon General, Circular No. 9, June 12, 1912, enclosed with AGO Docfile 1964550, filed with AGO Docfile 1045985, RG 94, Entry 25, NARA.

60. War Department, General Order No. 31, September 12, 1912, enclosed with AGO Docfile 1964550, filed with AGO Docfile 1045985, RG 94, Entry 25, NARA.

61. The only apparent exceptions were an extremely small number of courts-martial for commissioned officers during World War I in France. No commissioned officers were court-martialed for failure to receive venereal treatments in Hawaii.

62. The treatments were described in a variety of army documents but are laid out most clearly and in detail in Weston P. Chamberlain and Frank W. Weed, *Sanitation*, vol. 6 of U.S. Surgeon-General's Office, *The Medical Department of the United States Army in the World War*, ed. M. W. Ireland (Washington, DC: Government Printing Office, 1926), 938–949.

63. For an example, see the testimony of First Sergeant Joseph Moret in court-martial record of Private William A. Adkins, Court-Martial 97696, RG 153, Entry 15, NARA.

64. Court-martial record of Private James Hartford Jr., Court-Martial 97400, RG 153, Entry 15, NARA.

65. Court-martial record of Private Frederick Poindexter, Court-Martial 96446, RG 153, Entry 15, NARA, NARA.

66. Richard A. Greer, "Collarbone and the Social Evil," *Hawaiian Journal of History* 7 (1973): 3–17; Joan Hori, "Japanese Prostitution in Hawaii during the Immigration Period," *Hawaiian Journal of History* 15 (1980): 113–124; Ted A. Chernin, "My Experiences in the Honolulu Chinatown Red-Light District," *Hawaiian Journal of History* 34 (2000): 203–217; Beth L. Bailey and David R. Farber, *The First Strange Place: The Alchemy of Race and Sex in World War II Hawaii* (New York: Free Press, 1992), 98.

67. Greer, "Collarbone and the Social Evil," 4.

68. Chernin, "My Experiences," 206; Bailey and Farber, *First Strange Place*, 100.

69. Bailey and Farber, *First Strange Place*, 112.

70. A discussion of all the Honolulu Vice Squad's rules for prostitutes can be found in ibid., 108–109.

71. Ibid., 99.

72. See Bailey and Farber, *First Strange Place*, 192, for a demographic analysis; and Linn, *Guardians of Empire*, 253–254.

73. Quoted in Linn, *Guardians of Empire*, 129.

74. Quoted in ibid., 128.

75. Quoted in ibid.

76. Red-light districts were also shut down elsewhere in the continental United States, its territories, and the Philippines during the war. Greer, "Collarbone and the Social Evil," 3–17.

77. More discussion of life in the Hotel Street area during the late 1930s and the World War II era can be found in Bailey and Farber, *First Strange Place*, 95–132.

78. Ibid., 130–132.

79. Chernin, "My Experiences," 207, 211; Bailey and Farber, *First Strange Place*, 112.

80. Chernin, "My Experiences," 211–212.

81. Bailey and Farber, *First Strange Place*, 36.

82. James Jones, *From Here to Eternity: The Restored Edition* (New York: Open Road, 2011); Bailey and Farber, *First Strange Place*, 46–47.

83. Court-martial records of Private Robert L. Dancy, Court-Martial #112394, RG 153, Entry 3, Box 149, NARA II; and Private Luther H. Williams, Court-Martial #112399, RG 153, Entry 2, Box 149, NARA II.

84. The two men were, respectively, Private Robert L. Dancy and Private Luther H. Williams.

85. Court-martial record of Private John Manego, Court-Martial 91013, RG 153, Entry 15, NARA.

86. Court-martial records of Private Charles E. Coleman, Court-Martial 91015, RG 153, Entry 15, NARA; and Private Isidore Abrahams, Court-Martial 92453, RG 153, Entry 15, NARA.

87. Note that these statistics differ sharply from those of Brian McAllister Linn, who states that there were only 140 courts-martial for sodomy in the entirety of the U.S. Army from 1922 to 1941 (and only 34 in Hawaii during this period). Linn, *Guardians of Empire*, 280n105. Linn's statistics are off by roughly an order of magnitude because he appears to have relied solely on the General Court-Martial Ledger Sheets, RG 153, NARA. These ledger sheets include only a small fraction of the army's total number of courts-martial and cannot be used to calculate the total number of courts-martial either in specific locations or across the army as a whole. To obtain a complete census of all courts-martial of a given type, one must examine every volume of each U.S. Army Department's published compilations of court-martial summaries, generally published annually. This onerous process produces a much more complete picture of military justice across the army and shows that the total number of cases was much larger than has been previously understood.

88. Court-martial records of Sergeant John Gaufin and Private Jesse W. Durham, Court-Martial 103520, RG 153, Entry 15B, NARA II (both tried in same court-

martial); and Private William Myers, Court-Martial 103522, RG 153, Entry 15B, NARA II.

89. Court-martial record of Private Charles Johnson, Court-Martial 89369, RG 153, Entry 15, NARA.

90. Havelock Ellis and John Addington Symonds, *Sexual Inversion: A Critical Edition*, ed. Ivan Crozier (Basingstoke, UK: Palgrave Macmillan, 2008), 96.

91. Court-martial record of Privates Harold Albert and Dewey Passmore, Court-Martial 101446, RG 153, Entry 15B, NARA II (both tried in same court-martial).

92. Court-martial record of Private Harry J. Higdon, Court-Martial 91701, RG 153, Entry 15, NARA.

93. Court-martial record of Private Andrew Moreland, Court-Martial 92212, RG 153, Entry 15, NARA.

94. Court-martial record of Private Elmer E. Armstead, Court-Martial 98017, RG 153, Entry 15, NARA.

95. Court-martial record of Private James W. Sullivan Jr., Court-Martial 210854, RG 153, Entry 15B, NARA II.

96. In Hawaii as in other locales, army officials used the term *prophylaxis* to refer to venereal treatments administered shortly after sexual contact (and therefore after infection had already occurred) to prevent symptoms from appearing.

97. See, for example, the case of Private Alfred Larue, who was charged with propositioning seven other privates with oral sex, and the case of Private Ellis Wakeland, who was alleged to have allowed eleven other soldiers—none of whom were charged—to orally penetrate his mouth. Court-martial records of Private Alfred Larue, Court-Martial 85604, RG 153, Entry 15, NARA; and Private Ellis Wakeland, Court-Martial 109323, RG 153, Entry 15B, NARA II.

98. As examples, see two separate cases from 1927, each involving entirely different sets of men, in which four men were said to have had sex with a fifth man. In neither case was the fifth man court-martialed. Court-martials 177310 and 177311, RG 153, Entry 15B, NARA II.

99. Coffman, *Regulars*, 121.

100. Jones, *From Here to Eternity*. The new edition is discussed in Benedicte Page, "Censored Gay Sex in *From Here to Eternity* Restored for New Edition," *Guardian*, April 5, 2011.

Conclusion. Ongoing Concerns with Soldiers' Sexualities and Sexual Cultures

1. In a famous address, Patton is known to have said, "An Army is a team. It lives, sleeps, eats, and fights as a team. This individual heroic stuff is pure horse shit. The bilious bastards who write that kind of stuff for the *Saturday Evening Post* don't know any more about real fighting under fire than they know about fucking!" George S. Patton Jr., "Address to the Third Army" (June 5, 1944, Great Britain).

2. Many Americans conceived of the pre–World War I U.S. Army as full of rough, hard-drinking, womanizing outcasts and misfits mostly unable to find honest work in civilian society. While the war's massive mobilization brought more than four million more men into the army from across American society—and with them increased respectability for the institution—relatively few Americans maintained more than a

modicum of respect for those professional soldiers who chose to remain in the army at war's end.

3. This is not to suggest that men engaging in same-sex sexual practices, or who considered themselves to be homosexuals, did not participate in the U.S. Army; they clearly did, and in significant numbers. But the army as an institution increasingly constructed and imagined itself as a heterosexual one. Margot Canaday, *The Straight State: Sexuality and Citizenship in Twentieth-Century America* (Princeton, NJ: Princeton University Press, 2009).

4. "Venereal Diseases and Alcoholism in the Regular Army in the United States," undated chart, AGO Docfile 1915426, filed with AGO Docfile 1045985, RG 94, NARA. Note that this does not necessarily mean that 9 percent of all soldiers in the U.S. Army were admitted for newly contracted venereal diseases each year. Some soldiers might be admitted more than once during a calendar year for the same or a different venereal disease, and a man might be readmitted for a flare-up of a venereal disease contracted previously.

5. Data on Philippine posts taken from Surgeon General to the Adjutant General, "Rates for Venereal Disease in the Second Division," letter, November 19, 1914, AGO Docfile 2230647, filed with AGO Docfile 1045985, RG 94, NARA. Data on U.S. domestic posts taken from Surgeon General to the Adjutant General, "Venereal Disease in the Army," table A, letter, September 30, 1915, AGO Docfile 2225425, filed with AGO Docfile 1045985, RG 94, NARA. The topic is discussed further in Serafin E. Macaraig, *Social Problems* (Manila: Educational Supply, 1929), 156–157.

6. Court-martial record of Private First Class Willie O. Hill and Sergeant Charles W. Manning, Court-Martial 83218, RG 153, Entry 15, NARA (both tried in same court-martial).

7. *Army and Navy Journal*, January 29, 1916, and February 5, 1916; Edward M. Coffman, *The Regulars: The American Army, 1898–1941* (Cambridge, MA: Belknap Press of Harvard University Press, 2004), 132–133.

8. Noncommissioned officers existed in a space midway between these worlds, enjoying some privileges over junior enlisted soldiers but never being treated as social equals by commissioned officers.

9. U.S. Department of War, *A Manual for Courts-Martial, Courts of Inquiry, and of Other Procedure under Military Law*, approved by the U.S. Congress on June 4, 1920, and effective February 4, 1921 (Washington, DC: Government Printing Office, 1920).

10. For example, even some officers tasked with giving sexual education lectures refused to advocate abstinence. Disciplinary action was taken against these officers. Allan M. Brandt, *No Magic Bullet: A Social History of Venereal Disease in the United States since 1880*, expanded ed. (New York: Oxford University Press, 1987), 68.

11. Canaday, *Straight State*; Nathaniel Frank, *Unfriendly Fire: How the Gay Ban Undermines the Military and Weakens America* (New York: Thomas Dunne Books, 2009).

12. Situational homosexuality (and other situational sexual behaviors) has been widely observed by scholars in a variety of settings, many exclusively or predominantly same-sex environments. It has been studied most closely in prisons and other carceral settings, though it has also been observed in military, educational, and religious settings, among others. Joseph F. Fishman, *Sex in Prison: Revealing Sex Conditions in American Prisons* (New York: National Library, 1934); Christopher Hensley, ed., *Prison Sex:*

Practice and Policy (Boulder, CO: Lynne Rienner, 2002); Paula C. Rust, ed., *Bisexuality in the United States: A Social Science Reader* (New York: Columbia University Press, 2000).

13. George Chauncey Jr., *Gay New York: Gender, Urban Culture, and the Making of the Gay Male World, 1890–1940* (New York: Basic Books, 1994); George Chauncey Jr., "Christian Brotherhood or Sexual Perversion? Homosexual Identities and the Construction of Sexual Boundaries in the World War I Era," in *Hidden from History: Reclaiming the Gay and Lesbian Past*, ed. Martin Bauml Duberman, Martha Vicinus, and George Chauncey Jr. (New York: New American Library, 1989), 294–317. The army's perspective on same-sex acts during this period is in sharp contrast with the U.S. military's actions toward alleged homosexuals during World War II, as chronicled by historian Allan Bérubé, who describes the military's inadvertent role in helping to create a homosexual identity and, following the war, a coherent community. Allan Bérubé, *Coming Out under Fire: The History of Gay Men and Women in World War Two* (New York: Plume, 1990).

14. World War II and the unprecedented American war mobilization and conscription efforts opened up new opportunities and possibilities for male and female homosexuals during their wartime service. Bérubé, *Coming Out under Fire*; Leisa D. Meyer, *Creating GI Jane: Sexuality and Power in the Women's Army Corps during World War II* (New York: Columbia University Press, 1996). After the war, the dawning of the Cold War and increasing national security concerns about the dangers of homosexuality (and its alleged linkages with communism) closed off many of the opportunities for homosexuals within the U.S. military and national security apparatus. Canaday, *Straight State*; John D'Emilio, *Sexual Politics, Sexual Communities: The Making of a Homosexual Minority in the United States, 1940–1970*, 2nd ed. (Chicago: University of Chicago Press, 1998); Gary L. Lehring, *Officially Gay: The Political Construction of Sexuality by the U.S. Military* (Philadelphia: Temple University Press, 2003).

15. The "underlife" of an institution is a concept first defined by sociologist Erving Goffman to describe the tendency of members of a total institution, like the U.S. Army, to resist the formal regulations of the institution. Erving Goffman, *Asylums: Essays on the Social Situation of Mental Patients and Other Inmates* (Chicago: Aldine, 1962), 201–203; Erving Goffman, *The Goffman Reader*, ed. Ann Branaman and Charles C. Lemert (Malden, MA: Blackwell, 1997).

16. Suzanna M. Rose, "Same- and Cross-Sex Friendships and the Psychology of Homosociality," *Sex Roles* 12, no. 1 (January 1985): 63–74; Eve Kosofsky Sedgwick, *Between Men: English Literature and Male Homosocial Desire* (New York: Columbia University Press, 1992); Eve Kosofsky Sedgwick, *Epistemology of the Closet*, updated ed. (Berkeley: University of California Press, 2008).

17. For an example of such a case, see summary court-martial record of Private Julius Sherman, February 20, 1906, RG 393, Entry 3017, Part 1, Box 10, NARA.

18. It is increasingly clear that many men—especially working-class men like enlisted soldiers—who might have considered themselves to be primarily or mainly sexually attracted to women regularly or occasionally engaged in a variety of sexual acts with other men, sometimes in commercial arrangements, without considering themselves to be queer or homosexual. Clearly some soldiers and sailors in places like New York City sometimes earned money as a kind of prostitute, or "trade," in the parlance of the day. Barry Reay, *New York Hustlers: Masculinity and Sex in Modern America* (Manchester: Manchester University Press, 2010); Chad C. Heap, *Slumming: Sexual and Racial Encoun-*

ters in American Nightlife, 1885–1940 (Chicago: University of Chicago Press, 2009); Sedgwick, *Epistemology of the Closet*; Kevin White, *The First Sexual Revolution: The Emergence of Male Heterosexuality in Modern America* (New York: New York University Press, 1993); John Howard, *Men Like That: A Southern Queer History* (Chicago: University of Chicago Press, 1999); Matt Houlbrook, *Queer London: Perils and Pleasures in the Sexual Metropolis, 1918–1957* (Chicago: University of Chicago Press, 2005).

Bibliography

Manuscript and Unpublished Primary Sources

National Archives and Record Administration (NARA), Washington, DC

Record Group (RG) 94: Records of the Adjutant General's Office, 1780s–1917
    Entry 2: General Court-Martial Orders
    Entry 25: Adjutant General's Office Document Files
Record Group (RG) 153: Records of the Office of the Judge Advocate General
    (Army)
    Entry 15: Court-Martial Case Files
    Entry 17: Indexes to Court-Martial Cases, 1891–1917
Record Group (RG) 393: Records of U.S. Army Continental Commands, 1821–1920
    Entry 3017: Fort Riley Summary Courts-Martial
Record Group (RG) 395: Records of U.S. Army Overseas Operations and Com-
    mands, 1898–1942
    Entry 2061: General Orders, Special Orders, and General Court-Martial Orders
    Entry 2071: General Court-Martial Orders
    Entry 6040: General Court-Martial Orders

National Archives and Record Administration (NARA) II, College Park, MD

Record Group (RG) 120: Records of the American Expeditionary Forces (World War I)
    Entry 29: Records of the AEF Medical Department
Record Group (RG) 153: Records of the Office of the Judge Advocate General
    (Army)
    Entry 15B: Court-Martial Case Files
    Entry 31: Briefs of the AEF Court-Martial Cases, 1918–20
Record Group (RG) 165: Records of the War Department General and Special Staffs
    Entry 393: Commission on Training Camp Activities (CTCA)
    Entry 395: Reports Relating to Training Camp Activities
Record Group (RG) 350: Records of the Bureau of Insular Affairs
    Entry 5: General Classified Files, 1898–1945
    Entry 2039: General Classified Files, 1898–1945

Government Newspapers and Magazines

Amaroc News
Army and Navy Journal
Stars and Stripes

Other Newspapers and Magazines

The Crisis
Fortune
Literary Digest
New York Times

Published Primary Sources

Government Publications

American Battle Monuments Commission. *American Armies and Battlefields in Europe: A History, Guide, and Reference Book*. Washington, DC: Government Printing Office, 1938.

Anderson, George J. *Making the Camps Safe for the Army*. Washington, DC: Government Printing Office, 1919.

Ayres, Leonard Porter, ed. *The War with Germany: A Statistical Summary*. 2nd ed., with data rev. to August 1, 1919. Washington, DC: Government Printing Office, 1919.

[Bagby, Philip H.]. *American Representation in Occupied Germany, 1920–21*. 2 vols. Washington, DC: Government Printing Office, 1921.

Center of Military History, U.S. Army. *United States Army in the World War, 1917–1919*. 17 vols. Washington, DC: Center of Military History, U.S. Army, 1988–1992.

Commission on Training Camp Activities. *Committee on Protective Work for Girls*. Washington, DC: Government Printing Office, 1917.

——. *Keeping Fit to Fight*. Washington, DC: Government Printing Office, 1918.

——. *Report of the Chairman on Training Camp Activities to the Secretary of War, 1918*. Washington, DC: Government Printing Office, 1918.

——. *Women's Share in a National Service*. Washington, DC: Government Printing Office, n.d., ca. 1918.

Federal Bureau of Investigation. *Uniform Crime Reports*. Accessed August 6, 2018. http://www.fbi.gov/about-us/cjis/ucr/ucr.

Gibson, Campbell J., and Emily Lennon. *Historical Census Statistics on the Foreign-Born Population of the United States: 1850–1990*. Washington, DC: U.S. Bureau of the Census, Population Division, February 1999. http://www.census.gov/population/www/documentation/twps0029/twps0029.html.

Gillett, Mary C. *The Army Medical Department, 1865–1917*. Washington, DC: Center of Military History, U.S. Army, 1995.

Headquarters, American Forces in Germany, Office of Civil Affairs, U.S. Army, and I. L. Hunt. *American Military Government of Occupied Germany, 1918–1920: Report of the Officer in Charge of Civil Affairs, Third Army and American Forces in Germany*. Washington, DC: Government Printing Office, 1943.

Kreidberg, Marvin A., and Merton G. Henry, eds. *History of Military Mobilization in the United States Army, 1775–1945*. Washington, DC: Center of Military History, U.S. Army, 1984.

Patton, George S., Jr. "Address to the Third Army." June 5, 1944, Great Britain.

Pride, W. F. *The History of Fort Riley*. Fort Riley, KS: U.S. Army Cavalry School, Book Department, 1926.

Teller, Henry Moore. *The Problem in the Philippines: Speech of Hon. Henry M. Teller, of Colorado, in the Senate of the United States, February 11, 12, and 13, 1902*. Washington, DC, 1902.

U.S. Census Bureau. *Outlying Territories and Possessions: Number and Distribution of Inhabitants, Composition and Characteristics of the Population, Occupations, Unemployment, and Agriculture*. Washington, DC: Government Printing Office, 1932.

U.S. Census Bureau, Population Division. *1990 Census of Population and Housing*. Washington, DC: U.S. Census Bureau, Population Division, 1998. https://www.census.gov/prod/www/decennial.html.

U.S. Department of Defense, Statistical Service Center. *Principal Wars in Which the United States Participated: U.S. Personnel Serving and Casualties*. Washington, DC: Government Printing Office, 1957.

U.S. Department of the Army. *The Army Family*. Washington, DC: Chief of Staff, U.S. Army, 1983.

——. *Fort Riley: Its Historic Past*. Washington, DC: Government Printing Office, 1984.

U.S. Department of the Army, General Staff, Military Intelligence Division. *U.S. Military Intelligence Reports: Germany, 1919–1941*. Edited by Robert Lester and Dale Reynolds. Frederick, MD: University Publications of America, 1983.

U.S. Department of War. *Annual Report of the War Department*. Multiple volumes. Washington, DC: Government Printing Office, 1898–1941.

——. *Fourth Annual Report of the Philippine Commission, 1903*. Washington, DC: Government Printing Office, 1904.

——. *A Manual for Courts-Martial, Courts of Inquiry, and of Other Procedure under Military Law*. Washington, DC: Government Printing Office, 1917.

——. *A Manual for Courts-Martial, Courts of Inquiry, and of Other Procedure under Military Law*. Washington, DC: Government Printing Office, 1918.

——. *A Manual for Courts-Martial, Courts of Inquiry, and of Other Procedure under Military Law*. Washington, DC: Government Printing Office, 1920.

——. *A Manual for Courts-Martial, Courts of Inquiry, and Retiring Boards, and of Other Procedure under Military Law*. Rev. ed., 1901. Washington, DC: Government Printing Office, 1902.

——. *A Manual for Courts-Martial, Courts of Inquiry, and Retiring Boards, and of Other Procedure under Military Law*. Rev. ed., 1908, corrected to August 1910. Washington, DC: Government Printing Office, 1910.

——. *Regulations for the Army of the United States, 1913 Corrected to 1917*. Washington, DC: Government Printing Office, 1917.

U.S. Department of War, Office of the Surgeon-General. *Annual Report of the Surgeon-General*. Multiple volumes. Washington, DC: Government Printing Office, 1898–1941.

U.S. Provost Marshal General. *Second Report of the Provost Marshal General to the Secretary of War on the Operations of the Selective Service System to December 20, 1918*. Washington, DC: Government Printing Office, 1919.

U.S. Surgeon-General's Office. *The Medical Department of the United States Army in the World War*. Edited by M. W. Ireland. 15 vols. Washington, DC: Government Printing Office, 1921–1929.

Letters, Memoirs, Diaries, Autobiographical Fiction, and Other Personal Accounts

Allen, Henry T. *My Rhineland Journal.* Boston: Houghton Mifflin, 1923.

Baker, Newton D. *Frontiers of Freedom.* New York: George H. Doran, 1918.

Chernin, Ted A. "My Experiences in the Honolulu Chinatown Red-Light District." *Hawaiian Journal of History* 34 (2000): 203–217.

Fosdick, Raymond B. *Chronicle of a Generation: An Autobiography.* New York: Harper, 1958.

Franck, Harry A. *Roaming in Hawaii: A Narrative of Months of Wandering among the Glamorous Islands That May Become Our 49th State.* New York: Frederick A. Stokes, 1937.

Gatewood, Willard B., Jr. *"Smoked Yankees" and the Struggle for Empire: Letters from Negro Soldiers, 1898–1902.* Urbana: University of Illinois Press, 1971.

Harrison, Francis Burton. *Origins of the Philippine Republic: Extracts from the Diaries and Records of Francis Burton Harrison.* Edited by Michael Paul Onorato. Ithaca, NY: Cornell University Press, 1974.

Hazlett, A. Lester. *Affairs in the Philippine Islands: Hearings before the United States Senate Committee on the Philippines, Fifty-Seventh Congress, First Session, on Jan. 31, Feb. 1, 3–8, 10, 14, 15, 17–20, 25–28, Mar. 3–6, 11–13, 17–20, 1902.* Washington, DC: Government Printing Office, 1902.

Jones, James. *From Here to Eternity: The Restored Edition.* New York: Open Road, 2011.

Walker, George. *Venereal Disease in the American Expeditionary Forces.* Baltimore: Medical Standard, 1922.

Young, Hugh H. *Hugh Young: A Surgeon's Autobiography.* New York: Harcourt, Brace, 1940.

Other Publications

Adams, Romanzo Colfax. *Interracial Marriage in Hawaii: A Study of the Mutually Conditioned Processes of Acculturation and Amalgamation.* New York: Macmillan, 1937.

"Advice to Soldiers in Paris." *Social Hygiene* 5 (January 1919): 111–112.

Chicago Vice Commission. *The Social Evil in Chicago: A Study of Existing Conditions with Recommendations by the Vice Commission of Chicago.* Chicago: Vice Commission of Chicago, 1911.

Clarke, G. S. "Imperial Responsibilities a National Gain." *North American Review* 168 (February 1899): 129–141.

Cullum, George Washington. *Biographical Register of the Officers and Graduates of the U.S. Military Academy at West Point, New York since Its Establishment in 1802.* Edited by Wirt Robinson. Supplement, vol. 6A, *1910–1920.* Saginaw, MI: Seemann and Peters, 1920.

Daily, Edward L. *We Remember: U.S. Cavalry Association.* Paducah, KY: Turner, 1996.

Exner, Max J. "Prostitution in Its Relation to the Army on the Mexican Border." *Journal of Social Hygiene* 3 (1917): 205–219.

Freud, Sigmund. *Three Essays on the Theory of Sexuality.* Translated by James Strachey. New York: Basic Books, 1962.

Gulick, Luther H. *Morals and Morale.* New York: Association, 1919.

Johnson, Bascom. "Eliminating Vice from Camp Cities." *Annals of the American Academy of Political and Social Science* 78 (1918): 60–64.

Johnson, William B. *The Crowning Infamy of Imperialism.* Philadelphia: American League of Philadelphia, 1900.

Kidd, Benjamin. *The Control of the Tropics.* New York: Macmillan, 1898.

King, W. W. "Tropical Neurasthenia." Presented at the Annual Meeting of the American Society of Tropical Medicine, Philadelphia, March 24, 1906. *Journal of the American Medical Association* 46, no. 20 (1906): 1518–1519.

Kinsey, Alfred C., Wardell B. Pomeroy, and Clyde E. Martin. *Sexual Behavior in the Human Male.* Philadelphia: W. B. Saunders, 1948.

Kinsey, Alfred C., Wardell B. Pomeroy, Clyde E. Martin, and Paul H. Gebhard. *Sexual Behavior in the Human Female.* Philadelphia: W. B. Saunders, 1953.

Kipling, Rudyard. "The White Man's Burden." *McClure's,* February 1899.

Macaraig, Serafin E. *Social Problems.* Manila: Educational Supply, 1929.

Morse, C. F. "The Prevalence and Prophylaxis of Venereal Diseases at One Military Post." *Military Surgeon* 27, no. 3 (September 1910): 268–273.

Shea, Nancy. *The Army Wife.* 1941. 4th ed. New York: Harper and Row, 1966.

Snow, William F., and Wilbur A. Sawyer. "Venereal Disease Control in the Army." Presented at the Section on Preventive Medicine and Public Health at the Sixty-Ninth Annual Session of the American Medical Association, Chicago, June 1918. *Journal of the American Medical Association* 71, no. 6 (1918): 456–463.

Washburn, William S. "Health Conditions in the Philippines." *Philippine Journal of Science* 3, no. 4 (September 1908): 269–284.

Whitmarsh, Phelps. "In Pampanga Province." *Outlook,* February 17, 1903.

Wolbarst, Abraham. "Discussion." *Transactions of the American Society for Sanitary and Moral Prophylaxis* 3 (1910): 34.

Woodruff, Charles E. *The Effects of Tropical Light on White Men.* New York: Rebman, 1905.

Secondary Sources

Books

Abrahamson, James L. *America Arms for a New Century: The Making of a Great Military Power.* New York: Free Press, 1981.

Adams, Kevin. *Class and Race in the Frontier Army: Military Life in the West, 1870–1890.* Norman: University of Oklahoma Press, 2009.

Allen, Frederick Lewis. *Only Yesterday: An Informal History of the Nineteen Twenties.* New York: Harper and Row, 1964.

Alvah, Donna. *Unofficial Ambassadors: American Military Families Overseas and the Cold War, 1946–1965.* New York: New York University Press, 2007.

Anderson, Warwick. *Colonial Pathologies: American Tropical Medicine, Race, and Hygiene in the Philippines.* Durham, NC: Duke University Press, 2006.

Asbury, Herbert. *The French Quarter: An Informal History of the New Orleans Underworld.* 1936. Reprint, New York: Old Town Books, 1989.

Askin, Kelly Dawn. *War Crimes against Women: Prosecution in International War Crimes Tribunals*. The Hague: Kluwer Law International, 1997.

Bailey, Beth L. *From Front Porch to Back Seat: Courtship in Twentieth-Century America*. Baltimore: Johns Hopkins University Press, 1988.

Bailey, Beth L., and David R. Farber. *The First Strange Place: The Alchemy of Race and Sex in World War II Hawaii*. New York: Free Press, 1992.

Barbeau, Arthur E., and Florette Henri. *The Unknown Soldiers: Black American Troops in World War I*. Philadelphia: Temple University Press, 1974.

Bayer, Ronald. *Homosexuality and American Psychiatry: The Politics of Diagnosis*. Princeton, NJ: Princeton University Press, 1987.

Bederman, Gail. *Manliness and Civilization: A Cultural History of Gender and Race in the United States, 1880–1917*. Chicago: University of Chicago Press, 1995.

Bender, Thomas, ed. *Rethinking American History in a Global Age*. Berkeley: University of California Press, 2002.

Bérubé, Allan. *Coming Out under Fire: The History of Gay Men and Women in World War Two*. New York: Plume, 1990.

Blight, David W. *Beyond the Battlefield: Race, Memory, and the American Civil War*. Amherst: University of Massachusetts Press, 2002.

——. *Race and Reunion: The Civil War in American Memory*. Cambridge, MA: Belknap Press of Harvard University Press, 2001.

Blumenthal, Walter Hart. *Women Camp Followers of the American Revolution*. Philadelphia: G. S. MacManus, 1974.

Boemeke, Manfred F., Roger Chickering, and Stig Förster, eds. *Anticipating Total War: The German and American Experiences, 1871–1914*. Cambridge: Cambridge University Press, 1999.

Bosanac, Stephen E., and Merle Jacobs, eds. *The Professionalization of Work*. Whitby, ON: De Sitter, 2006.

Boyer, Paul S. *Urban Masses and Moral Order in America, 1820–1920*. Cambridge, MA: Harvard University Press, 1978.

Brands, H. W. *Bound to Empire: The United States and the Philippines*. New York: Oxford University Press, 1992.

Brandt, Allan M. *No Magic Bullet: A Social History of Venereal Disease in the United States since 1880*. Expanded ed. New York: Oxford University Press, 1987.

Bristow, Nancy K. *Making Men Moral: Social Engineering during the Great War*. New York: New York University Press, 1996.

Brod, Harry, ed. *The Making of Masculinities: The New Men's Studies*. Boston: Allen and Unwin, 1987.

Browne, George. *An American Soldier in World War I*. Edited by David L. Snead. Lincoln: University of Nebraska Press, 2006.

Burg, B. R. *Gay Warriors: A Documentary History from the Ancient World to the Present*. New York: New York University Press, 2002.

Burnham, John C. *Bad Habits: Drinking, Smoking, Taking Drugs, Gambling, Sexual Misbehavior, and Swearing in American History*. New York: New York University Press, 1993.

Burns, Eric. *The Spirits of America: A Social History of Alcohol*. Philadelphia: Temple University Press, 2004.

Butler, Judith. *Gender Trouble: Feminism and the Subversion of Identity.* New York: Routledge, 1990.

Canaday, Margot. *The Straight State: Sexuality and Citizenship in Twentieth-Century America.* Princeton, NJ: Princeton University Press, 2009.

Carnes, Mark C., and Clyde Griffen, eds. *Meanings for Manhood: Constructions of Masculinity in Victorian America.* Chicago: University of Chicago Press, 1990.

Chambers, John Whiteclay, II. *To Raise an Army: The Draft Comes to Modern America.* New York: Collier Macmillan, 1987.

Chauncey, George, Jr. *Gay New York: Gender, Urban Culture, and the Makings of the Gay Male World, 1890–1940.* New York: Basic Books, 1994.

Clark, J. P. *Preparing for War: The Emergence of the Modern U.S. Army, 1815–1917.* Cambridge, MA: Harvard University Press, 2017.

Clement, Elizabeth. *Love for Sale: Courting, Treating, and Prostitution in New York City, 1900–1945.* Chapel Hill: University of North Carolina Press, 2006.

Coffman, Edward M. *The Regulars: The American Army, 1898–1941.* Cambridge, MA: Belknap Press of Harvard University Press, 2004.

——. *The War to End All Wars: The American Military Experience in World War I.* Lexington: University of Wisconsin, 1986.

Cohen, Dara Kay. *Rape during Civil War.* Ithaca, NY: Cornell University Press, 2016.

Cohen, Stanley. *Folk Devils and Moral Panics: The Creation of the Mods and Rockers.* 3rd ed. London: Routledge, 2002.

Collier, Aine. *The Humble Little Condom: A History.* Amherst, MA: Prometheus Books, 2007.

Costello, John. *Virtue under Fire: How World War II Changed Our Social and Sexual Attitudes.* Boston: Little, Brown, 1985.

Crompton, Louis. *Homosexuality and Civilization.* Cambridge, MA: Belknap Press of Harvard University Press, 2003.

Crosby, Alfred W. *America's Forgotten Pandemic: The Influenza of 1918.* Cambridge: Cambridge University Press, 2003.

Cushman, Philip. *Constructing the Self, Constructing America: A Cultural History of Psychotherapy.* Boston: Addison-Wesley, 1995.

Dale, Rodney. *The Tumour in the Whale: A Collection of Modern Myths.* London: Duckworth, 1978.

Danbom, David B. *Born in the Country: A History of Rural America.* 2nd ed. Baltimore: Johns Hopkins University Press, 2006.

Day, Jared N. *Urban Castles: Tenement Housing and Landlord Activism in New York City, 1890–1943.* New York: Columbia University Press, 1999.

De Bevoise, Ken. *Agents of Apocalypse: Epidemic Disease in the Colonial Philippines.* Princeton, NJ: Princeton University Press, 1995.

D'Emilio, John. *Sexual Politics, Sexual Communities: The Making of a Homosexual Minority in the United States, 1940–1970.* 2nd ed. Chicago: University of Chicago Press, 1998.

D'Emilio, John, and Estelle B. Freedman. *Intimate Matters: A History of Sexuality in America.* 2nd ed. Chicago: University of Chicago Press, 1997.

Dobak, William A. *Fort Riley and Its Neighbors: Military Money and Economic Growth, 1853–1895.* Norman: University of Oklahoma Press, 1998.

Dobak, William A., and Thomas D. Phillips. *The Black Regulars, 1866–1898*. Norman: University of Oklahoma Press, 2001.

Dorsey, Leroy G. *We Are All Americans, Pure and Simple: Theodore Roosevelt and the Myth of Americanism*. Tuscaloosa: University of Alabama Press, 2007.

Douglas, Ann. *The Feminization of American Culture*. New York: Noonday, 1998.

Duberman, Martin Bauml, Martha Vicinus, and George Chauncey Jr., eds. *Hidden from History: Reclaiming the Gay and Lesbian Past*. New York: New American Library, 1989.

Dyer, Thomas G. *Theodore Roosevelt and the Idea of Race*. Baton Rouge: Louisiana State University Press, 1980.

Ellis, Havelock, and John Addington Symonds. *Sexual Inversion: A Critical Edition*. Edited by Ivan Crozier. Basingstoke, UK: Palgrave Macmillan, 2008.

Ellis, Mark. *Race, War, and Surveillance: African Americans and the United States Government during World War I*. Bloomington: Indiana University Press, 2001.

Engel, Jonathan. *American Therapy: The Rise of Psychotherapy in the United States*. New York: Gotham Books, 2008.

Enloe, Cynthia H. *Bananas, Beaches and Bases: Making Feminist Sense of International Politics*. Updated ed. Berkeley: University of California Press, 2000.

——. *Maneuvers: The International Politics of Militarizing Women's Lives*. Berkeley: University of California Press, 2000.

Erenberg, Lewis A. *Steppin' Out: New York Nightlife and the Transformation of American Culture, 1890–1930*. Westport, CT: Greenwood, 1981.

Fass, Paula. *The Damned and the Beautiful: American Youth in the 1920's*. New York: Oxford University Press, 1977.

Faulkner, Richard S. *Pershing's Crusaders: The American Soldier in World War I*. Lawrence: University Press of Kansas, 2017.

Fidell, Eugene R., Elizabeth L. Hillman, and Dwight H. Sullivan, eds. *Military Justice: Cases and Materials*. Newark, NJ: LexisNexis, 2007.

Filene, Peter G. *Him/Her/Self: Sex Roles in Modern America*. 2nd ed. Baltimore: Johns Hopkins University Press, 1986.

Fishman, Joseph F. *Sex in Prison: Revealing Sex Conditions in American Prisons*. New York: National Library, 1934.

Flacelière, Robert. *Love in Ancient Greece*. Westport, CT: Greenwood, 1973.

Ford, Nancy Gentile. *Americans All! Foreign-Born Soldiers in World War I*. College Station: Texas A&M University Press, 2001.

Foster, Gaines M. *Ghosts of the Confederacy: Defeat, the Lost Cause, and the Emergence of the New South, 1865–1913*. New York: Oxford University Press, 1987.

Foucault, Michel. *The History of Sexuality*. Vol. 1, *An Introduction*. New York: Vintage Books, 1990.

Frank, Nathaniel. *Unfriendly Fire: How the Gay Ban Undermines the Military and Weakens America*. New York: Thomas Dunne Books, 2009.

Frankel, Noralee, and Nancy S. Dye, eds. *Gender, Class, Race, and Reform in the Progressive Era*. Lexington: University Press of Kentucky, 1991.

Gay, Peter. *Freud for Historians*. New York: Oxford University Press, 1985.

Go, Julian, and Anne L. Foster, eds. *The American Colonial State in the Philippines: Global Perspectives*. Durham, NC: Duke University Press, 2003.

Goffman, Erving. *Asylums: Essays on the Social Situation of Mental Patients and Other Inmates*. Chicago: Aldine, 1962.

——. *The Goffman Reader*. Edited by Ann Branaman and Charles C. Lemert. Malden, MA: Blackwell, 1997.

Goldman, Nancy L., and David R. Segal, eds. *The Social Psychology of Military Service*. Beverly Hills: Sage, 1976.

Goldstein, Joshua S. *War and Gender: How Gender Shapes the War System and Vice Versa*. Cambridge: Cambridge University Press, 2001.

Gray, J. Glenn. *The Warriors: Reflections on Men in Battle*. 2nd ed. New York: Harper and Row, 1970.

Greenberg, Amy S. *Manifest Manhood and the Antebellum American Empire*. Cambridge: Cambridge University Press, 2005.

Gurstein, Rochelle. *The Repeal of Reticence: A History of America's Cultural and Legal Struggles over Free Speech, Obscenity, Sexual Liberation, and Modern Art*. New York: Hill and Wang, 1996.

Haas, Edward F. *Political Leadership in a Southern City: New Orleans in the Progressive Era, 1896–1902*. Ruston: Louisiana Tech University, 1988.

Hagemann, Karen, and Stefanie Schüler-Springorum, eds. *Home/Front: The Military, War, and Gender in Twentieth-Century Germany*. Oxford: Berg, 2002.

Hale, Nathan G. *The Rise and Crisis of Psychoanalysis in the United States: Freud and the Americans, 1917–1985*. New York: Oxford University Press, 1995.

Heap, Chad C. *Slumming: Sexual and Racial Encounters in American Nightlife, 1885–1940*. Chicago: University of Chicago Press, 2009.

Hegarty, Marilyn E. *Victory Girls, Khaki-Wackies, and Patriotutes: The Regulation of Female Sexuality during World War II*. New York: New York University Press, 2008.

Hensley, Christopher, ed. *Prison Sex: Practice and Policy*. Boulder, CO: Lynne Rienner, 2002.

Hicks, George L. *The Comfort Women: Sex Slaves of the Japanese Imperial Forces*. London: Souvenir, 1995.

Higham, John. *Strangers in the Land: Patterns of American Nativism, 1860–1925*. 2nd ed. New Brunswick, NJ: Rutgers University Press, 1988.

Hillman, Elizabeth Lutes. *Defending America: Military Culture and the Cold War Court-Martial*. Princeton, NJ: Princeton University Press, 2005.

Hobson, Barbara Meil. *Uneasy Virtue: The Politics of Prostitution and the American Reform Tradition*. Chicago: University of Chicago Press, 1990.

Hofstadter, Richard. *The Age of Reform: From Bryan to F.D.R.* New York: Knopf, 1955.

Hoganson, Kristin L. *Fighting for American Manhood: How Gender Politics Provoked the Spanish-American and Philippine-American Wars*. New Haven, CT: Yale University Press, 1998.

Höhn, Maria. *GIs and Fräuleins: The German-American Encounter in 1950s West Germany*. Chapel Hill: University of North Carolina Press, 2002.

Höhn, Maria, and Seungsook Moon, eds. *Over There: Living with the U.S. Military Empire from World War Two to the Present*. Durham, NC: Duke University Press, 2010.

Holmes, Richard. *Acts of War: The Behavior of Men in Battle*. New York: Free Press, 1989.

Houlbrook, Matt. *Queer London: Perils and Pleasures in the Sexual Metropolis, 1918–1957*. Chicago: University of Chicago Press, 2005.

Howard, John. *Men Like That: A Southern Queer History*. Chicago: University of Chicago Press, 1999.

Howell, Philip. *Geographies of Regulation: Policing Prostitution in Nineteenth-Century Britain and the Empire*. Cambridge: Cambridge University Press, 2009.

Hunt, Michael H. *Ideology and U.S. Foreign Policy*. New Haven, CT: Yale University Press, 2009.

Hynes, Samuel. *The Soldiers' Tale: Bearing Witness to Modern War*. New York: Viking Penguin, 1997.

Isaksson, Eva, ed. *Women and the Military System*. New York: St. Martin's, 1988.

Jacobson, Matthew Frye. *Barbarian Virtues: The United States Encounters Foreign Peoples at Home and Abroad, 1876–1917*. New York: Hill and Wang, 2000.

Jarvis, Christina S. *The Male Body at War: American Masculinity during World War II*. DeKalb: Northern Illinois University Press, 2004.

Jessup, Philip C. *Elihu Root*. 2 vols. New York: Dodd, Mead, 1938.

Jones, Richard E., and Kristin H. Lopez. *Human Reproductive Biology*. 3rd ed. San Diego: Academic, 2006.

Kauanui, J. Kēhaulani. *Hawaiian Blood: Colonialism and the Politics of Sovereignty and Indigeneity*. Durham, NC: Duke University Press, 2008.

Keene, Jennifer D. *Doughboys, the Great War, and the Remaking of America*. Baltimore: Johns Hopkins University Press, 2001.

——. *The United States and the First World War*. Harlow, UK: Longman, 2000.

Keire, Mara L. *For Business and Pleasure: Red-Light Districts and the Regulation of Vice in the United States, 1890–1933*. Baltimore: Johns Hopkins University Press, 2010.

Keith, Jeanette. *Rich Man's War, Poor Man's Fight: Race, Class, and Power in the Rural South during the First World War*. Chapel Hill: University of North Carolina Press, 2004.

Keller, Morton. *Regulating a New Society: Public Policy and Social Change in America, 1900–1933*. Cambridge, MA: Harvard University Press, 1994.

Kennedy, David M. *Over Here: The First World War and American Society*. New York: Oxford University Press, 1980.

King, Desmond S. *Making Americans: Immigration, Race, and the Origins of the Diverse Democracy*. Cambridge, MA: Harvard University Press, 2000.

Koistinen, Paul A. C. *Arsenal of World War II: The Political Economy of American Warfare, 1940–1945*. Lawrence: University Press of Kansas, 2004.

——. *Beating Plowshares into Swords: The Political Economy of American Warfare, 1606–1865*. Lawrence: University Press of Kansas, 1996.

——. *Mobilizing for Modern War: The Political Economy of American Warfare, 1865–1919*. Lawrence: University Press of Kansas, 1997.

——. *Planning War, Pursuing Peace: The Political Economy of American Warfare, 1920–1939*. Lawrence: University Press of Kansas, 1998.

Kornweibel, Theodore. *"Investigate Everything": Federal Efforts to Compel Black Loyalty during World War I*. Bloomington: Indiana University Press, 2002.

Kramer, Paul A. *The Blood of Government: Race, Empire, the United States, and the Philippines*. Chapel Hill: University of North Carolina Press, 2006.

Krist, Gary. *Empire of Sin: A Story of Sex, Jazz, Murder, and the Battle for Modern New Orleans*. New York: Crown, 2014.

Lacey, Jim. *Pershing*. New York: Palgrave Macmillan, 2008.

Landau, Emily Epstein. *Spectacular Wickedness: Sex, Race, and Memory in Storyville, New Orleans*. Baton Rouge: Louisiana State University Press, 2013.

Langley, Lester D. *The Banana Wars: United States Intervention in the Caribbean, 1898–1934*. Wilmington, DE: Scholarly Resources, 2002.

Langum, David J. *Crossing over the Line: Legislating Morality and the Mann Act*. Chicago: University of Chicago Press, 1994.

Laqueur, Thomas W. *Solitary Sex: A Cultural History of Masturbation*. New York: Zone Books, 2003.

Lehring, Gary L. *Officially Gay: The Political Construction of Sexuality by the U.S. Military*. Philadelphia: Temple University Press, 2003.

Lentz-Smith, Adriane. *Freedom Struggles: African Americans and World War I*. Cambridge, MA: Harvard University Press, 2009.

Levine, Philippa. *Prostitution, Race, and Politics: Policing Venereal Disease in the British Empire*. New York: Routledge, 2003.

Linn, Brian McAllister. *Guardians of Empire: The U.S. Army and the Pacific, 1902–1940*. Chapel Hill: University of North Carolina Press, 1997.

——. *The Philippine War, 1899–1902*. Lawrence: University Press of Kansas, 2000.

——. *The U.S. Army and Counterinsurgency in the Philippine War, 1899–1902*. Chapel Hill: University of North Carolina Press, 1989.

Long, Alecia P. *The Great Southern Babylon: Sex, Race, and Respectability in New Orleans, 1865–1920*. Baton Rouge: Louisiana State University Press, 2004.

Lord, Alexandra M. *Condom Nation: The U.S. Government's Sex Education Campaign from World War I to the Internet*. Baltimore: Johns Hopkins University Press, 2010.

Lowry, Thomas P. *The Story the Soldiers Wouldn't Tell: Sex in the Civil War*. Mechanicsburg, PA: Stackpole Books, 1994.

Lutz, Catherine, ed. *The Bases of Empire: The Global Struggle against U.S. Military Posts*. Washington Square, NY: New York University Press, 2009.

Lynn, John A. *Women, Armies, and Warfare in Early Modern Europe*. Cambridge: Cambridge University Press, 2008.

MacDonald, Keith M. *The Sociology of the Professions*. London: Sage, 1995.

Mackey, Thomas C. *Red Lights Out: A Legal History of Prostitution, Disorderly Houses, and Vice Districts, 1870–1917*. New York: Garland, 1986.

Mayer, Holly A. *Belonging to the Army: Camp Followers and Community during the American Revolution*. Columbia: University of South Carolina Press, 1996.

McBee, Randy. *Dance Hall Days: Intimacy and Leisure among Working-Class Immigrants in the United States*. New York: New York University Press, 2000.

McCoy, Alfred W. *Policing America's Empire: The United States, the Philippines, and the Rise of the Surveillance State*. Madison: University of Wisconsin Press, 2009.

McCoy, Alfred W., and Francisco A. Scarano, eds. *Colonial Crucible: Empire in the Making of the Modern American State*. Madison: University of Wisconsin Press, 2009.

Melzer, Arthur M., Jerry Weinberger, and M. Richard Zinman, eds. *Politics at the Turn of the Century.* Lanham, MD: Rowman and Littlefield, 2001.

Meyer, Leisa D. *Creating GI Jane: Sexuality and Power in the Women's Army Corps during World War II.* New York: Columbia University Press, 1996.

Miller, Stuart Creighton. *"Benevolent Assimilation": The American Conquest of the Philippines, 1899–1903.* New Haven, CT: Yale University Press, 1982.

Millett, Alan R., Peter Maslowski, and William B. Feis. *For the Common Defense: A Military History of the United States of America from 1607 to 2012.* 3rd ed. New York: Free Press, 2012.

Modell, John. *Into One's Own: From Youth to Adulthood in the United States, 1920–1975.* Berkeley: University of California Press, 1989.

Moon, Katharine H. S. *Sex among Allies: Military Prostitution in U.S.-Korea Relations.* New York: Columbia University Press, 1997.

Musicant, Ivan. *The Banana Wars: A History of United States Military Intervention in Latin America from the Spanish-American War to the Invasion of Panama.* New York: Macmillan, 1990.

Musto, David F. *The American Disease: Origins of Narcotic Control.* 3rd ed. New York: Oxford University Press, 1999.

Naimark, Norman M. *Fires of Hatred: Ethnic Cleansing in Twentieth-Century Europe.* Cambridge, MA: Harvard University Press, 2001.

Odem, Mary E. *Delinquent Daughters: Protecting and Policing Adolescent Female Sexuality in the United States, 1885–1920.* Chapel Hill: University of North Carolina Press, 1995.

Okihiro, Gary Y. *Island World: A History of Hawai'i and the United States.* Berkeley: University of California Press, 2008.

Okrent, Daniel. *Last Call: The Rise and Fall of Prohibition.* New York: Scribner, 2010.

Omi, Michael, and Howard Winant. *Racial Formation in the United States: From the 1960s to the 1990s.* 2nd ed. New York: Routledge, 1994.

O'Neill, William L. *Everyone Was Brave: The Rise and Fall of Feminism in America.* Chicago: Quadrangle Books, 1969.

Palmer, Frederick. *Newton D. Baker: America at War.* 2 vols. New York: Dodd, Mead, 1931.

Peiss, Kathy. *Cheap Amusements: Working Women and Leisure in Turn-of-the-Century New York.* Philadelphia: Temple University Press, 1985.

Pettigrew, Richard F. *The Course of Empire.* New York: Boni and Liveright, 1920.

Pfister, Joel, and Nancy Schnog, eds. *Inventing the Psychological: Toward a Cultural History of Emotional Life in America.* New Haven, CT: Yale University Press, 1997.

Pickus, Noah M. J. *True Faith and Allegiance: Immigration and American Civic Nationalism.* Princeton, NJ: Princeton University Press, 2005.

Pivar, David J. *Purity and Hygiene: Women, Prostitution, and the "American Plan," 1900–1930.* Westport, CT: Greenwood, 2002.

——. *Purity Crusade: Sexual Morality and Social Control, 1868–1900.* Westport, CT: Greenwood, 1973.

Qiu, Peipei. *Chinese Comfort Women: Testimonies from Imperial Japan's Sex Slaves.* Vancouver: University of British Columbia Press, 2013.

Rajchman, John, ed. *The Identity in Question*. New York: Routledge, 1995.

Reay, Barry. *New York Hustlers: Masculinity and Sex in Modern America*. Manchester: Manchester University Press, 2010.

Reddy, William M. *The Navigation of Feeling: A Framework for the History of Emotions*. Cambridge: Cambridge University Press, 2001.

Reimers, David M. *Unwelcome Strangers: American Identity and the Turn against Immigration*. New York: Columbia University Press, 1998.

Renda, Mary A. *Taking Haiti: Military Occupation and the Culture of U.S. Imperialism, 1915–1940*. Chapel Hill: University of North Carolina Press, 2001.

Resch, John, and Walter Sargent, eds. *War and Society in the American Revolution: Mobilization and Home Fronts*. DeKalb: Northern Illinois University Press, 2007.

Roberts, Mary Louise. *What Soldiers Do: Sex and the American GI in World War II France*. Chicago: University of Chicago Press, 2013.

Rodgers, Daniel T. *Atlantic Crossings: Social Politics in a Progressive Age*. Cambridge, MA: Belknap Press of Harvard University Press, 1998.

Roediger, David R. *The Wages of Whiteness: Race and the Making of the American Working Class*. Rev. ed. London: Verso, 2007.

Rose, Al. *Storyville, New Orleans, Being an Authentic, Illustrated Account of the Notorious Red-Light District*. Tuscaloosa: University of Alabama Press, 1974.

Rosen, Ruth. *The Lost Sisterhood: Prostitution in America, 1900–1918*. Baltimore: Johns Hopkins University Press, 1982.

Rosenzweig, Roy. *Eight Hours for What We Will: Workers and Leisure in an Industrial City, 1870–1920*. Cambridge: Cambridge University Press, 1983.

Rotundo, E. Anthony. *American Manhood: Transformations in Masculinity from the Revolution to the Modern Era*. New York: Basic Books, 1993.

Rust, Paula C., ed. *Bisexuality in the United States: A Social Science Reader*. New York: Columbia University Press, 2000.

Ryan, Garry D., and Timothy K. Nenninger, eds. *Soldiers and Civilians: The U.S. Army and the American People*. Washington, DC: National Archives and Records Administration, 1987.

Salman, Michael. *The Embarrassment of Slavery: Controversies over Bondage and Nationalism in the American Colonial Philippines*. Berkeley: University of California Press, 2001.

Sammons, Jeffrey T., and John H. Morrow Jr. *Harlem's Rattlers and the Great War: The Undaunted 369th Regiment and the African American Quest for Equality*. Lawrence: University Press of Kansas, 2014.

Scott, James C. *The Moral Economy of the Peasant: Rebellion and Subsistence in Southeast Asia*. New Haven, CT: Yale University Press, 1976.

Scott, Joan W. *Gender and the Politics of History*. Rev. ed. New York: Columbia University Press, 1999.

Sedgwick, Eve Kosofsky. *Between Men: English Literature and Male Homosocial Desire*. New York: Columbia University Press, 1992.

——. *Epistemology of the Closet*. Updated ed. Berkeley: University of California Press, 2008.

Silbey, David. *A War of Frontier and Empire: The Philippine-American War, 1899–1902*. New York: Hill and Wang, 2007.

Silva, Noenoe K. *Aloha Betrayed: Native Hawaiian Resistance to American Colonialism.* Durham, NC: Duke University Press, 2004.

Smith, Gene. *Until the Last Trumpet Sounds: The Life of General of the Armies John J. Pershing.* New York: Wiley, 1998.

Smythe, Donald. *Pershing, General of the Armies.* Bloomington: Indiana University Press, 1986.

Spears, Timothy B. *Chicago Dreaming: Midwesterners and the City, 1871–1919.* Chicago: University of Chicago Press, 2005.

Spiro, Jonathan Peter. *Defending the Master Race: Conservation, Eugenics, and the Legacy of Madison Grant.* Burlington, VT: University Press of New England, 2009.

Stewart, Richard W., ed. *American Military History.* 2 vols. Washington, DC: Center of Military History, U.S. Army, 2005.

Stoler, Ann Laura, ed. *Haunted by Empire: Geographies of Intimacy in North American History.* Durham, NC: Duke University Press, 2006.

Tanaka, Toshiyuki. *Japan's Comfort Women: Sexual Slavery and Prostitution during World War II and the U.S. Occupation.* London: Routledge, 2002.

Terry, Jennifer. *An American Obsession: Science, Medicine, and Homosexuality in Modern Society.* Chicago: University of Chicago Press, 1999.

Thompson, E. P. *The Making of the English Working Class.* New York: Vintage Books, 1963.

Trask, David F. *The AEF and Coalition Warmaking, 1917–1918.* Lawrence: University Press of Kansas, 1993.

——. *The War with Spain in 1898.* New York: Macmillan, 1981.

Tyrrell, Ian R. *Reforming the World: The Creation of America's Moral Empire.* Princeton, NJ: Princeton University Press, 2010.

Vandiver, Frank Everson. *Black Jack: The Life and Times of John J. Pershing.* 2 vols. College Station: Texas A&M University Press, 1977.

Van Nuys, Frank. *Americanizing the West: Race, Immigrants, and Citizenship, 1890–1930.* Lawrence: University Press of Kansas, 2002.

Walker, Stanley. *The Night Club Era.* New York: Frederick A. Stokes, 1933.

Walkowitz, Judith R. *Prostitution and Victorian Society: Women, Class, and the State.* Cambridge: Cambridge University Press, 1980.

Wall, Richard, and Jay Winter, eds. *The Upheaval of War: Family, Work, and Welfare in Europe, 1914–1918.* Cambridge: Cambridge University Press, 1988.

Walsh, Margaret. *The American West: Visions and Revisions.* Cambridge: Cambridge University Press, 2005.

Weaver, John D. *The Brownsville Raid.* New York: W. W. Norton, 1970.

Welch, Richard E., Jr. *Response to Imperialism: The United States and the Philippine-American War, 1899–1902.* Chapel Hill: University of North Carolina Press, 1979.

Weston, Rubin Francis. *Racism in U.S. Imperialism: The Influence of Racial Assumptions on American Foreign Policy, 1893–1946.* Columbia: University of South Carolina Press, 1972.

Wheeler, Leigh Ann. *Against Obscenity: Reform and the Politics of Womanhood in America, 1873–1935.* Baltimore: Johns Hopkins University Press, 2004.

White, Kevin. *The First Sexual Revolution: The Emergence of Male Heterosexuality in Modern America.* New York: New York University Press, 1993.

Willeford, Charles Ray. *Something about a Soldier*. New York: Random House, 1986.

Williams, Chad L. *Torchbearers of Democracy: African American Soldiers in the World War I Era*. Chapel Hill: University of North Carolina Press, 2010.

Willis, Henry Parker. *Our Philippine Problem: A Study of American Colonial Policy*. New York: Henry Holt, 1905.

Wintermute, Bobby A. *Public Health and the U.S. Military: A History of the Army Medical Department, 1818–1917*. New York: Routledge, 2011.

Wynn, Neil A. *From Progressivism to Prosperity: World War I and American Society*. New York: Holmes and Meier, 1986.

Yoshimi, Yoshiaki. *Comfort Women: Sexual Slavery in the Japanese Military during World War II*. Translated by Suzanne O'Brien. New York: Columbia University Press, 2000.

Zeiger, Susan. *Entangling Alliances: Foreign War Brides and American Soldiers in the Twentieth Century*. New York: New York University Press, 2010.

Journal Articles

Anderson, Warwick. "Immunities of Empire: Race, Disease, and the New Tropical Medicine, 1900–1920." *Bulletin of the History of Medicine* 70 (Spring 1996): 94–118.

Barrett, James R., and David R. Roediger. "In Between Peoples: Race, Nationality and the 'New Immigrant' Working Class." *Journal of American Ethnic History* 16 (1997): 3–44.

Brock, Darla. "Memphis's *Nymphs Du Pave*: 'The Most Abandoned Women in the World.'" *West Tennessee Historical Society Papers* 50 (1996): 58–69.

Burnham, John C. "Medical Inspection of Prostitutes in America in the Nineteenth Century: The St. Louis Experiment and Its Sequel." *Bulletin of the History of Medicine* 45 (May 1971): 203–218.

Cole, Jeannine. "'Upon the Stage of Disorder': Legalized Prostitution in Memphis and Nashville, 1863–1865." *Tennessee Historical Quarterly* 68, no. 1 (March 2009): 40–65.

Davis, Jeffrey S. "Military Policy toward Homosexuals: Scientific, Historical, and Legal Perspectives." *Military Law Review* 131 (Winter 1991): 55–109.

Dery, Luis C. "Prostitution in Colonial Manila." *Philippine Studies* 39, no. 4 (1991): 475–489.

Dubbert, Joe. "Progressivism and the Masculinity Crisis." *Psychoanalytic Review* 61 (Fall 1974): 433–455.

Glass, Leonard L. "Man's Man / Ladies' Man: Motifs of Hypermasculinity." *Psychiatry* 47, no. 3 (1984): 260–278.

Greenwood, Anna. "Looking Back: The Strange History of Tropical Neurasthenia." *Psychologist* 24, no. 3 (March 2011): 226–227.

Greer, Richard A. "Collarbone and the Social Evil." *Hawaiian Journal of History* 7 (1973): 3–17.

Habib, Douglas F. "Chastity, Masculinity, and Military Efficiency: The United States Army in Germany, 1918–1923." *International History Review* 28, no. 4 (December 2006): 737–757.

Hacker, Barton C. "Women and Military Institutions in Early Modern Europe: A Reconnaissance." *Signs* 6 (1981): 643–671.

Hori, Joan. "Japanese Prostitution in Hawaii during the Immigration Period." *Hawaiian Journal of History* 15 (1980): 113–124.

Hunt, Alan. "The Great Masturbation Panic and the Discourses of Moral Regulation in Nineteenth- and Early Twentieth-Century Britain." *Journal of the History of Sexuality* 8, no. 4 (April 1998): 575–615.

Imber, Michael A. "The First World War, Sex Education, and the American Social Hygiene Association's Campaign against Venereal Disease." *Journal of Educational Administration and History* 16, no. 1 (1984): 47–56.

Jones, James B., Jr., "A Tale of Two Cities." *North and South: The Magazine of Civil War Conflict* 10, no. 5 (March 2008): 64–70.

Kramer, Paul A. "Power and Connection: Imperial Histories of the United States in the World." *American Historical Review* 116, no. 5 (December 2011): 1348–1391.

Kuhlman, Erika. "American Doughboys and German *Fräuleins*: Sexuality, Patriarchy, and Privilege in the American-Occupied Rhineland, 1918–23." *Journal of Military History* 71 (October 2007): 1077–1106.

Leuchtenburg, William. "Progressivism and Imperialism: The Progressive Movement and American Foreign Policy, 1898–1916." *Mississippi Valley Historical Review* 39, no. 3 (December 1952): 483–485.

Levine, Philippa. "Women and Prostitution: Metaphor, Reality, History." *Canadian Journal of History* 28, no. 3 (December 1993): 479–494.

McGovern, James R. "David Graham Phillips and the Virility Impulse of Progressivism." *New England Quarterly* 39 (1966): 334–355.

Mosher, Donald L., and Mark Sirkin. "Measuring a Macho Personality Constellation." *Journal of Research in Personality* 18 (1984): 150–163.

Mosher, Donald L., and Silvan S. Tomkins. "Scripting the Macho Man: Hypermasculine Socialization and Enculturation." *Journal of Sex Research* 25 (1988): 60–84.

Page, Benedicte. "Censored Gay Sex in *From Here to Eternity* Restored for New Edition." *Guardian*, April 5, 2011.

Pivar, David J. "The Military, Prostitution, and Colonial Peoples: India and the Philippines, 1885–1917." In "History and Sexuality," special issue, *Journal of Sex Research* 17, no. 3 (August 1981): 256–269.

Reddy, William M. "Against Constructionism: The Historical Ethnography of Emotions." *Current Anthropology* 38, no. 3 (June 1997): 327–351.

Rees, John. "'The Multitude of Women': An Examination of the Numbers of Female Camp Followers with the Continental Army." *Minerva: Quarterly Report on Women and the Military* 14, no. 2 (Summer 1996): 1–47.

Rose, Suzanna M. "Same- and Cross-Sex Friendships and the Psychology of Homosociality." *Sex Roles* 12, no. 1 (January 1985): 63–74.

Schlueter, David A. "The Court-Martial: An Historical Survey." *Military Law Review* 87 (1980): 129–166.

Stoler, Ann Laura. "Colonial Archives and the Arts of Governance." *Archival Science* 2 (2002): 87–109.

Terry, Jennifer. "Theorizing Deviant Historiography." *differences* 3 (Summer 1991): 55–74.

Thompson, E. P. "The Moral Economy of the English Crowd in the 18th Century." *Past and Present* 50 (February 1971): 76–136.

Wilson, Peter H. "German Women and War, 1500–1800." *War in History* 3 (1996): 127–160.

Dissertations

Abalahin, Andrew Jimenez. "Prostitution Policy and the Project of Modernity: A Comparative Study of Colonial Indonesia and the Philippines, 1850–1940." PhD diss., Cornell University, 2003.

Allsep, L. Michael, Jr. "New Forms for Dominance: How a Corporate Lawyer Created the American Military Establishment." PhD diss., University of North Carolina at Chapel Hill, 2008.

Hussey, Michael. "'Do You Know What It Means When a Man Uses Another Man as a Woman?': Sodomy, Gender, Class, and Power in the United States Navy, 1890–1925." PhD diss., University of Maryland, College Park, 2002.

Lukasik, Sebastian Hubert. "Military Service, Combat, and American Identity in the Progressive Era." PhD diss., Duke University, 2008.

Miller, Heather Lee. "The Teeming Brothel: Sex Acts, Desires, and Sexual Identities in the United States, 1870–1940." PhD diss., Ohio State University, 2002.

Robert, Gerald Franklin. "The Strenuous Life: The Cult of Manliness in the Era of Theodore Roosevelt." PhD diss., Michigan State University, 1970.

INDEX